Epistle on Worship

OTHER TITLES BY IBN TAYMIYYA
PUBLISHED BY THE ISLAMIC TEXTS SOCIETY

The Goodly Word:
Al-Kalim al-Ṭayyib

OTHER TITLES BY IBN QAYYIM AL-JAWZIYYA

The Invocation of God:
Al-Wābil al-Ṣayyib min al-Kalim al-Ṭayyib

Medicine of the Prophet

IBN TAYMIYYA

Epistle On Worship

Risālat al-ʿUbūdiyya

Translated by James Pavlin

ISLAMIC TEXTS SOCIETY

This first edition published 2015 by

THE ISLAMIC TEXTS SOCIETY
MILLER'S HOUSE
KINGS MILL LANE
GREAT SHELFORD
CAMBRIDGE CB22 5EN, UK.

British Library Cataloguing-in-Publication Data.
A catalogue record for this book is
available from the British Library.

ISBN: 978 1903682 487 cloth
ISBN: 978 1903682 494 paper

Printed by mega Printing in Turkey

CONTENTS

INTRODUCTION

Ibn Taymiyya and his Epistle on Worship VII
Ibn Taymiyya's Methodology XXIV
Ibn Taymiyya's Theology LIV
Preliminary Comments to the Translation XCIII

THE EPISTLE ON WORSHIP

PART I

The Definition of Worship I

PART II

The Slavery of a Heart 34
The Interaction of Love: Worship and Reliance 47
The *Fanā'* of the Prophets and Saints 71
The Summation of Correct Worship 87

BIBLIOGRAPHY 119

INDEX 133

INTRODUCTION

IBN TAYMIYYA AND HIS EPISTLE ON WORSHIP

When Abū al-ʿAbbās Taqī al-Dīn Aḥmad b. ʿAbd al-Ḥalīm b. Taymiyya died in 728/1328, the prominent scholars and judges of Damascus gathered up all of his writings and distributed them among themselves. From this point there began a debate over his legacy that continues into our own times. Ibn Taymiyya remains one of the most controversial Islamic thinkers to this day, not only for his supposed influence on many fundamentalist movements, but also for the ongoing challenge his ideas pose to any form of conservatism that rests entirely on accepted traditions. He understood Islam to be a dynamic belief system that could be effectively applied to the ever-changing conditions of human society, but Ibn Taymiyya and his beliefs were themselves often misunderstood. For instance, one such element of his thinking that was frequently misinterpreted was the apparent contradictions that were seen in his arguments when they were only given a cursory study. For on the one hand, an insistence that the Qur'ān and *Sunna* had to be the starting point for all discussions in any field of human thought was clearly at the core of Ibn Taymiyya's thinking; consequently, he defended a type of conservatism that did not deviate from the foundations of Islam as presented by the Righteous Predecessors of the community (*al-salaf al-ṣāliḥ*[1]). Yet on the other hand, he was fully aware of all subsequent developments in Islamic legal thought, theology, philosophy and mysticism up to his own time. This is made clear by his constant engagement with all these developments throughout his writings. In some cases he willingly adopted new ideas while at other times he vigorously refuted them.

A further point of misunderstanding was related to Ibn Taymiyya's method of debate. By way of illustration, whenever he analysed the institutionalised rulings of the legal schools (*madhāhib*), the positions of the theologians or the claims of the Ṣūfīs, he would challenge one and all to prove that what they said could be grounded in the beliefs and practices of the earliest generations of Muslims. However, his arguments were not broadly applied in generic attacks on his opponents; instead, whether dealing with his contemporaries or criticising past scholars, he would praise or castigate, and support or refute, based solely on each individual statement made by any person or group. Thus, he could be in total agreement with Abū Ḥāmid al-Ghazālī on one point, and then denounce him on another. He could give credit to what he saw as the beneficial aspects of Muḥyī al-Dīn Ibn al-ʿArabī's writings and then denounce him for what he considered to be heretical beliefs. He could insist on the perpetual need for independent judgement (*ijtihād*) and nonetheless maintain that the legal schools were needed. He could reject the ideas of the Ṣūfīs and yet reformulate the concept of annihilation (*fanā'*) that was associated with them in order to conform to the beliefs of the Righteous Predecessors. This multifaceted nature of Ibn Taymiyya's methods is what underlies the challenge in understanding him and it explains why his statements could be misappropriated by supporters and critics alike.

One important step in overcoming the difficulties in understanding Ibn Taymiyya is to provide greater access to his beliefs and opinions as expressed in his own writings; one must absorb the full range of his thought processes, rather than only looking at snippets of his ideas. I hope to begin filling this gap by presenting this annotated translation of one of his most important epistles on the theology of worship, his *Risālat al-ʿubūdiyya*.

Ibn Taymiyya's *Epistle on Worship* was presented by him as an exegesis of Q.II.21, 'O people! Worship your Lord […],' and his student, Ibn ʿAbd al-Hādī (d. 744/1343), referred to the *Risāla* as a 'principal statement concerning the discourse on this verse and a most significant statement on predestination.'[2] The use of Q.II.21 as the basis of Ibn Taymiyya's discourse on worship was quite appropriate because it was considered by Sunnī exegetes to be an important statement indicating God's oneness, the creation of all things out of nothingness, and the obligation of people to worship only the one true God.[3] This verse was important because, as the philologist and Qur'ān reader Kisā'ī (d. 189/804) pointed out, it is the only one in the Qur'ān in which the phrase, 'O people' (*yā ayyuhā al-nās*), is followed by the command, 'worship your Lord' (*uʿbūdū rabbakum*).[4] Moreover, the exegete Ibn ʿAṭiyya (d. 546/1152) highlighted the significance of this wording when he stated that the verse called on people to 'single out their Lord' (*waḥḥidūhu*) and to 'specify Him for worship' (*khaṣṣūhu bi'l-ʿibāda*),[5] noting that the use of '*rabbakum*' referred to God's attribute as Creator, which was an attribute of God that the pagan Arabs confirmed, but then did not respond to with exclusive worship. Ibn ʿAṭiyya continued by saying that Q.II.21 was a call to the 'natural disposition' (*fiṭra*) of humans, for by worshipping God they would stay in this natural disposition and remain pious.[6] These are important concepts that Ibn Taymiyya developed in the *Risāla*. A further significance of the verse for Ibn Taymiyya was that it was preceded by a description of believers, disbelievers and hypocrites in the first twenty verses of the sura (Q.II.1–20) that provided Ibn Taymiyya (with his penchant for classifying all groups and individuals) with a starting point in revelation for his division of humanity into a hierarchy based on worship.[7]

The purpose of Ibn Taymiyya's *Risāla* was to elucidate all of the issues that he considered to be necessary for the proper understanding of worship. In the process of explaining worship in light of the Qur'ān and the *Sunna* according to orthodox interpretation, he mentioned various groups and individuals who, in his opinion, were either followers of orthodoxy or were those who had erred; however, polemical refutation was not the overriding theme of the *Risāla*. More significantly, the key element throughout the work was his concern to help each worshipper actualise what he considered to be the beliefs and practices of the Prophet and his Companions. Thus, polemics notwithstanding, this work shows how Ibn Taymiyya used the Qur'ān, the *Ḥadīth* and the Arabic language to develop arguments in support of his interpretation of Sunnī Islam.

The Banū Taymiyya

Abū al-ᶜAbbās Taqī al-Dīn Aḥmad b. Taymiyya[8] was born in Harran in what is today northern Syria on 10 Rabīᶜ al-Awwal 661/22 January 1263.[9] He was the eldest son of Shihāb al-Dīn ᶜAbd al-Ḥalīm b. Taymiyya (627/1230–682/1284) and was the newest member of a famous and well-respected family of Ḥanbalī scholars.[10] In order to sketch the history of the Banū Taymiyya, and the scholarly reputation of this family, we must begin with the paternal uncle of Ibn Taymiyya's grandfather. Fakhr al-Dīn Muḥammad b. al-Khāḍir Abū al-Qāsim b. Muḥammad b. Taymiyya (542/1147–622/1225)[11] was one of the foremost scholars and ascetics of the Ḥanbalī legal school (*madhhab*). After completing his initial studies in Harran, he travelled to Baghdad where he mastered the sciences of exegesis, *ḥadīth* and jurisprudence. During this time he became a close follower of the famous Ḥanbalī scholar, Abū al-Faraj b. al-Jawzī (d. 597/1201), and when Fakhr al-Dīn returned to Harran he was appointed as a prayer leader and preacher. As one of the prominent Ḥanbalī scholars of his time, he remained in contact with other leading figures of the *madhhab*. In particular, he kept up correspondence with the Ḥanbalī scholar, Muwaffaq al-Dīn b. Qudāma (d. 620/1223), in Damascus.[12] Consequently, with his roots firmly established in Ḥanbalī traditionism, Fakhr al-Dīn passed on to his descendants a corpus of learning based on the orthodoxy of the

Salaf in relation to the Qur'ānic exegesis, *hadīth* interpretation and pietistic attitude associated with this *madhhab*.

However, besides his scholarly reputation, Fakhr al-Dīn also had certain affiliations with Sufism. According to various reports, either Fakhr al-Dīn or his father was considered to be one of the forty *abdāl* in the Ṣūfī hierarchy of saints.[13] Notwithstanding this apparent Ṣūfī affiliation, Fakhr al-Dīn played a much more significant role in the transmission of pietistic and ascetic literature that condemned desire (*hawā*) and passion (*ᶜishq*), which was an activity more expected of Ḥanbalī pietists. Thus, from this early point in the history of the Banū Taymiyya, there emerged a clear trend toward the type of asceticism that avoided pantheistic mysticism. A brief look at some of the issues related to the education of Fakhr al-Dīn will help to distinguish the type of Sufism with which he was involved.

There are two important personal connections relating to this issue of asceticism worth mentioning in order to highlight the lineage of the traditionist teachings passed down from generation to generation among the Banū Taymiyya. In Baghdad, Fakhr al-Dīn studied with two of the most famous pietists and transmitters of literature censuring desire and passion: the first was Shuhda bint Aḥmad b. al-Faraj b. ᶜUmar (d. 574/1179)[14] and the second was Ibn al-Jawzī. Shuhda, a famous female scholar of sixth century Baghdad, was a student of Abū Muḥammad Jaᶜfar b. Aḥmad al-Ḥusayn al-Sarrāj al-Qārī (d. 500/1107), and was instrumental in transmitting his work, *Maṣāriᶜ al-ᶜushshāq*, which she received directly from him.[15] Shuhda also played a prominent role in Ibn al-Jawzī's work, *Dhamm al-hawā*, for in the chapter entitled, 'Accounts of Those Whom *ᶜIshq* Killed,' he related approximately half of the stories directly from her. It appears likely that the Sufism of both Shuhda and Fakhr al-Dīn was what Schimmel calls 'voluntaristic' Sufism;[16] that is, an asceticism devoid of mysticism, and the traditionalist education of Fakhr al-Dīn points in this direction. The links between the censure of passionate love and mystical love were brought out, for example, in the *Masāriᶜ al-ᶜushshāq*, for Sarrāj reported on those who were 'smitten by mystical rapture.'[17] It is also important to keep in mind that Ibn al-Jawzī was fiercely opposed to mysticism, yet advocated piety and asceticism. Giffen points out that Ibn al-Jawzī drew heavily from two earlier works, the *Iᶜtilāl al-qulūb* of Kharā'itī and the *Masāriᶜ al-ᶜushshāq*.[18]

Throughout Ibn al-Jawzī's *Dhamm al-hawā*, he expounded on the '...evils and dangers of passionate cravings for anything, and unbridled sexual lust in particular.'[19] He also spoke of the superiority of the intellect (*ᶜaql*) over desire (*hawā*), and of the need to control the soul. As a student of Ibn al-Jawzī, Fakhr al-Dīn was most assuredly familiar with the former's famous work, *Talbīs Iblīs*, which contains a lengthy section on the condemnation of mystical Sufism.[20] Thus, it is safe to say that Fakhr al-Dīn's education and training was in the traditional Ḥanbalī school of pietism and asceticism,[21] and his legacy to his descendants was his reputation as a pre-eminent upholder of orthodox Islam as based on its conception by the Righteous Predecessors.

The next member of the Taymiyya family to gain a reputation as one of the great scholars of the Ḥanbalī *madhhab* was Aḥmad b. Taymiyya's grandfather, Majd al-Dīn ᶜAbd al-Salām b. Taymiyya (590/1194–652/1254).[22] Although it was reported that Fakhr al-Dīn wrote many books,[23] it was Majd al-Dīn who left the first tangible legacy of important works in various fields of the Islamic sciences. According to Brockelmann,[24] there are six manuscripts attributed to him that mainly concern issues of jurisprudence (*fiqh*) and ḥadīth collection and criticism .[25] These books by Majd al-Dīn represent some of the most important works of the Ḥanbalī *madhhab* and were well appreciated and utilised by its students.

Aḥmad b. Taymiyya's father, Shihāb al-Dīn, continued in the tradition of the Banū Taymiyya. While residing in Harran, he had two more sons, Zayn al-Dīn and Sharaf al-Dīn,[26] but the family did not spend much more time in their ancestral homeland because in 667/1269, they were forced to flee Harran in advance of the invading

Mongol army. They then settled in Damascus, which had long been the home of a strong Ḥanbalī tradition,[27] and there Shihāb al-Dīn became the director of the Ḥanbalī school of *ḥadīth*, al-Sukkariyya. Although he was considered to be a great scholar in his own right, Shihāb al-Dīn was ultimately overshadowed by both his father, Majd al-Dīn, and his son, Taqī al-Dīn Aḥmad b. Taymiyya, in the history of the Ḥanbalī *madhhab*.[28]

Ibn Taymiyya's Conflicts and Trials

Although the Arabic sources mention several incidents from Ibn Taymiyya's early years, there is nothing immediately relevant to this study. I therefore focus on the most important period in the development of his ideas: the period in which he wrote the *Risāla*. These were the years of his conflicts with the Mamluk authorities and the religious leadership of his day between 698/1299 and 709/1311. This period represents his transition from the role of a young lecturer and scholar in a college (*madrasa*) to one of social activist and reformer. Driven by historical events and the strength of his convictions, Ibn Taymiyya went on to leave much more than simply a legacy of scholarly writings as his forefathers had done. Instead, he came to be viewed by history as a sharp critic of religious beliefs, social customs and political policies that he considered to have deviated from the Islam of the Companions (*ṣaḥāba*). His ideas of a pure Islam were confronted by a multitude of complex historical circumstances that worked both in his favour and against him. Yet ultimately, Ibn Taymiyya challenged his fellow Muslims to reform society along the lines of the orthodoxy of the Righteous Predecessors amid, on the one hand, the Mongol invasions and Mamluk court intrigue, and, on the other, the popularity of mystical Sufism and the institutionalism of the four schools of jurisprudence.[29] Through his activities and writings, he emerged as a vital player in shaping both Mamluk and Islamic history, which compels us to gain a better understanding of the man and his beliefs.

Probably the earliest controversy in which Ibn Taymiyya became a target of attack was prompted by a lecture that he gave at the Umayyad Mosque in Damascus in 690/1291. We know only that 'some opponents' tried to stop him from speaking about the attributes of God.[30] The incident came to a quick end after the Shāfiʿī chief judge Shihāb al-Dīn al-Khuway (d. 693/1294) supported his position.[31] This isolated event was, however, a portent of things to come.

The next controversy came in 693/1294 and gave rise to a much more volatile situation. It involved accusations that a Christian secretary to an influential emir of the family of ʿAlī had insulted the Prophet Muḥammad,[32] and, as a result, Ibn Taymiyya and the Shāfiʿī shaykh of the Dār al-Ḥadīth, Zayn al-Dīn al-Fāriqī, led a crowd to the viceregal palace demanding the Christian's execution.[33] Although assurances were given by the governor, ʿIzz al-Dīn Aybak al-Hamawī, that the matter would be handled according to Islamic law, no action was taken after the emir complained to the governor of attacks against himself and his home. There followed a week of scattered violence that was blamed on Ibn Taymiyya and Fāriqī, who were then imprisoned and beaten. Meanwhile, the governor sought the Mamluk sultan's advice and obtained a legal ruling from some of the Shāfiʿī judges stating that the Christian would be safe upon his conversion to Islam.[34] This brought the incident to an end because the leaders of the four schools of jurisprudence could not arrive at a unanimous decision.

One more incident occurred before the period of Mongol invasions that indicates the complexities of the relations between the *ʿulamāʾ*, including Ibn Taymiyya, and the ruling elite. In this case, Ibn Taymiyya's close relationship with an interim governor of Damascus, Jāghān,[35] disturbed his opponents sufficiently that they initiated a series of actions against him. In Rabīʿ al-Awwal 698/December 1297, a group of jurists accused Ibn Taymiyya of anthropomorphism because of statements he had made in his recently written creed, *al-ʿAqīda al-hamawiyya al-kubrā*,[36] and they insisted that he appear before the Ḥanafī chief judge Jalāl al-Dīn al-Qazwīnī (d. 739/1339). Ibn

Taymiyya responded by saying that initiating an investigation into points of creed was not within the jurisdiction of a judge (*qāḍī*), and his response caused the Ḥanafī chief judge to publicly declare that the *Hamawiyya* creed was heretical because it was worded in such a way as to indicate that Jalāl al-Dīn was incompetent to judge matters like these. In order to stop impending street demonstrations by supporters of both shaykhs, the governor Jāghān had the announcer of Jalāl al-Dīn's decision beaten. Ibn Taymiyya then met with the Shāfiʿī chief judge Imām al-Dīn al-Qazwīnī, the brother of Jalāl al-Dīn, to discuss the *Hamawiyya*, and after a day-long meeting, the Shāfiʿī chief judge declared that the *Hamawiyya* was sound. The affair ended when Imām al-Dīn said that whoever slandered Ibn Taymiyya would become his own enemy, and Jalāl al-Dīn added that they would punish whoever spoke badly of the Ibn Taymiyya.[37]

During the years 699/1300–704/1305, Damascus and all of Syria were under continual threat of attack by the Mongols who were led by the Ilkhan Ghazan (d. 704/1305), a descendant of Genghis Khan through his grandson, Hulagu.[38] Since Ibn Taymiyya's attention—and that of almost everyone—was turned toward the Mongol threat, there was little reported about his conflicts with the authorities. It is clear, however, that he was very much involved in defending Damascus and in negotiating with the Mongols. A brief review of some of his major actions will suffice to show that his defence of Islam was in action as well as in word, and that he did not hesitate to risk his life in order to defend Islam and the Muslims.

In the first of Ghazan's incursions into Syria (Rabīʿ al-Awwal 699/December 1299), the Mamluk forces under Sultan al-Nāṣir Muḥammad were badly defeated.[39] Damascus was left to defend itself, and a delegation which included Ibn Taymiyya met with Ghazan to sue for peace in Rabīʿ al-Thānī 699/January 1300. When they were brought before Ghazan, Ibn Taymiyya boldly chastised the Mongol khan who had recently accepted Islam. His bravery greatly impressed Ghazan who granted amnesty to the city.[40] Damascus was placed for a very short time under the military governorship of the Mongol generals, Sayf al-Dīn Qibjaq and Qutlughshāh. However, by Jumādā al-Ūlā 699/February 1300, Ghazan returned to Persia and the Mamluks quickly reoccupied Syria.[41]

After the Mamluks reestablished their control of Syria, the governor of Damascus, Jamāl al-Dīn Aqūsh al-Afram, led a successful expedition against the Shīᶜī inhabitants of Kasrawān who had aided the Mongols and attacked the retreating Egyptian and Syrian armies. Ibn Taymiyya accompanied the army on this campaign which lasted from Shawwāl to Dhū al-Qaᶜda 699/July to August 1300,[42] and he preached on the merits of military action against the Shīᶜī sects by pointing out the corruptions of their intentions and beliefs. However, the jubilation of this victory did not last long, for a second Mongol invasion occurred from Ṣafar to Jumādā al-Ūlā 700/October 1300 to February 1301. During this invasion, Ibn Taymiyya travelled to Egypt to demand that the sultan, who had been reluctant to get involved in another war with the Mongols, send troops to Syria. However, by the time the sultan conceded to Ibn Taymiyya's demands, the Mongols had already retreated from Syria.[43]

In spite of his efforts to defend Damascus, there were still a few attempts to condemn Ibn Taymiyya as his growing popularity with all levels of society was also accompanied by the rising hostility of his opponents toward him. This most likely encouraged some of them to act against him. One such incident occurred in Jumādā al-Ūlā 702/December 1302, when some of Ibn Taymiyya's opponents forged a letter implicating him in a conspiracy against the governor of Damascus and then accused him of corresponding with the Mongols. This letter stated that Ibn Taymiyya along with the Ḥanafī judge, Shams al-Dīn al-Ḥarīrī, the Shāfiᶜī shaykh, Ibn al-Zamlakānī, and Kamāl al-Dīn b. al-ᶜAṭṭār alongside several emirs were plotting to overthrow Afram and bring back the deposed emir Qibjaq. However, the truth was discovered and the perpetrators (two Ṣūfī mendicants, Yaᶜfūrī and Aḥmad al-Ghanārī) and a scribe (al-Tāj al-Munādīlī) were severely punished.[44] According to Ibn Kathīr, this event occurred shortly after the death of the Shāfiʿī chief judge of Egypt, Ibn Daqīq al-ʿĪd, whose demise sparked a period of uncertainty as the religious leadership in Egypt and Syria underwent changes. Subsequently, the chief judge of Damascus, Ibn Jamāʿa, was called to Cairo to serve as the new Shāfiʿī chief judge and was accompanied by the governor, Afram.[45] Meanwhile, in Damascus, this meant that Ibn Ṣaṣarī,[46] who strongly opposed Ibn Taymiyya, was appointed as chief judge to replace Ibn Jamāʿa. This change in the religious leadership was the first in a series of appointments of people antagonistic toward Ibn Taymiyya to high office.[47]

However, any efforts to condemn Ibn Taymiyya were disrupted by the third invasion of the Mongols, which occurred in Ramaḍān 702/April 1303. Finally, at the Battle of Shaqhab on the plain of Marj near Damascus, the combined Mamluk armies of Syria and Egypt decisively defeated Ghazan's army headed by his general Qutlughshāh, and stopped any further Mongol incursions into Mamluk territory.[48] Before accompanying the army to battle, Ibn Taymiyya issued an important ruling stating that it was a duty to fight Ghazan—even though he had converted to Islam—because he was acting in a similar manner to the Khawārij by oppressing and abusing Muslims.[49] His efforts in bringing about this great victory and his prominent role in defending Damascus brought Ibn Taymiyya the renewed love and respect of the people and many of the ruling and religious elite throughout Egypt and Syria. However, at the same time, this only increased the hostility of his opponents toward him and it was after the Mongol threat had passed that his most critical controversies with the authorities occurred.

In 704/1305, the year before his trials began, Ibn Taymiyya managed to supply his opponents with several reasons to believe that he was becoming too influential in both religious and political spheres. Firstly, he had increased his polemical activities against the adherents of mystical Sufism by stopping many of their public displays[50] and by writing against the monism of Ibn ʿArabī (d. 638/1241).[51] Secondly, he greatly enhanced his influence with government authorities in Dhū al-Ḥijja 704/June 1305 when he accompanied the governor, Afram, on a second expedition against the Shīʿa of Kasrawān, who later capitulated. Thirdly, Ibn Taymiyya began to request that the Mamluk sultan and the governor follow Islamic law more closely in the newly reconquered areas, in matters ranging from the subdivision of provinces to the appointment of callers to prayer.[52] In all, this level of influence proved too much for his opponents to bear.

In order to understand this period of Ibn Taymiyya's life, it would be best to look at the events of 705/1306 to 709/1310 as a whole; that is, as a connected series of trials. The apparent cause of these events began in Jumādā al-Ūlā 705/November 1305, when a group of mystics of the Rifāʿiyya order came to the governor, Afram, demanding that Ibn Taymiyya stop his attacks against them. This led to a debate at the viceregal palace where Ibn Taymiyya denounced their beliefs and practices,[53] while the leading Rifāʿī shaykhs, Ṣāliḥ and Munaybiʿ, claimed that his objections were merely a matter of legal opinion because they were Shāfiʿī whereas Ibn Taymiyya was a Ḥanbalī. On hearing this, Ibn Taymiyya responded by persuading a leading Shāfiʿī scholar called Ibn al-Zamlakānī to also denounce them. As a result, the governor ruled in Ibn Taymiyya's favour and the mystics were forced to curtail their activities.[54]

Shortly thereafter, in Rajab 705/January 1306, Ibn Taymiyya was called before a council of judges from the four schools of jurisprudence in Damascus to answer questions concerning his creed, a work known as *al-ʿAqīda al-wāsiṭiyya* which became a focal point of the trials.[55]. The *ʿAqīda* was a short treatise outlining the fundamentals of the Salafī creed (i.e., the beliefs of the Righteous Predecessors) that he wrote in 698/1299 in response to questions posed by several judges from the city of Wāsiṭ. Apparently, the trial in Damascus was initiated from Cairo by his main opponents, Naṣr al-Manbijī (d. 718/1319) and Ibn Makhlūf (d. 719/1319), who had the support of the Commander-in-Chief of the Mamluk army in Egypt, Baybars al-Jāshangīr. The intervention of these two men in Damascene affairs seems to have been prompted by a letter that Ibn Taymiyya wrote to Manbijī in 704/1305 and by certain points of his creed.[56] This letter constituted part of Ibn Taymiyya's recent doctrinal attacks on the monism of Ibn ᶜArabī, of whom Manbijī was an adherent. At this first council, Ibn Taymiyya defended his *ᶜAqīda* by arguing that what he had said concerning the attributes of God was in fact true to the beliefs of the *Salaf*, and not just of Ibn Ḥanbal. To his, his judges were unable to respond so they suggested that he write down his answers and present them at a second council.[57]

The first council was followed by two others, with the eventual outcome that there was reluctant agreement among the judges that Ibn Taymiyya's creed was orthodox. As for the second trial, the reports are conflicting: some versions claim that Ibn Taymiyya converted to Ashᶜarism, while others state that he was victoriously carried off from the council.[58] The confusion over the trial's outcome was most likely what prompted a third council, which seems to have been more decisive but no less confrontational. For example, during the proceedings the Shāfiᶜī shaykh, Ṣadr al-Dīn b. al-Muraḥḥil (d. 716/1317), reluctantly admitted that Ibn Taymiyya was correct in stating that Imam Shāfiᶜī believed that the Qur'ān was the literal word of God (*kalām lafẓī*) and that whoever rejected this was a disbeliever. This testimony caused an uproar among some of the Shāfiᶜī shaykhs because it implied that the famous Shāfiᶜī scholar, Juwaynī (d. 478/1085), was a disbeliever, because he had maintained that the Qur'ān was an expression of the meaning of God's essential knowledge (*kalām nafsī*).[59] However, in spite of some dissenting opinions, the matter of Ibn Taymiyya's creed was settled by default. His arguments that his beliefs were those of the Righteous Predecessors of Islam, and not just those of Ibn Ḥanbal, were neither whole-heartedly accepted nor clearly refuted. His enemies could prove nothing against him on this occasion, and so he was freed for the time being. But Ibn Taymiyya's status quickly changed when he was called to Cairo on the insistence of Ibn Makhlūf, the Mālikī chief judge, in Ramaḍān of the same year.

At the first council in Cairo (Ramaḍān 705/April 1306), Ibn Taymiyya was kept from speaking except to give direct answers to specific questions,[60] but after pointing out that Ibn Makhlūf was both his accuser and judge, he refused to answer any questions. On hearing this, Ibn Makhlūf was furious and had him imprisoned for the first time.[61] Ibn Taymiyya remained under arrest for approximately a year and a half. During this time, the Shāfiʿī chief judge, Ibn Jamāʿa, made public what he viewed as an official Shāfiʿī doctrine, in which everyone had to acquiesce. Part of this statement was his ruling that the creed of Ibn Taymiyya was to be officially condemned and that everyone, particularly the Ḥanbalīs, had to denounce him and his creed. This decree was effective in Egypt and Syria.[62]

A year later, in Shawwāl 706/April 1307, a second council was convened at the behest of the governor of Egypt, Sallār, who wanted Ibn Taymiyya to be freed.[63] Ibn Taymiyya was not present at the council when it was decided that he could be freed if he denounced his own creed. Afterwards, six offers were made to him to come and discuss the matter, but he refused to attend as long as they insisted on this condition. Sallār persisted in his efforts and finally a third council was called in Ṣafar 707/August 1307, in which Ibn Taymiyya met with the Shāfiʿī chief judge, Ibn Jamāʿa.[64] After a lengthy conversation with him, Ibn Taymiyya still stuck to his original demands and refused to leave the prison.[65] Thus, Sallār's intervention on behalf of Ibn Taymiyya ended without success.

However, a second effort to free him was more successful. In Rabīʿ al-Awwal 707/September 1307, the Syrian Emir, Ḥusām al-Dīn Muḥanna b. ʿĪsā (d. 735/1335), secured the sultan's permission to have Ibn Taymiyya released.[66] However, his release was immediately followed up by three more councils, which were essentially discussions between the governor and various scholars without the participation of any judges since they felt that these talks were useless now that the sultan had already freed him. For example, at the second council the judges actually sent excuses for not coming—some even stating that they were sick.

After the third council in Rabīᶜ al-Thānī 707/October 1307, Ibn Taymiyya was free to lecture once again.[67] This freedom would not last long. In Shawwāl 707/April 1308, a group of Ṣūfīs led by Karīm al-Dīn al-Amūlī (d. 710/1310–11), the chief shaykh of Khānqāh Saᶜīd al-Suᶜadā', and the Ṣūfī shaykh, Ibn ᶜAtā' Allāh al-Iskandarī (d. 709/1310), demonstrated against Ibn Taymiyya's denouncements of various forms of pantheism (*ittiḥād*)—especially that of Ibn ᶜArabī—at the Cairo citadel. This led to a new trial once again headed by Ibn Jamāᶜa. Although nothing could be proved against Ibn Taymiyya,[68] numerous complaints eventually forced the authorities to do something about him, and he was given three alternatives: to go to Alexandria, to Damascus, or to prison. But when no judge was willing to issue an order against him he himself volunteered to return to prison for the benefit of all.[69] He was detained for a short time and then released at the request of various shaykhs. During this period of detention, as before, Ibn Taymiyya was permitted to have a servant, as well as visitors, and he continued to lecture and write from his cell. This was one reason why his opponents felt it would be better to have him out of Cairo altogether; this was accomplished when political turmoil brought his adversary, Baybars al-Jāshangīr, to the sultanate in Shawwāl 708/April 1309.

A period of exile for Ibn Taymiyya coincided with the short reign of Jāshangīr. Although this Mamluk sultan supported Naṣr al-Manbijī and Ibn Makhlūf, he still sought the approval of Ibn Taymiyya and other *ᶜulamā'* for the legitimacy of his reign. However, Ibn Taymiyya responded by saying that the sultan's 'days are numbered, his leadership is finished and his rule is drawing to a close.'[70] This statement, compounded by his continued attacks on the monism of Ibn ʿArabī, led to him being exiled to Alexandria in Ṣafar 709/August 1309. Once there, he was detained at the sultan's palace, in a room with one window overlooking the sea and the other opened to the city in the hope that someone would expedite his demise.[71]

Notwithstanding these devious stratagems on the part of his opponents, the eight months that Ibn Taymiyya spent in Alexandria were actually very productive, for he was able to meet with visitors and write numerous letters and essays. He held various meetings with leading Mālikī and Ẓāhirī scholars and with the Ṣūfī followers of Ibn ʿArabī and Ibn Sabʿīn (d. 669/1271)— some of whom Ibn Taymiyya was able to gain as supporters.[72] Meanwhile elsewhere, events were progressing toward the downfall of Baybars al-Jāshangīr and Naṣr al-Manbijī. Al-Nāṣir Muḥammad regained control of Damascus in Shaʿbān 709/January 1310 and returned victoriously to Cairo as sultan in Shawwāl/March of that year. On returning to power, he invited Ibn Taymiyya to the royal court and treated him as a honoured guest.[73] This brief period in which he enjoyed the favour of the sultan meant that he was no longer in direct confrontation with the authorities, but it did not guarantee that he remained free of opposition.

At this point, Ibn Taymiyya remained in Cairo for a few years and continued teaching. But trouble and controversy were never far behind, and there were several incidents in which he was accosted and beaten by angry mobs.[74] One particular incident in Rajab 711/December 1311 almost caused a riot as Ibn Taymiyya's supporters came to his rescue. However, the fact that he forgave his attackers and ordered that no revenge be taken against them brought the turmoil to an end. Finally, in Shawwāl 712/February 1313, he left Egypt and returned to Damascus where he remained until his death in Dhū al-Qaʿda 728/September 1328.

During these final years in Damascus, Ibn Taymiyya concerned himself mostly with teaching and writing. However, there were two further episodes that led to his imprisonment on both occasions. The first incident concerned his ruling against the oath of divorce (*ḥilf bi'l-ṭalāq*). Once again a major problem arose because Ibn Taymiyya diverged from contemporary thinking on this issue among the four schools of jurisprudence.[75] For his part, he refused to accept that a man could divorce his wife based on an oath unrelated to the marriage situation. In what had become a common practice, a man could declare that if he performed a certain action or failed to do so, he would divorce his wife, but for Ibn Taymiyya, this was nothing less than wagering one's marriage in pursuit of a particular goal.[76] Influenced by lbn Taymiyya's opponents, Sultan al-Nāṣir ordered him to stop giving legal rulings on this topic, and as might be expected, he refused to remain quiet, regarding his beliefs on the matter to outweigh any potential repercussions. In response, three councils were convened over a two-year period to discuss his position. Finally, at the third council the governor of Damascus, Tankiz,[77] ordered Ibn Taymiyya arrested for his persistent disobedience and he was imprisoned for six months between Rajab 720/August 1320 and Muḥarram 721/February 1321.[78]

The second incident that led to Ibn Taymiyya's imprisonment related to his views on the visitation of graves (*ziyāra*).[79] When some of his opponents circulated a ruling he had written seventeen years earlier strictly prohibiting the visitation of graves for the purpose of worship, the populace of Syria and Egypt were in turmoil. In this case, his opposition was led by the Mālikī chief judge, Muḥammad b. Abī Bakr al-Ikhnā'ī (d. 732/1332), who had been a protégé of Ibn Taymiyya's former opponent in Egypt, Naṣr al-Manbijī. Ikhnā'ī had become one of the sultan's closest advisers and pressed for a strong response against the Ḥanbalī shaykh. Although Ibn Taymiyya accused Ikhnā'ī of intentionally spreading lies about his opinion on this matter, the accompanying public disturbances forced the sultan to order Ibn Taymiyya's imprisonment in Shaʿbān 726/July 1326. Thus condemned, he obligingly entered the citadel, which would remain his final abode until his death.

During this last period of imprisonment, there was a great outpouring of support for Ibn Taymiyya. Scholars from Baghdad and other cities beyond the Mamluk empire petitioned the sultan to release him.[80] But the situation deteriorated as Ibn Taymiyya's opponents grew increasingly frustrated by his relentless attacks written from his comfortable cell in the citadel. By Jumādā al-Ākhira 728/April 1328, the sultan was persuaded to forbid him from possessing any books or writing materials; this order was carried out in Shawwāl/August.[81] By Dhū al-Qaᶜda, Ibn Taymiyya fell ill, and on the 20th of the month (27 September), the sixty-five-year-old Ḥanbalī scholar passed away. After the announcement of his death was made from the minarets of Damascus, the gates of the city were opened to accommodate the crowds coming for his funeral. Ultimately, and in spite of the controversies surrounding his final imprisonment, the funeral procession of this beloved shaykh turned out to be one of the largest in Damascus.[82]

IBN TAYMIYYA'S METHODOLOGY

In order to fully comprehend the ideas presented in Ibn Taymiyya's *Risāla*, it is first necessary to understand how he arrived at them. To that end, this section identifies the major sources that formed the basis of his religious views and explains how he made use of these sources in formulating his beliefs. When reading through Ibn Taymiyya's writings, it quickly becomes apparent five elements formed the foundation of his religious thought. These were (1) the Qur'ān, (2) the *Sunna* of the Prophet, (3) the practice and statements of the Companions, (4) the opinions of the Followers (*tābiᶜūn*), and (5) the Arabic language. By using these sources, Ibn Taymiyya developed an understanding of Islam based on what he claimed was clearly identifiable with the beliefs and practices of the Prophet and his Companions.

Although there was nothing unique about his use of these sources as a basis for Muslim theology,[83] the particular methodology that he derived from these sources—which he claimed was in accordance with the methodology of the Righteous Predecessors—placed his discourse on theology within a clearly defined historical trend and distinguished it from the practice of other Islamic sects. In attempting to define the boundaries of theological discourse, Ibn Taymiyya utilised a traditionist approach to these sources, following the methodology of the *Ahl al-Ḥadīth* in general and of the Ḥanbalī *madhhab* in particular. However, he not only adhered to this traditionist methodology of the Predecessors, but stood out as its pre-eminent spokesman at the beginning of the eighth/fourteenth century.[84] His arguments to support his interpretation of the revealed texts, which for him meant both the Qur'ān and authentic *Ḥadīth* corpus, were based on this orthodox tradition, and, as he repeatedly pointed out, represented the methodology and beliefs of the four imams—Abū Ḥanīfa, Mālik, Shāfiʿī and Ibn Ḥanbal, and other great scholars of early Islam. For Ibn Taymiyya, the faith, knowledge and practice that were derived from these five sources constituted the entirety of the legitimate understanding of Islam. His position was that Muslims generally, and scholars especially, had to utilise the methodology of the Predecessors in matters of creed and practice. Yet, as indicated in the discussion of his life above, this stance placed him in opposition to those jurisprudents of the four *madhhab*s who sought to codify the law by using dialectical arguments borrowed from *kalām* as the basis for legal reasoning (*uṣūl al-fiqh*); it also set him at odds with the Ashʿarī theologians who sought to promote *kalām* arguments concerning theology.[85]

A further distinguishing feature of Ibn Taymiyya's writings on legal and theological issues was that they were based on the principle that revelation and methodology were intricately and necessarily linked together.[86] His premise was that within revelation itself was to be found the means to understand, interpret and practice that revelation; thus, no sources or methods outside the totality of Islamic revelation were permitted for the interpretation and practice of that revelation. He argued that the Qur'ān was manifested in the statements and actions of the Prophet, and that it was his *Sunna* which was scrupulously followed by the Companions. Accordingly, the Companion's manifestation of Islam represented the highest attainable religious state for which any Muslim could hope. For this reason, the Companions and, according to Ibn Taymiyya, the Followers were the model by which all other groups were to be judged.

In explaining Ibn Taymiyya's position relative to these five sources and the methodology derived from them, this discussion has been divided into three parts: the first deals with his approach to understanding the Qur'ān and includes a discussion of his hermeneutics and classification of the exegetes; the second focuses on the use of the Prophet's *Sunna* and the role of the Companions and the Followers as reliable transmitters of it; and the third describes the manner in which he used the Arabic language as a further means of defining the scope of theological discourse.

The Qur'ān

HERMENEUTICS

For Ibn Taymiyya, and by the unanimous agreement of Muslims, the Qur'ān was considered to be the actual word of God that was revealed directly to the Prophet by way of the archangel Gabriel. He therefore accepted that portions of it had been written down during the Prophet's lifetime and that ʿUthmān's edition of the text had been transmitted without corruption and in its totality by an uninterrupted chain of reciters.[87] As God's final revelation, the Qur'ān was held to necessarily contain the complete body of religious knowledge needed by a Muslim, and to provide him with practical advice combined with spiritual guidance in order to conduct his worldly affairs in a manner that elevated and perfected the soul for its return to its Lord. In addition, Ibn Taymiyya stipulated that the Qur'ān must be interpreted in the context of the *Sunna* of the Prophet and the statements of the earliest Muslims. His views on this may be further elucidated by looking at his discussion of exegesis (*tafsīr*).[88]

In the essay, *Muqaddima fī uṣūl al-tafsīr*, Ibn Taymiyya set out his fundamental position relative to the principles of the Islamic sciences, whether exegesis, law, or *kalām*.[89] He stated that the first thing a Muslim scholar ought to know in order to understand the Qur'ān properly was that the Prophet had explained its meaning fully and completely.[90] As proof of this, he mentioned that the Prophet's mission was defined in the verse, '…In order to explain to people what has been sent down to them' (Q.XVI.44). He further explained that the Companions used to learn ten verses from the Prophet but no more until they also learned what the verses said about knowledge and action.[91] This brief presentation of evidence[92] linked Ibn Taymiyya's methodology to a fundamental principle of the traditionists' hermeneutics; namely, that the Prophet fully explained the Qur'ān. This principle was used by Ibn Taymiyya, as it had been used by Ṭabarī (d. 310/923) before him, to refute the claims of the 'People of Opinion' (*Ahl al-Ra'y*) that human reason was needed to explain the Qur'ān. The *Ahl al-Ra'y* held the view that the Prophet had explained very little of the Qur'ān and so they developed a form of exegesis that became known as 'exegesis by opinion' (*tafsīr bi'l-ra'y*). This group was opposed by those scholars who maintained that the Prophet's exegetical role was all-encompassing and who therefore believed that the exegete's primary role was to relate the authentic statements associated with each verse of the Qur'ān. Due to this, their method of exegesis became known as 'exegesis by transmission' (*tafsīr bi'l-ma'thūr*).[93]

Consequently, Ibn Taymiyya's association with exegesis by transmission in asserting that the Prophet was the pre-eminent exegete was the first step he took in defining the boundaries of exegesis. His second step was to clarify the most correct way to proceed with an exegesis of the Qur'ān. So then, of the four steps that he mentioned, the first two forged an initial link between the Qur'ān and the *Sunna*, and further served to define the ranks of those capable of performing exegesis. In conjunction with steps one and two, he included steps three and four, which related to the statements of the Companions and the Followers, in order to complete the limitations he placed on exegesis.[94] The first step was to 'explain the Qur'ān by the Qur'ān,' as what was not mentioned in one spot was explained in another.[95] He said little else on this point because it was not a controversial issue. One limitation presupposed here was that an exegete should have memorised most of the Qur'ān—if not all of it, which in itself was a minor factor considering that memorisation of the Qur'ān was a common part of a scholar's training. However, another assumption of his concerning the exegesis of the Qur'ān by the Qur'ān was that an exegete must also know the 'causes of revelation' (*asbāb al-nuzūl*) and the science of abrogation (*al-nāsikh wa'l-mansūkh*).[96] These sciences related to both the Qur'ān and the *Ḥadīth* and were necessary for an exegete to know in order to properly evaluate the evidence from various sources relating to a given issue. This assumption suggests that Ibn Taymiyya intended to link exegesis to the sciences of *Ḥadīth*; a point more fully brought out in his second step, as we shall see.[97]

Ibn Taymiyya's second step in delimiting the science of exegesis went much further than the first in defining the skills needed by an exegete. He stated that if the first step were not sufficient to produce an answer, then a Muslim exegete must look to the *Sunna* of the Prophet, since that served as a commentator on, and clarifier of, the Qur'ān. Ibn Taymiyya supported this view by first quoting the verse, '...We did not send the book down to you except that you explain to them about which they differed, for it is a guidance and a mercy to people who believe' (Q.XVI.64). He then went on to mention a *ḥadīth* in which the Prophet said that he had been given the Qur'ān and its similitude;[98] the similitude here being the *Sunna*, which, when combined with the Qur'ān, was considered to constitute God's revelation in its entirety. Importantly for Ibn Taymiyya, this was also the opinion of Imam Shāfiʿī.[99] This second step presupposed that an exegete must also be an expert in the sciences of *Ḥadīth* in order to be able to discriminate between authentic *ḥadīth*s and weak or fabricated ones,[100] and Ibn Taymiyya further emphasised this point in his third step.

When an exegete was unable to find the answer he was looking for in either the Qur'ān or the *Sunna*, Ibn Taymiyya stated that his third step was to turn to the statements of the Companions on account of the fact that they were the most-informed Muslims concerning exegesis as they had witnessed the revelation of the Qur'ān, they were distinguished by their spiritual states and they possessed a complete understanding of Islam in terms of correct knowledge and righteous deeds. He mentioned in particular that Muslims should follow the statements of the four Rightly Guided Caliphs and the most knowledgeable Companions, such as ʿAbd Allāh b. Masʿūd (d. 32/653), who knew when each verse was revealed and with whom it was concerned. Ibn Taymiyya then made special mention of ʿAbd Allāh b. ʿAbbās (d. 68/688), on whose behalf the Prophet had supplicated to God to give him 'understanding in religion and knowledge of interpretation (*ta'wīl*).'[101] Thus, this third step further emphasised Ibn Taymiyya's insistence that an exegete must either be a *Ḥadīth* scholar, or at least rely on them when presenting an exegesis of the Qur'ān. Moreover, in order to distinguish the authentic statements of the Companions, the exegete was required to have the same skills as were needed to identify the authentic *ḥadīth*s of the Prophet. Thus, in the methodological and ideological struggle concerning exegesis, Ibn Taymiyya clearly intended to put the proponents of exegesis by opinion on the defensive with this step and the one following it.

Ibn Taymiyya's fourth step referred to the Followers of the Companions, who he saw as the last generational group to have sound knowledge of the Qur'ān. In particular, he mentioned Followers such as Mujāhid b. Jabr (d. 102/721), who studied with Ibn ʿAbbās, and ʿIkrima (d. 107/726), who was a client of Ibn ʿAbbās. He also mentioned ʿAtā' b. Abī Rabāḥ (d. 114/733), Saʿīd b. Jubayr (d. 95/714), al-Ḥasan al-Baṣrī (d. 110/729), Saʿīd b. al-Musayyab

(d. 92/711 or 94/713), Abū al-ʿAliyya (d. 93/712 or 106/725), al-Rabīʿ b. Anas (d. 139/757), Qatāda b. Diʿāma (d. 117/735), al-Ḍaḥḥak b. Muzāḥim (d. 102/721) and Masrūq b. al-Ajdaʿ (d. 63/683).[102] Although Ibn Taymiyya did not consider the Followers to be an independent source for the purposes of Qur'ānic exegesis because he thought that their statements had to be understood in context by means of the prior three steps. However, several specific problems arose with this fourth step and Ibn Taymiyya had to resolve internal conflicts in order to maintain consistency in his hermeneutics.[103] When looking at the statements of the Followers, it became clear to him that they often used terminology that differed from the statements of the Companions. In explaining what appeared to be contradictions, he expanded the scope of exegesis while simultaneously limiting the ranks of the exegetes because they also had to be experts on the statements of the Followers in addition to the *Ḥadīth* and the statements of the Companions.

When faced with the fact that the Followers sometimes used different terms from the Companions to explain the meaning of a verse, Ibn Taymiyya had to reconcile an obvious contradiction to his belief in faithfully following the statements of the Prophet and his Companions. He did so firstly by dismissing those who claimed that these discrepancies were real contradictions by countering that they were people without knowledge of the *Ḥadīth* sciences. Secondly, he began the process of reconciling the inconsistent terminology by clarifying that: 'some of them [the Followers] explained a matter by its connotative meaning or by what is similar to it (*bi-lāzimihi aw naẓīrihi*). Others stipulated a matter by its denotative meaning (*bi-ʿaynihi*).'[104] This statement had a two-fold effect on Ibn Taymiyya's exegesis: (1) it made allowance for some limited variation in explanation on the part of the Followers, and (2) it established their opinions as a form of evidence in the formulation of exegesis. Consequently, in the *Muqaddima* he was compelled to explain his use of the exegetical statements of the Followers in the light of Shuʿba b. al-Ḥajjāj's contention that if the opinions of the Followers were not to be used as evidence in jurisprudence, how could they then be used as evidence in exegesis?[105] Ibn Taymiyya's answer sought to justify his position while defining the meaning and use of personal opinion, which would then serve as guidelines for the exegete.

Ibn Taymiyya restricted the use of the statements of the Followers by saying that their opinions must conform to the understanding of a verse as elaborated in steps one to three. This meant that an exegete could not present one of their opinions as evidence (*ḥujja*) over another in the case of differences. But the statements of the Followers could be used as evidence when they agreed on an issue. Thus, Ibn Taymiyya widened the circle of sound knowledge by including unanimous opinions of the Followers with the other sources—the Qur'ān, the *Sunna*, the statements of the Companions and the Arabic language. His assumption again was that in order to accurately assess the validity of the statements of the Followers, an exegete had to be a fully competent *Ḥadīth* scholar; otherwise, he had to at least rely on the judgements of the *Ḥadīth* scholars concerning the authentication of traditions. Then, having reiterated this proviso of knowledge of the *Ḥadīth* sciences, Ibn Taymiyya then was in a position to delimit knowledge and opinion. He stated that if an exegesis of a verse of the Qur'ān was not based on the knowledge of the traditionists, then it fell into the category of 'mere opinion,' which Ibn Taymiyya said was strictly forbidden.[106] As evidence for this, he quoted a *ḥadīth* in which the Prophet stated that whoever talks about the Qur'ān without sound knowledge would take his place in the Hellfire. He also mentioned several *ḥadīth*s indicating that if an exegete were to give the correct explanation of a verse, but reached this explanation without recourse to sound knowledge, he would still be destined to the Hellfire.[107]

The hermeneutics involved in his fourth step allowed Ibn Taymiyya to successfully limit the ranks of those who were genuinely capable of conducting exegesis by his insistence that the exegete must be a *Ḥadīth* scholar. Yet at the same time, he allowed for a narrow door to sound reasoning (*ijtihād*) in exegesis by citing the use of personal opinion as strictly carried out by the Followers. Overall, by defining these four steps of hermeneutics, Ibn Taymiyya accomplished his goal of casting doubt on the validity of other hermeneutical approaches to the Qur'ān. With these principles of exegesis in hand, he was now in a position judge the authenticity of various exegetes, and in doing so, he also carefully classified individuals and groups according to his notion of Islamic sects.

CLASSIFYING THE EXEGETES

The four steps of Ibn Taymiyya's hermeneutics—the Qur'ān, the *Ḥadīth* of the Prophet, the statements of the Companions, and the opinions of the Followers—formed the basis of his thinking in all fields of the Islamic sciences. Curtis has shown that these were the principles of the Ḥanbalī *madhhab* in matters of theology, law and exegesis.[108] Lamotte presents an argument that these four principles were the basis of Ibn Taymiyya's epistemology, for they represent a movement from the absolute certainty of the Qur'ān to a lesser state of certainty to be found in the opinions of the Followers.[109] Although the details of the way in which Ibn Taymiyya applied these principles to the various Islamic sciences is extremely interesting, I shall have to limit my discussion here to his use of them in the classification of various Islamic sects. I shall show that adherence to these principles was the criterion Ibn Taymiyya used to judge the authenticity of the beliefs of known historical sects and of individual scholars. In this section I shall focus on the exegetes and in what follows, I shall expand the topic of classification to include a discussion of his judgements regarding who belonged to the People of the *Sunna* and the Congregation (*Ahl al-Sunna wa'l-Jamāʿa*). The ultimate purpose of this discussion is to identify for the reader the criteria used by Ibn Taymiyya to classify the ranks of worshippers in his *Risālat al-ʿubūdiyya*.

In the *Muqaddima*, Ibn Taymiyya began his discussion on the ranks of exegetes by stating that the most knowledgeable Muslims on this topic were the scholars of Mecca who were the companions of Ibn ʿAbbās.[110] After confirming the pre-eminent position of Ibn ʿAbbās as an exegete, Ibn Taymiyya identified the next tier of exegetes as being the scholars of Kufa, who were the companions of Ibn Masʿūd, and the scholars of Medina—especially those associated with Zayd b. Aslam (d. 136/754), who was the client of Ibn ʿUmar.[111] Up until the time of the Followers, Ibn Taymiyya was able to neatly arrange the early exegetes around the famous Companions; however, the task of classifying those who came after them was more complicated. For Ibn Taymiyya, exegesis became intricately linked to the sciences of *Ḥadīth* criticism from the time after the Followers onwards, as we have seen above. Based on this *Ḥadīth* connection, he explained that two groups of exegetes began to deviate from the traditionist methodology in exegesis, the best practioner of which was Ṭabarī.[112] But before elaborating on the deviant exegetes, it is necessary to point out two issues regarding Ibn Taymiyya's loyalty to Ṭabarī's methodology.

As mentioned above, McAuliffe and Speight have argued for the continuity of hermeneutics between Ṭabarī and Ibn Kathīr, but without crediting Ibn Taymiyya for the articulation of the principles of exegesis by transmission. Curtis, on the other hand, has shown that Ibn Taymiyya was indeed the architect of the Salafī principles of exegesis, and that Ibn Kathīr was his direct heir. I would add here that Ibn Taymiyya's high estimation of Ṭabarī highlights two important aspects of his own approach to methodology in the Islamic sciences: firstly, he disdained the use of opinion that was not grounded in the ordered principles of the Salafī methodology, and secondly, for him, adherence to this methodology superseded any loyalty to an established *madhhab*.

Concerning the first point, both Ṭabarī and Ibn Taymiyya must be seen as conservative *Ḥadīth* scholars who were appalled by what they considered to be the spread of personal opinion in the matter of exegesis, as well as in other Islamic sciences. While Ṭabarī was responding to the Muʿtazila, Ibn Taymiyya was primarily responding to the Ashʿariyya. Accordingly, by building on the juridical arguments of Imam Shāfiʿī (which established the role of the *Sunna* as embodied in the *Ḥadīth* as necessarily explaining the Qur'ān), Ṭabarī incorporated the idea that the Prophet, as an exegete, had explained everything in the Qur'ān. Additionally, in discussing some statements narrated from the Companions and Followers that indicated that they did not talk about the Qur'ān, Ṭabarī clarified that they did not speak about a verse unless they knew an authentic statement from the Prophet.[113] Later, when opposing the arguments of the Ashʿarī theologians that the Qur'ān required logic in order to be understood, Ibn Taymiyya advanced Ṭabarī's claim that the Prophet had explained the entire Qur'ān. Furthermore, both scholars met the challenge posed to traditionalism by the use of personal opinion by arguing for the need to rely on the statements of the Followers in explaining the Qur'ān.

Ibn Taymiyya's allegiance to the exegesis of Ṭabarī placed him at odds with many of his fellow Ḥanbalīs who did not care much for Ṭabarī.[114] Nonetheless, adhering to what he believed to be religious truth was more important to Ibn Taymiyya than adhering to the opinions of his *madhhab* affiliation. According to Abū Zahra, Ibn Taymiyya held that it was not permissible for a 'student of the truth' to prefer the ruling of his own *madhhab* when he knew that the truth lay elsewhere.[115] On a more practical note, he divided Muslims into three groups concerning the issue of following a *madhhab*. The first group consisted of those who 'know the detailed evidences' (*al-adillat al-tafṣīliyya*) needed to judge particular issues. For this group, following the truth instead of a *madhhab* was obligatory. The second group was made up of those who were 'incapable of extracting rulings for themselves' (*laysa lahu qudra ʿalā al-istinbāt*) because they did not know all judgements related to a particular issue or all the sciences needed to make judgements, such as the science of abrogation. This group included the majority of Muslims, who had to refer to more knowledgeable people and follow their opinions. The Muslims in this group could differ from their *madhhab* when they became convinced by the arguments of a particular case. The third group consisted of those who went from *madhhab* to *madhhab* looking for an opinion matching their desires. This was, of course, forbidden, and Ibn Taymiyya considered these people to be sinners.

Returning to the issue of the two groups of exegetes who deviated from exegesis by transmission, Ibn Taymiyya identified the first group as those who were weak in the *Ḥadīth* sciences and did not rely on the *Ḥadīth* scholars, and who therefore had drifted away from authentic transmissions. As examples of this group, he stated that Wāḥidī was far from being a safe transmitter and far from following the Predecessors.[116] Likewise, Ibn Taymiyya mentioned that Thaʿlabī was a good and religious man, but he blindly recorded everything he found in the books of exegesis, regardless of whether it was authentic, weak or fabricated.[117] However, Baghawī[118] later produced an abridged exegesis of Thaʿlabī's work which, according to Ibn Taymiyya, was safeguarded from fabricated *ḥadīth*s and innovated opinions because Baghawī was a scholar of *Ḥadīth*. Consequently, this ranking indicates that the error of the first group in the eyes of Ibn Taymiyya was primarily their weakness as *Ḥadīth* scholars and not any particular error in their theology.

The second group of exegetes whom Ibn Taymiyya criticised was composed of those whose theology was erroneous because they valued deduction based on human reason over authentic transmissions. In other words, they interpreted the Qur'ān according to their own reasoning which was not a source based on authentic transmission. In connection with this he referred to groups such as the Jahmiyya, the Muʿtazila, the Qadariyya and the Murji'a.[119] In his view, these groups erred in the matter of 'evidence and indicated meanings' (*al-dalīl wa'l-madlūl*); that is, they either disregarded the sound knowledge contained in the *Ḥadīth*, or they applied it in a manner contradicting that of the *Ḥadīth* scholars.[120] Thus, he thought that they held beliefs which were in opposition to the truth that the earliest generations of scholars had followed. Furthermore, by following their own school of thought and their own opinions, they interpreted verses without sound evidence or by distorting the meaning of words.

Ibn Taymiyya particularly focused on the Muʿtazila as the most egregious example of the deviation of the People of Opinion, and in connection with Muʿtazilī exegesis, he mentioned the works of: ʿAbd al-Raḥmān b. Kaysān al-Asamm (d. 190/806), Ibrāhīm b. Ismāʿīl b. ʿAliyya (d. 218/833), Abū ʿAlī al-Jubbā'ī (d. 303/915), al-Qaḍī ʿAbd al-Jabbār b. Aḥmad al-Ḥamadānī (d. 415/1025), ʿAli b. ʿIsā al-Rummānī (d. 384/995) and Abū al-Qāsim al-Zamakhsharī (d. 539/1144). The Muʿtazila were known for five principles and Ibn Taymiyya considered their explanation of these principles to be the cause of their deviation.[121] They were their concepts of (1) 'oneness' (*tawḥīd*), (2) 'justice' (*ʿadl*), (3) 'the position between the two positions' (*al-manzila bayn al-manzilatayn*), (4) 'executing the punishment' (*infādh al-waʿīd*) and (5) 'commanding good and forbidding evil' (*al-amr bi'l-maʿrūf wa'l-nahy ʿan al-munkar*). From these five principles, Ibn Taymiyya discussed the concepts of oneness, justice, and executing the punishment in relation to the exegesis of the Qur'ān.[122] As for the Muʿtazilite concept of oneness, he said that this was the oneness of the Jahmiyya, for it was a denial of all God's attributes. He also said that they claimed that God does not see, that the Qur'ān was created and not above the creation and that knowledge, power, life, hearing, seeing, speech, will and other attributes were not established in God's essence.[123] Ibn Taymiyya then explained that their principle of justice stemmed from their denial that God created all things. In particular, the Muʿtazila did not believe that God created the actions of people—neither their good deeds nor their bad.[124] The consequence of this doctrine was their advocacy of the absolute free will of a person to obey or disobey God, Who is then is obliged to reward or punish accordingly. Ibn Taymiyya connected this doctrine to the principle of executing the punishment, which he explained in association with the doctrines of the Khawārij. According to this, the Muʿtazila accepted the notion that God would not allow intercession on behalf of grave sinners and that He would not remove them from the Hellfire.[125] Unsurprisingly, Ibn Taymiyya rejected these beliefs because they were in opposition to the beliefs of the *Ahl al-Sunna wa'l-Jamāʿa*.[126] Accordingly, in his classification system, the Muʿtazila (as proponents of exegesis by opinion) were associated with those exegetes who held erroneous doctrines that had no basis in the beliefs and practices of the Companions and the Followers; instead, he saw their beliefs as mere opinion and which distorted their interpretation of certain verses and *ḥadīth*s.

As examples of exegetes who possessed either a correct or incorrect creed, Ibn Taymiyya mentioned the soundness of the exegesis of Ibn ʿAṭiyya, who followed the *Sunna*, as opposed to the false exegesis of Zamakhsharī, who interpreted the Qur'ān according to the innovations of his Muʿtazilī principles. Likewise, the speculative theologians, who were closer to the *Salaf* than the Muʿtazila, varied in their interpretations according to whether they followed the statements of the Companions and Followers, or the principles of their school of thought.[127] Thus, the methodology and conclusions of the Companions and the Followers functioned as the sole measure for judging the soundness of any exegesis, and this ultimately determined the soundness of theological doctrines. Ibn Taymiyya believed that the Companions and the Followers were the most knowledgeable Muslims concerning the meaning of the Qur'ān;[128] thus, he held whoever diverged from their statements to have erred in the matter of evidence and indicated meanings and to have mentioned something by way of rational confusion (*shubha ʿaqliyya*) or misunderstanding authentically transmitted texts (*shubha samʿiyya*).[129] Finally, although it was an infrequent occurrence, something else that Ibn Taymiyya mentioned in relation to exegesis was the possibility of erring in the matter of evidence (*dalīl*) while still discovering the correct indicated meaning (*madlūl*). This referred to the *ḥadīth* about the punishment of an exegete who gave the correct exegesis but without using sound knowledge. With no further elaboration, he remarked that this was what happened to some of the Ṣūfīs, such as Abū ʿAbd al-Raḥmān al-Sulamī (d. 412/1022) in his *Ḥaqā'iq al-tafsīr*.

In summary, Ibn Taymiyya considered there to be four different possibilities in the matter of the exegesis of the Qur'ān: one of them followed correct hermeneutics while the other three were deviations from the first. According to the first possibility, the exegete followed the Salafī principles as elaborated by the *Ḥadīth* scholars and would have correct evidence that leads to the proper indicated meanings. The second possibility referred to the exegete who did not know the sciences of *Ḥadīth*, or ignores them. This type of exegesis consisted of the reporting of all narrations without discrimination and this exegete necessarily mixed truth and falsehood. The third possibility was the exegesis of the People of Opinion, which entailed the exegete starting from a position of incorrect theology and consequently placing personal opinion above authentic transmissions. Furthermore, this exegete used incorrect evidence and arrived at incorrect indicated meanings. Ibn Taymiyya's fourth possibility, which was less common than the first three, concerned when an exegete used incorrect evidence but arrived at a sound interpretation. Ibn Taymiyya believed that although his interpretation might be correct in its conclusions, it posed a danger because it served to confuse people by spreading weak or fabricated narrations from the Prophet and his Companions. Thus, Ibn Taymiyya held that an exegete could be judged as to the soundness of his statements on a verse by verse basis.

The Prophet and His Companions

It is clear from the previous discussion of Ibn Taymiyya's understanding of the exegesis of the Qur'ān that he relied heavily on the *Ḥadīth* of the Prophet and on the statements and practices of the earliest generations of Muslims in order to develop his own exegesis. This represented what he saw as sound exegesis, which was based on Salafī principles and was accordingly restricted to the scholars who relied on the sciences of the *Ḥadīth*. Ibn Taymiyya then made allowance for these scholars to employ a limited form of independent reasoning that was similar to what had been practised by the Followers. By applying these same Salafī principles to theology, Ibn Taymiyya was able to develop his entire theology based on two traditionally fundamental concepts: (1) the existence of a 'clear revelation,' and (2) the unaltered transmission of that revelation within the Muslim community. The Qur'ān and the *Sunna* represented the totality and completeness of Islam, and the Righteous Predecessors represented the safeguarding of their transmission to future generations. In particular, it was the Companions who were deemed responsible for receiving Islam from the Prophet, for embodying it on a personal and communal level, and for passing it on to the next generation. Thus, those Muslims who adhered to these concepts became the truest and most perfect members of the Prophet's religious community. These people made up the group known as the *Ahl al-Sunna wa'l-Jamāʿa* and their views formed the foundation of Islamic orthodoxy.[130] The core of Ibn Taymiyya's ideas concerning the existence of an orthodox community revolved around his understanding of the *ḥadīth*s describing the three earliest generations of Muslims.

Ibn Taymiyya based his concept of the Righteous Predecessors on various authentic *ḥadīth*s in which the Prophet said that his generation was the best, then the following generation and then the following generation.[131] These three generations are referred to as the Companions, the Followers and the Followers of the Followers (*tābiʿ al-tābiʿīn*). Although not mentioned by Ibn Taymiyya in this context, further justification for identifying an orthodox community could be found in the *ḥadīth*s about the community of the Prophet Muḥammad being divided into 73 sects, all of which were in the Hellfire except 'the saved sect' (*al-firqat al-nājiya*). There was a difference of opinion among the *Ḥadīth* scholars as to which groups constituted the other

72 sects and whether any or all of them would remain eternally in the Hellfire or eventually be saved. However, the one 'saved sect' was associated with the more common name, *Ahl al-Sunna wa'l-Jamāʿa*.[132] As he had done with the exegetes, Ibn Taymiyya also classified (albeit on a larger scale) the various Muslim groups according to their adherence to the *Sunna* of the Prophet.

In his book, *Ṣiḥḥat uṣūl madhhab ahl al-Madīna*, Ibn Taymiyya identified the groups he believed to be most protective of the *Sunna* and the places in which he thought innovations began. Differing slightly from his classifications of the exegetes, he stated that the people of Medina held the highest rank in the matter of following the Prophet's teachings, saying that their behaviour was more authentic than that of all other towns.[133] He therefore considered Medina to be the geographical and spiritual centre of Muḥammad's religious community, and for this reason he freely compared Medina with other places where Muslims had settled but from which arose various types of innovations.[134] These places were Kufa, Basra and Syria (curiously, although he included Mecca in his list of places of knowledgeable people, he discussed neither the virtues nor the innovations associated with it). Ibn Taymiyya's accusation was that innovations from the places where the Companions and Followers had settled had diverted some people from following the knowledgeable scholars. As for the other regions, Kufa, he said, was the origin of the Shīʿa and the Murji'a. As for Basra, he identified it as the source of innovations concerning predestination (*al-qadar*) as related to the Muʿtazila and also as the point of origin for innovated acts of worship (*al-nask al-fāsid*).[135] As for Syria, it was the place where hatred of ʿAlī (*al-naṣb*) and fatalism arose.[136] In addition to these three places, Ibn Taymiyya mentioned that the Jahmiyya first appeared in the region of Khorasan.[137] Interestingly, in commenting on these regions, he explained that the innovations associated with them become worse the further one travelled from Medina, and that these innovations first began to appear in the last years of the time of the Companions, during the last years of Ibn ᶜUmar, Ibn ᶜAbbās and Jābir.[138]

Ibn Taymiyya's classification of these 'regions of innovations' in relation to the purity of Medina was the geographical counterpart to the exegetical innovations in relation to his hermeneutics. This represented a fundamental aspect of his thought in which the pure community was besieged by deviant sects. He then continued to build on his theory of a physical and spiritual centre of Islam by describing the various levels of adherence to the *Sunna*. For this purpose, he argued that the early scholars of the *Ahl al-Sunna* agreed that the opinions of the Companions and the Followers (particularly among the people of Medina) were sound, and that this reflected the superiority of these first two generations.

In the *Ṣiḥḥat*, Ibn Taymiyya discussed the position of the four imams, Abū Ḥanīfa (d. 150/767), Mālik (d. 179/796), Shāfiᶜī (d. 204/820) and Ibn Ḥanbal (d. 241/856), concerning the *Sunna* of the Prophet and the practice of the Companions in relation to the issue of the consensus of the people of Medina. His lengthy discussion cannot be fully repeated here, but I shall present his main points in order to highlight his view that the scholars of the *Ahl al-Sunna*, particularly those of earlier centuries as opposed to his own time period, were in full agreement concerning principles of belief (*ᶜaqīda*) and methodology (*minhāj*). They maintained this agreement concerning principles even though they differed on rulings related to specific cases. His claim that there was agreement among the four imams on methodological principles proved to be very useful to Ibn Taymiyya's overall view of the *Salaf* because it allowed him to focus on the idea of unity without being too distracted by particular differences. Consequently, it was relatively straightforward for him to argue that there were four levels of authority concerning the consensus of the people of Medina.[139]

Ibn Taymiyya's first level was the acceptance of customary practices of the Prophet as related by the people of Medina. As an example of this, he cited the size of dry measures and the fact that alms tax (*zakā*) was not collected on vegetables or endowed property; according to the four imams, there was complete agreement on this. This was actually a generalised view based on his assertion that the four imams agreed on the principles of jurisprudence. His emphasis on principles is clear from the special care that he took to show that Abū Ḥanīfa did not prefer analogy over authentic *ḥadīth*s, and which enabled him to maintain his claim of agreement between the four of them. As proof of this, he stated that when Abū Yūsuf (d. 182/798), the pre-eminent student of Abū Ḥanīfa, met with Mālik and heard *ḥadīth*s from him, he changed many of his opinions which he had held in accordance with the teachings of Abū Ḥanīfa.[140] Abū Yūsuf is then quoted as saying that if his master had heard what he had heard, he would have also changed his opinion.[141]

Ibn Taymiyya's second level of authority of the people of Medina referred to their actions that took place during the period before the death of ᶜUthmān.[142] For him, the leading role of Medina in propagating the Prophet's *Sunna* was based on his belief that the Rightly Guided Caliphs would not have allowed false practices or beliefs to spread among the Muslims. In holding this opinion, he was following the classical Sunnī theory of the early caliphate as first formulated by pre-eminent Followers such as al-Ḥasan al-Baṣrī and Ibn Sīrīn (d. 110/729). To summarise, this theory posited that the consensus of the Companions, and the judgements of the foremost among them, took precedence over all later opinions put forth by other scholars. This lofty opinion of the Rightly Guided Caliphs functioned as a pillar of Ibn Taymiyya's Sunnī world view. Consequently, it played a critical role in his efforts to undermine Shīᶜī theories of the Imamate.[143] However, his polemics against the Shīᶜa compelled him to perform a historical balancing act in his treatment of ᶜAlī (d. 40/661), whose caliphate created problems for Ibn Taymiyya's theory of the consensus of the people of Medina. For instance, in the *Ṣiḥḥat*, he was able to sidestep the issue by pointing out that ʿAlī was not included in the second level of authority because the seat of his caliphate was in Kufa, not Medina. This manner of deferring judgement seemed to be typical of the way that Ibn Taymiyya dealt with this extremely sensitive issue. In forging a 'mediating position' concerning the fourth caliph, he had to defend ʿAlī from certain Sunnī opinions in which the latter was judged to be an incompetent and unjust caliph on the one hand, and on the other, from Shīʿī claims that he was denied his prophetically appointed right to the caliphate by apostatising Companions.[144] In doing so, Ibn Taymiyya commended ʿAlī for the way in which he handled the turmoil of his caliphate, while at the same time he used that turmoil to separate ʿAlī from the first three caliphs for the purpose of upholding the authority of the people of Medina at the second level.

At the third level of authority, which referred to the time after ʿUthmān, Ibn Taymiyya admitted that the agreement on principles among the *Ahl al-Sunna* began to falter. A difference of opinion occurred concerning whether a jurisprudent must give preponderance to evidence in the form of *ḥadīth*s transmitted from the people of Medina and to their legal rulings based on analogy when alternative indicators existed for resolving a case.[145] Ibn Taymiyya stated that at this level, the four imams differed as to the use of the *ḥadīth*s and opinions of the people of Medina as elements in the principles of jurisprudence: he said that whereas Mālik and Shāfiʿī accepted giving preponderance to the evidence transmitted by the people of Medina, Abū Ḥanīfa did not. The Ḥanbalīs were divided on this point, with the majority claiming that Ibn Ḥanbal preferred giving preponderance to the statements of the people of Medina, while Abū Yaʿlā (d. 458/1066) and Ibn ʿAqīl (d. 513/1120) said that no preponderance should be given to them.

The final level of authority referred to the actions of the people of Medina from later times.[146] Ibn Taymiyya was not specific as to the time period to which he was referring, but I assume he means after the time of the Companions. In any case, he stated that there was again unanimity among the four imams, but this time they agreed that these later actions were no longer to be taken as constituting legal proof (*ḥujja sharʿiyya*).[147] Thus, in Ibn Taymiyya's understanding of the early Muslim community, the *Ahl al-Sunna* of the first three centuries (i.e., up to, and including, the four imams) formed a coherent group with common beliefs and only minor differences in methodology. These differences notwithstanding, he portrayed the *Ahl al-Sunna* as the representatives of a 'pure' Islam that stood against emerging sects such as the Khawārij, Shīʿa, Muji'a, Jahmiyya and Muʿtazila.

In order to indicate the implications of Ibn Taymiyya's view of the *Ahl al-Sunna*, I shall present some of his opinions which were consistent with the *Sunna* as laid down by the Companions and the Followers, but which opposed the accepted practices of the Muslims of his day. Many of his opinions on the topic of innovation are found in his work, *Kitāb iqtidā' al-ṣirāṭ al-mustaqīm li-mukhālafat aṣḥāb al-jahīm*.[148] Since discussing Ibn Taymiyya's relentless campaign against innovations is a formidable task that can only be hinted at here, I will focus on his insistence on following the way of the *Salaf* and highlight a few points brought out in this book. According to Memon, '...the test of all practice and ideal is, according to Ibn Taimiya, its compatibility with Islam of the Koran, the *Sunna*, and the conduct of the *Salaf*.'[149] For example, with regard to festivals, this meant that the practices of Muslims could become un-Islamic. Ibn Taymiyya considered there to be three elements involved in the definition of a festival, time (*waqt, zamān*), location (*makān*) and rites (*aʿmāl*), and to deviate or innovate on any of these points constituted an unacceptable or sinful act.[150] One example of this was that the Prophet and his Companions never practised or recommended acts such as congregational supererogatory prayers.[151] This, Ibn Taymiyya said, was venerating a time period not mentioned in the law and specifying the manner in which the prayers must be performed.

Likewise, the *Salaf* never celebrated the Prophet's birthday.[152] This, said Ibn Taymiyya, was tantamount to elevating a memorable day to the level of a festival with its accompanying rites and practices. Similarly, adhering to the way of the *Salaf* also included not venerating places that were not hallowed by the law, such as the tombs of prophets and saints.[153] Ibn Taymiyya's reasoning was that, first of all, this made no sense because the exact location of a tomb was often not known, and even when it was known, there was nothing in the law or in the practice of the Companions to indicate any benefit from carrying out devotions at the grave of a prophet or saint. In fact, the behaviour of the Companions indicated the exact opposite.[154] As for visiting the Prophet's grave, both Ibn Ḥanbal and Mālik stated that only salutations could be given and that when one had a personal prayer to make, he should not face the tomb but rather turn and face the Kaaba. These examples must suffice to show how Ibn Taymiyya used the practice of the Righteous Predecessors as a litmus test for everything a Muslim should do. He also claimed that no consensus or ruling could ever overturn the statements and habits of the Companions and Followers. On this point, Ibn Taymiyya referred to a statement by imam Mālik who said, 'Later Islam can approve only what early Islam did approve.'[155] Significantly, for Ibn Taymiyya, approving what early Islam approved also included the proper use of the Arabic language, to which I shall now turn.

The Arabic Language

In addition to the four methodological principles from which Ibn Taymiyya built his exegesis and his definition of the *Ahl al-Sunna*, he considered the correct use of the Arabic language to be a fifth indispensable tool for interpreting the Islam of the Prophet and the Companions. By taking such a stance, he aligned himself squarely with the classical grammarians, of whom al-Khalīl b. Aḥmad (d. 175/791) and Sībawayh (d. 188/804) were his authoritative references in the *Risālat al-ʿubudiyya*.[156] Although Ibn Taymiyya did not write a single work specifically on grammar (just as he did not write a complete exegesis), his views on the Arabic language can be assembled from various discussions throughout his works, especially those dealing with the Qur'ān. In the *Risāla*, he twice referred to specific aspects of Arabic in relation to worship. In both cases, he used Arabic as a means to define the proper boundaries of worship in accordance with the language of the Qur'ān and the *Ḥadīth*. This use of Arabic presupposed the authority of the first four principles and indicated that the language itself was an established aspect of revelation. Thus, it is not hard to imagine that Ibn Taymiyya would have fully accepted the notion that 'language control is "worship" control.'[157] In reference to exegesis, his use of Arabic was meant to serve the same purpose as his use of the four prior principles; namely, to restrict the ranks of the exegetes and to limit the range of flexibility for independent reasoning and opinion. In order to present Ibn Taymiyya's views on the Arabic language, I shall focus on two main issues. The first is his overall view of Arabic in reference to its origin and special role as the means by which God revealed His final revelation. The second issue concerns his understanding and usage of a few key linguistic terms and grammatical points which were essential to his theology.

For Ibn Taymiyya, human speech was a created act similar to the creation of a person's deeds. In the matter of reciting the Qur'ān, there was no comparison between God's speech, which is one of His eternal attributes, and the utterances that a person makes at the time of recitation.[158] God inspired human beings with language and understanding just as He inspired animals with their own form of language and understanding.[159] Thus, God is the 'Positor' of language, for all human languages are with Him eternally.[160] As for the issue of a written language, Ibn Taymiyya stated that there was no writing until the time of the Prophet Idrīs, as was reported by many of the *Salaf*. The family of Adam could neither read nor write. God taught Adam the names of all things by speaking to him with ordered speech (*kalām manẓūm*). Although there were several theories purporting to explain the origin of the Arabic script, Ibn Taymiyya was of the view that there were no authentic reports from the Prophet to indicate how the script originated.[161] He placed the accounts of these theories in the same category as the stories about the exegesis of the meaning of the letters appearing before certain Suras—in other words, he considered them to be baseless. What was important for Ibn Taymiyya, however, was that Arabic was the language chosen by God as the vehicle for His final revelation.

Ibn Taymiyya considered the proper use and understanding of Arabic to be vital for Muslims; specifically, knowing the Arabic of the Qur'ān and the way in which the Prophet and his Companions had used it would help save Muslims from the Hellfire. This was contrary to the Arabic of the pre-Islamic period, which by itself, he said, would lead to the Hellfire. In encouraging the Muslims to study Arabic, which he saw as a collective duty,[162] he said that when the people of the Arabic language turned away from its foundation they were at the level of the pre-Islamic poets, the companions of the Seven Odes, who were wood for the fire.[163] With such a statement, Ibn Taymiyya was clearly saying that, as with every issue related to Islam, the role of the Prophet and the Companions in using Arabic and defining the boundaries of discourse was of the utmost importance. It was not enough to know Arabic—a Muslim had to know the Arabic of the *Salaf*.

One clear example of how Ibn Taymiyya favoured the statements of the Companions and Followers, as opposed to those of some of the later lexicographers, concerned the definition of the word *ṣamad* in Q.CXII.2. The Companions, the Followers and the lexicographers gave two basic meanings for *ṣamad*: 'a being with no interior' (*lā jawfa lahu*)[164] and 'the lord on whom all depend in times of need' (*al-sayyid alladhī yuṣmadu ilayhi fī al-ḥawā'ij*). Ibn Taymiyya observed that the first meaning was used by most of the *Salaf* and a small group of lexicographers in reference to this sura, while the second was used by most of the lexicographers and a small group of the *Salaf*.[165] His list of the *Salaf* who favoured the first definition included many of the familiar names from the Companions and Followers, such as Ibn Masʿūd, Ibn ʿAbbās, al-Ḥasan al-Baṣrī, Mujāhid, Saʿīd b. Jubayr, ʿIkrima, Ḍaḥḥāk, Qatāda, and Saʿīd b. al-Musayyab. Given this evidence, Ibn Taymiyya made the concept of *lā jawfa lahu* the basis for his exegesis of this sura, but he also clarified that the two definitions complemented each other.[166] By referring to these statements of the Righteous Predecessors about the definition of *ṣamad*, Ibn Taymiyya made use of Salafī principles to define the acceptable boundaries in which the Arabic language was to be used in the discussion of this term, and he applied the same methodology when discussing other aspects of Arabic.

The role of Arabic grammar in Ibn Taymiyya's methodology conformed to his use of Salafī principles. Thus, he insisted that certain linguistic terms such as 'literal meaning' (*ḥaqīqa*), 'figurative speech' (*majāz*), 'unqualified' (*muṭlaq*), 'qualified' (*muqayyad*), 'general' (*ʿāmm*) and 'specific' (*khāṣṣ*),[167] must be understood in accordance with the grammar and usage of the earliest generations of Muslims. Nevertheless, Ibn Taymiyya made allowance for the technical terminology of the grammarians, as he had done with the technical terminology used in the other Islamic sciences—even though it was developed after the time of the Companions and Followers. This acceptance manifested itself in the erudite way in which he was able to discuss nearly every aspect of Islamic thought in the language of the specialists, whether jurisprudents, philosophers, or Ṣūfīs.[168] Based on the broad range of his studies, it seems that he accepted the use of technical terminology, but then sought to restrict, and at times to redefine, those terms within the boundaries of his Salafī principles as we shall see in the discussion of grammatical, theological and mystical terms.

One of the most prominent issues of Arabic grammar that Ibn Taymiyya considered was that of literal and figurative meanings. Following the traditional Ḥanbalī position that the Qur'ān and

Ḥadīth contained almost no figurative meanings,[169] Ibn Taymiyya clearly stated in his *Kitāb al-īmān* that the division of expressions according to a *ḥaqīqa-majāz* dichotomy first occurred in the speech of scholars after the third century AH (ninth century CE).[170] Furthermore, he regarded this dichotomy to be merely a 'terminological convention' (*istilāḥ ḥādith*) since the terms were not used by either the early imams, such as Mālik, Awzāʿī (d. 157/774), Abū Ḥanīfa and Shāfiʿī, or by the early grammarians, such as Abū ʿAmr b. al-ʿAlā' (d. 154/770), al-Khalīl b. Aḥmad (d. 175/791) and Sībawayh (d. 188/804).[171] The first person to use the term *majāz* was Abū ʿUbayda Maʿmar b. al-Muthannā (d. 209/824), who did not use it as a counterpart to *ḥaqīqa*; rather, he used it in reference to explaining one verse by the use of another.[172] According to Ibn Taymiyya, it was the Muʿtazila and other speculative theologians who began to use *majāz* as a technical term in order to explain their innovated beliefs. This explanation corresponded well with his view of history, for it allowed him to maintain the idea of the 'purity' of the early *Salaf* in opposition to the innovative practices of deviant sects.[173]

As for using a word differently to what was originally posited, Ibn Taymiyya said that this occurred only by way of an 'associative indication' (*qarīna*). His use of this term, although still a terminological convention, indicated his preference for the language of legal scholars over that of rhetoricians,[174] and illustrates the way in which his theological and legal affiliations influenced both his choice of terms and his use of language. For Ibn Taymiyya, an allowable associative indication occurred when one used the words 'lion' or 'donkey' in reference to a brave or stupid man, respectively. In such cases, first a word has been posited for a specific meaning, for which it is commonly used, then the word is carried over to another meaning for which it was not originally posited. For this reason, it was well-known that every figure of speech must necessarily have a literal meaning, but every literal meaning did not necessarily have a figurative use[175]. Thus, when a word appeared alone, one first thought of its literal meaning, and only when there was an associative indication did one think of its figurative meaning.[176] In this way, Ibn Taymiyya limited the use of associative indication to the narrowest applications of definition and grammar. A few examples will suffice to demonstrate his position.

One such case of referring to a word in the Qur'ān as *majāz* occurred with the word 'taste' (*dhawq*). Ibn Taymiyya noted that some people said that taste could only refer to the physical sensation in the mouth,[177] and they therefore held that when God says that the unbelievers will taste His punishment (as in Q.LIV.37 and 39), this must be a figure of speech. But Ibn Taymiyya refuted this by saying that this was a qualified definition, since taste indicates any type of physical sensation, and in support of his own definition, he mentioned that al-Khalīl b. Aḥmad defined *dhawq* as 'finding the savour of a thing.' He then went on to say that the various uses of the word *dhawq* in the Qur'ān indicated this broader meaning of 'savouring anything through the senses.' Besides referring to 'tasting punishment' (Q.III.106, Q.XXXII.21 and Q.LXV.9), the Qur'ān also referred to believers who will 'not taste death except the first death' (Q.XLIV.56) and to disbelievers who will 'not taste coolness or any drink except boiling water and paralysing cold' (Q.LXXVIII.24–25). This definition of *dhawq*, which included all physical sensation, was an important part of Ibn Taymiyya's views on faith and worship, because he believed that these aspects of religion could be experienced in this life. For example, three times in the *Risāla* he referred to a *ḥadīth* in which the Prophet mentioned those believers who would 'find the sweetness of faith.' In one of these three instances, he interpreted 'finding' (*wujūd*) as 'tasting' (*yadhūq*). However, this definition of *dhawq* clearly went against the accepted usage of the word as reported by later generations of lexicographers.[178] But for Ibn Taymiyya, it was more important to derive definitions from the Qur'ān, *Ḥadīth* and the statements of the *Salaf*. Accordingly, in deriving his definition of *dhawq*, he also referred in the *Risāla* to another *ḥadīth* in which the Prophet mentioned those Muslims who would 'taste the savour of faith;' the usage of which clearly resembled the definition of *dhawq* given above by Khalīl. Thus, Ibn Taymiyya was able to draw an analogy between 'tasting' and 'finding' based on the usage of the words 'tasting' and 'finding' in the Qur'ān and *Ḥadīth*. For him, there was consequently no reason to assume that a figurative meaning for *dhawq* was necessary: by including all physical senses in the meaning of taste, he could maintain the experiential character of the word and avoid recourse to a *majāz* meaning that was not supported by an associative indication.

The previous example referred to what Ibn Taymiyya saw as a misuse of *majāz* because of the qualified definition used by certain scholars. In another example of the misuse of *majāz*, he was concerned with a misunderstanding of Arabic grammar. This example occurred with the word 'village' (*qarya*) in Q.XII.82. Although it stated, 'ask the village,' Ibn Taymiyya said that this was not a figurative use of the word 'village,' but simply the elision of the full genitive construction that should read 'ask the people of the village.'[179] Thus, regarding any claims that there were examples of figurative speech in the Qur'ān, Ibn Taymiyya used similar lexical or grammatical explanations to refute such notions. He therefore conformed with Ibn Ḥanbal's claim that there were no examples of *majāz* in the Qur'ān. On other aspects of Arabic grammar, he presented his views by following a similar line of argumentation, in which he used the concepts 'general' and 'specific,' and 'qualified' and 'unqualified,' within the framework of his Salafī principles.

Ibn Taymiyya's understanding of the terms 'general' and 'specific' was clarified in his explanation of the concepts of *islām* (submission), *īmān* (faith) and *iḥsān* (perfect devotion). He stated, based on the well-known *ḥadīth* of Gabriel,[180] that these three terms must be understood in the context of general and specific.[181] As connotative terms, *iḥsān* was in itself more general than *īmān*, and *īmān* was in itself more general than *islām*. However, as to the people denoted by these terms, the reverse was true, meaning that *iḥsān* was more specific than *īmān*, and *īmān* was more specific than *islām*. Thus, he was able to claim that every *muḥsin* was necessarily a *mu'min*, and every *mu'min* was necessarily a *muslim*; but that every *muslim* was not necessarily a *mu'min*, and every *mu'min* was not necessarily a *muḥsin*. Through this use of general and specific meanings, he was able to conclude that when a term such as '*īmān*' was used in an absolute sense (*mujarrad*), it connoted all of the characteristics denoted by the term '*islām*,' but not by the term '*iḥsān*'.[182] According to Ibn Taymiyya, the concepts of 'general' and 'specific' had to be kept in mind whenever one was trying to understand the Qur'ān and *Ḥadīth*. However, these terms also had to be used in connection with the concepts 'unqualified' and 'qualified'. Ibn Taymiyya elaborated on the concepts of unqualified and qualified statements in relation to his theory of coordinating a specific term to a general one. A very precise explanation of his ideas concerning this matter is given by Izutsu,[183] who explains Ibn Taymiyya's theory by giving the example of term *A* connoting five basic elements, *a*, *b*, *c*, *d* and *e*. When the word is used in an unqualified manner, it must include all five elements. However, words are often used in a qualified manner in which one or more of the basic elements are mentioned with the connotative term. Thus, there might be a statement such as '*A* and *a* and *d*.' This happened, said Ibn Taymiyya, with the use of 'good' (*maʿrūf*) and 'evil' (*munkar*) as connotative terms.[184] In Q.VII.156 and Q.III.110, *maʿrūf* connoted every type of good and *munkar* connoted every type of evil. However, in Q.IV.114, God mentioned that there was no value to people's conversations unless they '...command the giving of charity, *maʿrūf* and reconciling between people.' Likewise, in Q.XXIX.45, God mentioned that prayer prevents '...blatant sins and *munkar*.' In the first case, charity and reconciliation were part of *maʿrūf*; thus, *maʿrūf* was the connotative term *A* and 'giving charity' and 'reconciliation' were the elements *a* and *b*. In the second case, 'blatant sins' were part of *munkar*; thus, *munkar* was the connotative term *A* and 'blatant sins' was the element *a*. The specific elements were mentioned along with the connotative terms to focus the believers' attention on the particular benefit or harm of a given action. Ibn Taymiyya went on to explain that the coordination of specific terms to general terms occurred for different reasons depending on the issues involved.

Some other examples are as follows. As for acts of worship, when *ʿibāda* was used in an unqualified way, it connoted concepts such as reliance on God, seeking aid from Him, and doing everything that He and His Messenger had commanded. But in a verse such as Q.I.5, 'seeking aid' was explicitly associated with worship, or in Q.XI.113, 'reliance' was explicitly associated with it, highlighting the importance of seeking aid only from God and relying only on Him. Likewise, in Q.LVI.7, God's statement, '…they believe in God and His Messenger…' implies that they believed in all of the earlier scriptures and prophets. This was made clear when God associated the earlier scriptures and prophets with belief in Him, as in Q.II.255. Thus, it can be seen that Ibn Taymiyya's use of Arabic grammar conformed to his methodology of interpreting 'the Qur'ān by the Qur'ān.' By adding the Arabic language to Salafī principles, he was able to define the boundaries of exegetical and theological discourse within which the 'true' scholar—that is, the *Ḥadīth* scholar—could operate.

In summary, Ibn Taymiyya developed his theology based on a very precise understanding and use of sources and methodology. The Qur'ān, the *Sunna* and the practices of the Righteous Predecessors constituted both source and methodology. Ibn Taymiyya maintained this to the point that he believed that any discourse concerning religion must come from these sources and be used in a manner consistent with that of the *Salaf*. Even the Arabic language was utilised by him as a clearly defined tool for understanding revelation. To speak about religion by using words differently to the speech of the *Salaf*, or by using new terminology in a way that opposed their clear statements, led to unacceptable innovation in his view. With this in mind, I shall now turn to the major theological points of his *Risālat al-ʿubūdiyya*.

IBN TAYMIYYA'S THEOLOGY

In the previous section, I have shown that Ibn Taymiyya aligned himself with the *Ahl al-Ḥadīth* in his approach to the Qur'ān and the *Sunna*, and in his methodology for understanding these revealed sources. I have also indicated in my discussion of his exegesis and his concept of the *Ahl al-Sunna* that this methodology had a tremendous influence on his understanding of history, as well as the development of jurisprudence and the emergence of 'deviations' in creed. In this section, I shall further develop the connection between Ibn Taymiyya's use of Salafī principles and his theology, with particular reference to matters related to his concept of worship as presented in the *Risāla*. In order to accomplish this, I shall focus on two main themes that exemplify this connection.

The first part of this section is a review of the most important issues of creed, which Ibn Taymiyya traced back to the Qur'ān, the *Sunna* and the beliefs of the Companions. In order to establish that he did not deviate in these matters from the the eponym of his *madhhab*, namely, Aḥmad b. Ḥanbal, I present a comparison of Ibn Ḥanbal's creed with Ibn Taymiyya's to show that the latter was quite faithful to the earlier theologian's position. Then, with reference to the creed as elaborated here, I show how Ibn Taymiyya made use of it to formulate his description of worship in the *Risāla* in the second part of my discussion. There, I explain the manner in which Ibn Taymiyya assumed an intermediate position concerning the nature of God and the worship of Him between the speculative theologians on the one hand, and the mystical Ṣūfīs on the other. In order to formulate this intermediate position, Ibn Taymiyya had to reconcile the simpler statements of the *Salaf* with the more sophisticated arguments that had developed within *kalām* and mystical Sufism over the years. I show that his process of reconciliation proceeded from two premises: the first was his proposition that a Muslim must accept the necessity of the Salafī principles and beliefs as a matter of faith, and the second was that the theological positions of his opponents were untenable because they conflicted with this orthodox creed and ultimately led to self-contradictory beliefs. This explanation of Ibn Taymiyya's theology of worship thus places the *Risāla* in its proper perspective.

Although Ibn Taymiyya wrote several works that may be described as creeds, I focus on one in particular. In his creed of 698/1299, known as *al-ʿAqīda al-wāsiṭiyya*,[185] Ibn Taymiyya claimed that the principles of belief that he described were, in fact, the beliefs of the *Ahl al-Sunna wa'l-Jamāʿa*. The major portion of the creed, and the principles of belief that concern us directly, are related to the issues of God's names and attributes and how God interacts with His creation.

The Creed of Ibn Taymiyya

THE PRINCIPLES OF THE CREED OF THE AHL AL-SUNNA

In his own ʿAqīda work, Ibn Ḥanbal stated that his creed was based on the belief that God was one with no additions, parts, or divisions.[186] He believed that God was one in every aspect, and there was nothing other than He that was one. However, God was to be described exactly as obligated by authentic transmission and consensus,[187] and this formed the evidence that confirmed Him in His existence. As proof of this general principle, Ibn Ḥanbal referred to Q.XLII.11, which states, 'there is nothing like unto Him, He is the All-Hearing, the All-Seeing.' This verse confirmed that God and His Messenger had described Him with specific attributes and that there were no alterations of meanings, no anthropomorphism, or additions to, and detractions from, God's attributes.[188] Thus, Ibn Ḥanbal said that whoever declared that God had not been ascribed attributes until those who described Him began to ascribe them to Him had left the religion. For Ibn Ḥanbal, to say such a thing was tantamount to denying God's eternal oneness because it was as if someone said that God was not one until others began describing Him as one, and this was false.[189] Thus, according to Ibn Ḥanbal, God's attributes were eternal (*qadīm*). In response to the question of whether the one being described with attributes was one eternal being and an attribute was another eternal being, he said that the question itself was a mistake, because it was not permitted to separate the True One from His attributes.[190] He thus confirmed the concept of the oneness of God's names and attributes, for to attribute a self, an essence or a will to God was no different than attributing a hand or a face to Him.[191]

For his part, Ibn Taymiyya restated Ibn Ḥanbal's principles by confirming that faith concerning God's names and attributes must be based on accepting 'what God has ascribed to [H]imself in the Scripture as well as what [H]is Messenger ascribed to [H]im.'[192] He further stated that this meant that a Muslim must approach the names and attributes of God without altering the meanings of the texts, without stripping God of His attributes, without questioning how the attributes existed in God's essence, and without making analogies to any part of creation. The manner in which a Muslim accepted the names and attributes of God was based on the belief that God used both negation and affirmation in reference to Himself. In other words, just as the assertion of God's oneness was based on a negation, 'there is no deity,' followed by an affirmation, 'except God,' so too did God employ this method in the verses in which He described Himself. Ibn Taymiyya referred to verse Q.XLII.11, which was mentioned above, and cited it in relation to God's attributes to show that a Muslim must accept the attributes as they were described in the Qur'ān and *Ḥadīth*. Thus, for Ibn Taymiyya and Ibn Ḥanbal, this verse represented the intermediate position assumed by the *Ahl al-Sunna* between the extremes of stripping God of His attributes and anthropomorphism.

Ibn Ḥanbal and Ibn Taymiyya quoted many verses of the Qur'ān as proofs for their understanding of God's names and attributes.

These verses affirmed His attributes, such as His infinite knowledge, omnipotence, love, wrath, face, hands, hearing, seeing, transcendence and divinity, His exaltedness above creation and His speech. Ibn Ḥanbal began his discussion in his *ʿAqīda* by referring to the attributes of omnipotence, living and knowledge. He confirmed that God was powerful, living and knowing based on God's verses in the Qur'ān that described Him as such. For example, God said that 'He is the living, there is no deity other than He' (Q.XL.65), 'God has power over all things' (Q.XVIII.45), and, 'God knows all things' (Q.XXXIII.40).[193] On the issue of God knowing by means of knowledge, Ibn Ḥanbal stated that God attributed knowledge to Himself in saying, 'they encompass nothing of His knowledge' (Q.II.255), and, 'if they do not answer your prayer, then know that it is revealed only in the knowledge of God' (Q.XI.14). God's knowledge, as with His other attributes, was different from any created knowledge; thus, according to Ibn Ḥanbal, it did not change, was not prone to forgetfulness and was not situated in a place such as the heart.[194]

Ibn Taymiyya confirmed these attributes in the *Wāsiṭiyya* and presented other verses such as, 'put your confidence in the Living One who does not die' (Q.XXV.58), 'no female bears [a child] or brings [it] forth except by His knowledge' (Q.XXXV.11), and, 'if God had so willed they would not have fought one another, but God does what he wills' (Q.II.253).[195] However, after confirming that God exists eternally with all His names and attributes, both theologians found it necessary to explain to some extent what they both claimed to be beyond human comprehension. In the face of beliefs that deviated from those of the *Ahl al-Ḥadīth*, Ibn Ḥanbal and Ibn Taymiyya sought to describe the manner in which God's attributes existed in His essence.

God's Will

On the issue of God's will, Ibn Ḥanbal and Ibn Taymiyya distinguished between His volition (*irāda*) and His creative will (*mashī'a*).

Ibn Ḥanbal confirmed that God never ceases to be a willer (*murīd*) and that His volition (*irāda*) is an attribute in His essence. Volition is an attribute of praise because an essence (*dhāt*) that does not will does not know that it exists, which is a defect. It is known that God wills because He says in the Qur'ān, 'but His command, when He wills a thing, is that He says to it "Be" and it is' (Q.XXXVI.82).[196] This volition was related to, but not the same as, God's creative will, which was directly associated with His omnipotence. Ibn Ḥanbal stated that if God so willed, He could stop a person from committing an act that He disliked. Also, if He so willed, He could gather all creation together so that everyone would have the same belief. For his proof, he referred to what God said in the Qur'ān, 'If We had so willed, We could have given every soul its guidance…' (Q.XXXII.13), and, '…if God had so willed, He could have gathered them all on guidance…' (Q.VI.35). In other words, God could will (*shā'*) into existence whatever He wanted, and it was through His volition (*irāda*) that He chose a certain thing at a certain time. Thus, God's will could not be defeated or conquered, and there was no fault or weakness in it. Also, when God withheld something from someone, it was not out of greed or stinginess, for this was a defective attribute. God was so eminently gracious that He bestowed his favours as He willed, based on His perfect knowledge.[197]

In the *Wāsiṭiyya*, Ibn Taymiyya discussed God's will in the context of determinism (*qadar*).[198] He considered there to be two aspects to determinism; one related to God's eternal foreknowledge, and the other related to God's creative will. Regarding God's eternal foreknowledge, he firstly made the point that God knew in advance what His creatures would do; whether they would be obedient or not, and whether they would be blessed with good fortune or instead suffer misfortune. He further stated that all of this had been recorded in the 'Guarded Tablet' (*lawḥ maḥfūẓ*). Secondly, he made the point that God's eternal foreknowledge encompassed both the universal and the particular. Regarding the other aspect of determinism, Ibn Taymiyya referred to God's creative will, specifying that it was His 'effective will' (*mashī'a nāfidha*). He stated that whatever God wills, will be, and whatever He does not will, will not be. The second point refers to God's volition. Ibn Taymiyya also maintained that God used His volition to bring a certain thing into existence at a particular time.[199] Of course, the problem that logically follows from a belief in God's absolute will to determine all things is the question of human will, which for each theologian meant a person's ability to choose either faith and obedience on the one hand, or disbelief and disobedience on the other.

Human Volition

According to Ibn Ḥanbal, God's omnipotence and creative will did not conflict with the application of His justice concerning the reward and punishment of a worshipper. Although a person's actions were created by God, each individual was responsible for performing his actions based on the promise of reward and the threat of punishment. A close look at his arguments shows that he maintained this position without attempting to explain the nature of the relationship between God's will and human volition. Unencumbered by Ashᶜarī arguments concerning the 'acquisition' (*kasb*) of a person's deeds to which Ibn Taymiyya would later have to respond, Ibn Ḥanbal needed only to craft a strong argument to counter the claims of the Jabriyya and the Qadariyya. Thus, by deriving his arguments from what appeared in the revealed texts, he concluded that, although God's will was absolute, a Muslim must still believe that he possessed his own volition; the exercise of which would be judged by God.

In his discussion on human volition, Ibn Ḥanbal began with a refutation of the Qadariyya, whose beliefs he dismissed by means of a brief argument. However, this refutation placed him in a difficult position when it came to arguing against the fatalism of the Jabriyya. In particular, to prove that God created the actions of, and conditions for, his creatures, he referred to verses such as, 'the Creator of all things' (Q.VI.102), 'We made compassion and mercy in the hearts of those who followed him' (Q.LVII.27), and, 'it may be that God will make friendship between you and those with whom you have enmity' (Q.LX.7),[200] all of which showed that it was not permitted to specify God's creative omnipotence for some things but not for others, as this would mean that He was the deity for some things but not for others. In other words, the concept of an absolute free will, which made man the creator of his actions, meant that God would not be the creator of those actions, and thus would not be the deity ruling over them. But whereas these verses proved to Ibn Ḥanbal that God had created the inner and outer conditions of a person's experiences, he was not ready to accept any concept of fatalism that denied human volition (and consequently, responsibility), because these verses had to be reconciled with the fact that God also referred to man's capability (*istiṭāʿa*) for performing an action.

More precisely, the Qur'ān spoke in terms of a person not having capability and Ibn Ḥanbal referred to verses which stated that a person's lack of capability meant the non-performance of an action. These verses were: 'see how they give parables to you, but they go astray, not capable of finding a way' (Q.XXV.9), 'that is the interpretation of what you were unable to be patient about' (Q.XVIII.82), and, 'you will not be capable of dealing justly with women, even if you were to desire this' (Q.IV.129). According to Ibn Ḥanbal, this incapacity to act indicated that created beings were impotent (*ʿajz*) and had no power over things, except through a capability that God had given them. Thus, he believed that capability was given for each action—a belief that suggests some similarity to the Muʿtazilite concept of capability, but with an important distinction: Ibn Ḥanbal's concept of capability still subjected the individual to God's will, for it was God who granted it or withheld it.[201]

In order to strengthen his argument against the fatalism of the Jabriyya, Ibn Ḥanbal had to refer to the concept of God's justice. He did so by maintaining that reward and punishment were part of God's justice, which was something that could not be comprehended by the rational faculties.[202] He then used this concept of the inability of created beings to understand the nature of God as the basis for his claim that God's justice (*ʿadl*) did not permit people to describe Him with injustice (*jawr*), for He was above such things. This point indicates that Ibn Ḥanbal ultimately relied on the formula *bi-lā kayf* ('do not ask how') in reference to the issue of God's will and human volition. His authority on the matter was a narration from ʿAlī b. Abī Ṭālib in which ʿAlī was asked about which actions of created beings deserved God's reward or punishment. ʿAlī answered by saying, 'Actions are acts from the worshippers and creations [are] from God, and do not ask anyone about this after having asked me.'[203]

In formulating his discussion on human volition, Ibn Taymiyya added to Ibn Ḥanbal's arguments by emphasising the moral nature of free will. He confirmed that there was evidence in the Qur'ān and *Ḥadīth* for human volition and responsibility, as well as for God's omnipotence. He held that God created all things but human volition was required for moral behaviour, because God 'has called upon mankind to render voluntary obedience to him and his messengers, and discouraged disobedience.'[204] Also, in what should be seen as a reaction to antinomian Sufism, Ibn Taymiyya stressed the relationship between love for God and obedience to Him through observance of the law. He noted that God loved the pious and righteous but did not love unbelievers and those who were corrupt; thus, God rewarded the believers and punished the disbelievers without ever being unjust. As was the case with Ibn Ḥanbal, Ibn Taymiyya ultimately believed that a Muslim must accept as a matter of faith that God's omnipotence and human volition were both active qualities that affected the human condition. Accordingly, he stated that '[m]en are actors in the genuine sense of that term; however, God is the Creator of their actions.'[205] His position was that a person was an active agent who would be held responsible before God, even though He was the Creator of each person's acts. This must be accepted *bi-lā kayf*, for created beings simply could not comprehend the manner in which God's omnipotence and justice were manifested in creation. Ibn Taymiyya therefore rejected the Ashᶜarī concept of the acquisition of one's actions (*kasb*, *iktisāb*) because that was an attempt to explain the nature of this manifestation.

Laoust is correct in pointing out that Ibn Taymiyya opposed the concept of acquisition as formulated by the speculative theologians, particularly Ashᶜarī (d. 323/935).[206] Ibn Taymiyya considered this concept to be 'pointless and futile.'[207] In particular, he rejected the Ashᶜarī distinction between God's creation (*khalq*) of an act and a person's acquisition of it (*kasb*, *iktisāb*), claiming that it amounted to a denial of a person's power over his acts. For Ibn Taymiyya, to claim that a person merely acquired an act bordered on fatalism; instead, he insisted that a person had to be a 'true agent' (*fāᶜil*).[208] However, rather than of simply relying on *bi-lā kayf*, it seems as if Ibn Taymiyya allowed himself to get drawn further into this theological debate. This is because he formulated a description of human acts in terms of causes (*asbāb*) and potentialities (*quwā*), both of which were created by God, in response to the Ashᶜarī theory of acquisition. In an example taken from the *Risāla*, he stated that hunger was the cause of a person's desire to eat, and it was through this person's volition, which was the potentiality in him, that he then acted on this cause by actually eating. Yet Ibn Taymiyya noted that God created both the cause and potentiality; consequently, a person only realised his acts through a 'preponderant factor' (*murajjiḥ*) or a 'particulariser' (*mukhaṣṣiṣ*), which was the divine volition. In other words, 'God creates the act that man chooses consciously.'[209] This theory, of course, did not solve the paradox of God's will and human volition, since it still left a person entirely dependent on God's will in order to perform an action; but this, I believe, was Ibn Taymiyya's intention. Through his theory, he was simply trying to maintain that God's omnipotence and His justice were compatible in His essence but unknowable to human understanding, which was his position concerning all of God's names and attributes.

God's Face and Hands

In dealing with specific attributes of God, both scholars included a discussion of the attributes that had caused the most controversy in terms of stripping God of His attributes (*taʿṭīl*) and anthropomorphism (*tashbīh*). For Ibn Ḥanbal, the confirmation of God's attributes as they appeared in the Qur'ān and the authentic *Ḥadīth* extended to every description He gave of Himself. For instance, he accepted the fact that God has a face based on the verse, 'everything will perish except His face' (Q.XXVIII.88). Although Ibn Ḥanbal relied on the doctrine of *bi-lā kayf* concerning God's attributes, he advanced several propositions about the face of God. Firstly, he said that God's face was not a body (*jism*) and was not like any formed shapes (*al-ṣuwar al-muṣawwara*) or defined particulars (*al-aʿyān al-mukhaṭṭaṭa*). Furthermore, he said that it was an everlasting face that had a reality befitting God, and His face was not to be interpreted metaphorically or allegorically (*dūna al-majāz*). Thus, he warned that whoever altered the meaning of face disbelieved and whoever transferred the meaning of it to the meaning of 'self' (*nafs*) also disbelieved.

Ibn Ḥanbal affirmed the existence of God's hands in a similar fashion. He said that His two hands were an attribute in His essence (*fī dhātihi*), which were not limbs, extensions, or compound bodies. He also said that one could not make any statements about them that were not in the Qur'ān and authentic *Ḥadīth*. For example, no analogies could be drawn, such as claiming that God had an elbow or upper arm. But he remarked that the Muslims knew from an authentic *ḥadīth* that, according to the Prophet, God's two hands were both right hands.[210]

With reference to verses in the Qur'ān, Ibn Taymiyya also affirmed that God had a face and hands. For example, he mentioned verses such as, 'the face of the Lord of might and glory will remain' (Q.LV.27), 'everything will perish except His face' (Q.XXVIII.88), 'what prevents you from prostrating before what I have created with My Own hands' (Q.XXXVIII.75), and, 'but [God]'s hands are spread wide open in bounty' (Q.V.64).[211] Ibn Taymiyya also mentioned a number of authentic *ḥadīth*s that referred to God's laughing and His leg. Ibn Taymiyya maintained that these attributes, as well as any others mentioned in the Qur'ān and *Ḥadīth*, had to be accepted without altering the meaning of the texts, stripping God of His attributes, or questioning how the attributes existed in God's essence, and without drawing analogies with any part of creation. In this way, Ibn Taymiyya defended the 'intermediate position' of the *Ahl al-Sunna* concerning the attributes of God because he considered it to be the only safe position between the extremes of those who denied God's attributes and those who engaged in anthropomorphism.

God's Hearing and Seeing

As part of his creed on the attributes of God, Ibn Ḥanbal repeatedly affirmed that there were attributes that could only be known through revelation and knowledge of them could not be obtained through intellectual inquiry. God's hearing and seeing were just such attributes. He pointed out that God had said, 'He is All-Hearing and All-Seeing' (Q.XLII.11) and he observed that such verses were easily accepted by the believers because God only informed them about Himself in a way that rational minds could believe. And, he continued, a rational mind knew that God's attributes, such as hearing and seeing, could not be compared with any other type of perception that existed in creation. Furthermore, a Muslim had to affirm that God hears with hearing and sees with sight just as He knows with knowledge. Ibn Ḥanbal then mentioned that all of God's attributes were specific attributes that could not share the same meaning. He rejected, for example, the claim of those who said that the attribute 'All-Hearing' actually meant 'All-Knowing,' because God said, 'and if they decide on divorce, then [God] is All-Hearing, All-Knowing' (Q.II.227). Ibn Ḥanbal's argument was that God used both terms together in one verse so therefore the terms had to carry separate meanings.[212]

Concerning God's attributes of hearing and seeing, Ibn Taymiyya presented numerous verses in the *Wāsiṭiyya* to confirm these attributes.[213] For example, he referred to: 'patiently wait on your Lord's decree for you indeed are in Our sight' (Q.LII.48), '[God] has heard the saying of the one who disputes with you concerning her husband and complains to [God]; indeed, [God] hears the discussion between you' (Q.LVIII.1), and, 'Lo, I am with you, I hear and I see' (Q.XX.46). But elsewhere, he mentioned the verse, 'He is with you wherever you are, for [God] sees what you do' (Q.LVII.4), which generated a new set of problems for Ibn Taymiyya and led him to give a more detailed discussion about the relationship between God's essence and attributes on the one hand, and His creation on the other. This discussion was prompted by God's statement, 'He is with you wherever you are,' which could be used to justify the concept of God's immanence in the world if it were not understood in accordance with Salafī principles. Ibn Taymiyya stated that this verse did not mean that God was 'diffused throughout (*mukhtaliṭ*) His creation,'[214] and to believe otherwise was to contradict what the *Salaf* had declared about the manner in which God manifested Himself to creation.

Transcendence

God's transcendence was one of the pillars of the creed of the *Ahl al-Sunna* and was vigorously defended by the scholars of the *Ahl al-Ḥadīth*.[215] On this issue, Ibn Ḥanbal stated that God in His essence and His attributes was completely different than His creation. He declared that God knows everything and controls all things without intermixing (*mukhālaṭa*) with them or interpenetrating (*muwālaja*) them. He further rejected any concept of immanence by stating that God is exalted above all things and detached (*munfarid*) from them. He supported his belief in God's 'aboveness' (*fawqiyya*) by referring to verses such as, 'He is the Conqueror above His worshippers' (Q.VI.18, 61), 'to Him good words ascend, and He raises up the pious deed' (Q.XXXV.10), and, 'they fear their Lord above them and do what they are commanded' (Q.XVI.50).[216] Of all the verses that indicated God's transcendence, the most convincing proofs for Ibn Ḥanbal were the verses indicating that God has risen above His throne. In discussing the phrase, 'rising above the throne' (*istawā ʿalā al-ʿarsh*), which appears, for example, in Q.X.3, Ibn Ḥanbal explained that 'rising' meant 'transcendence' (*ʿulūw*) and 'ascendency' (*irtifāʿ*). However, as with all of God's attributes, He never ceased to be lofty (*ʿalī*), which had been one of His eternal attributes even before the creation of the throne. Ibn Ḥanbal noted that the throne held a special position over all creation and also that God praised Himself by being above the throne. Furthermore, he said, it was not permitted to say that the 'rising above the throne' occurred by way of touching (*mumāssa*) or encountering (*mulāqā*). God undergoes no change or alteration, and no boundaries (*ḥudūd*) have ever confined Him, neither before the creation of the throne nor after it. Thus, Ibn Ḥanbal rejected the idea that God was in any particular place by His essence (*bi-dhātihi*) because a place is necessarily limited.[217] Nevertheless, God was a unique entity who had described Himself as being an individual 'self' or 'soul' (*nafs*).

For Ibn Ḥanbal, the issue of God's complete transcendence had to be understood in terms of the affirmation of the attribute of 'self' and the denial of any form of body (*jism*). He stated that God had a *nafs* that was unlike the *nafs* in bodies; rather, His *nafs* was an eternal attribute in His essence, and Ibn Ḥanbal supported this view by citing verses such as, 'God warns you of His "self"' (Q.III.28, 30), and, 'your Lord has written mercy upon His "self"' (Q.VI.12). Also, to prove the distinction between God's 'self' and the self of others, he referred to Jesus's statement in the verse, 'You know what is in my "self" but I do not know what is in Your "self"' (Q.V.116), and then added that Ibn ʿAbbās had explained that 'my self' meant the 'created self' (*al-nafs al-makhlūqa*), while 'Your self' meant 'Your divine self' (*nafsuka al-malakūtiyya*).[218] As for the concept of God having or being a body, Ibn Ḥanbal rejected the use of this term in relation to God because it did not appear in the lawful texts. According to the law and the Arabic language, the term 'body' was used for anything possessing extension, accidents, thickness and image, and anything compound and formed. Consequently, since God was far removed from such things and was outside the meaning of 'corporeality,' it was not permitted for God to be described with the term *jism*.

Ibn Taymiyya upheld God's transcendence in a very similar manner. In the *Wāsiṭiyya*, he presented verses describing God's rising above the throne in order to confirm His 'aboveness,' such as, 'the Infinitely Merciful has risen above the throne' (Q.XX.5), and, 'your Lord is [God] who created the Heavens and the earth in six days and then rose above the throne' (Q.X.3). Ibn Taymiyya also confirmed God's 'aboveness' by citing verses such as Q.XXXV.10, which was mentioned above. Further confirmation of God's transcendence could be found in various authentic *ḥadīth*s in which God and His Messenger attributed the motions of ascent and descent to Him. Accordingly, Ibn Taymiyya presented the *ḥadīth* about God's descent (*nuzūl*) to the lowest Heaven in the last third of the night to prove this point.[219] Importantly, he saw no contradiction in believing that God was transcendent yet near, and above the throne yet descending and ascending. 'Every facet of what God has said regarding himself,' he stated, 'corresponds to His reality and has no need of being altered.... It is necessary to add, however, that what the Qur'ān and the *Sunna* affirm regarding God's proximity to (*qurb*), and presence with (*maʿiya*), humankind in no way contradicts their emphasis on His transcendence and otherness (*fawqīya*), for His qualities can be compared to nothing that exists. He is transcendent in His nearness (*dunūw*) and near (*qarīb*) in His transcendence.'[220]

In another important issue related to God's essence, transcendence and self, both Ibn Ḥanbal and Ibn Taymiyya upheld the belief in the beatific vision, which means actually seeing the face of God and not just awaiting the effects of His mercy and compassion. In his creed, Ibn Ḥanbal applied the methodology of the Salafī principles to confirm that God would be perceived by the inhabitants of Paradise. He first referred to the verse, 'faces that day will be glowing, toward their Lord looking (*nāẓira ilā*)' (Q.LXXV.22–23),[221] and then commented that if God had not meant 'vision with the eye' (*al-naẓar bi'l-ʿayn*), then He would not have associated a direction with it. Furthermore, by analysing the Arabic grammar used here, Ibn Ḥanbal rejected the meaning of 'waiting' or 'anticipating' (*intiẓār*) to explain *nāẓira* in this verse, because the use of the preposition 'ilā' excluded the possibility of the idea of waiting or anticipating. He then proceeded to employ the hermeneutics of explaining the Qur'ān by the Qur'ān by comparing this verse to other verses that contained a form of the root '*naẓara*' without the preposition *ilā* with the meaning of waiting or anticipating (e.g., Q.XXXVI.49 and Q.XXVII.35). To further support his interpretation, he stated that the beatific vision was confirmed by many *ḥadīth*s related to verses that mentioned seeing God in the hereafter, and it was precisely such *ḥadīth*s that Ibn Taymiyya used to confirm the beatific vision. He asserted that 'the faithful will see God with their very eyes on the day of resurrection just as they see the sun when the sky is clear, or the moon when it is full....Later they will see Him again when they enter Paradise in accordance with God's will.'[222]

God's Speech

One final point of theology that was critical for both theologians was that of God's speech (*kalām*). As would be expected, Ibn Ḥanbal considered God's speech to be an attribute in His essence and referred to the fact that God had praised Himself with speech, whereas false deities were dumb and speechless. In addition, he noted that God had faulted those who worshipped idols that could not speak when He said, 'Did they not see that it did not speak to them nor guide them to any way; they chose it and became wrong-doers' (Q.VI.148). As for the issue of the Qur'ān itself, Ibn Ḥanbal referred to the exegesis of Ibn Masʿūd and Ibn ʿAbbās concerning the verse, 'an Arabic Qur'ān containing no crookedness, perhaps they will become pious' (Q.XXXIX.28), in which they said that this meant it was not created. Furthermore, he stated that the Qur'ān could not be described as an 'explanation' (*ʿibāra*) of God's speech or a 'reproduction' (*hikāya*) of it; clearly he intended this to be a refutation of the theory of Ibn Kullāb (d. 241/855).[223] Thus, continued Ibn Ḥanbal, when God said that He spoke to Moses in the Qur'ān (Q.IV.174), a Muslim must accept the statements of the Companions and their Followers who believed in God's speech without mentioning anything about it being revealed as explanation or reproduction.[224]

We have already discussed Ibn Taymiyya's views concerning the Qur'ān as the eternal speech of God and the Arabic language as the created speech of humans, so here I shall briefly review his position on the speech of God as presented in the *Wāsiṭiyya*. Ibn Taymiyya confirmed that God attributed speech to Himself by citing numerous verses from the Qur'ān and in presenting them he affirmed that God speaks and that the Qur'ān is the word of God. The verses he referred to include the following: 'who is more true than God in discourse' (Q.IV.87), 'who is more true than God in speech' (Q.IV.122), 'when Moses arrived at the time appointed by Us, his Lord spoke to him' (Q.VII.143), and, 'recite what was revealed to you of the Book of your Lord, no one can change His word' (Q.XVIII.27).[225] Ibn Taymiyya went on to confirm that 'the Qur'ān is the word of God, revealed but uncreated, having its origin in [H]im and that this Qur'ān is the very same one which [H]e revealed to Muḥammad.' He also specifically stated that 'it is not permissible to characterise this word as a reproduction of the original word of God, or [as] an explanation of it.' Furthermore, in both recitation and transcription, the Qur'ān never ceased to be the word of God, 'for a statement can only be attributed to the one who originally uttered it.' He specified that the Qur'ān was 'the word of God in respect both of its letters (*ḥurūf*) and of its meaning (*maʿānī*). The word of God does not consist of letters without meaning, or meaning without letters.'[226]

The Istiqāma *and Ibn Taymiyya's View of Worship*

Based on his fundamental creed outlined above, Ibn Taymiyya spent the rest of his life defending those beliefs as God's truth as revealed to the Prophet. As a consequence, any thoughts or concepts that he felt infringed upon those basic beliefs became a target of his attacks. Although it is clear that Ibn Taymiyya knew exactly which beliefs he needed to defend, the manner in which he presented his arguments developed over the course of his life. As mentioned earlier in this introduction, his most prolific period was in the years following his return to Damascus in 712/1313, so his most sophisticated arguments were formulated during the last 15 years of his life. However, in this section, I present the arguments that Ibn Taymiyya made while in Egypt against the claims of those who he felt had deviated from his understanding of orthodoxy; that is, as deriving from the Righteous Predecessors. For this purpose, I focus on one of his major works of that period, *al-Istiqāma*, which represents a major link in the development of his arguments and clarifies many of the points raised in the *Risāla*.[227] Although a precise chronological relationship between the two works cannot be established with certainty at present, the ideational relationship between them is quite clear. I also refer to several of his other works from the later Damascus period in order to clarify certain points.

In the *Istiqāma*, Ibn Taymiyya began by stressing the obligation to follow the Qur'ān and the *Sunna* in matters of belief, action and acts of worship. His position was that the Qur'ān and *Sunna* contained the principles on which the religion was based and he held that there was no need to utilise other systems of thinking such as *kalām* and Greek logic.[228] A reliance on these outside sources was responsible, in his view, for deviation in jurisprudence and beliefs. He stated that innovated opinions (*al-ra'y al-muḥdath*) concerning the principles or practical rulings of jurisprudence were a result of the influence of *kalām* on legal reasoning (*uṣūl al-fiqh*), while the innovated opinions in matters of worship were related to a form of Sufism that had adopted a similar use of *kalām*.[229] Although Ibn Taymiyya did not discuss *kalām* in his *Risāla*, he did make certain generalisations about the speculative theologians in reference to free will and predestination. His discussions on determinism were, however, an important stepping-stone in his development of ideas concerning love and worship. Thus, I present an overview of Ibn Taymiyya's thoughts on *kalām* below in order to provide sufficient background information for his generalisations.

IBN TAYMIYYA'S CRITIQUE OF *KALĀM*

In the opening pages of *al-Istiqāma*, Ibn Taymiyya refuted the speculative theologians who thought that the Qur'ān and *Sunna* alone did not suffice to articulate the principles of religion or thought that the principles of religion benefitted from rational analogy (*qiyās ʿaqlī*) and rational evidence (*dalīl ʿaqlī*). However, this did not mean that Ibn Taymiyya completely rejected the use of rational analogy and rational evidence, for he sought only to limit the use of these methods as being secondary to the greater religious truths of revelation.[230] Consequently, he particularly objected to statements such as, 'analogy is necessary for most of the law because there is limited textual evidence for legal judgements (*al-aḥkām al-sharʿiyya*).'[231] In response, Ibn Taymiyya first made a general objection to excessive use of analogy by claiming that every scholar was ultimately compelled to return to the Qur'ān and the *Sunna*. This was apparent because every group claimed to be based on the *Sunna* while accusing other groups of practising innovations. But even the groups most obviously following innovations, such as the Khawārij and the Rawāfiḍ, did not make such exaggerated claims about the need for analogy. Second, to further push his point, he stated that imam Shāfiʿī did not resort to *kalām* and noted that he was in fact one of the scholars of *Ḥadīth* who followed the intermediate position of the *Ahl al-Sunna*.[232] More specifically, he offered three points to refute the claim that the law was in need of rational analogy.

Ibn Taymiyya's first point was that the divinely revealed texts, being God's final revelation, had to necessarily indicate solutions to new cases that did not originate in the texts themselves. His second point was that if a scholar missed this first point, he would proceed to decide new cases based on 'corrupt' principles, such as were used in *kalām*, and which often led to decisions that opposed the law as understood by the *Ahl al-Ḥadīth*. His third point resulted from observing the practical aspects of the first two points, for he said that whoever attempted to give hundreds of rulings in a day would find that ruling according to the revealed texts would benefit the Muslims far more than relying on opinion. As proof of this last point he called attention to the fact that the rulings of the People of Opinion from Kufa were considered to be of less value to the Muslims despite the large number of Kufian scholars.[233] He also specified that the direct cause of this over-reliance on analogy was that the sound methodology and rulings of early scholars such as Mālik, Shāfiʿī, Ibn Ḥanbal, Ibn al-Mubārak (d. 181/798), Ḥammād b. Zayd (d. 179/796) and Awzāʿī were mixed with innovative principles and beliefs so that what the earlier scholars had condemned then became accepted as part of the *Sunna* by later scholars.[234] Furthermore, the underlying cause for the prevalent use of *kalām* by scholars of the later generations was the spread of misconceptions about prophethood.

For Ibn Taymiyya, the misunderstanding of prophecy stemmed from the philosophers' claim that the prophets, despite knowing 'the essence of universal theological science' (*al-ʿulūm al-ilāhiyya al-kulliyya*), spoke to the masses in symbolic language.[235] He objected to their characterisation of prophecy as being based on the faculty of imagination (*takhayyul*), by which the prophets communicated philosophical truths that they received from the Active Intellect to the masses in an allegorical manner. Although Ibn Taymiyya recognised the subtle distinctions between the philosophers themselves, such as between Fārābī (d. 339/951) and Ibn Sīnā (d. 429/1038), he nonetheless condemned their assertion that the literal meaning of the Qur'ān was merely a metaphorical device for explaining reality to those incapable of understanding philosophy. Ibn Taymiyya then traced the influence of this general idea of the allegorical nature of prophecy back to the speculative theologians, who were misled into thinking that the Prophet had not explained all aspects of the religion in detail. He mentioned in particular how Ghazālī allowed for a wide range of interpretation—all the way from the literalism of the Ḥanbalīs to the laxity of the philosophers.[236] Thus, he said, the speculative theologians sought proofs for the religion from knowledge that did not originate in the revealed texts due to the fact that they did not believe that the texts themselves contained all necessary proofs. Consequently, as far as Ibn Taymiyya was concerned, this meant that they no longer had any claim to certainty.

The next part of Ibn Taymiyya's argument against *kalām* in the *Istiqāma* concerned the relationship between religion and knowledge. He contended that the revealed texts offered the only sound knowledge on which one could rely for deducing the principles of law and belief. Thus, resorting to *kalām* was the same as arguing about religion without revealed knowledge, which was forbidden, and not relying on revealed knowledge meant that one was arguing based on doubts. By this he meant the sources of knowledge used by the logicians, such as 'conclusions based on pure reason' (*maʿqūlāt*), 'demonstrative proofs' (*barāhīn*) and 'syllogisms' (*aqyisa*). He objected to relying on these forms of argument drawn from the purely rational sciences because those who used them claimed that revelation had not provided evidence that could either validate or invalidate the proofs drawn from pure reason. This also meant that revelation was assigned an inferior position to pure reason.[237] Another undesirable outcome of disregarding revealed knowledge was that one could end up relying on personal feelings—by which he meant traditional Ṣūfī 'sources' of knowledge such as 'unveilings' (*mukāshafāt*), 'ecstatic experiences' (*mawājīd*) and 'mystical tastings' (*adhwāq*). For although the Ṣūfīs claimed that the knowledge received during these states was more certain than that obtained through dialectics, Ibn Taymiyya dismissed this as merely being a false interpretation.[238] Ultimately, he argued that all of the proofs mentioned here—whether they were advanced by the logicians or by the Ṣūfīs—were used without authority from the Qur'ān and the *Sunna*. In leading up to this conclusion he presented numerous verses of the Qur'ān condemning the practice of arguing about God without the authority (*bi-ghayr sulṭān*) given by Him to do so, and stated that knowledge could only come from revealed texts and those who argued from other sources did so without authority from God.[239]

Ibn Taymiyya then presented his own proofs to show that the principles of *kalām* did not lead to certainty. He first said that the speculative theologians differed among themselves regarding principles and case law. They also differed in their judgements about fundamental issues of belief such as the status of various Muslim sects, the modes of argumentation used in declaring other Muslims to be disbelievers, and the permissibility of cursing other Muslims and mutual hatred between them.[240] To disagree on fundamental issues was a warning sign for Ibn Taymiyya because differences of opinion were a clear indication of deviation from God's path. He indicated this in the *Istiqāma* by referring to the verse, 'do not be like those who divided into sects and differed with each other after the clear signs came to them, they will have a tremendous punishment' (Q.III.105).[241]

After arguing that disagreement over principles was a deviation from what the Prophet had brought by way of the Qur'ān and the *Sunna*, Ibn Taymiyya advanced a moral argument against those Muslims who had adopted a rigid stance on the issue of differences of opinion. In what may well have been an allusion to his own difficulties with fellow scholars and the authorities, Ibn Taymiyya called for a more tolerant attitude on the part of Muslims in their relations with those who held opposing opinions to their own, which was necessary, he believed, to avoid levelling accusations of disbelief (*takfīr*) against other Muslims. According to him, two of the most important reasons why disagreements on principles arose were injustice and transgression. Due to the fact that people were prone to err and to forget, God had not placed undue restrictions on the Muslims in religion; thus, if there were a difference of opinion among Muslims, and both groups sought to resolve the problem with one being right and the other being wrong, then this would be a forgivable difference. Only injustice led to turmoil, disbelief or accusations of sinful deviation (*tafsīq*).[242]

In the *Istiqāma*, Ibn Taymiyya concluded his arguments against the speculative theologians by stating that *kalām* was dangerous because it transformed jurisprudence from a sound religious science (*ʿilm*) into a matter of opinion (*ẓunūn*).[243] This occurred because the speculative theologians claimed that Islamic jurisprudence was based on the judgements of singularly transmitted *ḥadīth*s (*khabar al-wāḥid*), analogy, generalisations (*ʿumūm*) and literal meanings (*ẓawāhir*), which they considered to be inferior to the methods of the logicians. Of these four principles, the use of singularly transmitted *ḥadīth*s in jurisprudence was clearly the most controversial and Ibn Taymiyya's defence of their use as sound evidence may be traced back to the arguments of Shāfiʿī and Ibn Qutayba (d. 276/890). Schacht points out that Shāfiʿī referred to those who rejected the *ḥadīth*s altogether as the *Ahl al-Kalām* or the Muʿtazila.[244] As the speculative theologians came to find it more difficult to reject the *ḥadīth*s outright, a distinction emerged between, on the one hand, the extremists who rejected all *ḥadīth*s, and, on the other, a moderate group of the *Ahl al-Kalām* who rejected only the *khabar al-wāḥid ḥadīth*s. Eventually, even some of the speculative theologians of later generations, such as Āmidī (d. 631/1234), came to accept the use of singularly transmitted *ḥadīth*s with certain restrictions.[245] But for Ibn Taymiyya, the authenticity of the *khabar al-wāḥid ḥadīth*s (as determined by the *Ḥadīth* scholars) was undeniable. Thus, he argued that since they were to be included among the sound evidence of the revealed *Sunna*, a jurist could arrive at certainty in a particular case by using analogy based on such a *ḥadīth*. His particular stance on this issue was that the syllogistic reasoning favoured by the logicians was not a more formidable means of arriving at certainty than that of argument by analogy as used by the jurisprudents of the *Ahl al-Ḥadīth*.[246] Finally, Ibn Taymiyya refuted the claims of the speculative theologians by once again referring to judgements in actual cases, saying that the number of legal issues that had been clearly determined by referring to the revealed texts and consensus far exceeded those that had been resolved by individual opinion or had resulted in differences of opinion.[247]

In summary, Ibn Taymiyya's critique of *kalām* stemmed from his unwavering acceptance of Salafī principles. At the core of these principles lay the belief that the Prophet had explained the entire religion of Islam, including its operating principles and general beliefs. Based on this, Ibn Taymiyya asserted that only revealed knowledge could lead to certainty, whereas the methods of the logicians were unnecessary for a Muslim scholar. However, the real danger of *kalām* when it was applied to the issues of belief and worship, because it gave rise to beliefs about God that differed from the creed of the *Ahl al-Sunna*, as well as to acts of worship not practised by the *Salaf*. But before turning to this controversy, one final point must be addressed in order to show the continuity of Ibn Taymiyya's thinking when it came to classifying groups and individuals.

As he had done with the exegetes and in analysing the relationship of various groups to the *Ahl al-Sunna*, Ibn Taymiyya also classified the speculative theologians.[248] In their case, he perceived there to be a stronger deviation in their methods and opinions the nearer they came to the philosophers, which also corresponded to a greater distance in time from the earliest generations of Muslims. As a result, he placed Ibn Kullāb (d. 241/855) closest to the Salaf, followed by Ashʿarī (d. 323/935), who in turn was followed by Bāqillānī (d. 403/1013). After the latter scholar, Juwaynī (d. 478/1086) had gone even further in his deviations stemming from *kalām*, then finally, Ibn Taymiyya placed Rāzī (d. 606/1210) and Amidī (d. 631/1233) closest to the philosophers. But it is important to note that, in keeping with his tolerant attitude, Ibn Taymiyya still referred to the speculative theologians as people of oneness who had faltered when it came to certain aspects of their understanding of divinity (*ulūhiyya*) in relation to God's names and attributes. And in any case, he considered them to be better than the philosophers for not accepting philosophical cosmologies. Finally, so as not to leave anything unclassified, Ibn Taymiyya also stated that the philosophers from the People of the Book and the Muslims were better than the pagan philosophers.

IBN TAYMIYYA'S CRITIQUE OF THE ṢŪFĪS

Ibn Taymiyya's *Istiqāma* presents a precise summary of his understanding of the development of Ṣūfī beliefs. In this work he focused on Qushayrī's *Risāla* as the basis of his discussion with his major criticism of it being that Qushayrī (d. 465/1072) followed the beliefs of the speculative theologians, particularly, the Kullābiyya and the Ashʿariyya.[249] For Ibn Taymiyya, this established an important link between *kalām* and Sufism, and to support his contention he added that Qushayrī had received his knowledge of *kalām* from the Ashʿarī scholars Ibn Fūrak (d. 406/1015) and Abū Isḥāq al-Isfarāyīnī (d. 418/1027).[250] However, Ibn Taymiyya recognised that there were different kinds of Ṣūfīs and, for him, the great Ṣūfī shaykhs were those who agreed with what the pious Predecessors had taught. According to his Salafī standards for classifying people and groups, Ibn Taymiyya developed a hierarchy of the Ṣūfīs: in his opinion the best of them were al-Fuḍayl b. ʿIyād (d. 187/803), Abū Sulaymān al-Darānī (d. 215/830), Yūsuf b. Asbāt (d. 199/814 or 196/811), Ḥudhayfa al-Marʿishī, Maʿruf al-Karkhī (d. 200/815), al-Junayd b. Muḥammad (d. 297/910 or 298/911) and Sahl b.

ʿAbd-Allāh al-Tustarī (d. 283/896 or 273/886), all of whom had condemned *kalām* and had opposed the Kullābiyya and the Ashʿariyya.[251] The statements of these shaykhs were collected in the most reliable books of the Ṣūfīs, such as the works of Kalābādhī (d. 380/990 or 384/994), Muʿammar b. Ziyād al-Asfahānī (d. 418/1027) and Abū ʿAbd al-Raḥmān al-Sulamī (d. 412/1021).[252] As the opposite of these 'orthodox' Ṣūfīs, Ibn Taymiyya pointed to those Ṣūfīs who had succumbed to an ecstatic experience (*wajd*) and thereby lost sight of the truth. This is what had happened to Ḥallāj (d. 310/922) and Abū Bakr al-Shiblī (d. 334/944); they tried to differentiate between Creator and creation, but after being overcome by their ecstatic experience, they were never able to differentiate between truth and falsehood. Thus, it was not permitted to accept their statements without also referring to the sound views of the righteous shaykhs.[253] This led Ibn Taymiyya to a lengthy discussion of some of the statements attributed to Ḥallāj [254] and Ghazālī's comments on ecstatic expressions (*shaṭaḥāt*).

Ibn Taymiyya quoted certain parts of Ghazālī's discussion concerning ecstatic expressions in the *Iḥyā' ʿulūm al-dīn*. After mentioning that Ghazālī had identified two types of ecstatic expressions innovated by some Ṣūfīs, he cited the following: 'The first type are protracted claims about passionate love (*ʿishq*) for God and about a lover's union (*wiṣāl*) that frees him from external acts of obedience. This eventually results in claims of union with God (*ittiḥād*), of lifting the veil between God and man, of witnessing a vision of the divine and of oral expressions about the experience. By making these claims, they imitate Ḥallāj, who was crucified because he blurted out words of this type.'[255]

Ibn Taymiyya skipped over Ghazālī's short discussion about some of the *shaṭaḥāt* attributed to Abū Yazīd al-Bisṭāmī (d. 261/875) and continued to quote from Ghazālī's discussion of the second type of *shaṭḥ*: '[This] consists of incomprehensible statements that are outwardly impressive but contain appalling explanations (*ʿibārāt hā'ila*). There is nothing useful behind such statements. This type of *shaṭḥ* is either incomprehensible to the speaker himself (who produces it out of madness and derangement because there is a paucity of meanings in the speech which has reached his ears, and this is the most common type), or it is understandable to him, but he is incapable of making it understood and citing it with explanations to indicate what is in his mind.'[256] After this quotation, Ibn Taymiyya expressed his agreement with Ghazālī by saying that ecstatic expressions contained falsity, ambiguity, distorted and useless statements, as well as truth; consequently, the best and surest way to follow this truth was to avoid the way of Ḥallāj.

Ibn Taymiyya's warnings echoed the position of the orthodox community concerning the *shaṭaḥāt*. A brief discussion of the implications of these expressions must suffice to clarify this point. The ecstatic expressions of the Ṣūfīs were intricately linked to what they claimed was an experience of the annihilation of self (*fanā'*). During *fanā'*, 'a transfiguring occurs which gives one an intermittent divine investiture, thus consenting forever to a dialogue of love between God and man;' that is, between 'Thee and me.' What then occurs is the 'divinely inspired utterance which this supernatural commotion extracts from the subject.'[257] Unsurprisingly, from Ibn Taymiyya's point of view, it was easy to judge the *shaṭaḥāt* themselves to be heretical. In fact, Ṣūfīs such as Ḥallāj and ʿAyn al-Quḍāt al-Hamadhānī (d. 525/1131) actually realised the need of their own executions.[258]

In order to explain why the ecstatic expressions of the Ṣūfīs were considered to pose such a danger for the orthodox community I now present some of the most famous examples of them. Abū Yazīd al-Bisṭāmī (d. 261/875) was reported to have said, 'My "I am" is not "I am," because I am He, and I am "he is He" (*huwa huwa*).' Also attributed to him is the statement, '...I saw Him in every state, to such a degree that it was as if I were He.' Similarly, Ḥallāj was quoted as saying, 'My spirit mixes with Your spirit, in nearness and in distance, so that I am You, just as You are I.' Finally, there is the well-known statement of Ḥallāj, which was also attributed to Bisṭāmī, 'I am the Truth" (*anā'l-ḥaqq*).[259]

These expressions entailed the complete denial of the orthodox distinction between Creator and created. In essence, everything that was held to be normal or proper by the orthodox theologians was turned inside out and upside down by the monistic Ṣūfīs.[260] From the perspective of those who had not experienced the states of ecstasy and intoxication of the Ṣūfīs, the main problem arising from these ecstatic expressions was the heretical content that they contained. The *shaṭaḥāt* were alleged to be expressions of a spiritual state '...in which the speaker is God, testifying to His own unity on the tongue of His lover.' In analysing such expressions, the element of 'intoxication' could not be explained in a 'sober' state; thus, it was unavoidable '...that a literal understanding of ecstatic expressions would lead to heresy....' This was acknowledged by later Ṣūfīs, who cautioned against uttering comments about one's experiences. For example, Hujwīrī (d. 464/1071) warned that '...expression only produces an unreal notion and leads the student mortally astray.' Similarly, ʿAyn al-Quḍāt alluded to the problem in the following terms: '...the lover and the beloved are one in divine reality, but separate on the level of discursive thought."[261] These last two statements expressed the idea that if the experience was ineffable, then the mystic should remain silent. This type of warning did not deny the Ṣūfī's experience, but warned that the moment the mystic spoke, his statements entered into the domain of scrutiny and investigation; in other words, what he claimed to be reality was open for others to analyse.[262]

Ibn Taymiyya obviously felt compelled to investigate ecstatic expressions in order to show that what the monistic Ṣūfīs claimed to be reality was contrary to the Qur'ān and the *Sunna*. According to him, the heretical dimension of ecstatic expressions was the idea of the elimination of the ego during a state in which the mystic believed he had attained self-identity with God.[263] Based on Ibn Taymiyya's acceptance of the creed of the Salaf that God in no way intermixes with His creation, he had no choice but to condemn ecstatic expressions as a product of false belief.[264] He therefore associated the exaggerated claims of some Ṣūfīs with the concept of *fanā'*, the mystical annihilation of self. However, before entering into a discussion of *fanā'*, he had to address two major issues that he believed to be critical for avoiding deviation in religious experiences. The first was a proper understanding of the distinction God made between good and evil, which Ibn Taymiyya related to the concepts of predestination and free will. The second was a proper understanding of the role of love in relation to worship and obedience.

Ibn Taymiyya's arguments concerning these issues not only arose from his theological convictions about the nature of God, but also from his moral attitudes. Ibn Taymiyya objected to the concept of union with the divine on account of the fact that the Ṣūfī fell into unbelief by abandoning God's law while being so absorbed in the thought of the beloved that he lost consciousness. The loss of consciousness meant that the lover no longer knew how to approach the beloved; for Ibn Taymiyya, this meant that the Ṣūfī no longer knew how to follow the *Sunna*.[265] This act of disbelief was exemplified by the Ṣūfīs who had rejected the authority of the Qur'ān and the *Sunna*, thinking that there was some greater truth or reality than those two revealed sources. This false assumption was the basis for Ṣūfīs such as Abū Yaᶜqūb al-Maghribī saying, 'Being is One, and that is God. I don't see the One, I don't see God,' and, 'the [Qur'ān] and *Sunna* speak about Duality of Being, while Being is One, without dualism.' Also, Tilimsānī (d. 690/1291) said, 'The [Qur'ān], all of it, is polytheism (*shirk*), with no element of monotheism ([*al-tawḥīd*]) whatsoever; [*al-tawḥīd*] is but in our utterances....The [Qur'ān], at best, leads to Paradise, but our utterances to God Himself.'[266] Such statements indicated that truth, or some aspect of it, lay outside or beyond the Qur'ān and the *Sunna*. From his view of the all-encompassing nature of God's revelation, it is easy to understand why Ibn Taymiyya was outraged by these types of claims.

Ibn Taymiyya continued his moral arguments by insisting on the necessary distinction between good and evil and the necessity of repentance for acts of disobedience.[267] His position concerning good and evil revolved around the fact that God had made a clear distinction between good and evil deeds, as well as between those who obeyed Him and those who disobeyed Him. This distinction was permanent and could not be breached by the attainment of spiritual states. This was the crux of his moral argument, which he used as a form of reductio ad absurdum to show that anything other than the belief in the distinction between the Creator and the created would lead to a denial of the clear statements of the Qur'ān and the *Sunna*, and thus to moral decay.[268] As he pointed out in his *Risāla*, it was the polytheists and innovators who attempted to evade God's commands and obscure what He defined as good or evil; thus, the distinction between good and evil also indicated the importance of commanding good and forbidding evil.

Ibn Taymiyya included a lengthy discussion of commanding good and forbidding evil in the *Istiqāma* and his emphasis on the topic is a direct reflection of his polemics against the antinomian Ṣūfī groups that existed during the seventh/thirteenth and eighth/fourteenth centuries. Extreme antinomian tendencies in Sufism were Ibn Taymiyya's proof of the dangers that could result from deviations in creed and practice. Regrettably, even a short review of the history of the antinomian Ṣūfī groups existing prior to, and during, the lifetime of Ibn Taymiyya is not feasible within the present work. However, I feel it is necessary to identify some of the major groups that most clearly represented antinomianism and with which Ibn Taymiyya had direct contact.[269] It was these antinomian groups who were the living example of everything that the Ḥanbalī theologian saw to be wrong in monistic Sufism.

Ibn Taymiyya was involved in confrontations with fanatical groups that practised extreme forms of unconventional behaviour, ranging from a complete disregard for Islamic law to body piercing, fire walking and other similar practices. The Rifāʿiyya in particular were famous for these latter practices.[270] Memon details some of the actions Ibn Taymiyya took against them and notes that he was incensed by their claims to be able to perform miracles because of their overwhelming love for, and closeness to, God. Two other Ṣūfī groups that engaged in unconventional behaviour were the Qalandariyya and the Malāmatiyya.[271] The premise of their beliefs was that in order to focus all their attention on God they had to intentionally draw public censure upon themselves. They accomplished this by renouncing everything in this world, including the law and social norms, which allowed them to fulfil what they believed to be the true meaning of worshipping only God.

Although these two groups had common origins in the third/ninth century and, at times, have been viewed as indistinguishable from each other, their approaches to renunciation were different. The Qalandariyya sought to deviate publicly from the law through the non-performance of religious rituals and the performance of well-known prohibitions. The Malāmatiyya, on the other hand, performed the obligations of the law in order to hide their true spiritual state. However, on occasion, they would intentionally commit blameworthy acts so that people would censure them and shun them.[272] As far as Ibn Taymiyya was concerned, these deviations stemmed not only from corrupt beliefs but also from misguided love.

Therefore, Ibn Taymiyya incorporated his theory of the relationship between the love for God and His oneness into his moral and theological arguments advocating for a distinction between God and creation, and between good and evil. This theory included the idea that love for God had to evoke in the worshipper a desire to follow the Prophet and as evidence for this he referred to the verse of the Qur'ān, 'Say: If you love God then follow me, God will love you and forgive you your sins' (Q.III.31). He explained that the meaning of this verse was that God has made the love of the worshipper for

Him a cause for following the Prophet, which in turn brought God's love to His worshipper.[273]

As for the connection between a worshipper's love for God and the concept of oneness, Ibn Taymiyya contended that this love occurred between two separate beings with no possibility of existential or ontic union between them. He believed this was confirmed by the opening sura of the Qur'ān, which, according to an authentic *ḥadīth*, God has divided into two parts. The first part consists of the praises of the worshipper for his Lord and the second part concerns the seeking of guidance by the worshipper.[274] Based on this, he argued that all the activities of a worshipper, such as obedience, humility, love and hope, had to be directed to God. For this reason, a believer worships God and seeks aid from Him by continually saying, 'It is You alone we worship and from You alone we seek help' (Q.I.4). Ibn Taymiyya's argument was that the love evoked by the Qur'ān and the *Sunna* distinguishes itself from love resulting from polytheism. Thus, he concluded that there was a polytheistic form of love, in which the identity of the lovers was united, and which was related to polytheism in the matter of belief. He therefore added that such beliefs compromised monotheism and elaborated on this point through a discussion of intimate love (*khulla*).[275]

Ibn Taymiyya considered the fulfilment of worship and love to be the realisation that God, in His essence, had to be the focus of one's love. He described the process of loving God as a movement that paralleled the process of worshipping Him alone and without associating partners with Him, explaining this as a process of moving from an unqualified love (*maḥabba muṭlaqa*) to an exclusive, intimate love. He described this intimate love in the *Risāla* as follows: 'Intimacy (*khulla*) is the perfection of the love (*maḥabba*) required from a worshipper and the perfection of worship for God; and from the Lord, glorified be He, it is the perfection of Lordship toward His worshippers whom He loves and who love Him. This highest level of perfection occurred to Abraham and Muḥammad, may God bless them and grant them peace. For this reason, he [Muḥammad] did not have an intimate friend from the people of the earth, for intimacy cannot bear partnership....'

Ibn Taymiyya's conclusion was that, for a Muslim, love, worship and oneness formed an organic, integrated whole; and thus, whatever affected one would necessarily affect the others. Consequently, the realisation of faith depended on the exclusive nature of a Muslim's love and worship for the one deity. He argued that intimacy was exclusive and did not allow for any share to be given to another beloved. Furthermore, intimacy was a specific kind of love, for it was a complete or perfect love. The lover would be permeated by intimacy to the point that what he loved would only be loved for itself and not for any other thing; accordingly, the Prophet loved other people for the sake of God, but his sense of intimacy was for God alone. Intimacy had to be intended for God in His essence and not for the sake of anything else. In this sense, a worshipper had to love God for Himself and love others for His sake, a point stressed by Ibn Taymiyya in no uncertain terms. In order to worship God one had to love Him, because love was necessarily connected with worship, and intimacy was the perfection of love and worship.

According to Ibn Taymiyya, this link between love, worship and oneness was also reflected in the language of supplications.[276] He believed that the law had been revealed to establish the proper guidelines for worship and the proper concepts of oneness. For instance, the Prophet had taught the believers to remember God by means of statements such as, 'God is great,' 'Glory be to God' and, 'All praise is for God.' Likewise, he also taught the believers to supplicate Him with statements such as, 'O Lord, I have wronged myself, forgive me.' Importantly, all of these statements were based on a distinction between the Creator and His creation. It therefore followed that if a Muslim's concept of love and oneness did not preserve this distinction, then he was being led astray. This judgement was the basis of Ibn Taymiyya's criticism of those who claimed that their love for

God had done away with all distinctions. He held this to be a misguided love that stood in opposition to the perfection of love. In the *Risāla*, Ibn Taymiyya explained why he considered such statements concerning love to be erroneous:

> [S]ome shaykhs say that 'love is a fire that burns everything in a heart except a desire for the beloved.' They mean that God wills the existence of the whole universe, and thus they imagine that the perfection of love is that a worshipper should love everything including disbelief, depravity, and rebellion. But it is impossible for someone to love everything that exists. On the contrary, a person loves what suits him and benefits him and hates what is incompatible to him and harms him. However, from this error (*ḍalāl*) they take advantage of following their passions (*aḥwā*), for they love what they desire, such as images, leadership, excess wealth and misleading innovations. All the while, they maintain that these are part of love of God, but love of God includes the hatred of what He and His Messenger hate and the striving of His people with soul and wealth.[277]

Ibn Taymiyya associated erroneous notions about love with the monistic Ṣūfīs who only paid attention to God's creative will and neglected His religious decrees. He believed that the confusion of the monists was due to their failure to apprehend a distinction between God's will and the thing willed, as was the case when they regarded the existence of the universe to be the same as the existence of God. For him, one could only be considered a true lover and worshipper of God by following His legislation as it pertained to both practices and beliefs. He explained that God had made a clear distinction between good and evil, as well as between obedience and disobedience, so the believer must likewise maintain these distinctions.

Erroneous ideas about love were directly related to the experience of *fanā'* (annihilation of the self), along with a loss of consciousness and the ecstatic expressions that resulted from it. For the Ṣūfīs, mystical *fanāʾ* 'culminated in the belief that contemplation of God's pure essence, stripped of all attributes, constituted the highest degree of witnessing (*shuhūd*).'[278] In both the *Istiqāma* and the *Risāla*, Ibn Taymiyya discussed the issue of annihilation by identifying three types of *fanāʾ*: a praiseworthy type, a defective type and a condemnable type.[279] Notably, his conception of *fanāʾ* subtly diverged from the traditional manner of describing it in Ṣūfī literature, making this a good example of how Ibn Taymiyya attempted to redefine Ṣūfī terminology in line with his Salafī beliefs. A brief review of the standard Ṣūfī descriptions of *fanāʾ* helps to highlight his reformulations.

Qushayrī described *fanāʾ* as a three-stage progression toward what he believed to be a more profound spiritual experience.[280] He describes this progression by referring to traditional Ṣūfī concepts related to *fanāʾ*. Firstly Qushayrī referred to the annihilation of the blameworthy self and the attributes of the worshipper by his subsisting in the attributes of the truth (i.e., the universal, eternally true attributes of God). Secondly he mentioned the annihilation of the attributes of the truth by means of witnessing the truth (i.e., the essential oneness of God). Thirdly he referred to the annihilation of the witnessing of annihilation by perishing (*istihlāk*) in the existence (*wujūd*) of the truth (i.e., by achieving union with God).

ʿAbd Allāh al-Anṣārī al-Harawī (d. 481/1089) was important because this fellow Ḥanbalī had such a clear influence on both Ibn Taymiyya and the latter's student, Ibn al-Qayyim (d. 751/1350), although they did not accept his statements unconditionally.[281] In his work entitled, *Manāzil al-sāʾirīn*, Harawī discussed the three stages of *fanāʾ*. He referred to the first stage as 'the *fanāʾ* of cognition in the thing cognised;' in other words, the annihilation of the subject in an object. The second stage was 'the *fanāʾ* of the witnessing of seeking because what is cognised is eliminated;' which is to say, the annihilation of the object. Like Qushayrī, Harawī's third stage was also 'the *fanāʾ* of the *fanāʾ*.' However, although Harawī did not suggest that this third stage was equivalent to an annihilation of existence into the one divine existence, Ibn al-Qayyim nonetheless rejected it as an error in Harawī's explanation of *fanā'*, remarking that this use of *fanā'* was associated with the people of union with the divine (*Ahl al-Ittiḥād*). Ibn al-Qayyim added that it stemmed from their misinterpretation of *fanā'*, which, he said, was merely the annihilation of a thing in the worshipper's intellectual and mental existence. By contrast, the *Ahl al-Ittiḥād*, he said, had interpreted it as the annihilation of a worshipper's existence in the existence of God. This third stage of the Ṣūfī concept of *fanā'* was therefore the point of departure for Ibn Taymiyya and Ibn al-Qayyim.

This rejection of the traditional Ṣūfī conception of annihilation was reflected in Ibn Taymiyya's reformulation of the experience of *fanā'*, where instead of identifying three progressive stages ending in the *fanā'* of the *fanā'*, or the *istihlāk*, he categorised the experience of annihilation according to his own notion of perfect worship. For him, the praiseworthy type of *fanā'* was that of the prophets, messengers and saints. It was the annihilation of the will for anything other than God; not an annihilation of it in an absolute sense.[282] Whoever attained this level brought himself into complete conformity with God's will while remaining conscious and maintaining a distinction between God and His creation; that is, a distinction, but not a desire, for anything other than God. He next described the defective type of *fanā'*, which fell short of the perfection of the first type, but was still suitable for the righteous. At this level, the seeker lost his witnessing of anything other than God—in other words, his awareness of God's creation—by concentrating only on Him. As Ibn Taymiyya explained in the *Risāla*, this was a state similar to that of Moses's mother when she became devoid (*fārigh*) of all thoughts except for her son (Q.XXVIII.10). The danger of the defective *fanā'* was that a seeker of the truth could become confused by his experiences, believing that his loss of witnessing anything other than God had brought him into a selfsame identity with Him. This led to the condemnable *fanā'*, which was the level of those who had followed the example of Pharaoh; that is, they believed themselves to be a god. At this level, the seeker was completely misled by his experiences and believed that God in His essence and existence was the only existence, the seeker being included in it. However, the multiplicity of particulars was merely an extension of God's being, with no reality outside His existence. For Ibn Taymiyya, 'this is the *fanā'* of the unbelievers, for it makes the existence of things to be the selfsame existence as the True One.'[283]

In comparison with the traditional Ṣūfī descriptions of *fanā'*, the purpose of Ibn Taymiyya's reformulation is clear. He was seeking to discredit the practice of falling unconscious during the *fanā'*, which he saw as the outward manifestation of a purported mystical union with God, and he did so by emphasising the sober qualities of worship as prescribed by Ḥanbalī pietism. In line with the teachings of Junayd, who Ibn Taymiyya respected as an 'orthodox' Ṣūfī, he believed that sobriety must prevail over intoxication.[284] Thus, Ibn Taymiyya elevated the first stage of the Ṣūfī experience (which typically referred to the annihilation of passions and desires) to a complete annihilation of the worshipper's will for anything other than what God willed. It was a state of consciousness and total submission. As mentioned above, the second stage described by the Ṣūfīs related to either an annihilation of witnessing or a loss of consciousness concerning one's attributes. It was at this stage that Ibn Taymiyya warned about the dangers of the annihilation of witnessing, which for him was a less perfect state that could lead to a permanently weakened intellect and discernment. Moreover, this condition prepared the way for a worshipper's lapse into the deceptions associated with the third stage of *fanā'*. Thus, what was praised by the monistic Ṣūfīs as *istihlāk* (or the *fanā'* of the *fanā'*) was, for Ibn Taymiyya, nothing more than a means of succumbing to the falsities of the notion of union with the divine.

The importance that Ibn Taymiyya placed on the role of consciousness in worship culminated in his theory concerning the Ṣūfī term *baqā'* (subsistence).[285] Although Ibn Taymiyya did not mention the term *baqā'* in the *Risāla*, he included a short discussion of the Ṣūfī concepts of *farq* and *jam*ᶜ, which are directly related to *fanā'* and *baqā'*.[286] In addition, his theory of *baqā'* may be derived from his later works and from statements made by his student, Ibn al-Qayyim, on the topic. In Ṣūfī descriptions, *jam*ᶜ ('concentration') was associated with *fanā'* and *farq* ('separation') with *baqā'*. These descriptions explained that as the Ṣūfī perished from himself, he concentrated on the Divine Reality, and as he separated from this experience, he subsisted—albeit transformed—in his former state.[287] By contrast, Ibn Taymiyya's ideas about subsistence were based on the need to maintain an explicit distinction between Creator and created. One assumption evident in his discussions was that *fanā'* and *baqā'* occurred simultaneously, which was yet another echo of Junayd's theory.[288] Ibn Taymiyya stated that the correct type of *fanā'* was conjoined with *baqā'*.[289] This experience would then remain true to the requirements of the testimony of faith, which was the constant realisation that there is no deity but God. This point was confirmed by the way he concluded his discussion of correct witnessing in the *Risāla* where he stated that it was the negation in the heart of the divinity of everything other than God and simultaneously the confirmation in the heart of the divinity of the Truth (*ulūhiyyat al-Ḥaqq*).

Ibn al-Qayyim similarly explained *fanā'* in terms of this definition of oneness and said that it was a confirmation of the divinity of God and a negation of the divinity of everything else. He then stated that the negation was the *fanā'* while the confirmation was the *baqā'*.[290] Consequently, for Ibn Taymiyya and Ibn al-Qayyim, the perfection of worship became the perfection of the *fanā'-baqā'* experience; that is, the annihilation of the worshipper's will and desire so that he subsisted in conformity with God's will while never losing awareness of His distinction from His creation. As mentioned above, this was a path of complete sobriety and yet also of complete submission.

At the heart of *fanā'*, according to Ibn Taymiyya, lay the conflict between intoxication (*sukr*) and sobriety (*sahw*) in relation to religious experiences.[291] Losing consciousness, or intoxication, was not praiseworthy because it meant the presence of delight (*ladhdha*) and an absence of distinction (*tamyīz*). He considered this to be blameworthy because God praises knowledge, intellect and understanding while censuring the absence of these qualities.[292] Thus, with respect to sobriety and intoxication, Ibn Taymiyya's guiding principle was adherence to the Qur'ān and the *Sunna* as literally understood. In this matter, the best path was that of the prophets and saints who maintained sobriety in worship, followed in superiority by that of the Companions, who strove to remain sober while worshipping God in the best manner.

Ibn Taymiyya also classified the types of people who fell into some kind of unconscious state. The blameless ones were those who were afflicted naturally and could not resist. The next group consisted of those who were afflicted but were able to resist, with the resistance itself considered to be a good deed even if one slipped into a temporary loss of consciousness. Finally, the best type was the one who was afflicted but did not lose consciousness. As for those who sought *sukr* or *fanā'*, Ibn Taymiyya belied that they were actually being punished, whereas those who resisted and retained consciousness were closest to the condition of the Prophet and his Companions. As proof of this, he related the *ḥadīth* describing how Muḥammad was raised to Heaven and experienced what no one could imagine, yet remained conscious, whereas Moses had fallen unconscious when God spoke to him and revealed Himself to the mountain. Accordingly, although Moses's position was lofty, the Prophet's was superior.[293] Thus, Ibn Taymiyya redefined *fanā'* by appropriating a Ṣūfī term and adapting its definition in compliance with the boundaries of Ḥanbalī pietism.

One underlying theme of Ibn Taymiyya's discussion of worship was a rejection of the concepts of 'union with the divine,' 'incarnation' and 'the unity of being;' the terms that he used to designate them being *ittiḥād*, *ḥulūl* and *waḥdat al-wujūd* respectively, with the last of these terms representing a particular aspect of the more general topic.[294] It is therefore important to consider Ibn Taymiyya's understanding of the unity of being, albeit briefly. Although he was clearly aware of the subtle differences between various aspects of these beliefs, he employed the terms interchangeably when not discussing the concepts in detail. He referred to the monists collectively as the *Ahl al-Ittiḥād* or *Ahl al-Waḥda* and generally described their principles as being 'incarnation and union and whatever comes near to that, as in the statement of the unity of being, as those who say that existence is one and that the necessary existence of the Creator is the possible existence of the created.'[295]

This definition summarised Ibn Taymiyya's belief that the Avicennian concept of the Necessary Existent (*wājib al-wujūd*) and the Muʿtazilī concept of denying the divine attributes (*taʿṭīl*) underpinned the philosophy of monistic Sufism. He discerned a close connection between the philosophers' description of God on the one hand, and that of the Ṣūfīs on the other. Ibn Taymiyya knew that the philosophers viewed God as the 'First Principle from which all existence flows whose only activity is eternal self-contemplation…,'[296] so he associated this idea of One Absolute Reality devoid of all positive attributes with the philosophical monism that was professed by the Ṣūfīs. In particular, he identified a close correspondence between Ibn Sīnā's definition of God and that of Ibn ʿArabī. Ibn Taymiyya based this observation on Ibn ʿArabī's conception of God as the absolute existence, in which, like Ibn Sīnā, Ibn ʿArabī conceived of God as the 'absolute existence (*al-wujūd al-muṭlaq*)…[which is] existence in itself, unconditioned and unaffected by anything (*lā bi-sharṭ shay'*).'[297] From this concept of an Absolute Being devoid of attributes, Ibn ʿArabī developed a metaphysical system in which the 'Perfect Man' becomes a mirror of the Divine Names, which he considered to be distinct from the Absolute Being yet flowing out of it.[298] Likewise, he believed that all creation, including man, was distinct from the

Absolute Being yet flowing out of it. However, for Ibn Taymiyya, who believed in God's complete distinction from creation, such a philosophical mysticism could not be tolerated. It was therefore inevitable that he could only view it as deviating from the Salafī principle of not questioning the nature of God's attributes (*bi-lā kayf*).

According to Ibn Taymiyya, the belief in the distinction between the Creator and the created (*al-tamyīz bayn al-khāliq wa'l-makhlūq*) was the ultimate truth. An equally vital aspect of that truth was the interrelationship between God's essence, names and attributes, which formed a holistic or organic oneness, as opposed to the philosophers' mathematical oneness. Thus, any belief based on the denial of God's distinction from creation and the denial of His attributes in the manner of *taʿṭīl* (stripping God of His names and attributes) was related to a belief in the eternity of the universe through emanation from Him. Ibn Taymiyya's refutation of belief in any form of unity of being was based on the fact that those who held such beliefs did not affirm 'to the Creator an existence dissimilar to the existence of the creature.'[299] For Ibn Taymiyya, affirming this 'dissimilar' nature of God meant that a Muslim had to affirm His uniqueness without demeaning Him through the concepts of 'the unity of being,' 'union with the divine' or 'incarnation.' But this was precisely what Ibn ʿArabī was doing when he professed that God was both the Real (*al-ḥaqq*) and the creation (*al-khalq*).[300] Ibn Taymiyya supported his position concerning God's distinction from creation by relying on the long-standing affirmation of this belief among the *Salaf*, from whom it was passed on through the *Ahl al-Ḥadīth*, who were Ibn Taymiyya's primary affiliation and source of justification.

PRELIMINARY COMMENTS TO THE TRANSLATION

There is virtually no information about the historical circumstances of the *Risālat al-ʿUbūdiyya* or Ibn Taymiyya's composition of it. However, the attribution of the work to him is corroborated by brief remarks made by two of his students: firstly, Ibn ʿAbd al-Hādī in his *al-ʿUqūd al-durriyya* and secondly, Ibn al-Qayyim in his *Asmāʾ muʾallafat Ibn Taymiyya*.[301] Unfortunately, neither of them gives any details about the work. In the text itself, there is no information to indicate a possible date for the *Risāla*, or for whom it was written, but it was most likely written during his years in Egypt or very shortly thereafter, as noted at the beginning of this introduction.

As for surviving manuscripts of the work, the only reference that I have come across is to a copy made by one Muḥammad b. ʿAbd Allāh b. ʿAbd al-Muḥsin in the year 947/1540, which was 212 years after Ibn Taymiyya's death, but no further information is available about the features of the text or its whereabouts.[302] Although Brockelmann lists *al-ʿUbūdiyya* in his *Geschichte der arabischen Litteratur*, his reference is to the earliest print edition whose editor, Muḥammad al-Ḥalabī, does not mention which manuscript he used as a base text for his edition either.[303] Consequently, my translation is based on the printed editions of the work.

The Printed Arabic Editions

In preparing this translation of the *Risālat al-ʿUbūdiyya*, I consulted the following five printed editions of the text:

1) *Al-ʿUbūdiyya fī al-islām*, Cairo: al-Maṭbaʿa al-Salafiyya, 1387/1967 (Edition 1).
2) '*Risālat al-ʿubūdiyya fī tafsīr qawlihi taʿālā yā ayyuhā al-nās uʿbudū rabbakum*,' in *Majmūʿ Rasāʾil*, ed. Muḥammad Badr al-Dīn Abū Firās al-Naʿsānī al-Ḥalabī, Cairo: al-Maṭbaʿa al-Ḥusayniyya al-Miṣriyya, 1323/1905, pp. 2–44 (Edition 2).
3) *Al-ʿUbūdiyya*, ed. Muḥammad Ḥāmid al-Faqī, Cairo: Maṭbaʿat al-Sunna al-Muḥammadiyya, 1367/1947 (Edition 3).
4) '*Al-ʿUbūdiyya fī al-islām*,' in *Majmūʿ fatāwā shaykh al-islām Aḥmad b. Taymiyya*, vol. x: *Kitāb ʿilm al-sulūk*, Riyadh: Maṭbaʿat al-Ḥukūma, 1386/1966, pp.149–237 (Edition 4).
5) *Al-ʿUbūdiyya*, ed. ʿAbd al-Raḥmān al-Bānī, Beirut: al-Maktab al-Islāmī, 1399/1979 (Edition 5).

While I found only minor differences in wording during the process of comparing these five editions, the one that served as the base text for my translation was Edition 1. Given that none of these five printed versions were critical editions, I preferred not to be influenced by the punctuation and paragraph divisions introduced by some of the editors, so Edition 1 was superior due to its lack of editorial features and was therefore selected as a base text.

Edition 1 contains few paragraph breaks and only sporadic punctuation. However, all of the Qur'ānic verses have been identified by the editor, who has listed the sura and verse numbers, which was an appreciable help in preparing the translation. Furthermore, the Qur'ānic verses and *ḥadīth* quotations were more fully transcribed in this edition, which also facilitated my task. Due to the unavailability of any manuscripts, the reasons why these distinguishing features are only found in Edition 1 remain unknown, but for the purposes of providing greater access to Ibn Taymiyya's writings, it was not a major concern.

Criteria Followed in Preparing and Presenting the Translation

In preparing this translation, I have noted most of the minor differences in wording between the five editions of the text and have listed the variants in the footnotes. However, I have overlooked what I considered insignificant differences, such as variations of phrases glorifying of God and the honorifics mentioned after the Prophet and the Companions, because this is not a critical edition of the Arabic text. For example, I do not indicate if 'Glory be to God' or 'May God bless him and grant him peace' is present or missing in the base text compared with the others. I also do not indicate variations in the use of the plural of the word 'messenger' (*rasūl*) when another text has the singular, or vice versa, unless these differences were pertinent to understanding a subtle nuance in the sentence. However, I have ensured that the use of 'the Messenger' (for *al-Rasūl*) has been consistently applied in reference to the Prophet Muḥammad.

Similarly, variations in the use of the perfect and imperfect tenses, or in the use of a verb and a verbal noun, have not been indicated since there was no significant change in the meaning of the sentence.

When indicating the textual differences in the footnotes, I have listed the variant readings found in the other editions so that the reader knows that there is some variation between the five editions. Then, if the wording of a variant alters the meaning of a sentence, I have provided an alternate translation. Occasionally, I have inserted an additional word or phrase found in one of the other editions consulted, or have replaced the wording in Edition 1 with that of other variants. In either case, insertions and replacements are indicated by the use of angle brackets < > and are accompanied by comments about the variants. Additions to the text to clarify an implied word or phrase in the translation are indicated by the use of square brackets [ ]. One last point in reference to the variations in the published editions must be made concerning the text edited by Muḥammad Ḥāmid al-Faqī (Edition 3). This edition contains numerous, and sometimes lengthy, insertions that do not appear in any of the other published editions. Although I have noted these insertions in the footnotes to the translation, I have rarely translated them or commented on them because they do not enhance the understanding of the text in any significant way.

With respect to the structure of the text, all of the published editions divide the work into two sections: an introductory section (about one third of the entire text, 'Part I' of the translation) followed by a more detailed discussion that is separated from the introduction with by the title, *faṣl* ('Part II' of the translation). Given this uniformity across all editions, I assume that this was Ibn Taymiyya's original arrangement. I consider the first section to be Ibn Taymiyya's introductory one because all of the topics touched on in it are dealt with in more detail in the remaining four sections. Because the Arabic text of Edition 1 contains no section headings other than that single *faṣl*, I have added descriptive headings of my own in order to aid the reader's navigation of the text. For simplicity's sake, these additional headings are not marked by square brackets, but they should be treated as insertions to the text in all cases.

A Note on Terminology

Before presenting the translation, it is appropriate to explain the basic meanings of, and translated terms for, the concepts of 'worship' (*ʿubūdiyya*), 'worshipping' (*ʿibāda*) and 'worshipper' (*ʿabd*) found in this translation. According to Ibn Manẓūr, the great Arabic lexicographer, the term *ʿabd* referred to any human being, whether freeman or slave, because everyone is a servant who is owned by his Creator. This was a basic definition that Ibn Taymiyya not only accepted, but used as the basis for his hierarchy of worshippers. The term also has a more specific meaning, in the sense of a person owned by someone else (*mamlūk*), but Ibn Manẓūr related a *ḥadīth* from Abū Hurayra stating that the Prophet said not to call your slave *ʿabd*. Thus, the meaning derived from this *ḥadīth* was that *ʿabd* (pl. *ʿabīd* or *ʿibād*), was to be used only in reference to serving and worshipping God.[304] Consequently, I translate *ʿabd* as worshipper and indicate when I translate it as slave by including the Arabic term.

As for the term *ʿubūdiyya*, Ibn Manẓūr stated that the origin of its meaning was subjection and self-abasement (*tadhallul*). I interpret this as being a state or a condition of a person and translate it as 'worship' or a 'state of worship' accordingly. With respect to *ʿibāda*, Ibn Manẓūr said that its basic meaning was obedience. Thus, I translate it as 'worshipping' or 'acts of worship.' With this in mind, I present the translation of Ibn Taymiyya's *Risālat al-ʿUbūdiyya*.

NOTES TO INTRODUCTION

1 Hereafter referred to as the *Salaf*.

2 Ibn ʿAbd al-Hādī, *al-ʿUqūd al-durriya*, Beirut: Dār al-Kutub al-ʿIlmiyya, 1975, p. 43.

3 For example, see Ibn Kathīr, *al-Bidāya wa'l-nihāya*, ed. Aḥmad Abū Māhim et al., 14 vols., Beirut: Dār al-Kutub al-ʿIlmiyya, 1407/1987, I, pp. 38–40.

4 The passage from Kisā'ī is taken from John E. Wansbrough, *Quranic Studies: Sources and Methods of Scriptural Interpretation*, Oxford: Oxford University Press, 1977, p. 213.

5 Ibn ʿAṭiyya, *al-Muḥarrar al-wajīz fī tafsīr al-kitāb al-ʿazīz*, ed. ʿAbd al-Salām ʿAbd al-Shāfī Muḥammad, Beirut: Dār al-Kutub al-ʿIlmiyya, 1413/1993, vol. I, p. 105.

6 For Ibn Taymiyya's views on the *fiṭra*, see Wael B. Hallaq, 'Ibn Taymiyya on the Existence of God,' *Acta Orientalia*, vol. LII, 1991, pp. 49–69. For a further elaboration on his theory of the *fiṭra*, see Livnat Holtzman, 'Human Choice, Divine Guidance and the *Fiṭra* Tradition: The Use of Hadith in Theological Treatises by Ibn Taymiyya and Ibn Qayyim al-Jawziyya,' in *Ibn Taymiyya and His Times*, ed. Yossef Rapoport and Shahab Ahmed, New York: Oxford University Press, 2010, pp. 163–188.

7 Toshihiko Izutsu discusses this three-way division of humanity in relation to the historical development of the concept of faith. On his discussion of Ibn Taymiyya's theory of faith, see *The Concept of Belief in Islamic Theology: A Semantic Analysis of Imān and Islām*, Yokohama: Yurindo Publishing Co. Ltd., 1965, pp. 50-56.

8 The origin of the name Taymiyya was reported by Ibn Rajab, ibid., vol. II, p. 161 and Ibn Khallikan, *Ibn Khallikan's Biographical Dictionary*, tr. W. Mac Guckin de Slane, 4 vols., repr., New York & London: Johnson Reprint Corporation, 1961, vol. III, p. 97. They mentioned that Fakhr al-Dīn Ibn Taymiyya said that his father or grandfather went on the pilgrimage to Mecca and had left his pregnant wife at home. When he reached the town of Taymā', which lay in the desert of Tabūk between Khaybar and Syria, he saw a little girl who attracted his attention. When he returned home, he learned that his wife had given birth to a girl. Upon seeing his daughter, she so reminded him of the little girl from Taymā' that he called out, '*Yā Taymiyya, yā Taymiyya*.' The daughter was thus called Taymiyya, which then became the family matronymic.

9 This date is given by Ibn Rajab, *Kitāb al-dhayl ʿalā ṭabaqāt al-ḥanābila*, 2 vols., Beirut: Dār al-Maʿrifa, [no date], vol. II, p. 387 and Ṣafadī, *Kitāb al-wāfī bi'l-*

wafayāt, 30 vols., Wiesbaden: Franz Steiner Verlag, 1974, vol. vii, p. 16. See also H. Laoust who mentions 12 Rabīʿ al-Awwal as another possible date; *Essai sur les doctrines sociales et politiques de Taḳī-d-Dīn Ahmad b. Taimīya*, Cairo: Imprimerie de l'Institut français d'archéologie orientale, 1939, p. 11.

10 For the biography of ʿAbd al-Ḥalīm, see Ibn Rajab, ibid., vol. ii, p. 310 and Ṣafadī, ibid., vol. xviii, p. 69.

11 For the biography of Fakhr al-Dīn, see Ibn Rajab, ibid., vol. ii, pp. 151–162, Ṣafadī, ibid., vol. iii, p. 37, and Ibn Khallikān, ibid., vol. iii, pp. 96–97.

12 Laoust, ibid., pp. 8–9.

13 Laoust says that Fakhr al-Dīn was one of the *abdāl*; ibid, p. 8. However, Ibn Rajab and Ibn Khallikān stated that it was Fakhr al-Dīn's father who was one of the *abdāl*. Ṣafadī makes no mention of this Ṣūfī connection. As for the hierarchy of Ṣūfī saints, Annemarie Schimmel explains that the highest spiritual authority is the 'pole' (*qutb*) or the 'help' (*ghawth*). He is surrounded by three 'substitutes' (*nuqabā'*), four 'pillars' (*awtād*), seven 'pious' saints (*abrār*), forty lesser 'substitutes' (*abdāl*), three hundred 'good' saints (*akhyār*) and four thousand hidden saints; *Mystical Dimensions of Islam*, Chapel Hill: University of North Carolina Press, 1975, pp. 200–202. For variations on this order, see also de Slane's comments in Ibn Khallikān, ibid., vol. iii, p. 98. Aḥmad Ibn Taymiyya completely rejected the idea of a Ṣūfī hierarchy and declared that all *ḥadīth*s related to such beliefs were weak or fabricated; see, for example, '*Al-Farq bayn awliyā' al-raḥmān wa-awliyā' al-shayṭān*,' in *Majmūʿ fatāwā shaykh al-islām Aḥmad b. Taymiyya*, vol. xi: *Kitāb al-taṣawwuf*, Riyadh: Maṭbaʿat al-Ḥukūma, 1386/1966, pp. 13–14.

14 For a biography of Shuhda bint Aḥmad, see Ibn Khallikān, ibid., vol. i, p. 625. As for her Ṣūfī connections, he stated that she was married to Abū al-Ḥasan ʿAlī b. Muḥammad b. Yaḥya al-Duraynī, who 'built a college for Shafites on the bank of the Tigris, at the gate of al-Ajz, and erected close by it a convent for Sufis.'

15 Sarrāj was a key figure in the development of ideas concerning the topic of love and the censure of desire and passion. According to Lois Anita Giffen, Sarrāj's work played a major role in the transmission of love theory within the Ḥanbalī *madhhab*; see *Theory of Profane Love Among the Arabs: the Development of the Genre*, New York: New York University Press, 1971, pp. 25–27. For a detailed account of the chain of narrators and the contents of the narrations reported by Sarrāj, see Joseph N. Bell, 'The Hanbalite Teaching on Love,' Ph.D. dissertation, Princeton University, 1971, pp. 24–58.

16 Schimmel, ibid., pp. 5–6.

17 Giffen, ibid., pp. 25–27.

18 Abū Bakr Muḥammad b. Jaʿfar al-Kharā'iṭī al-Sāmarrī (d. 327/938) wrote the *Iʿtilāl al-qulūb*. In strongly condemning desire (*hawā*), he represented an early orthodox reaction against the idealization of the notion of the martyrs of love as appeared in writers such as Ibn Dāwūd al-Ẓāhirī (d. 297/910), the author of the *Kitāb al-zahra*. Kharā'ṭī was also the first to base his book on the standards of

authenticating *ḥadīth*s as put forth by the *Ḥadīth* scholars who had compiled the six canonical collections of traditions; see Giffen, ibid, pp. 15–16.

19 Giffen, ibid, p. 76.

20 See D. S. Margoliouth's translation of *Talbīs Iblīs*, 'The Devil's Delusion of Ibn al-Jawzi,' *Islamic Culture*, vol. x, July, 1936, pp. 339–368, 633–647; vol. xi, April, 1937, pp. 267–273, 393–403, 529–533. For the relevant sections on ascetics and Ṣūfīs, see vol. x, July, 1936, pp. 339–368 and pp. 633–647; vol. xi, April, 1937, pp. 267–273, pp. 393–403, and pp. 529–533. Additionally, Walther Braune makes important observations about Ibn al-Jawzī's opposition to mystical Sufism. In particular, he points out that the Ḥanbalīs emphasized the destructive effects of not taking the concept of the world as a creative act of God seriously and stressed that a person must function within the limits of a created world; 'Ibn al-Ǧauzīs Streitschrift gegen den Sufismus,' *Annali dell'Istituto Universitario Orientale di Napoli*, Nuova Serie, vol. i, 1940, p. 313.

21 On the ascetic origins of the Hanbali madhhab and its connection with the development of early Sufism, see Christopher Melchert, 'The Ḥanābila and the Early Sufis,' *Arabica*, vol. xlviii, no. 3, 2001, pp. 352–367. For more on the early Hanbali Ṣūfīs, see A. G. Ravan Farhadi, *ʿAbdullah Ansārī of Herat (1006–1089 C.E.): An Early Sūfi Master*, Richmond, Surrey: Curzon Press, 1996 and Walther Braune, *Die Futūḥ al-Ġaib des ʿAbd al-Qādir*, Berlin & Leipzig: Walter De Gruyter & Co., 1933.

22 For the biography of ʿAbd al-Salām, see Ibn Rajab, ibid., vol. ii, p. 249 and Ṣafadī, ibid., vol. xviii, p. 482. According to Ibn Rajab, Majd al-Dīn married his cousin, Badra bint Fakhr al-Dīn. Fakhr al-Dīn also had two sons, Abū Muḥammad ʿAbd al-Ḥalīm (d. 603/1207) and Sayf al-Dīn Abū Muḥammad ʿAbd al-Ghanī (d. 639/1242); see Ibn Rajab, ibid., vol. ii, p. 39 and p. 222, respectively.

23 See Ibn Rajab, ibid., vol. ii, p. 153.

24 See Brockelmann, *GAL*, vol. i, p. 504 and *GAL Supplement*, vol. i, p. 690.

25 For further information on Majd al-Dīn's life and works, see Laoust, ibid., p. 9, and the introductions to two published works by Majd al-Dīn, *al-Muḥarrar fī al-fiqh ʿalā madhhab al-imām Aḥmad b. Ḥanbal*, ed. Muḥammad Ḥāmid al-Fiqī, 2 vols., Cairo: Maṭbaʿat al-Sunna al-Muḥammadiyya, 1369/1950, vol. i, pp. 11–15 and *al-Muntaqā min aḥādīth al-aḥkām*, Cairo: al-Maktaba al-Salafiyya, [no date], pp. 3–7.

26 Zayn al-Dīn was born in 663/1265 and died in Dhū al-Qaʿda 747/February 1347. Although he was a Ḥanbalī scholar, he seems to have paid more attention to his business affairs. In his biographical notice on Zayn al-Dīn, Ibn ʿImād al-Ḥanbalī mentions that he was detained along with his brother Aḥmad in Alexandria and Damascus out of love for him and to serve him; *Shadharāt al-dhahab fī akhbār man dhahaba*, 8 vols., Beirut: Dār al-Fikr, 1414/1994, vol. vi, p. 152. Ibn Kathīr also refers to him as *al-shaykh* and mentions that Zayn al-Dīn was imprisoned briefly in Egypt along with Aḥmad and his other brother in 705/1306; Ibn Kathīr,

Bidāya, vol. XIV, pp. 233 and 40 respectively. Sharaf al-Dīn was born in Muḥarram 666/September 1267 and became a well respected scholar and ascetic known for his expertise in *Ḥadīth* and the biographies of the Salaf. He died in Jumādā al-Ūlā 727/April 1327, a year before Aḥmad's death; see Ibn Rajab, ibid., vol. II, p. 382.

27 According to Laoust, one of the earliest Ḥanbalī teachers at Damascus was Abū Ṣāliḥ Mufliḥ (d. 333/942), who founded a mosque. The first college was founded by ʿAbd al-Wahhāb (d. 536/1142), whose father, Abū al-Faraj al-Shīrāzī (d. 486/1093), was instrumental in spreading Ḥanbalīsm in Syria and Palestine. See *EI2*, vol. III, s.v. '*Ḥanābila*.' Laoust also mentions that the prestige of the Ḥanbalī *madhhab* in Damascus was greatly enhanced when the Banū Qudāma migrated to the city in 551/1156; *Essai*, pp. 12–18. On the development of the Ḥanbalī *madhhab*, see Laoust 'Le hanbalisme sous le califat de Bagdad (241/855–656/1258),' *Revue des études islamiques* (*REI*), vol. XXVII, 1959, pp. 67–128 and 'Le hanbalisme sous les Mamlouks bahrides (658/1260–784/1382),' *REI*, vol. XXVIII, 1960, pp. 1–71.

28 Laoust, quoting Dhahabī, states that Shihāb al-Dīn's 'luster would pale between the moon, who was his father, and the sun, who would become his son;' *Essai*, pp. 10–11.

29 On the institutionalization of the legal schools in Damascus in the three centuries prior to Ibn Taymiyya, see J. E. Gilbert, 'Institutionalisation of Muslim Scholarship and Professionalization of the *ʿUlamā'* in Medieval Damascus,' *Studia Islamica*, vol. LII, 1980, pp. 105–134. In her conclusion (p. 131) she states, 'The rulers of late eleventh, twelfth, and thirteenth-century Damascus, who generally failed to achieve political or administrative continuity, took advantage of the opportunity to help shape social institutions. These rulers and their households institutionalized international scholarship and professionalized the *ʿulamā'* in Damascus and then sought to bureaucratize, hierarchize, and further dominate the *ʿulamā'* by making areas once in the hands of scholars dependent on government.' A general overview of the role of the *ʿulamā'* under the Mamluks is given by Laoust, ibid., pp. 41–42.

30 Up to this time, Ibn Taymiyya followed the standard training of the *ʿulamā'* class. According to Ḥasan Qāsim Murād, Ibn Taymiyya 'was licensed to give *fatāwa* by a Shāfiʿī *muftī*, Sharaf al-Dīn al-Maqdisī (d. 694), before he was twenty years of age;' 'Miḥan of Ibn Taymiyya: A Narrative Account based on a Comparative Analysis of Sources,' M.A. thesis, McGill University, Montreal, 1968, p. 74. Ibn Kathīr mentions the licensing under Maqdisī's funeral notice of 694/1295 without indicating that it was given in that year; *Bidāya*, vol. XIII, p. 361. Laoust, translating Ibn Kathīr, concludes that the licensing took place in 694; see 'La biographie d'Ibn Taimīya d'après Ibn Kaṯīr,' *Bulletin d'études orientales* (*BEO*), vol. IX, 1942, p. 118. However, Murād's opinion is given weight by the fact that Ibn Taymiyya had already given his first public sermon in Muḥarram 683/March 1285 when he was only twenty-two years old, which was shortly after the death of his father. It was

attended by the most prominent scholars of Damascus such as the Ḥanbalī shaykh Zayn al-Dīn b. al-Munajjā, the Shāfiʿī chief judge Bahā' al-Dīn b. al-Zakī and the Shāfiʿī shaykh Tāj al-Dīn al-Fazārī. The lecture was received with enthusiastic acclaim and established Ibn Taymiyya's reputation as a precise and powerful defender of orthodox tradition. See Ibn Kathīr, ibid, vol. XIII, p. 320, Laoust, ibid., p. 117, and Abul Hasan Ali Nadwi, *Saviours of Islamic Spirit*, ed. and trans. by Muhiuddin Ahmad. Lucknow, India: Academy of Islamic Research and Publications, 1977, p. 25.

31 Murād, ibid., p. 75.

32 There is some confusion concerning this incident and the people involved in it. Ibn Kathīr reported that the Christian's name was ʿAssāf while the emir was Ibn Aḥmad b. Hajjī, which is what Laoust likewise reports; see Ibn Kathīr, ibid., vol. XIII, p. 355 and Laoust, ibid., p. 118. However, Murād states that the emir's name was ʿAssāf b. Aḥmad b. Hajjī and that the Christian's name was not known; ibid., p. 75. His assertion is based on the testimony of one other source and the fact that Ibn Kathīr later reported that the emir ʿAssāf b. Aḥmad b. Hajjī, who had freed the Christian, had been killed; cf. Ibn Kathīr, ibid., p. 360.

33 It was the general opinion of most Muslim jurisprudents that anyone who insulted the Prophet should be executed, even non-Muslims; see, for example, Tarābūlusī, *Muʿīn al-ḥukkām*, Egypt: [no publisher], 1393/1973, p. 192. Ibn Taymiyya also discussed the matter in detail in response to the incident; see *al-Ṣārim al-maslūl ʿalā shātim al-rasūl*, ed. Muḥammad Muḥyī al-Dīn ʿAbd al-Ḥamīd, Tanta: Maktabat Tāj, 1379/1960. It should be noted that Ibn Kathīr referred to this work by the alternate title, *al-Sārim al-maslūl ʿalā sābb al-Rasūl*; ibid., vol. XIII, p. 355.

34 Murād, ibid., p. 76.

35 Jāghān was the temporary governor in Damascus after Sayf al-Dīn Qibjaq defected to the Mongols. Jāghān had supported the emir Lājīn in his bid to become sultan in 696/1297, and both he and Lājīn's governor in Egypt, Mankūtamur, plotted against Qibjaq. However, after Lājīn's brief reign, which ended with his murder in Rabīʿ al-Thānī 698/January 1299, al-Nāṣir Muḥammad returned to the sultanate for the second time. He replaced Jāghān (who suffered only a short imprisonment) with Aqūsh al-Afram, who also became a supporter of Ibn Taymiyya. For Jāghān's biography, see Laoust, *Essai*, p. 114. On the general history of the reign of Lājīn, see R. Irwin, *The Middle East in the Middle Ages: The Early Mamluk Sultanate, 1250–1382*, Carbondale & Edwardsville, IL: Southern Illinois University Press, 1986, pp. 90–100.

36 Laoust, ibid., p. 115, states that Ibn Taymiyya's opponents fabricated statements concerning his beliefs, as explained in the *Hamawiyya*.

37 The details of this event are reported in: Ibn Kathīr, ibid., vol. XIV, p. 5; Ibn Ḥajar al-ʿAsqalānī, *al-Durar al-kāmina fī aʿyān al-mi'at al-thāmina*, 5 vols., Cairo: Dār al-Kutub al-Ḥadītha, [no date], vol. I, p. 155; Laoust, ibid., pp. 111–117; and, Murād, ibid., pp. 77–78.

38 René Grousset, *The Empire of the Steppes: A History of Central Asia*, tr. Naomi Walford, New Brunswick, NJ: Rutgers University Press, 1970, p. 378.

39 According to Irwin, the Mamluk army was caught off guard by the winter invasion. After a forced march, which was interrupted by a revolt of the Mongol mercenaries, the Wāfidiyya, the Mamluk forces met the Mongol army at Wādī al-Khazindār north of Homs. Besides the defeat itself, two other factors came to play a role in Ibn Taymiyya's life. One was that the leader of the Mongol army was Sayf al-Dīn Qibjaq, who had been the Mamluk governor of Damascus in 698/1299. His defection to the Mongols was later used against Ibn Taymiyya in a conspiracy charge. Also, the retreating Mamluk army was harassed by the various Shīʿī sects of the Kasrawān region of Lebanon, against whom Ibn Taymiyya later instigated military action. See Irwin, ibid., p. 100.

40 See Laoust, 'La biographie d'Ibn Taimīya,' pp. 121–125 and Abul Hasan Ali Nadwi, *Saviours of Islamic Spirit*, ed. and tr. Muhiuddin Ahmad., Lucknow, India: Academy of Islamic Research and Publications, 1977, pp. 30–31.

41 Grousset, ibid., p. 382.

42 According to Ibn Kathīr, Ibn Taymiyya met with the leaders of the Shīʿa of Kasrawān, demanded their repentance, explained the correct beliefs of Islam to them and then forced them to return any booty they had taken from the retreating armies; ibid., vol. XIV, p. 13. See also Laoust, ibid., p. 125 and Nadwi, ibid., p. 33.

43 For the details of Ibn Taymiyya's activities during this incursion, see Laoust, ibid., pp. 126–127 and Nadwi, ibid., p. 34. This was the second winter campaign of the Ilkhanid ruler Ghazan in an attempt to recoup his position in northern Syria. However, the Mongols were forced to retreat because of heavy rains that year. Also, Ibn Taymiyya's efforts appear to have been somewhat superfluous, for neither Ghazan nor the Mamluk Sultan al-Nāṣir Muḥammad were interested in fighting. By the spring of 700/1301, they agreed to exchange embassies and establish peaceful commerce; see Irwin, ibid., p. 101.

44 Laoust, ibid., pp. 129–130; Murād, ibid., p. 80.

45 Ibn Daqīq al-ʿĪd was a famous traditionist with whom Ibn Taymiyya had studied; see Ibn Kathīr, ibid., vol. XIV, pp. 23-29. As for Ibn Jamāʿa, he was respectful toward Ibn Taymiyya but not outwardly supportive of him; see Laoust, ibid., p. 129.

46 This was Najm al-Dīn b. Ṣaṣarī, or Ṣaṣra, (d. 723/1323). According to Sherman A. Jackson, he belonged to one of the powerful families of Damascus and was inclined toward Ashʿarī beliefs; 'Ibn Taymiyyah on Trial in Damascus,' *Journal of Semitic Studies*, vol. XXXIX, no. 1, 1994, p. 46. Although Ibn Ṣaṣarī had had bitter arguments with Ibn Taymiyya, he supported him after his resignation as chief judge following the events of the third Damascus council, which I describe below.

47 Ibn Taymiyya's student, Abū Ḥafs ʿUmar b. ʿAlī al-Bazzār, compiled a list of his teacher's main opponents; see *al-Aʿlām al-ʿaliyya fī manāqib shaykh al-islām*

Ibn Taymiyya, ed. Ṣalāḥ al-Dīn al-Munajjid, Beirut: Dār al-Kitāb al-Jadīd, 1396/1976, pp. 85–87. The most prominent of the twelve people listed were: Jāshangīr (d. 709/1310), a Mamluk emir who usurped the sultanate in 709/1310; Ṣafī al-Dīn al-Ḥindī (d. 715/1315), a leading Shāfiʿī shaykh of Damascus; Taqī al-Dīn al-Subkī (d. 756/1355), a Shāfiʿī chief judge of Damascus; Taqī al-Dīn b. al-Ikhnā'ī (d. 732/1332), a Mālikī chief judge of Cairo; Ṣadr al-Dīn b. al-Muraḥḥil (d. 716/1316), a Shāfiʿī *muftī* of Damascus; Aḥmad b. Muḥammad al-Iskandarī (d. 709/13010), a leading Ṣūfī shaykh of Cairo; Naṣr al-Manbijī (d. 719/1319), a leading Ṣūfī shaykh of Cairo who followed the teachings of Ibn ʿArabī and who was Jāshangīr's spiritual guide; and, Zayn al-Dīn b. Makhlūq (d. 718/1318), a Mālikī chief judge of Egypt and a close friend of Manbijī. For further information on some of Ibn Taymiyya's opponents in Damascus, see Jackson, ibid., pp. 43–48.

48 Irwin, ibid., p. 101, and Grousset, ibid., p. 382.

49 The details were given by Ibn Kathīr, ibid., vol. xiv, p. 25. Ibn Taymiyya often made use of particular groups historically classed as heretics by the Muslims to crystallize his arguments on certain issues. This reflected his belief that all religious controversies were related to the deviations and schisms that had occurred during the first two centuries of Islam. For the effects of this ruling on Muslim thinking in modem times, see Emanuel Sivan, *Radical Islam*, New Haven & London: Yale University Press, 1990, pp. 94–107. On the history of the Khawārij, see G. Levi Della Vida, *EI2*, vol. iv, s.v. 'Khāridjites.'

50 Ibn Kathīr reported various actions taken by Ibn Taymiyya against the innovations and antinomian activities of certain Ṣūfī shaykhs. For example, he forced a certain shaykh named Mujāḥid Ibrāhīm al-Qaṭṭān, who was accused of using hashish, to remove an enormous turban, cut his hair, nails and moustache, and to conform to Islamic law in all his public affairs; ibid., vol. xiv, p. 36. See also Laoust, ibid., p. 133.

51 It was at this time that Ibn Taymiyya wrote his '*Risāla ilā Naṣr al-Manbijī*' concerning the errors of Ibn ʿArabī's monism. There are two printed editions of this treatise: '*Risāla ilā Naṣr al-Manbijī*,' in *Majmūʿ fatāwā shaykh al-islām Aḥmad b. Taymiyya*, vol. ii: *Kitāb tawḥīd al-ulūhiyya*, pp. 452–479 and '*Risāla ilā Naṣr al-Manbijī*,' in *Majmū'at al-rasā'il wa'l-masā'il*, vol. i, pp. 161–183. The date of AH 704 is based on a manuscript listed in the *Fihrist al-makhṭūṭāt*, ed. Fu'ād Sayyid, 3 vols., Cairo: Maṭbaʿat Dār al-Kutub, 1961–1963, vol. ii, p. 249. Although he did denounce certain aspects of Ibn ʿArabī's beliefs, his harshest attacks in this letter were directed at some of the followers of Ibn ʿArabī, such as Tilimsānī (d. 690/1291) and Ibn Sabʿīn (d. 669/1271). According to Murād, Ibn Taymiyya wrote the letter after his first reading of Ibn ʿArabī's *Fuṣūṣ al-ḥikam* in 703/1304; ibid., p. 83. Murād also states that Ibn Taymiyya wrote a refutation of Ibn ʿArabī around this time entitled *al-Nuṣūṣ ʿalā al-fuṣūṣ*.

52 Laoust, *Essai*, pp. 124–125.

53 On this occasion, Ibn Taymiyya challenged their claims to sainthood based on

their performance of miraculous deeds, such as fire walking. Knowing that they coated their skin with oil, he demanded that they bathe and then proceed with performing the fire walking. The mystics, of course, refused. See Ibn Kathīr, ibid., vol. XIV, p. 38.

54 Laoust, 'La biographie d'Ibn Taimīya,' p. 135, and Murād, ibid., pp. 81–82.

55 See Merlin Swartz, 'A seventh century (A.H.) Sunnī creed: The ʿAqīda Wāsiṭīya of Ibn Taymīya,' *Humaniora Islamica*, vol. 1, 1973, p. 99 and Jackson, ibid., pp. 49–51.

56 Murād, ibid., p. 83.

57 According to Murād, Ibn Taymiyya used this creed at the first Damascus council to prove that his beliefs had not changed over the years. He was prompted to do this because a forged creed was in fact sent to Baybars al-Jāshangīr; ibid., pp. 84–85.

58 The second council revolved around a lengthy discussion between Ibn Taymiyya and Ṣafī al-Dīn al-Ḥindī, who was not at the first trial. Ibn Taymiyya sought to prove that all of the great scholars of the past had accepted the Salafī creed as formulated by Ibn Ḥanbal, which denounced *ta'wīl*, *taḥrīf*, *taʿṭīl*, *takyīf* and *tamthīl* (these terms are defined below). He also produced a copy of Ibn ʿAsākīr's *Tabyīn kadhibi al-muftarī fīmā nuṣiba ilā al-Imām Abī al-Ḥasan al-Ashʿarī* to prove that Ashʿarī accepted the beliefs of Ibn Ḥanbal; see Jackson, ibid., pp. 51–53. Ibn Taymiyya's agreement with many points in the *Tabyīn* might well account for the confusion that resulted after the second council. Murād, describes many of the extremes to which people went; ibid., p. 126, n. 18.

59 According to Murād, the Shafiʿī shaykh Ibn al-Zamlakānī vigorously objected to this implication and sought the support of Ibn Ṣaṣarī. However, the latter refused to take a stance and, realizing he could not support the *madhhab*'s position, immediately resigned his post as chief judge; ibid., p. 90. See also Laoust, ibid., p. 138. It was at this time that Ibn Taymiyya came to the support of Ibn Ṣaṣarī.

60 The specific charges were related to 'Ibn Taymiyya's belief that God is really above the throne, and that He speaks by letter and sound, and that he can be pointed at in a physical sense;' Murād, ibid., pp. 90–92.

61 Nadwi, ibid., p. 43.

62 Murād, ibid., pp. 92–93.

63 In the brutal struggles between various Mamluk emirs as each attempted to claim the sultanate for himself, there were frequent, and at times confusing, shifts in allegiances. However, it seems clear that Sallār was engaged in a long power struggle with Jāshangīr. Although Sallār fulfilled his religious duties as a Muslim, it is not clear that his motives for supporting Ibn Taymiyya were purely for religious reasons; see Irwin, ibid., pp. 85–95.

64 A couple of months before this meeting, in Dhū al-Ḥijja 706/June 1307, Sallār arranged a meeting between Ibn Makhlūf and Ibn Taymiyya's two brothers who were imprisoned with him at that time. According to the reports, their

arguments were more convincing than Ibn Makhlūf's, but to no avail; see Laoust, ibid., p. 141 and Murād, ibid., p. 95.

65 Ibn Kathīr, ibid., vol. xiv, pp. 44–47.

66 Ibn Kathīr, referred to him as a king of the Arabs; ibid., vol. xiv, p. 47. In his obituary notice, he reported that Ḥusām al-Dīn had had a great love for Ibn Taymiyya, who was honored amongst the tribes of Syria (p. 182). See also Irwin, who indicates that Muḥanna b. ʿĪsā had his own difficulties with the ongoing power struggles between the Mamluks, having been treacherously imprisoned in 692/1293; ibid., p. 81. For more on Ibn Taymiyya's release from prison, see Laoust, ibid., p. 141 and Murād, ibid., p. 96.

67 It seems that Ibn Taymiyya had consented to an interdiction against public speaking on his part. However, on Friday, 30 Rabīʿ al-Awwal, he was pressed to give a talk after the Jumuʿa prayer. He answered the request by 'speaking until the evening on the meaning of *ʿibāda* and *istiʿāna*;' Murād, ibid., p. 97. This incident was most likely what had led to the third council on 6 Rabīʿ al-Thānī.

68 The main complaint made against him was that he claimed that seeking aid and intercession could not be sought from the Prophet on the basis that the Prophet, as with anyone who had died, could not benefit the living. Rather, the Prophet's intercession would only occur on the day of resurrection. Although Ibn Taymiyya's arguments could not be denied, Ibn Jamāʿa reprimanded him for sounding as though he were being disrespectful to the Prophet; see Laoust, ibid., p. 143. In 711/1312, Ibn Taymiyya wrote a letter on the topic of the Prophet's intercession that he later incorporated into his work, '*Qāʾida fīʾl-tawassul waʾl-wasīla*;' *Majmūʿ fatāwā*, vol. 1: *Kitāb al-rubūbiyya*, pp. 313–358.

69 Ibn Taymiyya originally chose to return to Damascus and had already set out for Syria when Ibn Makhlūf called him back to stand trial; see Ibn Kathīr, ibid., vol. xiv, p. 48 and Murād, ibid., p. 99. All of this occurred on 18 Shawwāl 707. Murād, contends that Ibn Taymiyya was detained continuously from Shawwāl 707 to Ṣafar 709 (including his transfer to Alexandria) and that Ibn Kathīr is wrong in stating that he was released in 707 and only sent to Alexandria when Jāshangīr came to power; ibid., pp. 99–101 and p. 130, n. 31. Laoust maintains the events as depicted by Ibn Kathīr; *EI2*, vol. iii, s.v. '*Ibn Taymiyya*.' I report the events according to Ibn Kathīr's version.

70 See Ibn Kathīr, ibid., vol. xiv, p. 52, Laoust, 'La biographie d'Ibn Taimīya,' p. 144 and Irwin, ibid., p. 96.

71 Ibn Kathīr, states that Ibn Taymiyya's friends and family were extremely anxious about his stay in Alexandria because he had no close supporters there, whereas the various Ṣūfī groups were very popular; ibid., vol. xiv, p. 52. See also Laoust, ibid., p. 145.

72 For a brief biography of Ibn Sabʿīn, see A. Faure, *EI2*, vol. iii, s.v. '*Ibn Sabʿīn*.'

73 Ibn Taymiyya's good treatment by al-Nāṣir Muḥammad was most likely in return for his resistance to Jāshangīr, but if Nāṣir had hoped to gain Ibn Taymiyya as a

loyal supporter, his hopes were soon disappointed. Although Ibn Taymiyya acted as an advisor to Nāṣir for some time, he refused to sanction any action that he felt contradicted Islamic law and did not hesitate to chastise the sultan on a number of occasions; see Murād, ibid., pp. 101–102.

74 Nadwi, ibid., p. 49.

75 Although his contemporaries accepted the validity of the oath of divorce, according to Ibn Taymiyya, there was a difference of opinion on the matter. Abū Ḥanīfa ruled that a divorce based on an oath should not take place, whereas Ibn Ḥanbal said that it should. Also, some Shāfiʿī and Mālikī scholars said that it should take place; see Victor Makari, 'The Social Factor in Ibn Taymiyyah's Ethics,' Ph.D. dissertation, Temple University, 1976, p. 109. This has also been published as *Ibn Taymiyyah's Ethics: the Social Factor*, California: The Scholars Press, 1983.

76 Ibn Taymiyya's legal reasoning related to *ḥilf bi'l-ṭalāq* can be summarized as follows: (1) a pronouncement of divorce must be intentional and unconditional; (2) a divorce oath does not have divorce as the ultimate end and so is ineffectual; (3) although the divorce oath is not valid, atonement for breaking the oath is required. For a complete discussion of Ibn Taymiyya's position concerning *ḥilf bi'l-ṭalāq*, as well as for the counterarguments of his opponents, see Makari, ibid., pp. 107–112 and Muḥammad Abū Zahra, *Ibn Taymiyya: hayyātuhu wa-ʿaṣruhu ārā'uhu wa-fiqhuhu*, Cairo: Dār al-Fikr al-ʿArabī, [no date], pp. 414–436.

77 Sayf al-Dīn Tankiz al-Ḥusāmī was the powerful, almost semi-independent, governor of Syria from 712/1313 until 740/1340. However, he remained quite loyal to Sultan al-Nāṣir Muḥammad. He established a period of calm in Syria that witnessed various reconstruction projects. He kept a neutral stance toward Ibn Taymiyya, occasionally intervening on his behalf, but his main concern was keeping order. When the sultan fell ill in 740, he feared that Tankiz would revolt, so he had him tortured and killed; see Irwin, ibid., p. 121. Nāṣir died in 741/1341.

78 According to Laoust, the first council took place on 1 Jumādā al-Ūlā 718/2 July 1318, the second on 29 Ramaḍān 719/14 November 1319 and the last on 12 Rajab 720/19 August 1320. He was released by order of the sultan on the 10th of Muḥarram, the day of ʿAshūra; *Essai*, pp. 144–145.

79 The details of Ibn Taymiyya's rulings on the visitation of graves and the act of supplicating to the dead are presented in Muhammad Umar Memon, *Ibn Taymiyyah's Struggle Against Popular Religion: With an Annotated Translation of his* Kitāb iqtidā' aṣ-ṣirāṭ al-mustaqīm li-mukhālafat aṣḥāb al-jahīm, The Hague & Paris: Mouton, 1976, pp. 263–297. To summarize, he allowed Muslims to visit graves as a reminder of death and in order to supplicate to God on behalf of the dead. But he forbade Muslims from making pilgrimages to graves with the aim of having the deceased intercede for the living or grant favors for the living, or out of the belief that supplications made at the graves of prophets and saints were more likely to be answered. All such acts that Ibn Taymiyya forbade were

in common practice during his time and had received the approval of many *ʿulamāʾ*. For a comparison of Ibn Taymiyya's views with those of Ghazālī, who permitted pilgrimages to graves but with similar restrictions as mentioned by Ibn Taymiyya, see Christopher Schurmann Taylor, 'The Cult of Saints in Late Medieval Egypt,' Ph.D. dissertation, Princeton University, 1989, pp. 120–137.

80 Nadwi, ibid., p. 56.

81 This move was instigated by the Mālikī chief judge Ikhnāʾī, who had in the meantime become the target of a harsh refutation from Ibn Taymiyya concerning the visitation of graves. As for the material that was taken from Ibn Taymiyya, Ibn Kathīr, reports that 60 volumes and 14 packages of notes were confiscated and brought to the ʿAdiliyya library. The works were reviewed by various shaykhs and judges, who divided them amongst themselves; ibid., vol. XIV, p. 140.

82 For descriptions of the events surrounding Ibn Taymiyya's funeral, see Ibn Kathīr, ibid., vol. XIV, pp. 141–146, Laoust, *Essai*, pp. 147–150 and 'La biographie d'Ibn Taimīya,' p. 159, and Nadwi, ibid., pp. 59–60.

83 Ibn Taymiyya was well aware that every Muslim group claimed to be following the *Sunna* and that each group viewed the others as engaging in innovations. See his comments in *al-Istiqāma*, ed. Muḥammad Rashād Sālim, 2 vols., Cairo: Maktabat al-Sunna, 1409/1989, vol. I, p. 13.

84 Roy Young Muhammad Mukhtar Curtis identifies a 'Salafī movement' that crystallized around Ibn Taymiyya at the beginning of the 8th/14th century and ended unofficially with the death of his student, the great Shāfiʿī traditionist Abū al-Fidāʾ b. Kathīr (d. 774/1373); 'Authentic Interpretation of Classical Islamic Texts: An Analysis of the Introduction of Ibn Kathīr's *Tafsīr al-Qurʾān al-ʿAẓīm*,' Ph.D. dissertation, University of Michigan, 1989, pp. 18 and 259, n. 111.

85 Laoust points out that Ibn Taymiyya criticized earlier Ḥanbalī scholars who had deviated from Ibn Ḥanbal's insistence on relying solely on the revealed texts; *Essai*, pp. 76–80. Ibn Taymiyya considered anyone who had accepted speculative theology and logic as being equal, or superior, to revelation to have deviated from Ibn Ḥanbal's position. Those Ḥanbalī scholars involved with *kalām* or with objectionable Ṣūfī practices were censured for these particular faults. His criticism in these matters was directed at certain scholars of the Ḥanbalī *madhhab*, such as Ibn ʿAqīl (d. 513/1120) for his use of *kalām* and Muwaffaq al-Dīn b. Qudāma (d. 620/1223) for his compliance with the Ṣūfī cult of saints. However, his criticism was limited to only those opinions that he found objectionable in the writings of these scholars, for he continued to utilize their works and those of other Ḥanbalīs. For a thorough analysis of his supporters and opponents based on the concept of traditionalist and rationalist camps, see Caterina Bori, 'Ibn Taymiyya wa-Jamāʿatuhu: Authority, Conflict and Consensus in Ibn Taymiyya's Circle,' in *Ibn Taymiyya and His Times*, pp. 23–52.

86 This was Ibn Taymiyya's guiding principle in reference to all aspects of the Islamic sciences. Thus, he applied the term '*kalām*' in a broader sense to describe any

principles and methodologies falling outside of his Salafī principles. The division of Islamic knowledge into the two categories of 'legal' (*fiqh*) and 'theological' (*kalām*) came about gradually at the end of the first century and the beginning of the second century of the Hijra. Harry A. Wolfson identifies this division as part of the development of *kalām* in its pre-Muʿtazilī stage; *The Philosophy of the Kalam*, Cambridge, MA: Harvard University Press, 1976, pp. 1 –5. Briefly stated, after the death of the Prophet, Muslims began discussing matters related to law and practice. Some scholars began to use analogy (*qiyās*) to help solve novel problems that arose. As the early community began to differ over the concepts of faith and the nature of God, some Muslims started using analogy to answer these problems. Thus, *kalām*, which in general aimed to arrive at a solution through reasoning, came to be solely associated with issues of faith and belief, in contradistinction to *fiqh*, which was the discussion of practical legal issues.

87 Laoust presents this view in connection with Ibn Taymiyya's use of the Qur'ān as a source for legal opinions; ibid., p. 231. Adrian Brockett indicates the existence of a preserved Qur'ān text since the time of Muḥammad in both an oral and a written tradition: 'There must have been a parallel written transmission limiting variation in the oral transmission to the graphic form, side by side with a parallel oral transmission preserving the written transmission from corruption. The transmission of the Qur'ān after the death of Muhammad was essentially static, rather than organic;' 'The Value of the Hafs and Warsh Transmissions for the Textual History of the Qur'ān,' in *Approaches to the History of the Interpretation of the Qur'ān*, ed. Andrew Rippin, Oxford: Clarendon Press, 1988, p. 44.

88 The term *tafsīr* is identifiable with exegesis and the term *uṣūl al-tafsīr* with hermeneutics. This distinction between exegesis and hermeneutics is defined by Jane Dammen McAuliffe in 'Quranic Hermeneutics: The Views of al-Tabarī and Ibn Kathīr,' in ibid., p. 47. In relation to Christian theology, she states, 'The practice of interpretation was equated with what we would now term "exegesis", while the term "hermeneutics" was used to denote the aims and criteria of that practice. In conventional theological usage, then, hermeneutics was the enterprise which identified the principles and methods prerequisite to the interpretation of texts.'

89 Laoust comments that Ibn Taymiyya used this principle to incorporate the views expressed in dogmatic theology, jurisprudence, the literalism of the Ẓāhiriyya and the esotericism of the Bātiniyya into his doctrines. For Laoust, this represents Ibn Taymiyya's syncretistic approach to divergent views in Islam. See Laoust, *Contribution à une étude de la méthodologie canonique de Taḳī-d-Dīn Aḥmad b. Taimīya*, Cairo: Imprimerie de l'Institut français d'archéologie orientale, 1939, p. 55, n. 22.

90 '*Muqaddima fī uṣūl al-tafsīr*,' in *Majmūʿ fatāwā*, vol. XIII: *Kitāb muqaddimat al-tafsīr*, p. 331. Curtis has shown that Ibn Kathīr not only used Ibn Taymiyya's *Muqaddima fī uṣūl al-tafsīr* in his own discussion of hermeneutics, but that Ibn Taymiyya had written this work specifically for him; ibid., chapters 5 and 6. However, Ibn

Kathīr did not mention Ibn Taymiyya as the source of his own hermeneutic section because, as Curtis points out, the opposition of the official'*ᶜulamā'* to the deceased Ḥanbalī scholar remained quite strong (pp. 17–20). The fact that Ibn Kathīr did not credit Ibn Taymiyya for the exposition on hermeneutics could explain why McAuliffe mentions only that he was influenced by Ibn Taymiyya without detailing the depths of that influence; ibid., p. 55. Thus, although she is correct in identifying the clear links between Ṭabarī (d. 310/923) and Ibn Kathīr concerning hermeneutics, she overlooks the fact that Ibn Taymiyya established that link through his formulation of *uṣūl al-tafsīr*. A detailed analysis of the *Muqadimma* and its place in the exegetical tradition is given by Walid A. Saleh, 'Ibn Tamiyya and the Rise of Radical Hermeneutics: An Analysis of *An Introduction to the Foundations of Qur'ānic Exegesis*,' in *Ibn Taymiyya and His Times*, pp. 123–162. For an opposing point of view concerning Ibn Kathīr's position relative to prior exegesis works, see the comments of Norman Calder who argues that Ibn Kathīr deviated significantly from the exegesis tradition started by Ṭabarī; 'Tafsīr from Ṭabarī to Ibn Kathīr: Problems in the Description of a Genre, Illustrated with Reference to the Story of Abraham,' in *Approaches to the Qur'ān*, pp. 101–139.

91 This narration was reported by Abū Jaᶜfar al-Ṭabarī in his discussion of hermeneutics ; *Jāmiᶜ al-bayān ᶜan tafsīr āy al-Qur'ān*, Cairo: Maktaba wa Maṭbaᶜat Muṣtafā al-Bābī al-Ḥalabī, 1373/1954, vol. 1, p. 35. It is the statement of the follower Abū ᶜAbd al-Raḥmān al-Sulamī (d. 72/692), who should not be confused with the famous fourth/tenth-century Ṣūfī with the same name. The Ṣūfī Sulamī (d. 412/1022) was also quoted by Ibn Taymiyya, who criticized him for the many errors he made in his exegesis of the Qur'ān, entitled *Ḥaqā'iq al-tafsīr*; see the *Muqaddima*, p. 362.

92 As Curtis, ibid., pp. 220 and 250, points out, the lack of details and explanations in Ibn Taymiyya's *Muqaddima* is most likely related to the fact that it was written for a like-minded scholar. Consequently, his usual style of presenting extensive evidence from the Qur'ān and *Ḥadīth* to prove his point was not utilized here.

93 The development of the concept of the Prophet's exegetical role is traced by McAuliffe from Ṭabarī to Ibn Kathīr, but she overlooks Ibn Taymiyya's role; see ibid., pp. 48–62. Similarly, R. Marston Speight overlooks Ibn Taymiyya's influence in 'The Function of *ḥadīth* as Commentary on the Qur'ān, as Seen in the Six Authoritative Collections,' in *Approaches to the History of the Interpretation of the Qur'ān*, ed. Andrew Rippin, Oxford: Clarendon Press, 1988, pp. 63–68. Muḥammad Ḥusayn al-Dhahabī has presented the arguments of the two groups as to whether the Prophet explained all, or just a little, of the Qur'ān; see *al-Tafsīr wa'l-mufassirūn*, 3 vols, Cairo: Dār al-Kutub al-Ḥadītha, 1396/1976, vol. 1, pp. 49–51.

94 Curtis has shown that Ibn Taymiyya faithfully followed Ibn Ḥanbal's methodology with respect to sources and order of precedence; ibid., p. 247.

95 *Muqaddima*, p. 363.

96 On the use of the *Ḥadīth* to determine the causes of revelation for the purpose

of exegesis, see Speight, ibid., pp. 68–72. On Imām al-Shāfiʿī's theory of abrogation in relation to the Qur'ān, see Majid Khadduri, *Al-Shāfiʿī's* Risāla: *Treatise on the Foundations of Islamic Jurisprudence*, Cambridge: Islamic Texts Society, 1987, pp. 123–130; in relation to the *Ḥadīth*, see pp. 195–202.

97 References to the terms and techniques of the *Ḥadīth* scholars are based on Muḥammad A. Ṣāliḥ, *Lamaḥāt fī uṣūl al-ḥadīth*, Beirut & Damascus: al-Maktab al-Islāmī, 1405/1985 and Mohammad M. Azami, *Studies in Early Ḥadīth Literature*, Indianapolis: American Trust Publications, 1978.

98 See *Muqaddima*, p. 363. This is the opening statement of a lengthier *ḥadīth*; see al- Khaṭīb al-Tibrīzī, *Mishkāt al-maṣābīḥ*, ed. Muḥammad Nāṣir al-Dīn al-Albanī, 3 vols., Beirut & Damascus: al-Maktab al-Islāmī, 1405/1985, vol. I, p. 57 and *Mishkat al-Masabih: English Translation with Explanatory Notes*, ed. and tr. James Robson, Lahore: Muhammad Ashraf, 1975, vol. I, P. 43.

99 On Imam Shāfiʿī's views concerning the relationship between the Qur'ān and the *Sunna*, and on the need to obey the Prophet, see Khadduri, ibid., pp. 109–122. In commenting on Q.II.146 in reference to the Prophet's teaching of 'the Book and Wisdom' (*al-kitāb wa'l-ḥikma*), Shāfiʿī said (p. 111) that 'it is not permissible for Wisdom to be called here [anything] save the *Sunna* of the Apostle of God.'

100 A *muḥaddith* was actually the one holding the middle rank in the three-tiered classification of the scholars of *Ḥadīth*. The lowest rank was that of the *musnid* and the highest rank was that of the *ḥāfiẓ*. There was a fourth category known as *amīr al-mu'minīn fī'l-ḥadīth*, which has only been given to a few scholars over the centuries, such as Ibn Ḥanbal (d. 241/856) and Bukhārī (d. 256/870). See Ṣāliḥ, ibid., pp. 103–109.

101 See *Muqaddima*, pp. 364–365. Some other authorities of interpretation were the Companions Ubayy b. Kaʿb (d. 22/643), Ibn ʿUmar (d. 74/693–4), Jābir b. ʿAbd Allāh (d. 78/698), Abū Saʿīd al-Khuḍrī (d. 74/694) and Abū Hurayra (d. 59/679). Bukhārī reported two *ḥadīths* about Ibn ʿAbbās's knowledge of the Qur'ān. In one, the Prophet said, 'O God, teach him wisdom,' and in the other, 'O God, teach him the Book;' see Ibn Ḥajar, *Fatḥ al-bārī sharḥ Ṣaḥīḥ al-Bukhārī*, 13 vols and introduction, Beirut: Dār al-Maʿrifa, [no date], vol. VII, P. 100. In another *ḥadīth*, Bukhārī reported that the Prophet said, 'Learn the Qur'ān from four people: ʿAbd Allāh b. Masʿūd, Sālim (the client of Abū Hudhayfa), Ubayy b. Kaʿb and Muʿādh b. Jabal;' see Ibn Ḥajar, ibid., p. 101. These authorities and others were also reported by Jalāl al-Dīn al-Suyūṭī, *al-Itqān fī ʿulūm al-Qur'ān*, Beirut: Dār al-Fikr, [no date], vol. II, p. 187.

102 See the *Muqaddima*, pp. 368–370. For a comparable, but less extensive list, see Ibn ʿAṭiyya, *al-Muḥarrar*, pp. 41–42.

103 On the topic of resolving such conflicts, Curtis summarizes Ibn Kathīr's procedure as follows: 'When source materials disagree, it is the duty of the exegete to relate (a) all the information, (b) evaluate its authenticity and tenableness, and (c) point out its benefits and consequences;' ibid., p. 82. These three points refer

to the sciences of *Ḥadīth*, particularly causes of revelation and abrogation. An exegete needed to know these sciences in order to justify why one statement was preferred over another.

104 See the *Muqaddima*, p. 369. Curtis translates this passage as, 'Some of them may express something by its intrinsic nature or by comparison to something else; some may describe an entity precisely.' See ibid., p. 102

105 Shuʿba b. al-Ḥajjāj (d. 160/777) was a prominent student of many of the Followers, such as Qatāda and Ḥammād b. Abī Sulaymān; see Azami, ibid., p. 165.

106 He states, *fa-amma tafsīr al-Qur'ān bi-mujarrad al-ra'y fa-ḥarām*; *Muqaddima*, p. 370. Curtis defines *ra'y* as including 'personal opinion, intuition, observation, or any reasoning devoid of substantiation by approved sources;' ibid., p. 82.

107 In the *Muqaddima*, he gave two examples of Companions who did not interpret a verse or even a single word because they did not know of an authentic statement of the Prophet; ibid., pp. 372–373. Abū Bakr did not comment on the word *abban* in Q.LXXX.31 because he did not know what it meant. Likewise, Ibn ʿAbbās refused to interpret the meaning of, 'a day whose measure is a thousand years' (Q.XXXII.5), or, 'a day whose measure is fifty thousand years' (Q.LXX.4) because the knowledge of these two verses was with God and he would not say a thing about the Qur'ān without knowledge.These two *ḥadīth*s are discussed by Speight in connection with the objections of the *Ḥadīth* scholars to the spread of exegesis by use of personal opinion; ibid., p. 66. Curtis discusses them in connection with Ibn Kathīr's similar position against the use of opinion when it was not based on sound reasoning, which may only be derived from the Qur'ān, *Ḥadīth* and statements of the Companions; ibid., pp. 82–84. Calder discusses the same *ḥadīth*s as presented by Qurtubī (d. 671/1273) and Ibn ʿAṭiyya (d. 546/1151); ibid., pp. 131–133. Calder attempts to show that their understanding of these *ḥadīth*s differed significantly from that of Ibn Taymiyya and Ibn Kathīr. However, he clearly misrepresents the views of the latter two by indicating they even rejected opinions based on sound reasoning. He also does not deal with the fact that Ibn Taymiyya held the exegesis of both Qurtubī and Ibn ʿAṭiyya in high esteem.

108 Curtis, ibid., pp. 248–259

109 Virginie Lamotte, 'Ibn Taymiyya's Theory of Knowledge,' M.A. Thesis, McGill University, 1994, pp. 4–5.

110 *Muqaddima*, pp. 347–350. The geographical aspect of classifying the exegetes was a point on which Ibn Taymiyya particularly focused. For example, he elaborated on it in his discussion about affiliations with the *Ahl al-Sunna*. His geographical classifications were also used by some later scholars. For instance, Suyūṭī quoted directly from Ibn Taymiyya's *Muqaddima* on this issue; ibid., vol. II, P. 190. See also Dhahabī, ibid., vol. I, P. 101.

111 Ibn Taymiyya's list of reliable transmitters from the Followers is rather lengthy, for it includes many of the well-known figures of that time. Besides the scholars already mentioned, there were Abū Ṣāliḥ al-Sammān (d. 101/720),

ʿAbd al-Raḥmān b. Ḥurmūz al-Aʿraj (d. 117/735), Sulaymān b. Yasār (d. 107/726), Muḥammad b. Sīrīn (d. 110/729) and al-Aswad b. Yazīd al-Nakhaʿī (d. 75/695).

112 This was Muḥammad b. Jarīr al-Ṭabarī (d. 310/923) and his exegesis is known as *Jāmiʿ al-bayān ʿan taʿwīl āy al-Qur'ān*. For a brief description of this scholar and his exegesis, see Mahmoud Ayoub, *The Qur'an and its Interpreters*, 2 vols., Albany: State University of New York Press, 1984, vol. 1, p. 3.

113 In order to strengthen his claim, Ṭabarī argued that the *ḥadīth* of ʿĀ'isha, in which she said that the Prophet did not explain the Qur'ān except for certain verses taught to him by Gabriel, was a weak *ḥadīth*; ibid., p. 39. It therefore could not be used as evidence because one of its narrators, Jaʿfar b. Muḥammad al-Zubayrī, was not known to the scholars of *Ḥadīth*. See also Didin Syafruddin, 'The Principles of Ibn Taymiyya's Qur'ānic Interpretation,' M.A. Thesis, McGill University, 1994, p. 108. However, Ibn ʿAṭiyya, whom Ibn Taymiyya also held in high esteem, accepted the *ḥadīth* of ʿĀ'isha, but explained it in relation to the *ḥadīth* in which the Prophet stated that whoever used opinion to discuss the Qur'ān had erred, even if his answer was correct. His conclusion was similar to that of Ṭabarī; in other words, that the *ḥadīth* of ʿĀ'isha was not evidence, but for a different reason. See Ibn ʿAṭiyya, ibid., p. 41.

114 Laoust indicates that Ibn Taymiyya differed from the majority of Ḥanbalīs in his high estimation of Ṭabarī; *Essai*, p. 73 n. 2. Related to this issue, Melchert discusses the conflicts between the Ḥanbalīs and Ṭabarī in connection with the activities of Abū Bakr b. Abī Dāwūd al-Sijistānī, the son of the famous traditionist who compiled one of the six canonical *Ḥadīth* collections; Melchert, ibid., pp. 14–15. On one particular occasion, for example, Abū Bakr led a group of Ḥanbalīs in blockading Ṭabarī's house and preventing people from studying *Ḥadīth* with him. Although there were no definitive reasons for the overall antagonism, it must have been a serious situation for the Ḥanbalīs and the followers of Ṭabarī remained in conflict with each other for a number of years after his death.

115 Abū Zahra, ibid., pp. 358–361.

116 This is Abū al-Ḥasan ʿAlī b. Aḥmad al-Wāḥidī (d. 468/1076) and his exegesis is known as *Asbāb nuzūl al-Qur'ān*. See Ayoub, ibid., vol. 1, p. 4.

117 *Muqaddima*, p. 354. This reference was to Aḥmad b. Ibrāhīm al-Thaʿlabī (d. 383/993). His exegesis is known as *al-Kashf wa'l-bayān ʿan tafsīr al-Qur'ān*; see Brockelmann, *EI*, vol. VIII, s.v. 'Thaʿlabī.'

118 This is Ḥasan b. Masʿūd al-Baghawī (d. 510/1116), and his exegesis is known as *Maʿālim al-tanzīl*. He was a well-known traditionalist who compiled the *Sharḥ al-sunna* and the *Maṣābiḥ al-sunna*, the latter of which was revised in 737/1337 by Khaṭīb Tibrizī under the more famous title, *Mishkāt al-maṣābiḥ*. For a biography of Baghawī and Khaṭīb Tibrizī, see the translation of the latter work by Robson who gives Baghawī's name as Ḥusayn and an alternative date of death as AH 516; ibid., vol. 1, pp. xii–xiv.

119 In reference to Qur'ānic exegesis, Ibn Taymiyya also mentioned the Shīʿa (*al-rāfiḍa*), philosophers and Karmathians (*al-qarāmiṭa*), but viewed them as separate groups outside Sunnī Islam. He said they had gone astray and had interpreted the Qur'ān in astonishing ways. He then listed various interpretations of verses attributed to the Shīʿa. For example, he stated that the Shīʿa interpreted Q.CXI.1, 'Perish the two hands of Abū Lahab,' as referring to Abū Bakr and ʿUmar. He also stated that any such interpretations referring to people were fabricated, even if they supported a Sunnī position. Thus, for example, he equally rejected the interpretation of Q.XCV.1–4, in which it was said that *al-ṭīn* referred to Abū Bakr, that *al-zaytūn* referred to ʿUmar, that *ṭūrī sīnīn* referred to ʿUthmān, and *hādhā al-balad al-amīn* referred to ʿAlī. See *Muqaddima*, pp. 359–360.

120 See *Muqaddima*, p. 356. In the context in which Ibn Taymiyya was speaking here, the term, *dalīl*, referred to the statements of the Prophet and the Companions while the term, *madlūl*, referred to the traditionists' interpretations derived from these statements. The basis for this understanding came from Ibn Taymiyya's definition of knowledge (*ʿilm*) given in his opening remarks of the *Muqaddima*, p. 329. He said that knowledge was either a trustworthy transmission from an infallible source or a statement drawn from known evidence. Everything else was either a spurious report which had to be rejected or an ambiguous statement about which one did not know whether it was spurious or had been proven false.

121 Ibn Taymiyya's arguments against the Muʿtazila are found in the *Muqaddima*, pp. 357–358. The Muʿtazila figured prominently in Ibn Taymiyya's thinking for they represented an extreme case of the dangers of using personal opinion in explaining revelation.

122 These five principles of Muʿtazilī thought are discussed by W. Montgomery Watt in *Islamic Philosophy and Theology*, Edinburgh: Edinburgh University Press, 1985, pp. 46–55. The two points that Ibn Taymiyya did not discuss were 'the position between the two positions,' and, 'commanding good and forbidding evil.' The former referred to the Muʿtazilī concept that grave sinners were neither believers nor disbelievers, but would nonetheless be in the hellfire. The latter referred to the concept of maintaining justice and opposing injustice by word and by action if one is able to do it.

123 See *Muqaddima*, p. 357. Watt states that the Muʿtazila considered the idea of attributes as 'introducing an element of multiplicity into the unity of God's nature or essence (*nafs*, *dhat*); ibid., p. 49. He says, for example, that according to Muʿtazilī belief, God did not know 'by any hypostatic Knowledge,' which was diametrically opposed to Ibn Taymiyya's concept of oneness in which God's attributes described His eternal essence.

124 See *Muqaddima*, p. 358. In connection with this issue of free will and justice, Ibn Taymiyya also mentioned that this was the belief of the Twelver

Shīʿa as represented by Shaykh al-Mufīd (d. 413/1022) and Abū Jaʿfar al-Ṭūsī (d. 460/1067). These two Shīʿī scholars represented the ascendency of the rationalist trend in Shīʿī thinking that was centered in Baghdad, as opposed to the traditionalist school of Qom. On this aspect of the development of Shīʿī thought, see Wilferd Madelung, *Religious Trends in Early Islamic Iran*, Albany, NY: Persian Heritage Foundation, 1988, pp. 82–83 and Said Amir Arjomand, *The Shadow of God and the Hidden Imam: Religion, Political Order, and Societal Change in Shiite Iran from the Beginning to 1890*, Chicago & London: University of Chicago Press, 1988, p. 28. For a review of Shīʿī hermeneutics and exegesis, see Ayoub, ibid., 177–198.

125 See *Muqaddima*, p. 358. According to Watt, this was a minor principle of Muʿtazilī thought, placed after the concepts of 'oneness' and 'justice;' ibid., p. 52. He refers to it as the doctrine of 'the promise and the threat,' and mentions that the Muʿtazila remained close to the Khawārij on this point, in opposition to the Murji'a.

126 It was a well-known position of the *Ahl al-Sunna* that all Muslims, even grave sinners, would eventually be taken out of the hellfire. See, for example, Khaṭīb Tibrīzī, who related a *ḥadīth* from Bukhārī and Muslim stating that even the fornicator and thief would eventually enter Paradise if they died holding the belief of oneness; see ibid., vol. I, P. 14 and the translation, ibid., vol. I, p. 11. On the many *ḥadīths* about the Prophet's intercession, see Ibn Ḥajar, ibid., vol. XI, pp. 414–444. Ibn Taymiyya dealt extensively with this topic in '*Qāʿida fī'l-tawassul wa'l-wasīla*,' ibid., vol. XII, PP. 142–368.

127 See *Muqaddima*, p. 361. The details of Ibn Taymiyya's arguments against the speculative theologians are dealt with below.

128 *Muqaddima*, p. 362.

129 Cf. Ghazālī's statements on the confusion and 'false *ra'y*' of the Muʿtazila in Richard Joseph McCarthy, *Freedom and Fulfillment: an Annotated Translation of al-Ghazālī's* al-Munqidh min al-Dalāl *and Other Relevant Works of al-Ghazālī*, Boston: Wayne Publishers, 1980, p. 327.

130 Laoust also stresses Ibn Taymiyya's complete dependence on the Salaf ('les pieux Anciens') for the development of every aspect of his beliefs and doctrines; *Essai*, p. 204. He points out (pp. 220–225) that for Ibn Taymiyya the *Ahl al-Sunna wa'l-Jamāʿ* was the moderate group that mediated between the diverse opinions of the Muslims. Ibn Taymiyya maintained that just as Islam had adopted the correct position between the Jews and Christians (*Ahl al-Kitāb*), so the *Ahl al-Sunna* had adopted the correct position on every issue within Islam. See Swartz for Ibn Taymiyya's comments on this issue in his work the *Wāsitiyya*; ibid., p. 115.

131 Ibn Taymiyya included a detailed discussion about these *ḥadīths* in his work entitled, *Ṣiḥḥat uṣūl madhhab ahl al-Madīna*, ed. Aḥmad Hijāzī Aḥmad al-Saqā, Cairo: Maktabat al-Thaqāfa al-Dīniyya, 1988, p. 27–30. He said that there were

two variations: one version mentioning the first three generations and the other mentioning the first four generations. In the later version, the narrators expressed some doubts as to whether the Prophet had said three or four generations. Thus, Ibn Taymiyya referred to the first three while accepting that the fourth generation might have been included in the Prophet's statement.

132 Ibn Taymiyya clearly associated *al-firqat al-nājiya* with the Ahl al-Sunna; see Swartz, ibid., p. 104, n. 1. For a full discussion of the *ḥadīth* of the 73 sects, see Abū Manṣūr ᶜAbd al-Qāhir b. Ṭāhir al-Baghdādī, *al-Farq bayn al-firaq*, Beirut: Dār al- Āfāq al-Jadīda, 1408/1987, pp. 4–11, which has been translated by Kate Chambers Seelye as *Moslem Schisms and Sects*, New York: AMC Press, Inc, 1966, pp. 21–24.

133 *Ṣihhat*, p. 31. Related to this issue, Ibn Taymiyya said that the consensus of the people of Medina was not proof that all Muslims should follow it. On this issue of Medina as the geographical 'centre' for the practice of the *Sunna*, see Joseph Schacht, *The Origins of Muhammadan Jurisprudence*, Oxford: Clarendon Press, 1959, pp. 8–9, 21–35, 172 and Azami, *On Schacht's Origins*, pp. 36–69.

134 *Ṣiḥḥat*, p. 34

135 This referred to false piety and corrupt asceticism. In his work, *al-Ṣūfiyya wa'l-fuqarā'*, Ibn Taymiyya clearly associated Basra with the rise of Sufism and all extreme forms of worship and devotion; *al-Ṣūfiyya wa'l-fuqarā'*, ed. Muḥammad Jamīl Ghāzī, Jeddah: Sūq al-Nādā, [no date]. He claimed that some of the Muslims in Basra began to make independent judgements (*ijtihād*) concerning acts of worship, which was absolutely forbidden according to the Qur'ān and *Sunna*.

136 Ibn Taymiyya was referring here to the idea of God's determining all events, including a person's acts, which was used by the Umayyads to legitimize their claims to the caliphate. This concept of predestination was the way *qadar* was originally used. After the Muᶜtazila (whose origins he located in Basra) began to argue that God did not create the acts of human beings and did not even know them until they occurred, the term *qadar* was applied to those Muslims who held such a view. Thus, they became known as the Qadariyya. Those who continued to support the concept of predestination to the total exclusion of any choice on the part of the individual, became known as the Jabriyya. See Watt, ibid., pp. 25–31.

137 According to Ibn Taymiyya, the Jahmiyya first appeared during the last years of the generation of the Followers, after the death of the Caliph ᶜUmar b. ᶜAbd al-ᶜAzīz and during the caliphate of Hishām b. ᶜAbd al-Mālik; *Ṣiḥḥat*, p. 35. The originator of this group was Jahm b. Safwān but the more famous propagator of his ideas was Jaᶜd b. Dirham. Ibn Taymiyya saw them as being responsible for the ideas related to *taᶜṭīl*, or 'stripping,' God of all His names and attributes. To highlight the enormity of this deviation from the understanding of the Salaf, he related the story of how Khālid b. ᶜAbd Allāh al-Qasrī, the governor

of Iraq, had sacrificed Ja^cd on the day of ʿĪd al-Aḍḥā because he claimed that God had not taken Abraham as an intimate friend and had not spoken directly to Moses. The same story was related by Baghdādī; ibid., p. 262.

138 Baghdādī said that these three Companions, as well as others such as Abū Hurayra and Anas b. Mālik, refused to greet or to pray the funeral prayer over those known to hold the beliefs of the Qadariyya; ibid., p. 15.

139 *Ṣiḥḥat*, p. 36.

140 According to al-Sayyid Sābiq, Abū Ḥanīfa maintained that *zakā* was due on 'every type of produce of the land including vegetables;' *Fiqh us-Sunna: az-Zakāh and as-Siyām*. tr. Abdul-Majid Khokhar, Muhammad Saʿeed Dabas and Jamal al-Din M. Zarabozo. Indianapolis: American Trust Publications, 1412/1991, p. 23. He continued by saying that Abū Yūsuf and Muḥammad al-Shaybānī (d. 189/805) differed from their teacher, because they maintained that produce that 'does not last a whole year, such as [...] cucumbers and watermelons' had no *zakā* due on them.

141 See *Ṣiḥḥat*, p. 37. In connection with formulating opinions in opposition to authentic *ḥadīth*s, Ibn Taymiyya said there were about twenty valid excuses for doing this. He referred the reader to his work, *Rafʿ al-malām ʿan al-a'immat al-aʿlām*, for a full discussion of this point. In the *Ṣiḥḥat* he mentioned a few possible scenarios, such as that a scholar did not know of a particular *ḥadīth*, that he knew of the *ḥadīth* only through a weak chain of narrators, that he did not believe the *ḥadīth* to constitute evidence in judging a particular case, that he thought another *ḥadīth* was stronger evidence in judging a case, or that he thought that the *ḥadīth* had been abrogated.

142 *Ṣiḥḥat*, p. 42.

143 See Laoust, ibid., pp. 205–206.

144 The details of Ibn Taymiyya's views on ʿAlī are presented by Laoust as part of the chapter entitled, 'les Salaf;' ibid., pp. 213–218.

145 *Ṣiḥḥat*, p. 43.

146 *Ṣiḥḥat*, p. 44.

147 Ibn Taymiyya made a special note in reference to Imam Mālik's opinion by stating that this was what had been reported by the most reliable followers of Mālik, such as al-Fāḍil ʿAbd al-Wahhāb (d. 422/1031). He went on to say that the followers of Mālik in North Africa held the opposite opinion, but that they had no authentic evidence for this and were simply people of blind imitation. He did not mention, however, whose opinion they were following.

148 I refer to the translation by Memon, ibid.

149 Memon, ibid., p. 24.

150 Memon, ibid., p. 11.

151 Memon mentions two prayers in particular, the *ṣalāt al-ragha'ib* offered in Rajab and the prayers of mid-Shaʿbān; ibid., p. 12. Ibn al-Jawzī discussed the various fabricated *ḥadīth*s related to offering special prayers in these two months;

see *Kitāb al-mawḍūʿāt*, 3 vols. Beirut: Dār al-Fikr, 1403/1983, pp. 123–130.

152 Memon, ibid., p. 13.

153 A very concise review of Ibn Taymiyya's opinions on the visitation of graves is given by Taylor, ibid., pp. 126–132.

154 Memon, ibid., pp. 14–17.

155 Memon, ibid., p. 19.

156 On the early history of the grammatical tradition in Islam, see Monique Bernards, *Changing Traditions: Al-Mubarrad's Refutation of Sībawayh and the Subsequent Reception of the* Kitāb, Leiden & New York: E. J. Brill, 1997.

157 This is my paraphrase of the title of Michael Carter's article, 'Language Control as People Control in Medieval Islam: the Aims of the Grammarians in their Cultural Context,' *al-Abhath: Journal of the Faculty of Arts and Sciences, American University of Beirut*, vol. XXXI, 1983, pp. 65–83.

158 In his work, '*al-Kaylāniyya*,' Ibn Taymiyya presented several reports related from Ibn Ḥanbal that there was total agreement among the *Ahl al-Sunna* that the actions and speech of human beings were created and not eternal; see '*al-Kaylāniyya*,' in *Majmūʿ fatāwā*, vol. XII: *Kitāb al-Qur'ān*, pp. 324–326. Ibn Taymiyya's arguments in this context were directed against a group referred to by Ibn Ḥanbal as the Lafẓiyya, who claimed that a person's recitation of the Qur'ān was not created. Thus, the Lafẓiyya denied that the recitation of Qur'ān was created human speech. This description of them differs from that given by Josef Van Ess, who says that Ibn Ḥanbal attacked the Lafẓiyya as being 'people who believed in the createdness of the pronunciation (*lafẓ*), i.e. the recitation of the Kur'ān;' *EI2*, Supp. fascicules 5-6, s.v. 'Ibn Kullāb.' I have not found much information about this particular group, which makes it difficult to resolve these two contradictory statements. But assuming both statements of Ibn Ḥanbal about the Lafẓiyya were accurate, he might have used the term in reference to two different groups. However, it could also be the case that both statements were directed against a group holding beliefs similar to those espoused by Ibn Kullāb, who held that the eternal speech of God was, in van Ess's words, a 'reproduction (*ḥikāya*) in historical reality, especially in a Holy Scripture.' This complicates the issue, for Ibn Kullāb discussed both the eternal speech of God and the created Qur'ān. I shall discuss Ibn Ḥanbal's and Ibn Taymiyya's beliefs concerning God's speech below.

159 In his *Kitāb al-īmān*, Ibn Taymiyya referred to verses such as Q.XXVII.16 and 18 to show that God gave birds and ants speech (*manṭiq*); *Kitāb al-īmān*, Beirut: Dār al-Kutub al-ʿIlmiyya, 1412/1991, pp. 82–83. He said that God does the same for humans as indicated in Q.LV.1–4 and Q.XLI.21.

160 The term 'Positor' is used by Adrian Gully in relation to his discussion of the Muslim theory of language; see *Grammar and Semantics in Medieval Arabic: A study of Ibn-Hisham's 'Mughni l-Labib'*. Richmond, Surrey: Curzon Press, 1995, p. 33. He places Ibn Taymiyya with the Ẓāhirīs and the Ḥanbalīs who 'assert the

ultimate belief in the divine origin of language.' Ibn Taymiyya stated in his *Kitāb al-īmān* (p. 86), in reference to Turkish, Hebrew and Arabic, that they were all the speech of God.

161 Ibn Taymiyya dealt with the issue of writing and the Arabic script in his essay, '*Mas'alat al-aḥruf allatī anzala Allāh ʿalā Ādam*,' in *Majmūʿ fatāwā*, vol. XII: *Kitāb al-Qur'ān* , pp. 56–59. He mentioned, for example, the stories related to the creation of the Arabic script by the Bedouins known as Abū Jād, Ḥawwāz and Ḥuṭṭī. Cf. the reports given by Abū al-Faraj Muḥammad b. Isḥāq al-Nadīm in *The Fihrist of al-Nadīm*, ed. and tr. Bayard Dodge, 2 vols., New York: Columbia University Press, 1970, vol. I, pp. 6–9.

162 According to Carter, this is the view expressed by Fakhr al-Dīn al-Rāzī (d. 606/1210) and implied by earlier grammarians such as Zajjājī (d. 337/949) and Ibn al-Anbārī (d. 577/1182); ibid., p. 80.

163 See Ibn Taymiyya, '*al-Furqān bayn al-ḥaqq wa'l-bāṭil*,' in *Majmūʿ fatāwā*, vol. XIII: *Kitāb muqaddimat al-tafsīr*, p. 207.

164 He also reported that some of the Salaf said that *ṣamad* meant *laysa lahu aḥshā'*; see Ibn Taymiyya, *Tafsīr ṣūrat al-ikhlāṣ*, ed. Ṭaha Yūsuf Shāhīn, Cairo: Dār al-Ṭibāʿa al-Muḥammadiyya, [no date], pp. 3–7.

165 See Abū Faḍl Jamāl al-Dīn Muḥammad Ibn Manẓūr, *Lisān al-ʿArab*, Beirut: Dār Ṣādir, [no date], s.v. '*ṣmd*.' He stated that *lā jawfa lahu* was not allowed to be used in reference to God.

166 Ibn Taymiyya reported most of the *ḥadīth*s to support his claim from the exegesis of Ibn Abī Ḥātim. By way of comparison, Bukhārī mentioned only the *ḥadīth*s that give the meaning of *ṣamad* as 'the lord on whom all depend in times of need;' see Ibn Ḥajar, *Fatḥ al-bārī*, vol. VIII, PP. 739–740. On Ibn Taymiyya's exegesis of this sura, see also the comments by Syafruddīn, ibid., pp. 88–97.

167 For the translation of these and other grammatical terms, I follow the translations used by Gully, ibid. Alternative translations for *muṭlaq* and *muqayyad* are 'absolute' and 'conditional,' respectively, which are used by Izutsu in *The Concept of Belief*, p. 71.

168 Makari mentions that even Ibn Taymiyya's opponents acquiesced in his superior skills as a debater and in mastering all sciences; ibid., p. 26.

169 Ghazālī wrote that Ibn Ḥanbal allowed for a non-literal interpretation of only three *ḥadīth*s and that the Ashʿarīs were the closest to the Ḥanbalīs in avoiding *majāz* interpretations; see *Fayṣal al-tafriqa bayna al-islām wa'l-zandaqa*, ed. Hogga Mustapha, Casablanca: Dār al-Naṣr al-Maghribiyya, 1983, pp. 16–17. See also McCarthy, ibid., pp. 155–156.

170 *Kitāb al-īmān*, pp. 79–81.

171 The expression, 'terminological convention,' is taken from Wolfhart Heinrichs, who summarizes the same passage from Ibn Taymiyya's *Kitāb al-īmān*; 'On the Genesis of the *Ḥaqīqah-Majāz* Dichotomy,' *Studia Islamica*, vol. LIX, 1984, p. 115. Ibn Taymiyya also refered to this dichotomy as being *min*

ʿ*awāriḍ al-alfāẓ*. Concerning Ibn Ḥanbal, Ibn Taymiyya said that he did use the expression *min majāz al-lugha* in reference to certain statements in the Qur'ān. However, he added that, according to the earliest followers of Ibn Ḥanbal, this meant what was allowable in the Arabic language (*min-mā yajūz fī'l-lugha*). The vast majority of the Ḥanbalīs agreed that there was no *majāz* in the Qur'ān or the *ḥadīths*, except as mentioned in the previous note. See *Kitāb al-īmān*, p. 81 and Heinrichs, ibid., p. 116.

172 Gully makes the same reference to Abū ʿUbayda's use of the term *majāz*; ibid., p. 40. He says that his use of the term might 'constitute a "prefiguration" of its later acceptance as figurative speech.' On Abū ʿUbayda's use of the term, *majāz*, see Heinrichs, pp. 117–130.

173 Heinrichs associates Ibn Taymiyya's account of the history of the *ḥaqīqa-majāz* dichotomy with his 'Salafī view-point,' and suggests that his use of *istilāḥ ḥādith*s to describe this dichotomy was very close to the meaning of innovation (*bidʿa*); ibid., p. 117. On the issue of whether language was merely the result of human convention, Gully states that Ibn Taymiyya 'believed that the conventionalist view of language had been invented to justify the concept of figurative (extended) usage (*majāz*);' ibid., pp. 33, 40–41 and 69 n. 21. On a related issue, Wael B. Hallaq points out that Ibn Taymiyya argued that to claim a distinction between essence and accident was merely based on convention (*waḍʿ*), which 'is nothing but the result of what a group of people invents (*takhtariʿ*) and agrees to use or accepts as a norm;' *Ibn Taymiyya against the Greek Logicians*, New York: Oxford University Press, 1993, p. xvii.

174 In tracing the development of the use of the terms *ḥaqīqa* and *majāz*, Heinrichs narrows down the discussions in the later Middle Ages to the use of the terms by legal scholars in *uṣul al-fiqh* works and rhetoricians in ʿ*ilm al-bayān* works; ibid., p. 114. These discussions included the differences in the way that the *bayāniyyūn* and the *uṣūliyyūn* used the term, *qarīna*, which helps to explain Ibn Taymiyya's position. The *bayāniyyūn* saw the *qarīna* as an integral part of the *majāz* and used it in ways that were irrelevant to the *uṣūliyyūn*, who limited it to being only a condition for the soundness of *majāz*.

175 *Kitāb al-īmān*, p. 81.

176 Ibid., p. 87.

177 Ibid., pp. 98–100.

178 See Ibn Manẓūr, ibid., s.v. '*dhwq*,' who used Q.XLIV.48–49, 'Then pour on his head the torment of boiling water. Taste! (*dhuq*) [...],' to argue that the use of 'taste' was *majāz*.

179 See *Kitāb al-īmān*, pp. 101–102. Cf. a similar argument concerning this verse in Gully, ibid., p. 41.

180 See Ibn Ḥajar, ibid., vol. 1, p. 114.

181 See *Kitāb al-īmān*, p. 11.

182 See *Kitāb al-īmān*., p. 15; and see Izutsu, ibid., pp. 59–60.

183 Izutsu, ibid., p. 71.

184 *Kitāb al-īmān*, pp. 142–151.

185 All quotations from the *Wāsiṭiyya* are from Swartz, ibid., pp. 91–131.

186 The specific points of Ibn Ḥanbal's creed are taken from *ʿAqīdat Aḥmad b. Ḥanbal bi-riwāyat Abī Bakr al-Khallāl*, ed. ʿAbd al-ʿAzīz ʿIzz al-Dīn al-Shīrawān, Damascus: Dār Quṭaybiyya, 1408/1988.

187 According to Ibn Ḥanbal, consensus (*ijmāʿ*) referred to the consensus of the Companions; ibid., p. 123.

188 Ibid., p. 42.

189 Ibid., p. 102.

190 Ibid., p. 112.

191 This refers to the concept of the oneness of the names and attributes (*tawḥīd al-asmāʾ wa'l-ṣifāt*); see Sayyid ʿAbd al-ʿAzīz al-Sīlī, *al-ʿAqīda al-salafiyya bayn al-imām Ibn Ḥanbal wa'l-imām Ibn Taymiyya*, Cairo: Dār al-Manār, 1416/1995, pp. 219–228.

192 See Swartz, ibid., p. 105.

193 Ibn Ḥanbal, ibid., p. 102.

194 Ibid., p. 105.

195 Swartz, ibid., pp. 107–108

196 Ibn Ḥanbal, ibid., p. 106.

197 Ibid., pp. 114–115.

198 I use 'determinism' for *qadar* and 'predestination' for *qaḍāʾ* in order to reflect a basic lexical distinction in meanings. Lane distinguishes between *qaḍāʾ* and *qadar* by referring to the former term as a general one and the latter term as a particular decree, predestination, fate or destiny; *Arabic-English Lexicon,* 8 vols., repr., Beirut: Librairie du Liban, 1980, '*qdr*.' L. Gardet explains the difference as being the 'eternal Decree' (*qaḍāʾ*) and the 'Decree given existence in time' (*qadar*) ; *EI2*, vol. IV, s.v. 'al-ḳaḍāʾ wa'l-ḳadar.' Elsewhere, however, Gardet and M. M. Anawati use 'prédétermination' for *qaḍāʾ* and 'décret' for *qadar*; *Introduction à la théologie musulmane: essai de théologie comparée*, Études de philosphie médiévale, 37, Paris: J. Vrin, 1970, p. 37. Watt uses both 'predetermination' and 'determinism' interchangeably for *qadar*; ibid., pp. 25–31.

199 See Swartz, ibid., pp. 121–122. For a general review of Ibn Taymiyya's beliefs concerning God's will, see Laoust, *Essai*, p. 165. He states that Ibn Taymiyya distinguished between 'la volonté créatrice au sens large (*mashīʾa*) et la volanté normative (*irāda*).' For a more nuanced discussion of Ibn Taymiyya's views on God's voluntary will, see Jon Hoover, 'God Acts by His Will and Power: Ibn Taymiyya's Theology of a Personal God in his Treatise on the Voluntary Attributes,' in *Ibn Taymiyya and His Times*, ed. Yossef Rapoport and Shahab Ahmed, New York: Oxford University Press, 2010, pp. 55–77.

200 Ibn Ḥanbal, ibid., p. 113.

201 Ibid., pp. 114–116. The Muʿtazilī belief in a person's receiving *istiṭāʿa* was

connected with their belief that 'God has no will in men's actions and men's actions are not created by God,' see Wolfson, ibid., pp. 622–623.

202 Ibn Ḥanbal, ibid., p. 116.

203 Ibid., p. 113.

204 Swartz, ibid., p. 122.

205 See Swartz, ibid., p. 123.

206 Laoust, ibid., pp. 165–167.

207 See Gardet, ibid., s.v. 'Kasb.'

208 See Nurcholish Madjid, "'Ibn Taymiyya on *Kalām* and *Falsafa*: A Problem of Reason and Revelation in Islam,' Ph.D. dissertation, University of Chicago, 1984, pp. 144–145. For an analysis of the problems associated with the concept of acquisition, see David B.Burrell, *Freedom and Creation in Three Traditions*, Notre Dame: University of Notre Dame Press, 1993, pp. 79–83.

209 See Madjid, ibid., pp. 143–144. The idea that a person 'chooses' the act must be qualified, for the choice is not independent of God's will. This explanation was Ibn Taymiyya's way of maintaining an intermediate position between the absolute free will of the Qadariyya and the fatalism of the Jabriyya, which in his time manifested itself in the passive *tawakkul* ('reliance') of the Ṣūfīs.

210 Ibn Ḥanbal, ibid., pp. 103–104.

211 Swartz, ibid., p. 109.

212 Ibn Ḥanbal, ibid., pp. 102–103.

213 Swartz, ibid., p.109.

214 Swartz, ibid., p. 117.

215 According to Ibn Ḥajar, Bukhārī added the last '*Kitāb*' to his *Ṣaḥīḥ*, entitled '*Kitāb al-Tawḥīd*,' in order to defend the creed of the *Ahl al-Sunna* against the *taʿṭīl* of the Muʿtazila and the *tashbīh* of the anthropomorphists; see Ibn Ḥajar, ibid., vol. XIII, PP. 344–346.

216 Ibn Ḥanbal, ibid., pp. 108–109.

217 Ibid., pp. 107–108.

218 Ibid., p. 110.

219 Swartz, ibid., pp. 110–112.

220 Ibid., p. 117. In Ibn Taymiyya's book *al-Istiqāma* (p. 70), which was written about ten years after the *Wāsiṭiyya*, he confirmed God's movement in relation to the attributes of motion and stated that it was confirmed by the *Ahl al-Sunna wa'l-Ḥadīth* but was denied by groups of jurisprudents and the speculative theologians. He added that 'it is well-known amongst the companions of Aḥmad that they do not interpret the attributes in the genus of movement such as arrival, descent and nearness' (p. 76).

221 Ibn Ḥanbal, ibid., p. 111.

222 Swartz, ibid., p. 118. Elsewhere in the *Wāsiṭiyya* (p. 114), Ibn Taymiyya presented a *ḥadīth* which stated, '[On the day of judgement,] you will see your Lord as clearly as you see the moon when it is full, and you will not need to crowd

together in order to see him.' Bukhārī presented many *ḥadīths* about the beatific vision in his chapter on Q.LXXV.22–23 in the '*Kitāb al-Tawḥīd*' of his *Ṣaḥīḥ*; see Ibn Ḥajar, ibid., vol. XIII, pp. 419–434.

223 I use the term, 'reproduction,' for *ḥikāya* as it is used by van Ess, ibid., s.v. 'Ibn Kullāb.' In discussing the controversies over the Muʿtazilī doctrine of the createdness of the Qur'ān, van Ess explains that Ibn Kullāb presented the idea of 'a distinction between the speech of God (*kalām Allāh*) and its realization.' Accordingly, the Qur'ān becomes 'the "trace" (*rasm*) of God's speech [and] its reproduction (*ḥikāya*) in historical reality.'

224 Ibn Ḥanbal, ibid., pp. 106–107.

225 Swartz, ibid., p. 111.

226 Ibid., p. 118.

227 *Al-Istiqāma* was considered by Ibn Taymiyya's students to have been one of his most important works; see Ibn ʿAbd al-Hādī, ibid., p. 29. He probably wrote it while in Egypt between the years 705/1305 and 709/1310; see the comments by Muḥammad Rashād Sālim in his introduction to the *Istiqāma*, ibid., p. 5. Ibn Taymiyya's arguments in the *Istiqāma* were an important link for his more detailed work on the reconciliation between pure reason and revelation in his *Dar' taʿāruḍ al-ʿaql wa'l-naql*, which he wrote in Damascus between 713/1314 and 717/1318; *Dar' taʿāruḍ al-ʿaql wa'l-naql*, ed. Muḥammad Rashād Sālim, Riyadh: Jāmiʿat al-Imām Muḥammad b. Saʿūd al-Islāmiyya, 1399/1979. On the dating of this work, see the comments by Sālim in his introduction (pp. 7–10). For a salient discussion of issues related to Ibn Taymiyya's arguments against the Ashʿariyya in the *Dar' taʿāruḍ*, see Racha el Omari, 'Ibn Taymiyya's "Theology of the Sunna" and his Polemics with the Ashʿarite,' in *Ibn Taymiyya and His Times*, pp. 101–119.

228 Ibn Taymiyya's claim was that any religious question must be referred back to the Qur'ān, the authentic *Sunna* of the Prophet and the opinions of the Companions. This is clearly stated, for example, in his response concerning the paths of the Ṣūfīs: 'It is for the Muslim to know that the best word is the Word of God, and the best guidance is the guidance of Muḥammad, and the best of the centuries is the one in which he was sent to them, and the most preferable of the paths (*ṭuruq*) and the ways (*subul*) to God is that which was with him and his Companions.' See *al-Ṣūfiyya wa'l-fuqarā'*, ibid., p. 20. Elsewhere he stated that the Qur'ān and the *Sunna* contained the fundamentals of religion including proofs, signs and arguments; see Laoust, *Contribution*, p. 72.

229 *Istiqāma*, vol. I, p. 3

230 Ibn Taymiyya held a dual view of the intellect (*ʿaql*). In attempting to maintain an intermediate position between extremes, he rejected the superior position given to the intellect by the philosophers and speculative theologians on the one hand, while advocating the necessity of preserving the intellect and faculties of discernment in opposition to the Ṣūfī claim of a mystical annihilation of the self on the other. For him, the intellect (or reason) was to be used in the service of

revelation. The independent status of the intellect has been defined as 'rational, non-religious' concepts by Hallaq, who refers to *dalīl ʿaqlī* as 'a rational, non-religious argument;' ibid., p. liii.

231 Ibn Taymiyya attributed this statement to the Shāfiʿī scholar Juwaynī; *al-Istiqāma*, vol. 1, p. 6. He also quoted a similar statement from Ghazālī; see Madjid, ibid., p. 116. For a closer investigation of Ibn Taymiyya's views on the relationship between revelation and reason, see M. Sait Özervarli, 'The Qur'ānic Rational Theology of Ibn Taymiyya and his Criticism of the *Mutakallimūn*,' in *Ibn Taymiyya and His Times*, pp. 78–100.

232 See *al-Istiqāma*, vol. 1, p. 13. Ibn Taymiyya claimed that imam Shāfiʿī held the opinion that those who used *kalām* should be beaten. He also claimed that some speculative theologians, such as Fakhr al-Dīn al-Rāzī, had repented on their deathbeds for having engaged in *kalām*. See Madjid, ibid., pp. 124–125.

233 See *al-Istiqāma*, vol.1, pp. 9–13. In *al-Ṣūfiyya wa'l-fuqarā'* (p. 22), Ibn Taymiyya distinguished between a Kufian school of jurisprudence and a Basrian school of worship. He said that just as certain scholars gathered in Kufa to exercise independent judgment (*ijtihād*) concerning legal matters, so too did certain scholars practice *ijtihād* in Basra concerning issues of piety and asceticism. Although practicing *ijtihād* concerning a particular issue was not wrong in jurisprudence, it was forbidden in worship.

234 Ibn Taymiyya gave three examples of this in *al-Istiqāma*, vol. 1, p. 14–16. The first was that Imam Mālik had defended the belief in God's rising above the throne, His speech and the beatific vision against the beliefs of the Jahmiyya. However, some later Mālikī scholars came to accept the denial of these beliefs. The second example was that Imam Shāfiʿī had denounced the people of *kalām*, but some of the later adherents of the Shāfiʿī *madhhab* came to embrace these principles. The third example was that the beliefs of Ibn Ḥanbal concerning the createdness of a worshipper's attributes—as opposed to the uncreatedness of God's attributes—were reversed by some of his later followers on two issues: some Ḥanbalīs came to believe (1) that a worshipper's recitation of the Qur'ān was uncreated, and (2) that God's attributes of movement were to be rejected.

235 Madjid, ibid., p. 114.

236 A brief presentation of Ibn Taymiyya's critique of the philosophers and speculative theologians may be found in Laoust, *Essai*, pp. 179–186 and *Contributions*, pp. 55–58. Ibn Taymiyya's beliefs on prophecy are laid out in his *Kitāb al-nubuwwāt* and his critique of philosophical-mystical cosmologies may be found in his *Kitāb bughyat al-murtād*. See *Kitāb al-nubuwwāt*, Lebanon: Dār al-Qalam, [no date] and '*Kitāb bughyat al-murtād*,' in *Majmūʿat fatāwā Ibn Taymiyya al-kubrā*, vol. v, Cairo: Dār al-Manār, 1408/1988, pp. 291–430. Fārābī's and Ibn Sīnā's theories of prophecy are described by Majid Fakhry in *A History of Islamic Philosophy*, New York: Columbia University Press, 1983, pp. 142–145. For Ibn Sīnā's views on prophecy, see his '*Fī ithbāt al-nubuwwa*,' in *Tisʿ rasā'il fī al-ḥikma*

wa'l-ṭabīʿiyyāt, Cairo: al-Maṭbaʿa al-Ḥindiyya, 1327/1908, pp. 120–132 and the translation by Michael Marmura, 'Avicenna: On the Proof of Prophecies and the Interpretation of the Prophet's Symbols and Metaphors,' in *Medieval Political Philosophy: A Sourcebook*, ed. Ralph Lerner and Muhsin Mahdi, New York: The Free Press, 1963, pp. 112–121. Ghazālī's five grades of allowable interpretation were presented in his *Faysal al-tafriqa*, pp. 8–11 and see the translation by McCarthy, ibid., pp. 150–152.

237 Hallaq, ibid., p. 122.

238 For a general description of the Ṣūfī states leading to mystical knowledge, see Reynold Nicholson, *The Mystics of Islam*, repr., New York: Schocken Books, 1975, p. 59 and Schimmel, ibid., pp. 178–192.

239 Some of the verses he referred to are the following: 'Those who argue concerning the verses of God without authority that came to them' (Q.XL.35), 'Have We revealed any authority that speaks about what they associate [with Him]' (Q.XXX.35), and, 'Do you have a clear authority; then bring forth your book, if you are truthful' (Q.XXXVII.156 –157). Ibn Taymiyya further developed this idea of authority in argumentation in his *Dar' taʿāruḍ al-ʿaql wa'l-naql*, vol. I, P. 57 AND VOL. V, P. 207.

240 See *al-Istiqāma*, vol. I, P. 24. Ibn Taymiyya often raised the point that the groups whom he opposed were not in agreement on even the principles to be applied in forming judgements; on the remark that the philosophers were constantly attacking each other's theories see Hallaq, ibid., pp. xlv and 122.

241 See *al-Istiqāma*, vol. I, P. 25.

242 See the *Istiqāma*, vol. I, p. 31. Ibn Taymiyya actually held a tolerant position toward many of his opponents regarding accusations of *takfīr* and *tafsīq* in spite of his harsh criticisms of them; see Ignaz Goldziher, *Vorlesungen über den Islam*, Heidelberg: Carl Winter's Universitätsbuchhandlung, 1910, p. 200 and George Makdisi, 'Hanbalite Islam,' in *Studies on Islam*, trans. Merlin Swartz, New York: Oxford University Press, 1981, pp. 252–253. On this point he was paralleling Ghazālī's views as presented in his *Faysal al-tafriqa*; see the translation by McCarthy, ibid., pp. 145–174.

243 In relation to this belief concerning jurisprudence, Ibn Taymiyya was referring to Ashʿarī scholars such as Abū Bakr al-Bāqillānī (d. 304/916), Juwaynī, Ghazālī, Fakhr al-Dīn al-Rāzī and Āmidī; see the *Istiqāma*, vol. I, pp. 49–51.

244 See Schacht, ibid., p. 41 and Azami, *On Schacht's Origins*, pp. 72–95.

245 For Āmidī's discussion of the *khabar al-wāḥid*, see Bernard Weiss, *The Search for God's Law: Islamic Jurisprudence in the Writings of Sayf al-Dīn al-Ḥmidī*, Salt Lake City: University of Utah Press, 1992, pp. 291–328. According to Āmidī, Ibn Ḥanbal, 'certain Ẓāhirīs' and 'certain *ḥadīth* specialists' were among those who maintained that the *khabar al-wāḥid*, 'yields the knowledge that it [the report] is true' (ibid, p. 294). According to Weiss (ibid, p. 306), Āmidī did not base the authority of the *khabar al-wāḥid* directly on revelation (i.e., at the level of the Qur'ān and *Sunna*),

but on the consensus of the community, which itself was derived from divine revelation. Thus, the *khabar al-wāḥid* did not yield certainty but only probability, which, for Āmidī, was acceptable in making legal judgements.

246 Ibn Taymiyya stated elsewhere that 'those who draw a distinction between analogy and the categorical syllogism attempt to show that analogy leads to probability when it is formed of a particular subject-matter' (Hallaq, ibid., pp. 127–128). Ibn Taymiyya contended that a subject-matter that leads to certainty would do so through both analogy and the categorical syllogism. Thus, he did not deny the 'validity of the deductive process' when the two premises of the syllogism were 'conceived and structured in a proper way.' However, he did attack the validity of the syllogism in deducing conclusions in metaphysics by denying the existence of universals outside the mind. See Madjid, ibid., pp. 190–191.

247 See the *Istiqāma*, vol. I, pp. 59–60.

248 For the discussion in this paragraph, see Madjid, ibid., pp. 147–149.

249 See *al-Istiqāma*, vol. I, pp. 82–85.

250 Ibn Fūrak and Isfarāyinī studied along with Bāqillānī under Abū al-Ḥasan al-Bāhilī in Baghdad. Afterwards, they went to Nishapur to establish Ashʿarī theology. It was there, according to Watt, *EI2*, vol. III, s.v. 'Ibn Fūrak,' that Ibn Fūrak secured 'the adoption of the Ashʿarite theology by a group of mystics,' which included Qushayrī.

251 See *al-Istiqāma*, vol. I, pp. 82–89.

252 Of the three authors mentioned here, Ibn Taymiyya stated that Kalābādhī, the author of *al-Taʿarruf li -madhhab ahl al-taṣawwuf*, was 'the best, the most correct, and the closest to the *madhhab* of the *Salaf*;' *al-Istiqāma*, vol. I, p. 83. See also Kalābādhī, *al-Taʿarruf li -madhhab ahl al-taṣawwuf*, ed. Maḥmūd Amīn al-Nawāwī, Cairo: Maktabat al-Kulliyyāt al-Azhariyya, 1389/1969

253 See *al-Istiqāma*, vol. I, p. 115.

254 It is beyond the scope of this book to review Ibn Taymiyya's detailed analysis of the many statements attributed to Ḥallāj. In the *Istiqāma*, he scrutinized each statement according to its chain of narrators and the contents of the narration; *Istiqāma*, vol. I, pp. 115–141. In general, he tended to give Ḥallāj the benefit of the doubt; that is, when the chain was weak or missing he said that one could not attribute the statement to Ḥallāj, and when it was a corrupt statement known to be from him, Ibn Taymiyya said that it arose from the influence of the ecstatic experience. Any sympathies notwithstanding, his overall opinion was that Ḥallāj was a sinner who deserved to be executed for heresy. If he did repent, it was a matter between him and God; see L. Massignon, *La Passion de Husayn Ibn Mansūr Hallāj*, trans. Herbert Mason as *The Passion of al-Ḥallāj: Mystic and Martyr of Islam*, 4 vols., Bollinger Series, vol. XCVIII, Princeton: Princeton University Press, 1982, vol. II, pp. 46–48. However, in the *Istiqāma*, he did have this to say about Ḥallāj: 'The best of what is said about him by his supporters is that he was "a righteous man on a correct path but was overcome

by an ecstatic experience and state so that he spoke confusedly because he did not know what he was saying." The speech of the intoxicant is set aside and not transmitted, for the one executed is a martyr and the executioner is a fighter in the cause of God.' See *Istiqāma*, vol. I, p. 116. The assumption, of course, was that the one executed would be a martyr if his repentance were sincere.

255 Ibn Taymiyya presented only Ghazālī's initial criticisms about the *shaṭḥ* in the *Istiqāma*, vol. I, pp. 119–121. See also Ghazālī's full discussion of *shaṭḥ* in his *Iḥyā' ʿulūm al-dīn*, 4 vols. Cairo: al-Maṭbaʿa al-Azhariyya al-Miṣriyya, 1316/1899, vol. I, pp. 31–32.

256 *Istiqāma*, ibid.

257 Massignon, *EI*, vol. VII, s.v. 'Shaṭḥ.'

258 This is reported by Carl Ernst, *Words of Ecstasy in Sufism*, Albany: State University of New York Press, 1985, p. 79. Nicholson records an anecdote from Jalāl al-Dīn al-Rūmī's *Masnavī* in which he wrote that Abū Yazīd al-Bistāmī, after being told of what he had said in an ecstatic state, ordered his followers to stab him if he ever said such offences again. However, when they obeyed his command and tried to stab him during his next ecstatic state, the knife blows were deflected from him and he remained unharmed; see Nicholson, ibid., p. 132.

259 The quotations are from Ernst, ibid., pp. 26–27 and 44. Schimmel discusses the impact of Bistāmī's *shaṭaḥāt*, which she calls 'theopathic locutions in ibid., pp. 47–50.

260 This is the view of Fazlur Rahman in *Islam*, London: Weidenfeld & Nicolson, 1966, p. 146.

261 The four previous quotations are also from Ernst, ibid., pp. 48, 49, 50 and 74, respectively. Schimmel refers to the sin of the mystic as being 'a lover's greatest sin: to divulge the secret of his love.' See ibid., p. 64.

262 This sentiment was also mentioned by the Anatolian Ṣūfī, Jalāl al-Dīn al-Rūmī (d. 672/1273), who was quoted as saying: 'When you say, "Words are of no account," you negate your own assertion through your words. If words are of no account, why do we hear you say that words are of no account? After all, you are saying this in words.' This quotation is from Steven T. Katz, who summarizes the problem of mystical language in this way: 'Mystics do not say what they mean and do not mean what they say.' See from Steven T. Katz, ed., *Mysticism and Language*, New York: Oxford University Press, 1992, p. 3.

263 Memon, ibid., pp. 29–34, presents various comments of Ibn Taymiyya concerning statements from Ḥallāj, Ibn Sabʿīn and Tilimsānī. I have summarized Ibn Taymiyya's arguments in this paragraph.

264 In the *Istiqāma*, Ibn Taymiyya criticized several specific statements, such as one made about the testimony of faith. He maintained that both testimonies must be uttered in order for someone to become a Muslim. The criticism stemmed from a claim by Qushayrī that Shiblī, after saying the call to prayer, said, 'If only You had ordered me not to mention another with You;' *al-Istiqāma*, vol. II, p. 15 and

see Schimmel, ibid., p. 79. The implication is that the statement, 'Muḥammad is the Messenger of God,' in the testimony of faith somehow detracted from the concept of God's oneness. Ibn Taymiyya rejected this on the basis that testifying only to 'There is no deity but God,' did not make one a Muslim because rejecting Muḥammad as Messenger was a rejection of God's revelation and law; ibid., vol. II, p. 20. He also refuted a claim by Qushayrī that Abū Sulaymān al-Darānī said that contentment was not to ask God for paradise and not to seek refuge with Him from the hellfire; ibid., vol. II, p. 65. According to Ibn Taymiyya, the righteous Ṣūfī shaykhs agreed with the *Salaf* concerning contentment, which meant to accept the calamities of this life with patience; ibid., vol. II, pp. 65–95. To prove that seeking paradise was part of the religion, he presented evidence from the Qur'ān and the *Sunna* for the reality of the beatific vision in the hereafter; ibid., vol. II, pp. 96–100. A final point he made on this topic was that God loves and is loved based on what He has revealed in the Qur'ān and the *Sunna* of Muḥammad. Those whom He loves were described in many verses and *ḥadīth*s as to their beliefs, statements and actions; ibid., vol. II, pp. 100–104.

265 In his *al-Ṣūfiyya wa'l-fuqarā'*, Ibn Taymiyya mentioned that some famous scholars fainted on hearing the recitation of the Qur'ān; ibid., p. 14. For example, he related a story from Ibn Ḥanbal that a certain Yaḥyā b. Saʿīd fainted upon hearing a recitation of the Qur'ān. But he noted that Yaḥyā was a most reasonable man and if anyone were able to resist fainting, it would be him. Ibn Taymiyya's point was that a Muslim must resist losing consciousness.

266 See Memon, ibid., p. 33 and Nicholson, ibid., p. 93. Based on such statements, Ibn Taymiyya directed his most vicious attacks against the Ṣūfīs who continually expressed these views in a sober state of mind. He did not consider them to be ecstatic expressions but rather carefully thought-out beliefs. He considered Ṣūfīs such as Ibn Sabʿīn, al-Ṣadr al-Rūmī al-Qūnawī (d. 672/1273, also known as Ṣadr al-Dīn al-Qūnawī), Balyānī (d. 686/1287) and Tilimsānī to be the worst offenders of orthodox beliefs. Ibn ʿArabī was associated with the others as denying the distinction between the Creator and the created, but was placed by Ibn Taymiyya in a rank closer to the beliefs of Islam because he maintained the need to follow the Qur'ān and the *Sunna*. See *Risāla ilā Naṣr al-Manbijī*, pp. 469–474.

267 Ibn Taymiyya's discussion of the distinction between good and evil deeds appears in the *Istiqāma*, vol. II., pp. 168–198. This is followed by his discussion of the need for commanding good and forbidding evil, pp. 198–311.

268 Joseph Bell has characterised Ibn Taymiyya's arguments in support of a 'moral purpose of creation' as a reduction to the absurd; see *Love Theory in Later Hanbalite Islam*, Albany: State University of New York Press, 1979, p. 64.

269 For a history of the antinomian Ṣūfī groups, see Ahmet T. Karamustafa, *God's Unruly Friends: Dervish Groups in the Islamic Later Middle Period, 1200–1550*, Salt Lake City: University of Utah Press, 1994.

270 See C. E. Bosworth, *EI2*, vol. VIII, s.v. 'Rifāʿiyya.'

271 See Tahsin Yazıcı, *EI2*, vol. IV, s.v. 'Ḳalandariyya' and F. de Jong and Hamid Algar, *EI2*, vol. VI, s.v. 'Malāmatiyya.' For a more detailed discussion of these groups, see also David Ludwig Martin, 'al-Fana' (Mystical Annihilation of the Soul) and al-Baqa' (Subsistence of the Soul) in the Work of Abū al-Qasim al-Junayd al-Baghdādī", Ph.D. dissertation, Los Angeles, University of California, 1984, pp. 258–283. Memon also mentions some of Ibn Taymiyya's confrontations with these two groups; see ibid., pp. 57–66.

272 Al-Hujwīrī (d. 464/1071) traced the belief of drawing blame on oneself back to the Prophet, who took on the role of the 'proto-type of the *malāmatī*;' Martin, ibid., p. 258. For the exact quotation, see ʿAlī b. ʿUthmān Hujwīrī, *Kashf al-maḥjūb*, tr. Reynold Nicholson as *The Kashf al-Maḥjūb: The Oldest Persian Treatise on Sufism*, London: Luzac, 1976, p. 62.

273 See *al-Istiqāma*, vol. I, pp. 261–265 and *Risāla ilā Naṣr al-Manbijī*, p. 453.

274 See his *Risāla ilā Naṣr al-Manbijī*, p. 455. For the *ḥadīth*, see Ibn Kathīr, *Mukhtaṣar tafsīr Ibn Kathīr*, 3 vols., ed. Muḥammad ʿAlī al-Ṣābūnī, Beirut: Dār al-Qur'ān al-Karīm, 1402/1981, vol. I, p. 15.

275 *Risāla ilā Naṣr al-Manbijī*, p. 456.

276 The wording of supplications was a very important issue for Ibn Taymiyya. He considered that the prayers in the Qur'ān, or which were taught by the Prophet, indicated the correct relationship between God and a worshipper. See ibid., p. 456.

277 Quotation from the section, 'The Criteria of Love,' in the translation.

278 See Memon, ibid., p. 33.

279 See *al-Istiqāma*, vol. II, pp. 142–148. Similar descriptions of *fanā'* may be found in Ibn Taymiyya's '*Ibṭāl waḥdat al-wujūd*,' in *Majmū'at al-rasā'il*, vol. I, pp. 82–84 and his *al-Risāla al-tadmuriyya*, Cairo: al-Maṭbaʿa al-Salafiyya, 1387/1968. He apparently maintained this belief throughout his life because he referred to it in one of the last books he wrote, '*al-Furqān bayn al-ḥaqq wa'l-bāṭil*,' in *Majmūʿ fatāwā*, p. 218.

280 See Qushayrī, *al-Risāla al-qushayrīyya fī ʿilm al-taṣawwuf*, ed. Zakariyyā al-Anṣārī, Cairo: Maktabat wa-Maṭbaʿat Muḥammad ʿAlī Sabīʿ wa-Awliyā'uh, 1382/1962, pp. 61–63 and Richard Gramlich, *Das Sendschreiben al-Qushayrīs über das Sufitum*, Wiesbaden: Franz Steiner Verlag, 1989, pp. 121–123.

281 ʿAbd Allāh al-Anṣārī al-Harawī wrote the *Kitāb manāzil al-sā'irīn*, French trans. S. de Laugier de Beaurecueil, Cairo: Institut français d'archéologie orientale, 1962. For the section on the *fanā'*, see the Arabic text, p. 104 and the French translation, p. 129. This work formed the basis of Ibn al-Qayyim's *Madārij al-sālikīn*, in which he also quoted extensively from Ibn Taymiyya; *Madārij al-sālikīn bayna manāzil iyyāka naʿbudu wa-iyyāka nastaʿīn*, 3 vols, Cairo: Dār al-Ḥadīth, [no date]. His commentary on Harawī's discussion of *fanā'* is found in vol. III, pp. 385–400.

282 Ibn Taymiyya's description of *fanā'* is more closely related to that of Kalābādhī because he did not talk about a *fanā'* of the *fanā'*, or about the *fanā'* of existence, as was indicated by Qushayrī's reference to *istihlāk*. See

Kalābādhī, ibid., pp. 147–157 and the English translation, *The Doctrine of the Sufis*, trans. Arthur J. Arberry, repr. New York: Cambridge University Press, 1977, pp. 120–132. Thus, when Ibn Taymiyya spoke of the 'annihilation of the will for other than God,' he was reflecting Kalābādhī's thinking on this topic. Kalābādhī's first stage was 'a state in which all passions pass away.' He then mentioned a *fanā'* from 'the very consciousness of discord (with God);' these translations are taken from Arberry. Kalābādhī's annihilation of 'passions' and 'discord' was Ibn Taymiyya's annihilation of 'the will for other than God.'

283 This quotation is from *al-Istiqāma*, vol. II, p. 142.

284 The sobriety and orthodoxy of Junayd is the picture commonly portrayed in the accounts of him and Ibn Taymiyya accepted this view. On the historical development of the concepts of sobriety and intoxication, see Jawid A. Mojaddedi, "Getting Drunk with Abū Yazīd or Staying Sober with Junayd: The Creation of a Popular Typology of Sufism,' *Bulletin of the School of Oriental and African Studies*, vol. LXVI, no. 1, 2003, pp. 1–13. However, Martin, ibid., p. 2, challenges this view when he writes, 'Nonetheless, the "safe" orthodoxy of Junayd is perhaps more attributable to ignorance of Junayd's comprehensive theosophy than to his actual "orthodoxy," which [...] is, at base, heterodox.'

285 In the texts of Kalābādhī, Qushayrī and Harawī, *baqā'* was discussed either in the same chapter of *fanā'* or in the chapter immediately following it. The term itself was directly related to *fanā'* and has been described as a 'persistence' or 'subsistence' in God after *fanā'*; see Schimmel, ibid., p. 143. Martin, ibid., also uses 'subsistence' for *baqā'*. Nicholson defines it as 'continuance' or 'abiding;' ibid., p. 61.

286 For the descriptions of *farq* and *jam*ᶜ, see: Gramlich, *Schlaglichter über das Sufitum: Abū Naṣr as-Sarrāğs* Kitāb al-lumaᶜ, Stuttgart: Franz Steiner Verlag, 1990, p. 329–330; Kalābādhī, ibid., pp. 57–58; Arberry, ibid., pp. 114–117; Qushayrī, ibid., pp. 208–210; Gramlich, *Das Sendschreiben al-Qushayrīs*, pp. 121–125; and, Harawī, ibid., pp. 109 (Arabic) and 135 (French). *Farq*, or sometimes *tafriqa*, is translated as 'Trennung' by Gramlich. Arberry translates *farq* as 'separation,' and Harawi's use of *tafriqa* is translated as 'dispersion' by de Beaurecueil. *Jam*ᶜ is translated as 'Vereinigung' by Gramlich and as 'concentration' by Arberry and de Beaurecueil.

287 This process is described by Schimmel, ibid., pp. 143–144.

288 Martin, ibid., 145–157.

289 *Al-Furqān bayn al-ḥaqq wa'l-bāṭil*, p. 218.

290 Ibn al-Qayyim, ibid., vol. III, p. 504.

291 Ibn Taymiyya related intoxication to a Muslim's mental and spiritual state. Anything that interfered with the normal, healthy functioning of the mind was considered to bean intoxicant. This included alcohol and hashish, as well as passions, ambitions and insanity; see *al-Istiqāma*, vol. II, PP. 147–148 AND *al-Ṣūfiyya wa'l-fuqarā'*, p. 16.

292 Ibn Taymiyya referred to the following verses, 'Say: Are those who know

the same as those who do not know?' (Q.XXXIX.9), 'They have hearts with which they do not understand, they have eyes with which they do not see, and they have ears with which they do not hear, they are like the cattle' (Q.VII.179), 'Then know that there is no deity except God' (Q.XLVII.19), and, 'Say: My Lord, increase me in knowledge' (Q.XX.114). See *al-Istiqāma*, vol. II, PP. 157–159.

293 See *al-Ṣūfiyya wa'l-fuqarā'*, p. 18.

294 Ibn Taymiyya's full discussion of this topic may be found in '*Ibṭāl waḥdat al-wujūd*,' ibid.

295 This statement is from the *Ibṭāl*, p. 66. Ibn Taymiyya associated this general statement with well-known monists such as Ibn ʿArabī, al-Ṣadr al-Rūmī al-Qūnawī, Ibn Sabʿīn, Ibn al-Fāriḍ (d. 633/1236), Tilimsānī and Balyānī.

296 Thomas Michel, 'Ibn Taymiyya's Critique of *Falsafa*,' *Hamdard Islamicus*, vol. VI, no. 1, 1983, p. 11.

297 See Hallaq, ibid., p. xxii.

298 The concept of the 'Perfect Man' was a common Ṣūfī notion that Ibn ʿArabī incorporated into his philosophical mysticism. For the Ṣūfīs, the Prophet was the model of the Perfect Man, who 'is necessary to God as the medium through which He is known and manifested;' Schimmel, ibid., p. 272. In relation to the Divine Names, the Perfect Man 'is he who has realized in himself all the possibilities of being;' ibid., p. 273. As for Ibn ʿArabī's concept of the Divine Names, William Chittick explains that he viewed them as 'a kind of *barzakh* between Oneness and manyness. There is but a single Being, yet the names represent a multiplicity of the faces that Being assumes in relation to the created things. The Essence Itself, or Being considered without the names, is what Ibn al-ʿArabī sometimes calls the Unity of the One (*aḥadiyyat al-aḥad*) in contrast to Being considered as possessor of the names, which is the Unity of Manyness (*aḥadiyyat al-kathra*). God as such, taking both perspectives into account, is the 'One/Many' (*al-wāḥid al-kathīr*).' Chittick, *The Sufi Path of Knowledge: Ibn al-ʿArabi's Metaphysics of Imagination*, Albany: State University of New York Press, 1989, p. 25

299 Michel, ibid., p. 3.

300 Fakhry says the following about Ibn Arabi's conception of the Real and the creation: 'The two, however—the one and the many, the first and the last, the eternal and the temporal, the necessary and the contingent—are essentially one and the same reality;' ibid., p. 252.

301 Ibn ʿAbd al-Hādī, ibid., p. 43 and Ibn al-Qayyim al-Jawziyya, *Asmā' mu'allafāt Ibn Taymiyya*, ed. Ṣalāḥ al-Dīn al-Munajjid, 2nd ed., Damascus: Maṭbūʿāt al-Majmaʿ al-ʿIlmī al-ʿArabī, 1372/1953, p. 10.

302 This information about the manuscript is given by Faqī in his edition of *al-ʿUbūdiyya*, ibid., p. 87.

303 See Brockelmann, *GAL*, vol. II, p. 120 and Ibn Taymiyya, '*Risālat al-ʿubūdiyya*,' in *Majmūʿ Rasā'il*, ibid., pp. 2–44.

304Ibn Manẓūr gave a lengthy discussion of the words derived from the root, '*ʿbd*,' in his *Lisān al-ʿArab*, s.v. ‘*ʿbd*.’ I summarize the main points related to the concept of worship. In the context of worshipping God, the term *ʿabd* has two plurals, *ʿibād* and *ʿabīd*. When the term is used in the context of obeying false deities, other forms of the plural are used. He referred to Q.V.60 (which reads, *ʿabada al-ṭāghūt*) in order to present various plurals by offering alternative readings such as, *ʿabūda al-ṭāghūt*, *ʿābidū al-ṭāghūt*, *ʿubuda al-ṭāghūt* and *ʿubbāda al-ṭāghūt*. Ibn Taymiyya seems to have held strictly to this classification of plurals.

EPISTLE ON WORSHIP

In the Name of God, Infinitely Merciful and Compassionate

PART I

The Definition of Worship

The shaykh, imam, scholar and most knowledgeable Abū al-ʿAbbās Aḥmad b. ʿAbd al-Ḥalīm b. Taymiyya, reviver of the *Sunna* and destroyer of innovation (may God be pleased with him),[1] was asked the following about this verse of God (Great and Glorious is He), 'O people! Worship your Lord…' (Q.II.21).[2] What is worshipping, and what are its branches? Is the whole of the religion (*dīn*) included in it, or not? What is the reality of worship? Is it the highest of stations (*aʿlā maqamāt*) in this world and in the hereafter, or is there any station above it? Please expound on this.

Ibn Taymiyya (may God be pleased with him) replied: All praise is for God, the Lord of the worlds. Worshipping is a term that comprises every apparent and hidden saying and deed that God loves and of which He approves, such as prayer, legislated almsgiving, fasting, pilgrimage, truthfulness in speech, trustworthiness, honouring parents, maintaining kind relationships with relatives, fulfilling pledges, enjoining good and forbidding evil, striving against disbelievers and hypocrites, beneficence to neighbours, orphans, the poor, <wayfarers,> and slaves and animals,[3] supplication, remembrance of God, recitation of the Qur'ān, and all similar acts. Likewise, the following actions are acts of worship for God: love of God and His Messenger, apprehension before God, turning repentantly to Him, sincerity of religion for Him, patience with His judgement, thankfulness for His bounties, contentment with His decree, reliance on Him, hope for His mercy, fear of His punishment, and all similar states. In fact, worshipping God is for Him the most beloved and pleasing purpose for which He created the creation, as He (Exalted is He) says, 'And I created jinn and humankind only that they should worship Me [alone]' (Q.LI.56).[4]

A DESCRIPTION OF WORSHIPPERS

He [God] sent all the messengers with this beloved purpose as Noah said to his people, '...Worship God! The only deity for you is He...' (Q.VII.59). Similarly, Hūd, Ṣāliḥ, Shuᶜayb and other prophets said this to their people as He (Exalted is He) says, 'We have certainly sent to every nation a messenger, "Worship God and avoid all false deities." Then God guided some of them, while others deserved to be led astray...' (Q.XVI.36) and 'We did not send any messenger before you (Muḥammad) but that We revealed to him, 'There is no deity except I, therefore worship Me alone'' (Q.XXI.25) and 'This is certainly your religious community, a single religious community, and I am your Lord, therefore worship Me alone' (Q.XXI.92) and 'O messengers! Eat good, allowable foods and do righteous deeds, for I am well-acquainted with all that you do; and this is certainly your religious community, a single religious community, and I am your Lord, therefore act piously out of fear of Me' (Q.XXIII.51–52).

God has made worshipping imperative for His messengers until death, as He says, 'Worship your Lord until certainty (*al-yaqīn*) comes to you' (Q.XV.99).[5]

By this special characteristic of worshipping, God describes His angels and prophets as He says, 'Everything in the Heavens and on earth belongs to Him. Those who are in His very presence are not too proud to worship Him and do not become weary. They exalt Him night and day, never slackening to do so' (Q.XXI.19–20) and 'Surely those who are in the very presence of your Lord are not too proud to worship Him; they celebrate His praises, and prostrate before Him' (Q.VII.206).

God disgraces those who are disdainful of worshipping as in His verse, '...Those who are too proud to worship Me will surely enter Hell in humiliation' (Q.XL.60).

God also describes the best of His creation with worship for Him as He (Exalted is He) says, 'The pious worshippers shall surely drink from a cup containing a mixture from *kāfūr*, a fountain from which the worshippers of God will drink, making it flow in unstinted abundance' (Q.LXXVI.5–6) and 'The worshippers of the Infinitely Merciful are those who walk on earth with reverence, and when ignorant ones address them, they say, "Peace!"' (Q.XXV.63).

When Satan said, '...O my Lord, because You sent me astray, I will surely make [disobedience] appear pleasing to them on earth, and I will lead them all astray except Your purified worshippers among them' (Q.XV.39–40), God replied, 'You do not have any power over My worshippers, only over the erring ones who follow you' (Q.XV.42).

Also, when describing the angels with [the attribute of] worship He says, 'They say, "The Infinitely Merciful has taken a son." Glorified be He! They are only honoured worshippers.[6] They do not speak prior to Him, and they act by His command. He knows what is before them and what is behind them, and they cannot intercede except for the one with whom He is pleased; and they tremble apprehensively in awe of Him' (Q.XXI.26–28) and 'They say, "The Infinitely Merciful has taken a son." Indeed, you have brought forth a terrible thing by which the Heavens are almost torn apart and the earth is split asunder and the mountains fall in utter ruin by ascribing a son to the Infinitely Merciful. But it is not suitable for the Infinitely Merciful that He takes a son. Everything in the Heavens and on earth comes to the Infinitely Merciful as a humbled servant. He has taken them all into account and has numbered them accurately. Each of them will come alone to Him on the day of resurrection' (Q.XIX.88–95).

Concerning the Messiah, about whom there are claims of divinity and the sonship[7] of the deity, God says, 'He [Jesus] was only a worshipper to whom We granted Our favour, and We made him a paradigm for the Children of Israel' (Q.XLIII.59). For this reason, the Prophet (may God bless him and grant him peace) said in an authentic *ḥadīth*, 'Do not flatter me as the Christians have flattered Jesus the son of Mary, for I am only a worshipper; therefore say, "The worshipper of God and His Messenger."'[8] God also describes him as being in a state of worship during his most perfect state. He says concerning the Night Journey, 'Glorified is the One who took His worshipper on a journey by night from the Sacred Mosque to the Farthest Mosque, the vicinity of which We have blessed so that We might show him Our signs. He is surely the All-Hearing the All-Seeing' (Q.XVII.1).

He says concerning the conveyance of revelation, 'Thus He revealed to His servant [Gabriel] what he then revealed [to Muḥammad]' (Q.LIII.10).[9]

Also, concerning the act of inviting to Islam, He says, 'When the worshipper of God stood up, calling to Him, they crowded around him' (Q.LXXII.19).[10] Regarding the challenge to those who doubt the mission of the Prophet, He says, 'If you are in doubt concerning what We have sent down to Our worshipper, then produce a sura like this one…' (Q.II.23).

THE COMPONENT PARTS OF WORSHIP

Therefore, the whole of the religion is included in worshipping. It has been confirmed in the *Ṣaḥīḥ*[11] that when Gabriel came to the Prophet in the guise of a Bedouin to ask him about submission (*islām*), faith (*īmān*) and perfect devotion (*iḥsān*),[12] he said, 'Islam is that you testify that there is no deity but God and that Muḥammad is the Messenger of God, and that you establish prayer, pay the legislated almsgiving, observe the fast of Ramadan, and perform the pilgrimage to the Kaʿba if you are able to bear the journey.' Gabriel then said, 'What is faith?' He replied, 'That you believe in God, His angels,

His books, His messengers, the resurrection after death and that you believe in determinism (*qadar*) for good and evil.' Gabriel then said, 'What is perfect devotion?'[13] He replied, 'That you worship God as if you see Him, for though you do not see Him, He surely sees you.' He [Muḥammad] remarked at the end of this *ḥadīth*, 'This was Gabriel. He came to instruct you about your religion.' Thus, he made all of this part of the religion.

The word 'religion' necessarily includes the meaning of subjection and humility. It is said, 'I subjugated him (*dintuhu*) and he became subjugated (*fa-dāna*).' That is, I humbled him (*adhlaltuhu*) and he became humble (*dhalla*). It is said, 'We obey God (*nadīnu Allāh*) and submit to Him (*nadīnu li'Llāh*).' That is, we worship God, we obey Him and subject ourselves to Him. Therefore, the religion of God is worshipping Him, obeying Him, and subjecting oneself to Him.

LOVE COMPLETES THE CONCEPT OF WORSHIP

Worshipping in its original meaning is also humility. It is said that a beaten path (*ṭarīq muʿabbad*) is the path that has been trodden by the trampling of feet. But the worshipping that is commanded necessarily includes the meaning of humility and love (*ḥubb*),[14] for it necessarily includes extreme humility before God with extreme love for Him. The final level of love is enslavement by love (*tatayyum*),[15] and its initial level is attachment (*ʿalāqa*) because the heart is first attached to the beloved. Next is deep affection (*ṣabāba*) because the inclination of the heart is toward the beloved. This is followed by ardent desire (*gharām*), which is an unavoidable love in the heart. Then comes passionate love (*ʿishq*), and finally enslavement by love.[16] Thus it is said that 'the enslaved lover of God' (*taym Allāh*) means 'the worshipper of God' (*ʿabd Allāh*) because the enslaved lover is the one who yields completely to his beloved.

One who submits to a person with hatred is not worshipping him. Also, if he were to love something without submitting to it, he would not be a worshipper of it; this is like a man who loves his son and friend. For this reason neither love nor submission alone are sufficient in worshipping God. Rather, it is obligatory that God is more beloved for a worshipper than everything else and that He is greater for him than all things. Furthermore, nothing deserves love and complete humility[17] except God. For if one's love for something is for other than the sake of God, then his love is corrupt, and if one's reverence of something is without the command of God, then his reverence is false. The Exalted One says, 'Say: If your fathers, your sons, your brothers, your wives, your kindred, the wealth that you have gained, the commerce in which you fear a decline and the dwellings in which you delight, are dearer to you than God and His Messenger and striving hard in His Cause, then wait until God brings about His command. God does not guide rebellious people' (Q.IX.24).

CLASSIFICATION OF EMOTIONS

Thus, general love (*jins al-maḥabba*) is for God and His Messenger. Likewise, obedience is for God and His Messenger and the act of pleasing (*irḍā'*) another is for God and His Messenger, '...But it is more fitting that they please God and His Messenger, if they are believers' (Q.IX.62). Also, the distribution of provisions is for God and His Messenger, 'If only they had been pleased with what God and His Messenger gave them...' (Q.IX.59).

However, worshipping and what is related to it, such as reliance and fear, must be only for God as the Exalted One says, 'Say: O People of the Scripture! Come to a proper agreement between us and you that we worship none but God, that we associate nothing in worship with Him and that none of us shall take others as lords besides God. Then if they turn away, say, "Bear witness that we are Muslims"' (Q.III.64) and 'But if only they had been pleased with what God and His Messenger gave them and had said, "God suffices for us; God and His Messenger will give us of His bounty; we are surely directing our wishes toward God alone"' (Q.IX.59).

Thus the distribution of provisions is the right of God and His Messenger as He says, '. . . Whatever the Messenger gives you, take it, and whatever he forbids you, avoid it; and act piously out of fear of God. God is certainly severe in punishment' (Q.LIX.7).

As for sufficiency (*ḥasb*), which is adequacy (*kāfī*), it is God alone, as the Exalted One says, '[The believers are] those to whom people said, "Men are surely gathering against you, so fear them." But this increased them in faith and they said, "God suffices for us, and how perfect a protector He is"' (Q.III.173) and 'O Prophet! God suffices for you and for any believers who follow you' (Q.VIII.64).

That is, God suffices for you [Muḥammad] and He suffices for those <Muslims[18]> who follow you. Whoever thinks that the meaning is 'the sufficer for you [Muḥammad] is God and the believers together' is surely making a tremendous error. We have explained this elsewhere.[19] Also, the Exalted One says, 'Is not God sufficient for His worshipper?. . .' (Q.XXXIX.36).

PREDESTINATION AND CLASSIFICATION OF HUMANITY

The clarification of this is that the term slave (*ʿabd*) refers to the subjugated one whom God subjugates, humbles, controls and disposes. In this respect, all created beings are actually slaves of God—the pious and the impudent, the believers and the unbelievers, the inhabitants of Heaven and the inhabitants of Hell—for He is the Lord of them all and their Owner. They cannot escape from His creative will (*mashī'a*), His determinism[20] and His perfect words, which no man, pious or sinner, can transgress. Whatever He wills, is, even though they did not will that; and whatever they will, is not, if He has not willed it, as the Exalted One says, 'Do they seek other than the religion of God while all that is in the Heavens and on earth have submitted to Him, willingly or unwillingly? And to Him all shall be returned' (Q.III.83).

He, glorified be He, is the Lord of the worlds, their Creator, the Provider of their sustenance, the One bestowing life to them and the One causing them to die, the Controller of their hearts and the Disposer of their affairs. He is the only Lord they have; they have no owner or creator[21] other than Him. [This is true] whether they acknowledge it or deny it and whether they know it or are ignorant of it. But the faithful believers among them know[22] it and acknowledge it.[23] This is contrary to the one who is ignorant of it or who disavows it while being arrogant toward his Lord. He neither confirms [his status as slave] nor submits to Him, although he knows that God is his Lord and his Creator. For cognising the truth while arrogantly disdaining to accept it, and even disavowing it,[24] is a great torment to such people as the Exalted One says, 'They disavowed them [God's signs] unjustly and arrogantly, though their souls were convinced by them. Then see what was the end of those who acted corruptly' (Q.XXVII.14) and 'Those to whom We gave the scripture recognise him (Muḥammad) as they recognise their sons. But a group of them knowingly conceal the truth' (Q.II.146) and '...But they do not deny you [Muḥammad], rather the transgressors disavow the signs of God (Q.VI.33).

Therefore, if a slave cognises[25] that God is his Lord and his Creator and that he is poor without Him and in need of Him, then he cognises that his worship is related directly to the Lordship of God. Such a slave asks for things from his Lord, beseeches Him and relies on Him. Nevertheless, he still might obey His command or he might disobey it and he still might worship Him while worshipping Satan and idols. This type of worship does not distinguish between the people of Paradise and the people of Hell. With this type of worship a man does not become a believer as God (Exalted is He) says, 'Most [people] only believe in God as polytheists' (Q.XII.106).

Indeed, the pagan Arabs used to confirm that God was their Creator and Provider while worshipping other than Him. God says, 'Certainly, if you ask them, "Who created the Heavens and the earth?" They will say, "God"...' (Q.XXXIX.38) and 'Say: To whom belongs the earth and whatever is on it, if you know? They will say, "To God!" Say: Will you then not be admonished? Say: Who is the Lord of the seven Heavens and the Lord of the Great Throne? They will say, "God!" Say: Will you then not fear God? Say: In whose Hand is the sovereignty of everything and He protects all while against Him there is no protector, if you know? They will say, "God!" Say: How then are you deceived?' (Q.XXIII.84–89).

Most of those who speak about reality and bear witness to it, bear witness to only this reality—the existential reality (*al-ḥaqīqa*[26] *al-kawniyya*)—in which the believer and the disbeliever, the upright and the impudent, participate. They share in the witnessing of it and the cognizance of it. Even Iblīs [Satan] and the people of Hell are cognizant of this reality, '[Iblīs] said, "My Lord! Give me respite then until the day they are resurrected"' (Q.XXXVIII.79), and, 'He said, "O my Lord! Because You sent me astray, I will surely make (disobedience) appear pleasing to them on earth and I will lead them all astray"' (Q.XV.39), and, 'He said, "I swear by Your might that I will lead them all astray"' (Q.XXXVIII.82), and, 'He said, "Do You see this one whom You have honoured above me? If You give me respite until the day of resurrection, I will surely bring his posterity under my authority,[27] all but a few"' (Q.XVII.62). There are many similar statements in which Iblīs confirms that God is his Lord and his Creator and the Creator of all others. Similarly, the people of the Hellfire will say, '...Our Lord! our misfortune overwhelmed us and we were an erring people (Q.XXIII.106). God says, 'If you could see when they [the disbelievers] will be detained in front of their Lord! He will say, "Is not this the truth?" They will confirm, "Yes, by our Lord!"...' (Q.VI.30).

PREDESTINATION AND RELIGIOUS OBLIGATIONS

Thus, whoever limits himself to this existential reality and the witnessing of it and does not perform the religious reality (*al-ḥaqīqa al-dīniyya*) that he is commanded to do—which includes worshipping Him as related to His divinity and obeying His command and the command of His messengers—will be in the same category as

Iblīs and the people of the Hellfire. Moreover, if he thinks that he is one of God's special elite and one of the possessors of cognizance and realisation,[28] one of those who believes that the legislated commands and prohibitions have been waived for them, then he is one of the most evil unbelievers and an apostate. Whoever thinks that Khaḍir[29] and others had the legislated commands waived for them because of witnessing the divine volition and things of this sort, is saying something more evil than the statements of the disbelievers in God and His messengers. He will remain [a disbeliever] until he enters into the second type of meaning of *ʿabd*; that is, a slave who is a worshipper. Then he will be a worshipper of God, not worshipping anything other than Him; he will obey His command and the command of His messengers, act loyally toward the believing, pious saints of God and bear enmity toward the enemies of God.[30] This worshipping is related to the divinity of God. For this reason, the declaration of oneness[31] is 'there is no deity except God.' This stands in contrast to the one who confirms God's Lordship but does not worship Him or who worships another deity alongside Him. For a deity is that which a heart deifies with perfect love, glorification, exaltation, respectfulness, fear, hope and the like.[32] This worshipping is what God loves and approves of, and by which He describes His chosen worshippers, and with which He sent His messengers. As for the other meaning of slave—regardless of whether one admits that status or denies it, it is a meaning that refers to both the believer and the disbeliever.

By differentiating between these two types of *ʿabd*, one can recognise the difference between, on the one hand, the religious realities, and on the other, the existential realities. The religious realities include worshipping God, His religion and His legislated commands. God loves these realities and approves of them and He grants His protection to the people of these realities and honours them accordingly.[33] The existential realities are those in which the believer and disbeliever, the upright and impudent, participate.

Whoever is satisfied with the existential realities without following the religious realities is one of the followers of the cursed Iblīs and one of the rejecters of the Lord of the worlds. Also, whoever is satisfied with them [the religious realities] in certain matters but not in others, or in a certain situation or circumstance but not in another, will have diminished faith in, and friendship with, God, in accordance with the diminishment of the religious realities. This is a serious situation in which many erring persons have been mistaken. Many seekers of the truth have been confused by this to the point that even great scholars associated[34] with realisation, oneness and cognition (*ʿirfān*),[35] have slipped because of it. No one can count their number except God, who knows the concealed and revealed matters.

PREDESTINATION AND FREE WILL

Shaykh ʿAbd al-Qādir[36] (may God be pleased with him), pointed to this matter as is reported from him, 'Many people hold back when they reach the subject of predestination and determinism, but not I. A window to it has been opened for me. I fight the determinations of the truth, by the truth, for the truth. A man is the one who fights determinism, not the one who conforms to it.'[37]

What the shaykh (may God be pleased with him) has mentioned is that which God and His Messenger have commanded. But many people have erred concerning it. Those who err might witness acts of disobedience and sins that have been determined for one of them, or that have been determined for others, even if it is disbelief. They witness that this is occurring through the will of God, His predestination and His determinism, and that it belongs to the judgement stemming from His Lordship and the requirement of His will. They think that submitting to this sin, conforming to it, being pleased with it and the like, is a religion, a path and an act of worship. Thus, they resemble the polytheists who said, '...If God had willed, neither we nor our fathers would have associated partners with Him and we would not have forbidden anything...' (Q.VI.148), and, '...Shall we feed those whom, if God so willed, He could feed?...' (Q.XXXVI.47), and, '...If the Infinitely Merciful had willed, we would not have worshipped them (the angels)...' (Q.XLIII.20).

If they were truly rightly guided, they would know that determinism commands us to be content and patient, despite its being the cause of calamities that afflict us, such as poverty, sickness and fear. The Exalted One says, 'Calamities occur only with God's permission, and He guides aright the heart of whoever believes in God...' (Q.LXIV.11).

Concerning this, some of the Righteous Predecessors said, 'It is the man who has been afflicted by a calamity, but knowing it is from God, is therefore content and at peace with it.' The Exalted One says, 'No calamity occurs on earth or in yourselves but that it is recorded in a book before We bring it forth into existence. That is easy for God. [He informs you of] this in order that you do not grieve over matters that pass you by, nor rejoice over matters that come to you...' (Q.LVII.22–23).

PREDESTINATION AND THE ḤADĪTH OF ADAM AND MOSES

It is reported in the two *Ṣaḥīḥs*[38] that the Prophet (may God bless him and grant him peace) said, 'Adam and Moses had an argument. Moses said, "You are Adam whom God created with His Hand, into whom He breathed by His spirit, to whom He made the angels prostrate, and to whom He taught the names of everything, so why have you expelled us and yourself from Paradise?" Adam replied to him, "You are Moses whom God favoured with His message and His words, have you not found that it had been determined for me before I was created?" Moses said, "Yes, indeed."' He [Muḥammad] said, 'So Adam got the better of Moses in the argument.'

Adam (may God grant him peace) did not argue against Moses by means of determinism and by thinking that a sinner can use determinism as an argument; neither a Muslim nor any intelligent person would say that. If it were an excuse, it would be an excuse for Iblīs as well as for Noah's people, Hūd's people and every disbeliever. Also, Moses did not blame Adam (may God grant him peace) for the sin itself, for God accepted the repentance of Adam,[39] favoured him and guided him. However, he blamed him for the calamity that afflicted them because of the mistake. For this reason, he said to Adam, 'Why have you expelled us and yourself from Paradise?' Adam replied that this had been written before he was created. Thus, an action and the calamity resulting from it are determined and one is obliged to submit to determined calamities. This is an aspect of complete contentment (*min tamām al-riḍā'*) with God as Lord. But as for sins, the worshipper should not be sinful; but if he does sin, he should ask forgiveness from God, repent of all his faults and be patient with calamities, as the Exalted One says, 'And so be patient (Muḥammad), for the promise of God is surely true, and ask forgiveness for your sin...' (Q.XL.55), and, '...But if you remain patient and pious, their cunning will not harm you at all...' (Q.III.120), and, '...And so remain patient and pious, for these are surely aspects of fixed determination' (Q.III.186). Also, Joseph said, '...As for the one who acts piously and is patient, then surely God does not neglect the reward of those who do good' (Q.XII.90).

As for the sins of the worshippers, it is obligatory that a worshipper command right conduct and forbid evil in accordance with his ability. He must strive in the cause of God against disbelievers and hypocrites, give allegiance to God's closest friends and have enmity for God's enemies, and love and hate for God (Exalted is He), as the Exalted One says, 'O you who believe! Do not take My enemies and your enemies as allies, offering them friendship while they disbelieve in the truth that has come to you and drive out the Messenger and yourselves [from Mecca] because you believe in God, your Lord, if you have come forth to strive in My way and to seek My good pleasure. You secretly offer them friendship while I am fully aware of what you conceal and what you reveal; any of you who does that has gone far astray from the right path.

If they gain an advantage over you, they would behave as enemies toward you, striking out at you, cursing you with evil and desiring that you should also become disbelievers. Neither your relatives nor your children will benefit you on the day of resurrection when He will judge among you. God sees all that you do. There is surely an excellent example for you in Abraham and those with him, when they said to their people, "We completely disown you and whatever you worship besides God; we reject you and there will always be hostility and hatred between you and us until you believe in God alone..."' (Q.LX.1–4), and, 'You will not find any people who believe in God and the last day offering friendship to those who oppose God and His Messenger even though they are their fathers, or their sons, or their brothers, or their kindred. These are the ones in whose hearts He has written faith and whom He strengthened with a spirit from Himself...' (Q.LVIII.22), and, 'Shall We then treat the submitting Muslims the same as the criminals?' (Q.LXVIII.35), and, 'Or shall We treat those who believe and do good deeds the same as those who act violently on earth? Or shall We treat those who act piously the same as the wicked?' (Q.XXXVIII.28), and, 'Or do those who seek to do evil deeds think that We shall treat them the same as those who believe and do good deeds, that their present life and after their death [will be the same]? What an awful judgement they make' (Q.XLV.21), and, 'The blind and the seeing are not alike. Darkness and light are not alike. The shade and the sun's full heat are not alike. The living and the dead are not alike...' (Q.XXXV.19–22), and, 'God puts forth a parable: a man belonging to many partners disputing with one another and a man belonging entirely to one master. Are these two equal in comparison?...' (Q.XXXIX.29), and, 'God puts forth a parable: a slave who has no power over anything and a man on whom We have bestowed good provisions from Ourselves and who spends some of it secretly and openly. Can they be equal? Praise be to God! No! And most of them do not know. God puts forth a parable of two men: one of them dumb, having no power over anything and being a burden to his master. Whichever way he directs him, he brings no good. Is such a man equal with one who commands justice and is on a straight path?' (Q.XVI.75–76), and, 'The dwellers of the Fire and the dwellers of Paradise are not equal; the dwellers of Paradise will be successful' (Q.LIX.20).

ANTINOMIANISM AND THE UNITY OF BEING

There are many similar verses in which God makes a distinction between the people of truth and falsehood, the people of obedience and disobedience, the people of righteousness and rebellion, the people of guidance and misguidance, the people of transgression and straightforwardness, and the people of truthfulness and lies. Therefore, the one who witnesses the existential reality without the religious reality will equate these types of people between whom God has made an ultimate distinction until he reaches the point [where[40]] he equates God with idols, as the Exalted One says about them, 'By God, we were truly in manifest error when we held you [false deities] as equals with the Lord of the worlds' (Q.XXVI.97–98).

Moreover, with them the matter reaches the point [where] they equate God with every existing being. They render His exclusive right to be worshipped and obeyed as a right for every existing thing because they make Him to be the existence of created things. This is the greatest disbelief and apostasy, and it is disbelief in the Lord of the slaves.[41] Disbelief with them reaches the point that they do not even bear witness that they are slaves, neither in the meaning of a subjected one nor in the meaning of a worshipper, because they witness that they themselves are the truth. Their false idols (*ṭaghāwīt*), such as Ibn ʿArabī, who wrote *al-Fuṣūṣ* [*al-Ḥikam*], and other slandering apostates such as Ibn Sabʿīn and those like him, have made this unambiguously clear.[42] They also witness that they themselves are both the worshippers and the ones being worshipped.

WITNESSING DETERMINISM AS AN EXCUSE FOR DISOBEDIENCE

But this is not the witnessing of reality—either the existential one or the religious one. Rather, it is deviation and blindness with regard to the witnessing of existential reality, for they have made the existence of the Creator the same as that of the created. They made every blameworthy and praiseworthy quality an attribute of both the Creator and the created, for they consider the existence of the former as being the same as the existence of the latter. But the believers in God and His Messenger, both ordinary and elite, are the people of the Qur'ān, as the Prophet (may God bless him and grant him peace) said, 'God certainly has favoured people among mankind.' He was asked, 'Who are they, O Messenger of God?' He replied, 'The people of the Qur'ān, they are the people of God and His elite.'[43]

These people know that God is the Lord, the Owner and the Creator of everything and that the Creator, Glory be to Him, is different from created beings. He does not reside in them,[44] He is not united with them and His existence is not the same as a created being's existence. In fact, God has declared the Christians to be disbelievers because they speak of an incarnation and unity with the Messiah in particular; how is it then for the one who does this generally with every creature? Furthermore, they[45] know that God orders obedience to Him and to His Messenger and forbids disobedience to Him and to His Messenger. They know that God does not love corruption and does not approve of disbelief on the part of His worshippers; and they know that it is necessary for creation to worship Him, obey His commands and ask for His help in fulfilling them as He says, 'You alone we worship and You alone we ask for help' (Q.I.5).

Commanding good, forbidding evil and striving for the sake of God against the people of disbelief and hypocrisy as much as possible, are part of worshipping God and obeying His command. They [the believers] strive to establish His religion, seeking help from Him in this. In this way, they are repelling and eliminating any evil that has been determined, removing any fearful consequences of that evil. This is the same as the one who removes actual hunger by eating and thereby drives away future hunger. Also, when he alleviates coldness, he repels it by wearing proper clothing. Likewise, he uses every means to drive away any harm just as they [the Companions] said to the Prophet (may God bless him and grant him peace), 'What do you think of the medicines we use to cure ourselves, the invocations we say as remedies and the shields we use to protect ourselves; do they thwart any of God's determinism?' He replied, 'They are aspects of God's determinism.'[46] Also, in another *ḥadīth*, he said, 'Supplications and afflictions confront each other and struggle between Heaven and earth.'[47]

This, then, is the state (*ḥāl*) of the believers in God and in His Messenger and of the worshippers of God. All of this is part of worshipping. Those who witness existential reality, [in other words], the Lordship of Him (Exalted is He) over everything and make it to be an obstruction to following His legislated religious commands are at different levels of being astray. The most extravagant ones use it [witnessing existential reality] unqualifiedly and generally. They use determinism in arguing against anything they oppose in the law. The discourse of these people is more evil than the discourse of the Jews and the Christians, and it is the same type as the discourse of the polytheists who said, '...If God had willed, neither we nor our fathers would have associated partners with Him and we would not have forbidden anything...' (Q.VI.148), and, '...If the Infinitely Merciful had willed, we would not have worshipped them (the angels)...' (Q.XLIII.20).

These people are the most self-contradictory people on earth. Moreover, anyone who argues using determinism [as a justification] is self-contradictory. It is impossible for him to approve of all actions of all people. When a tyrant oppresses [a person] and other people, [when he] spreads corruption through the land, starts shedding the blood of people, allows adultery, destroys civilisation and humanity, or practices any such types of harm that people cannot bear, [that person] must repel aggression and punish the aggressor by resisting his acts of aggression. It should be said to this person, 'If determinism is [acceptable] evidence in an argument, then let anybody do to you and to others whatever he likes. If, however, it is not evidence in arguing, then the premise of your utterance is proven false.'

The people of this kind of discourse who argue by way of existential reality are not consistent in their arguments and do not fully adhere to them. Rather, they act in accordance with their own whims and desires just as a certain scholar said about them, 'As regards obedience, you advocate free will and as regards disobedience, you are a fatalist. Whatever approach fits your desires you take as your approach.'

Another group of them makes a claim [concerning] realisation and cognizance. They assert that commanding and forbidding is only necessary for the one who witnesses in himself a capability to act and confirms in himself a creative power. But as for the one who witnesses that his actions are created or that he is compelled to perform them, and that God is the Disposer concerning him just as He moves all other moving things, [it is the case that] commanding and forbidding and the promise and the threat are removed from him. They might say that whoever witnesses the divine volition has been freed of legal responsibilities. They allege that Khaḍir was freed of legal responsibilities because of his witnessing the divine will. These people differentiate[48] between the common people and the elite, who have witnessed the existential reality. Thus, they witness that God is the Creator of the actions of worshippers and that He is the willer[49] for all beings. They might differentiate between the one who knows that intellectually (*ʿilm^an^*) and the one who has experienced it through witnessing.[50] They do not allow the suspension of legal responsibility for the one who believes in the witnessing of the existential reality and only knows about it, but they suspend it for the one who witnessed it and thus sees no action [as] originating from himself. In this way, these people make fatalism[51] and the affirmation of determinism a waiver for legal responsibility.

THE DELICATE BALANCE OF PREDESTINATION AND FREE WILL

Many sects associated with realisation, cognizance and oneness[52] have faltered concerning this matter. The reason for this is that they possess a narrow understanding (*ḍāqa niṭāquhum*) of the state of a worshipper who has been commanded to act contrarily to what has been determined for him. The understanding of the Muᶜtazila and the rest of the Qadariyya was similarly narrow concerning this matter. Thus, the Muᶜtazila affirmed the legislated commands and prohibitions while rejecting[53] predestination and determinism, which is the general will of God and His creation of a worshipper's deeds. The others affirm predestination but negate commands and prohibitions on behalf of the one who witnesses determinism, for it is impossible for them to negate it unqualifiedly. Their statement is worse than the statement of the Muᶜtazila. For this reason, no such people existed among the Salaf. These people make commands and prohibitions incumbent on unenlightened people (*maḥjūbūn*) who have not witnessed the existential reality. Thus they absolve the one who reaches this truth from the responsibilities of commands and prohibitions, for he is one of the elite. They frequently interpret His verse (Exalted is He) for this purpose, 'Worship your Lord until certainty comes to you' (Q.XV.99).

They interpret certainty (*yaqīn*) as the cognizance of this reality. The statement of these people is clear disbelief although some sects succumbed to this without knowing that it was disbelief. However, it is known by necessity that, according to the religion of Islam, commands and prohibitions are incumbent on every worshipper until he dies, so long as he is in possession of his intellect. Commands and prohibitions cannot be waived for him because of his witnessing determinism, or for any other reason. Thus, whoever does not recognise that must have it made known to him and explained to him. But if he persists in believing in the waiver of commands and prohibitions, he should be executed (*yuqtalu*).[54]

Statements such as these have become quite numerous among later generations. But such statements were not known among the earlier generations of this religious community, for these utterances are in opposition to God and His Messenger, [they are] an act of hostility toward Him, an obstruction on His path, an abandonment of Him, a denial of His messengers and a contradiction to Him in His judgement. Even if one used to say these utterances while being ignorant of this and believing that what he is following is the path of the Messenger and of the saints of God, [who are] the verifiers of truth, he would still be at the level of the one who believes that prayer is not incumbent on him because of his dispensing with it by way of the spiritual states (*al-aḥwāl al-qalbiyya*) that occur to him, or that wine is allowable for him because he is one of the elite who cannot be harmed by drinking it, or that adultery (*fāḥisha*) is allowable for him because he has become like a sea that cannot be spoiled by sin. And there are many similar claims.

DESIRES ARE RESPONSIBLE FOR CLAIMS OF WITNESSING *QADAR*

There is no doubt that the polytheists who denied the messengers fluctuated between innovation, which opposes the legislation of God, and using determinism as an argument to oppose the command of God. Thus, these types of people resemble the polytheists, whether they innovate or use determinism as an argument or combine the two matters; as the Exalted One says about the polytheists, 'When they commit a blatant sin, they say, "We found our fathers doing it and God has commanded us to do so." Say: No! God never commands blatant sins. Do you say of God what you do not know?' (Q.VII.28). And the Exalted One also says about them, 'Those who associate partners with God will say, "If God had willed, neither we nor our fathers would have associated partners with Him and we would not have forbidden anything..."' (Q.VI.148).

What is being mentioned is that the polytheists have introduced innovations in religion, such as permitting prohibitions and acts of worship that God did not legislate as, for example, in His verse, 'They say of their own accord that these cattle and crops are forbidden and that none will eat of them except those whom we allow, and that there are cattle forbidden to use for burden and cattle over which [at slaughter] the Name of God is not pronounced. These are lies attributed to Him (God)...' (Q.VI.138)

Also, in *Sūrat al-Aʿraf* [Q.VII.27–33], there are the verses of the Exalted One, 'O children of Adam! Do not let Satan deceive you in the way he led your parents out of Paradise...When they [the polytheists] commit a blatant sin, they say, "We found our fathers doing it and God has commanded it for us." Say: God does not command blatant sins; do you say of God what you do not know? Say: My Lord has commanded justice and has ordered you to direct yourselves [to Him] in every place of prayer, invoking Him only and being sincere to Him in religion, for as He made you, so too you will return [to Him]...O children of Adam! Wear your finest clothes to every mosque and eat and drink but do not be wasteful. God certainly does not like extravagant wasters. Say: Who has forbidden the adornments and the delightful provisions that God has produced for His worshippers? Say: These things are for those who, in this life, believe with sincerity in the day of resurrection. In this way we explain our signs to a people who know. Say: However, my Lord has forbidden blatant sins in public or private, disobedience, transgressions without just cause, that you associate partners with Him for which He has given no authority, and that you say things about God of which you have no knowledge' (Q.VII.27–33).

These people frequently call what they innovate truth; just as they call the determinism they witness truth. The path of truth according to them is a course of conduct in which its adherent is not restricted to the Legislator's commands and prohibitions. Instead, he restricts himself to whatever he sees, tastes, finds and other such things.[55] These people do not use determinism as an argument unqualifiedly. Rather, their intention is to follow their own opinions and desires, rendering what they see and desire as true. Their command is to follow these without following the commands of God and His Messenger. This is similar to the innovations of the speculative theologians (*Ahl al-Kalām*), such as the Jahmiyya and others, who render the statements which they innovate—which are opposed to the Book and the *Sunna*—as rational truths (*ḥaqā'iq ʿaqliyya*) requiring firm conviction without regard to what the transmitted revelation (*samʿiyyāt*) indicates. As for the Book and the *Sunna*, they either change them from their proper meaning or completely shun them. They do not endeavour to understand them properly or study them intelligently. Rather, they say, 'We entrust their meanings to God,' while believing the contrary of what is indicated by them. When the statements of these people are ascertained, the rational arguments (*ʿaqliyyāt*) that they maintain in opposition to the Qur'ān and the *Sunna* turn out to be ignorant arguments and corrupt beliefs.[56] Likewise, when their statements regarding truths that are opposed to the Qur'ān and the *Sunna* about the saints of God are ascertained, they are found to be vain desires that the enemies of God follow, not His saints.

TASTING FAITH AS OPPOSED TO LOVING ONE'S OWN DESIRES

The origin of misguidance of the one who errs is the prioritising of his reasoning (*taqdīm qiyāsihi*) above the text sent down from God and his choosing desire over following God's commandment. For things such as taste and passion are proportionately related to what a worshipper loves and every lover has a taste and passion related proportionately to his love. Thus, the people of faith have a taste and passion in accordance with what the Prophet (may God bless him and grant him peace) explained by his statement in an authentic *ḥadīth*, 'There are three qualities existing in the one who has found the sweetness of faith: He is the one to whom God and His Messenger are dearer than all else, who loves a person only for the sake of God, and who abhors returning to disbelief after God has rescued him from it as he abhors being cast into fire.'[57] Also, he (may God bless him and grant him peace) said in an authentic *ḥadīth*, 'The one who has tasted the savour of faith is the one who is well-pleased with God as Lord, with Islam as a religion and with Muḥammad as a prophet.'[58] As for the people of disbelief, innovation and lusts, each acts accordingly. It was said to Sufyān b. ʿUyayna,[59] 'What has happened to the people of desires that they have a strong love for their desires?' He replied with these words, or something similar to them, 'Did you forget the saying of God, "...Their hearts absorbed the calf because of their disbelief..."' (Q.II.93). Thus, the worshippers of idols love their false deities, as the Exalted One says, 'Some people set up rivals of God; they love them as they love God. But those who believe, love God more (than those others love their idols)...' (Q.II.165), and, 'But if they do not answer you, then know that they follow only their own lusts. Who is more astray than one who follows his own lusts without guidance from God?...' (Q.XXVIII.50), and, '...They follow only a guess and what their souls desire; and yet guidance from their Lord has already come to them!' (Q.LIII.23).

For this reason, these people incline toward listening to poetry[60] and melodious voices[61] that stimulate an unqualified love that is not appropriate for people of faith. Rather, all these people share in it [unqualified love]: the lover of the Infinitely Merciful, the lover of idols, the lover of the cross, the lover of nations, the lover of the brethren, the lover of beardless youths and the lover of women. These are the ones who follow their own tastes and passions without taking into account the Book, the *Sunna* and the way of the Righteous Predecessors of this religious community. Thus, the one who opposes what God has sent His messengers—which includes worshipping God, obeying Him and obeying His messengers—is not following a religion legislated by God, as He says, 'Then We have put you on the right path in this matter. Follow it and do not follow the desires of those who do not know. They will never benefit you against God, for the unjust disbelievers are protectors to one another; but God is the protector of those who act piously' (Q.XLV.18–19). He is actually following his own desire without any guidance from God, as the Exalted One says, 'Or do they have partners who have legislated for them in religion what God has not allowed?...' (Q.XLII.21).

THE GROUPS THAT ERR CONCERNING *QADAR*

In following desires, [at] one moment they are following an innovation that they call truth, which they prioritise above God's law, and [at] another moment they use determinism as related to existence (*al-qadar al-kawnī*) as an argument against God's law, as He (Exalted is He) has mentioned above about the polytheists. One group of these people is of the highest rank because they hold fast to religion[62] in the performance of well-known obligations and the avoidance of well-known prohibitions. However, they err greatly by abandoning the means [of worship] (*asbāb*) that they were commanded to carry out, and which are themselves acts of worship. They think that the cognizant one, when witnessing determinism, turns away from these means as, for example, [is the case for] the one who consigns reliance,[63] supplications and all such means to the stations of the common people but not to those of the elite, understanding that whoever witnesses determinism will know that what has been determined will be, so there is no need for these [actions]. This is a tremendous error, for God has determined things by their causes just as He has determined happiness and misfortune by their causes; as the Prophet (may God bless him and grant him peace) said, 'God has created a people for Paradise, having created it for them while they were still in their fathers' loins, and so they do the work of the people of Paradise; and He has created a people for Hell, having created it for them while they were still in their fathers' loins, and so they do the work of the people of Hell.'[64] Also, when the Prophet (may God bless him and grant him peace) informed them (the Companions) that God has recorded the determined measures of all things, they said, 'O Messenger of God! Should we not abandon work and just rely on the Book?' He replied, 'No! Work! For everyone is eased toward that for which he was created. The one who is of the people of happiness will be eased toward the work of the people of happiness, while the one who is of the people of misfortune, will be eased toward the work of the people of misfortune.'[65] Thus, the means that God has ordered for His worshippers are acts of worship, and reliance is associated with worshipping, as in the verses of the Exalted One, '...So worship Him and rely on Him...' (Q.XI.123), and, '...Say: He [God] is my Lord! There is no deity but He! I rely on Him and my repentance is to Him' (Q.XIII.30). And there is the statement of Shuᶜayb, '... I rely on Him and I repent to Him' (Q.XI.88).

There is another group that abandons recommended actions but not obligations. Therefore, they are diminished [in faith] in accordance with that.

There is yet another group that is deceived by the extraordinary events that occur to them, such as an unveiling (*mukāshafa*), or an answer to a supplication that borders on the miraculous and other such things.[66] Hence, a person of this group becomes distracted from acts of worship, gratitude and similar things that he is commanded to perform.[67] These matters frequently occur to the people of traversing and concentration (*Ahl al-Sulūk wa'l-Tawajjuh*).[68] A worshipper can only save himself from these matters by adhering in each moment[69] to God's command with which He sent His Messenger, as Zuhrī said, 'Those of our predecessors who have passed on used to say that clinging to the *Sunna* is a salvation.' This is so because the *Sunna*, as Mālik (may God be pleased with him) has said, is like the ark of Noah, for whoever rides it will be rescued and whoever misses it will drown.

THE TWO PRINCIPLES OF PERFECT WORSHIP

There is only one meaning for terms such as worshipping, obedience, uprightness and holding fast to the straight path, but they are based on two main principles. The first is that only God is to be worshipped and the second is that the worshipper must worship Him in the way that He commanded and legislated. He should not worship Him based on any other principles such as desires and innovations.[70] The Exalted One says, '...and so whoever hopes for the meeting with his Lord, let him do righteous work and not associate anyone in worshipping his Lord' (Q.XVIII.110), and, 'Certainly, whoever submits himself fully to God as a perfect devotee has his reward with his Lord; no fear will come to them and they shall not grieve' (Q.II.112), and, 'Who is better in religion than one who submits himself fully to God as a perfect devotee and who follows the way of Abraham as a sincere worshipper of God? Indeed, God took Abraham as an intimate friend' (Q.IV.125).

The righteous deed is perfect devotion, which is the performance of the best deeds; and the best deeds are those that God and His Messenger love. These are the obligatory acts and recommended acts that have been commanded by God and His Messenger, and which are not some unlegislated innovation in religion,[71] for God and His Messenger do not love these. They are neither the best deeds nor are they righteous deeds. This is similar to what are known as rebellious acts,[72] such as blatant sins and injustice. These matters are never considered to be good or righteous deeds.

As for His statements, 'and not associate anyone in worshipping his Lord' (Q.XVIII.110), and, 'Who submits himself fully to God' (Q.II.112 and Q.IV.125), they refer to the sincerity of religion for God alone. ʿUmar b. al-Khattāb (may God be pleased with him) used to say, 'O God! Make the whole of my deed righteous, make it pure for Your countenance and do not give anyone else a share of it.' Fuḍayl b. ʿIyāḍ[73] said the following about His verse, '...that He [God] may test you as to which of you is the best devotee in actions...' (Q.LXVII.2): '[The best deed] is the most sincere and the most proper. They asked, "O Abū ʿAlī! What is the most sincere and the most proper deed?" He said, "A deed that is sincere but not proper is not accepted and one that is proper but not sincere is not accepted. [There is no acceptance of deeds] until they are both sincere and proper. Sincerity means that they are for God alone and proper means that they are in compliance with the *Sunna*."'

GRAMMATICAL ANALYSIS OF THE COMMANDS TO WORSHIP

Now, were it said that if all that God loves is included in the term worshipping, why did He syntactically coordinate other terms with it, such as in His verses, 'You alone we worship and You alone we ask for help' (Q.I.5), and, '...So worship Him and rely on Him...' (Q.XI.123)? And there is the statement of Noah, 'Worship God and act piously out of fear of Him, and obey me' (Q.LXXI.3). There are similar statements from other messengers.

The response is that this occurs frequently [in the Qur'ān], as in the verses of God, '...Verily, prayer prevents blatant sin and reprehensible deeds...' (Q.XXIX.45), and, 'God surely commands justice, perfect devotion and giving to relatives; and He forbids blatant sin, reprehensible deeds and transgression...' (Q.XVI.90). In this verse, 'giving to relatives' is a part of justice and perfect devotion, just as 'blatant sin' and 'transgression' are aspects of reprehensible deeds. Also, there is His verse, 'And those who hold fast to the Book and are constant at prayer...' (Q.VII.170). However, being constant at prayer is one of the greatest forms of holding fast to the Book. Also, there is His verse, '...They used to rush to do good deeds and to call on Us with hope and fear...' (Q.XXI.90). The supplication [performed] with hope and fear is part of doing good deeds. Similar examples to these are numerous throughout the Qur'ān.

The use of syntactic coordination sometimes occurs when one of two terms is considered as a part of the other; thus, it is coordinated to the other term as a specification relevant to the need to make known a general meaning and a specific meaning. At other times, the meaning indicated by the term varies according to the [grammatical] rules for separating and associating [terms]: when the term is separate, its meaning is general, but when it is in association with another term, it has a specific meaning. For example, this occurs with the terms 'poor' (*faqīr*) and 'needy' (*miskīn*) as in these verses of the Exalted One, '[Charity is] for the poor (*fuqarā'*), who in God's cause are restricted [from travel]...' (Q.II.273), and, '...Feeding ten needy persons (*masākīn*)...' (Q.V.89). When one of these [terms] is used separately the meaning of the other is included in it. However, when they are associated with each other, as in this verse of the Exalted One, 'Charity is only for the poor and the needy...' (Q.IX.60), they have two distinct meanings.

It is [sometimes] said that when a specific term is coordinated with a general one, the condition of association is not included in the meaning of the general term; rather, it is part of this [condition of separation]. But the truth is that this is not necessarily so. The Exalted One says, 'Whoever is an enemy to God, His angels, His messengers, Gabriel and Michael...' (Q.II.98), and, '[Remember] when We made the covenant with the prophets and with you [Muḥammad] and with Noah, Abraham, Moses and Jesus, the son of Mary' (Q.XXXIII.7).

Mentioning the specific with the general can be for a variety of reasons. Sometimes a specific term might have a unique quality that does not exist in the other components of the general [term], as in the case of Noah, Abraham, Moses and Jesus. At other times, the general term might be indefinite and one cannot understand what details are contained in the general meaning, as in His verse, '...A guidance to those who act piously, who believe in the unseen, are constant at prayer and spend out of what We have provided for them, who believe in what has been sent down to you [Muḥammad] and in what was sent down before you…' (Q.II.2–4).

His statement, 'Who believe in the unseen,' comprises all the unseen in which one should believe. However, it is undefined. There is no indication that part of the unseen includes things such as 'in what has been sent down to you [Muḥammad] and in what was sent down before you.' [The statement, 'Who believe in the unseen'] might also mean that they believe in that which is reported, which is the unseen, and in the act of reporting about the unseen, which is 'what has been sent down to you [Muḥammad] and what was sent down before you.' Also [included] under this topic are the verses of the Exalted One, 'Recite what is revealed to you from the Book and be constant at prayer…' (Q.XXIX.45), and, 'Those who hold fast to the Book and are constant at prayer…' (Q.VII.170).

The recitation of the Book clearly means following it.[74] This is just as Ibn Masᶜūd said concerning His verse, 'Those to whom We have given the Book recite it with a true recitation…' (Q.II.121): 'They allow what it allows, they forbid what it prohibits, they believe in its obscure passages and they implement its firm commands.' Therefore, following the Book includes prayer and other duties. However, He specifically mentions prayer because of its distinguishable qualification. Likewise, there is His statement to Moses, 'In truth! I am God, there is no deity but I, so worship Me and be constant at prayer for My remembrance' (Q.XX.14). Here being constant at prayer for the remembrance of Him is one of the most exalted forms of worshipping Him. Also, there are the verses of the Exalted One, '…Act piously out of fear of God and always say what is righteous' (Q.XXXIII.70), and, '…Act piously out of fear of God and seek the means of approach to Him…' (Q.V.35), and, '…Act piously out of fear of God and be with the truthful ones' (Q.IX.119). All these matters are part of the perfection of acting piously out of fear of God. Also, there is His verse, '…So worship Him and rely on Him…' (Q.XI.123). Reliance and seeking help are aspects of worshipping God; however, they are specifically mentioned so that the worshipper may strive to attain them because of their special qualifications. This is [the case] because they are the means of assistance [in performing] all other aspects of worshipping, for He cannot be worshipped without His help.

SUMMARY OF THE DESCRIPTION OF PERFECT WORSHIP

If all of this is clear, then the perfection of the created being lies in the realisation of his worshipping God. The more a worshipper increases the realisation of worship, the more his perfection will increase and his rank will rise. Whoever imagines that a created being can escape from worship by any means, or that departing from it is more perfect, will be one of the most ignorant and erring of all creation. The Exalted One says, 'They say, "The Infinitely Merciful has taken a son." Glorified be He! They are only honoured worshippers. They do not speak before Him and they act by His command. He knows what is before them and what is behind them, and they cannot intercede except for the one with whom He is pleased; and they tremble apprehensively in awe of Him' (Q.XXI.26–28), and, 'They say, "The Infinitely Merciful has taken a son." You have surely brought forth a terrible thing by which the Heavens are almost torn apart and the earth is split asunder and the mountains fall in utter ruin, that you ascribe a son to the Infinitely Merciful. But it is not suitable for the Infinitely Merciful that He takes a son. Everything in the Heavens and on earth comes to the Infinitely Merciful as a humbled servant. He has taken them all into account and has numbered them accurately; and each of them will come alone to Him on the day of resurrection' (Q.XIX.88–95). The Exalted One says concerning the Messiah, 'He [Jesus] was only a worshipper to whom We granted Our favour and We made him an example for the Children of Israel' (Q.XLIII.59).

The Exalted One also says, 'Everything in the Heavens and on earth belongs to Him. Those who are in His very presence are not too proud to worship Him and do not weary [of it]. They exalt Him night and day, never slackening' (Q.XXI.19–20), and, 'The Messiah will never be disdainful of being a worshipper of God and neither will the angels who are near [to Him]. As for the one who is disdainful of worshipping Him and too proud for it, He will gather them all together to Himself. Then as for those who believe and do righteous deeds, He will give them their rewards and increase His bounty to them. But as for those who are disdainful and proud, He will punish them severely and they will not find any protector or helper for themselves besides God' (Q.IV.172–173), and, 'Your Lord said, 'Invoke Me and I will respond to you. Those who are too proud to worship Me will surely enter Hell in humiliation' (Q.XL.60), and, 'Some of His signs are the night and the day and the sun and the moon. Do not prostrate to the sun and the moon, but prostrate to God who created them, if you worship only Him. But if they are too proud for this, then those who are with your Lord glorify Him night and day, and they never tire' (Q.XLI.37–38), and, 'Remember your Lord in your soul, humbly and fearfully, without loudness in words, in the morning and in the evening; and do not be one of the neglectful ones. Surely those who are near to your Lord are not too proud to worship Him, they glorify Him and prostrate themselves before Him' (Q.VII.205–206).

Verses in which worshipping is ascribed to the best of creation, and in which those who deviate from it are condemned, are numerous in the Qur'ān. In fact, God states that He sent all the messengers with it. The Exalted One says, 'We did not send any messenger before you [Muḥammad] but that We revealed to him, "There is no deity except I, therefore worship Me alone"' (Q.XXI.25), and, 'We have certainly sent to every nation a messenger, "Worship God and avoid all false deities." Then God guided some of them, while others deserved to be led astray…' (Q.XVI.36).

The Exalted One said to the Children of Israel, 'O My worshippers who believe! My earth is certainly spacious. Therefore worship

Me alone' (Q.XXIX.56), and, '...and act piously out of fear of Me' (Q.II.41), and, 'O people! Worship your Lord Who created you and those who were before you, perhaps you will act piously' (Q.II.21), and, 'I created jinn and humankind only that they should worship Me alone' (Q.LI.56), and, 'Say: I have certainly been commanded to worship God, making religion pure for Him only; and I have been commanded to be foremost among the Muslims. Say: I surely fear, if I should disobey my Lord, the torment of a great day. Say: I worship God, making my religion pure for Him. Then worship what you like besides Him...' (Q.XXXIX.11–15).

Every messenger began his mission with the invitation to worship God, as in the statement of Noah and those who came after him, '...Worship God! There is no other deity for you but He...' (Q.VII.59).

Also, in the *Musnad*[75] it is reported from Ibn ᶜUmar (may God be pleased with him) from the Prophet (may God bless him and grant him peace) who said, 'I was sent with a sword just before the last hour so that God will be worshipped alone, with no partner. My sustenance was made under the shadow of my spear, and humiliation and lowliness were made for those who disobey my order.' He has shown that His worshippers are those who will find safety from Satan.[76] Satan says, '...O my Lord! Because You sent me astray, I will surely make [disobedience] appear pleasing to them on earth and I will lead them all astray except Your purified worshippers among them' (Q.XV.39–40). God, the Exalted, replied, 'You do not have any power over My worshippers, only over the astray ones who follow you' (Q.XV.42). Also, he [Satan] says, '...I swear by Your might that I will lead them all astray except Your chosen worshippers among them' (Q.XXXVIII.82–83).

He says concerning the truth of Joseph (peace be upon him), '...[We did this so] that We might turn evil and blatant sin away from him. Surely he was one of Our chosen worshippers' (Q.XII.24). He also says, 'Glory be to God, exalted above what they ascribe excepting the chosen worshippers of God' (Q.XXXVII.159–160), and, 'He [Satan] certainly has no power over those who believe and rely on their Lord. His power is only over those who take him as a friend and those who associate partners to Him [God]' (Q.XVI.99–100).

He describes those whom He has chosen from His creation, as in the verses of the Exalted One, 'Remember Our worshippers, Abraham, Isaac and Jacob, men of strength and understanding. We purified them for a special purpose: the remembrance of the hereafter' (Q.XXXVIII.45–46), and, '...and remember Our worshipper David, a man of strength; he was a sincere penitent' (Q.XXXVIII.17). He says concerning Solomon, '...how excellent a worshipper; he was a sincere penitent' (Q.XXXVIII.30). [He says] concerning Job, '...how excellent a worshipper; he was a sincere penitent' (Q.XXXVIII.44), and, 'Remember Our worshipper, Job, when he invoked his Lord...' (Q.XXXVIII.41). He says concerning Noah (peace be upon him), 'The offspring of those whom We carried with Noah; he certainly was a grateful worshipper' (Q.XVII.3).

He also says, 'Glorified is He who took His worshipper [Muḥammad] for a journey by night from the Sacred Mosque [of Mecca] to the Farthest Mosque [in Jerusalem]...' (Q.XVII.1), and, 'When the worshipper of God stood up, calling to Him...' (Q.LXXII.19), and, 'If you are in doubt concerning what We have sent down to Our worshipper...' (Q.II.23), and, 'Thus He [God] revealed to His servant [Gabriel] what he revealed' (Q.LIII.10), and, 'A fountain from which the worshippers of God will drink...' (Q.LXXVI.6), and, 'The worshippers of the Infinitely Merciful are those who walk on earth with reverence...' (Q.XXV.63). There are many verses that are similar to these in the Qur'ān.

PART II

The Slavery of a Heart

SECTION (*FAṢL*). Now that this [discussion] has been clarified for you, it should be known that people[77] differ greatly concerning this topic of worship. Their differences are according to the reality of faith and in this way they are divided into general and specific types. For this reason, with regard to the Lordship[78] of the Lord (Glory be to Him), people have generality, specificity and variety.[79] Thus, in this religious community, polytheism is more hidden than the crawling of an ant.[80] It is narrated in the *Ṣaḥīḥ*[81] from the Prophet (may God bless him and grant him peace) that he said: 'May the slave (*ʿabd*) of the dirham be wretched; may the slave of the dinar be wretched; may the slave of velvet cloth be wretched; may the slave of embroidered cloth be wretched. May he be wretched and degraded, and if such a one is pierced with a thorn, let it not be extracted. When he is granted his desires he is pleased and when he is denied them he is angered.'

The Prophet (may God bless him and grant him peace) labelled this person a worshipper of the dirham, a worshipper of the dinar, a worshipper of velvet cloth and a worshipper of embroidered cloth. In this *ḥadīth* he mentioned a supplication against and a description of [this person] by saying, 'May he be wretched and degraded, and if such a one is pierced with a thorn, let it not be extracted.' Extraction is the act of removing a thorn from a man and tweezers are the means by which a thorn is removed. This *ḥadīth* refers to the condition of the one who, when evil afflicts him, does not escape it and is not successful because he is wretched and degraded. Thus, he has neither attained his goal nor avoided harm. This is the state of the slave of wealth. He is so described because 'when he is granted his desires, he is pleased and when he is denied them, he is angered,' as the Exalted One says, 'Some of them accuse you (Muḥammad) concerning the matter of distributing alms, for if they are given something, they are pleased; but if they are not given anything, they suddenly are enraged' (Q.IX.58).

Thus, their contentment is for other than God and their rage is for other than God. This is the state of the one who is attached to positions of leadership, to an image, or to similar desires of the self. If he attains them, he is pleased and if he does not attain them, he is angered. Therefore, he is a worshipper of what he desires and a slave (*raqīq*) to it; for slavery and worship are in reality the slavery and worship of a heart. Thus, one is a worshipper to whatever enslaves one's heart and subdues it. For this reason it is said, 'The slave is a free man as long as he is content, and the free man is a slave as long as he is greedy.' Also, a poet said, 'I obeyed my desires, thus they subdued me; and if I had been content, I would have been free.'

It is said that greediness is an iron collar around the neck and a fetter around the leg. If the iron collar vanishes from around the neck, the fetter will also vanish from around the leg. It is narrated that ʿUmar b. al-Khaṭṭāb (may God be pleased with him) said, 'Greediness is poverty and renunciation is richness. If one of you renounces a thing, he will have no need of it.'

A person will find this condition [of greed and renunciation] within himself. If he has renounced a thing, then he will certainly not seek it or desire it. His heart will not remain in need of it or the person who might supply it. However, when a person has a desire concerning a certain matter and hopes for it, his heart becomes attached to it. Then he will be in need of obtaining it and whoever he believes might be the cause of obtaining it. This is the case for things such as wealth, fame and images. Al-Khalīl [Abraham] (May God bless him and grant him peace) said, '...therefore seek your provisions from God alone, worship Him and be grateful to Him, for you will be returned to Him' (Q.XXIX.17).

THE MEANING OF RELIANCE ON GOD

A slave must have provisions, for he is in need of them.[82] Thus, when he seeks his provisions from God, he becomes a worshipper of God and in need of Him. But when he seeks them from a created being, he becomes a worshipper of that created being and in need of him. For this reason, requesting things from a created being has been forbidden in principle and is only allowed under [conditions of] necessity. There are many *ḥadīths* in the *Ṣiḥāḥ*, *Sunan* and *Masānīd* about the prohibition of request[ing provisions].[83] He [Muḥammad] (may God bless him and grant him peace) said, 'Some of you will continue begging (*mas'ala*) so that on the day of resurrection you will come without any flesh on your faces.'[84] He said, 'Whoever begs from people while having enough [provisions] will have scratches on his face because of his begging.'[85] He said, 'Begging is only allowable when there is horrendous debt, debilitating injury, or emaciating poverty.'[86] This meaning is in the *Ṣaḥīḥ*, which also contains [the saying], 'It is better for one of you to take his rope and go to chop wood [for his livelihood] than to beg from people, whether they give him anything or deny him.'[87] He said, 'Whatever wealth comes to you without begging for it or aspiring to it, you may take. But do not let your soul follow any other wealth.'[88]

Thus, the Prophet disliked the taking of money based on a verbal request or an aspiration of the heart. He said in an authentic *ḥadīth*, 'God shall enrich whoever dispenses (with riches). God will make chaste the one who seeks chastity. God will grant surety to whoever is patient. No one has been given a gift better and more ample than patience.'[89] He also commanded his special companions not to request anything from people in principle. It is reported in the *Musnad* that when Abū Bakr al-Ṣiddīq (may God be pleased with him) used to drop <a whip[90]> from his hand, he would not ask anyone to give it to him, but would say, 'My intimate friend commanded me not to ask people for anything.' It is reported in *Ṣaḥīḥ Muslim* and elsewhere from ʿAwf b. Mālik that when the Prophet (may God bless him and grant him peace) accepted the pledge of allegiance from him and others, he whispered to them a secret saying, 'Do not ask people for anything.'[91] Thereafter, when a person of that group used to drop a whip from his hand, he would not say to anyone, 'Give it to me.' Thus the texts have indicated in many places that what has been commanded is to ask the Creator and what has been prohibited is to ask the created being, as His verse states, 'And so when you finish your obligations, persist in supplications; and make humble requests of your Lord' (Q.XCIV.7–8).

The Prophet (may God bless him and grant him peace) said to lbn ʿAbbās, 'When you ask for something, ask it of God; and when you seek help, seek it from God.'[92] The same thing appears in the statement of al-Khalīl [Abraham] (upon whom be peace), '...therefore seek from God alone your provisions...' (Q.XXIX.17). He did not say, 'seek your provisions from God,' because the pre-positioning of an adverb implies particularisation and restriction.[93] The meaning of the verse is the same as saying, 'Do not seek provisions except from God.' He, the Exalted, says, '...ask God for a portion His bounty...' (Q.IV.32).

A person must acquire the provisions he needs and he must prevent what harms him. It has been legislated for him that these two matters are to be supplicated from God. Thus, he should direct his requests to Him and complain only to Him,[94] as Jacob said, '...I complain of my grief and sorrow only to God...' (Q.XII.86).

PATIENCE AND RENOUNCEMENT

God (Exalted is He) mentions in the Qur'ān an honourable leaving, an honourable patience and an honourable forgiveness.[95] It is said that an honourable leaving is leaving without hurting anyone; an honourable forgiveness is forgiving without blaming anyone; and an honourable patience is patience without complaining to any created being. For this reason, it was mentioned to Aḥmad b. Ḥanbal during his sickness that Ṭāwūs[96] used to hate the moaning of a sick man and used to say it was a complaint. Thereafter, Aḥmad b. Ḥanbal did not groan until he died. But as for complaining to the Creator (Glory be Him), it does not contradict honourable patience, for Jacob, peace be upon him, said, '...Then an honourable patience (is best for me)...' (Q.XII.18 and 83) and '...I complain of my grief and sorrow only to God...' (Q.XII.86).

ᶜUmar b. al-Khaṭṭāb (may God be pleased with him) used to recite the suras *Yūnus* (Q.X), *Yūsuf* (Q.XII) and *al-Naḥl* (Q.XVI) in the dawn prayer. When he passed [the] verse [quoted above],[97] he cried so that his sobbing[98] was heard in the last rows. There is also the supplication of Moses (peace be upon him), 'O God! All praises are for You; all complaints are directed to You. You are the One from whom help is sought, from whom succour is sought and on whom is all reliance. There is no strength nor power except with You.'[99]

There is also the supplication that the Prophet (may God bless him and grant him peace) made when the people of Ṭā'if acted against him:

> O God! To You alone I complain of my helplessness, the paucity of my resources and my insignificance before mankind. O most Merciful One, You are the Lord of the oppressed and You are my Lord! O God! To whom would You entrust me? To a stranger who would scowl at me? To an enemy to whom You have given control over my affairs? But if Your wrath does not fall upon me, I am not concerned by it. For Your pardon is enough for me. I seek refuge in the light of Your countenance—by which all darkness is illuminated and due to which all affairs in this world and in the hereafter are right—should Your anger descend upon me or Your wrath afflict me. To You alone belongs the right of censure until You are pleased, for there is no power nor strength except with You.[100]

The more a worshipper's desire is strengthened concerning God's graciousness, mercy and pleasure in order to fulfil his need and prevent harm from reaching him, the more his worship of Him and his freedom from others increases. Similarly, his desire for a created being necessitates his worship of it, and his dispensing with it necessitates the renouncement of his heart for it. And so it is said,

'Dispense with whomever you will and you become his equal; have graciousness for whomever you will and you become his master; and have a need for whomever you will and you become his captive.' Likewise, the desire of a worshipper for his Lord and his hope in Him necessitates his worship of Him, and the aversion of his heart from asking God[101] and hoping in Him necessitates the diversion of his heart from the worship of God. This is particularly so for the one who has hope in a created being and not in the Creator. It occurs in such a way that his heart is dependent on his leadership position, his soldiers, his followers and his possessions, or on his family and friends, or on his wealth and treasures, or on his leaders and nobles such as his master, king, shaykh, employer, or any of those who have died or will die. He, the Exalted, says, 'Rely on the Living One who will never die and celebrate His praise; and it suffices that He is well informed about the sins of His worshippers' (Q.XXV.58).

Whoever attaches his heart to created beings so that they render him victorious, provide him with provisions or guide him, has a heart that surrenders to them. It becomes engaged in worshipping them according to the level of that submission, although in appearance he is the master, manager[102] and administrator over [those created beings]. But a thinking person looks at realities and not at appearances. Thus, when a man's heart becomes attached to a woman—even if she is lawful to him—it remains her captive; she has control over him[103] and manipulates him as she wills. In appearance he is her lord because he is her husband,[104] but in reality he is her captive and is possessed by her. This is particularly so when she is aware[105] of his need and passion (*ʿishq*) for her and [knows] that he will not substitute another woman for her. So she controls him in the same way [that] a domineering, oppressive master [controls] a dominated slave who cannot escape from him. It is even worse than this because the captivity of [the] heart is more severe than the captivity of [the] body and the subjugation of [the] heart is more severe than the subjugation of [the] body. For whoever is <physically[106]> subjugated, enslaved and captured[107] does not care when[108] his heart finds rest and serenity from that; moreover, there [always] exists the possibility of escape.

But when a heart, which is master <of the body[109]>, is subdued, enslaved and enthralled by love for [what is] other than God, then this is pure humiliation, captivity and [a form of] <degrading[110]> worship [made] to that which has subdued the heart. The state of a heart's worship and its captivity form the basis on which reward or punishment will be established. If a Muslim is captured by an unbeliever or is unjustly enslaved by an immoral person (*fājir*), it will not harm him so long as he can fulfil the obligations required of him. And whoever is legally subjugated while continuing to fulfil the rights of God and the rights of his master will be rewarded twice. Even if he is forced to declare [his] disbelief, [if he] pronounces it while keeping faith secure in his heart, [then] that will not harm him. But the one whose heart is subdued, thereby becoming a slave for [what is] other than God, will be harmed[111] by that, even if outwardly he is a king over the people. For freedom (*ḥurriyya*) is the freedom of the heart, and slavery (*ʿubūdiyya*) is the slavery of the heart. Similarly, richness is the richness of the heart. The Prophet (may God bless him and grant him peace) said, 'Richness is not how much wealth you have, but the richness of the soul.'[112]

FREEDOM AND PASSIONATE LOVE

This *ḥadīth*, by my life,[113] refers to when a person's heart is subjugated by an allowable image. [But] as for the one whose heart is subjugated by an unlawful image, [such as] a woman or a youth, then this is a torment that has no recompense.[114] These people are among the least rewarded and the most severely punished. Thus the one who is passionate (*ʿāshiq*)[115] toward an image and remains[116] attached to it and subdued by it, will be surrounded by all kinds of evil[117] and corruption that only the Lord of all slaves can count, even if he were safeguarded from committing the greatest blatant sin. For the continuous attachment of a heart to (an image) without committing a blatant sin is more harmful to him than committing a sin and then repenting of it, thus removing its trace from his heart. These people are similar to drunkards or to the insane, as it is said, 'A drunkard becomes intoxicated on passion or on wine, but though he tries to recover from the first, he is still out of his mind.' Elsewhere it is said, 'They said you were driven insane by that for which you have a passion. I replied, "Passion is more powerful than what affects the insane. As for passion, the obsessed one will never overcome this fate, whereas, only occasionally do the insane succumb to their insanity."'

THE WILL TO ACT LEADS TO TASTING FAITH

One of the greatest afflictions[118] is a heart's turning away from God. For when a heart tastes the savour of worshipping God and sincerity toward Him, then nothing will ever be sweeter, more delightful[119] and more enjoyable than that. A person will only leave a beloved thing for another beloved thing that is more beloved to him than the former or out of fear of a disliked thing. Therefore, a heart will only turn away from a corrupt love because of a righteous love or because of a fear of harm. The Exalted One says concerning the truth of Joseph (peace be upon him), '...thus [We showed him proof] in order to divert evil and blatant sin from him; he was certainly one of Our sincere worshippers' (Q.XII.24).

Thus, God deflects from His worshipper any inclination for, and attachment to, an image that could be evil for him. He also turns blatant sin away from him by replacing it with sincerity toward God. For this reason, before he tastes the sweetness of worship for God and sincerity toward Him, a worshipper's soul must gain mastery[120] over following its desires. Once he tastes the savour of sincerity, and it grows stronger in his heart, his passion will submit to him without any effort. God (Exalted is He) says, '...prayer certainly prevents blatant sins and reprehensible deeds, and the remembrance of God is greater...' (Q.XXIX.45).

Prayer is capable of repulsing harmful things, such as blatant sins and evil deeds, and it is capable of obtaining a beloved thing;[121] namely, the remembrance of God. The attainment of this beloved thing is greater than the repulsion of those harmful things, for the remembrance of God and a heart's worship of God [122] are goals in themselves (*maqsūda li-dhātihi*). However, repulsing evil from oneself is a goal for other than itself (*maqṣūd li-ghayrihi*), as a matter of [logical] subordination. A heart is a creature that loves the truth, wants it and seeks it. But when a desire for evil confronts it, a heart seeks the repulsion of that because a heart becomes corrupt just as cultivated land becomes corrupt with thickets. For this reason, He (Exalted is He) says, 'He who sanctifies it [his soul] surely succeeds; and he who corrupts it surely fails' (Q.XCI.9–10), and, 'He who sanctifies himself, remembers the Name of his Lord and performs prayer shall surely achieve success' (Q.LXXXVII.14–15), and, 'Tell the believing men to lower their gaze and preserve their chastity, that is purer for them...' (Q.XXIV.30), and, '...And had it not been for God's favour and His mercy on you, not one of you would have ever been purified...' (Q.XXIV.21).

Thus, He (Glory be to Him) has made lowering the gaze and preserving chastity the best means of purifying of the soul.[123] He has also explained that avoiding blatant sins is part of purifying the soul. The purification of souls necessarily includes the cessation of all evils such as blatant sins, injustice, polytheism and lying. Likewise, the heart of the seeker of leadership and domination on earth is a slave (*raqīq*) to those who help him. Although outwardly he is their leader and the one who is obeyed by them, in reality he has hope in them and fears them. Thus, he offers them wealth and governorships and pardons them[124] so that they will obey him and assist him. Therefore he appears to be an obeyed leader while in fact he is their obedient slave (*ʿabd*). The fact is that both groups manifest worship of each other and both have strayed from the reality of worshipping God. When they help each other to gain unjust domination on earth, then they are the same as those who help each other to commit blatant sins or to obstruct the path [of worship]. Hence, each of them desires that which subjugates him and enslaves him[125] to the other.

This is also the case of the seeker of wealth, for this <wealth[126]> subjugates and enslaves him. These cases are of two types. The first type of wealth is that for which a worshipper has a need, such as for food, drink, housing and marriage. He seeks these from God and requests them of Him. Thus, he uses this wealth for his needs just as he uses his donkey that he rides, or his mat on which he sits. Furthermore, he should use it just as he uses a bathroom, in which he satisfies his need without becoming subjugated to it. For he is in a state of anxiety and acts miserly when good touches him.[127]

The second type of wealth is that for which a worshipper does not have a need. It is not fitting for him to attach his heart to this type of wealth, for if his heart becomes attached to it, he becomes subjugated by it. Perhaps he will become dependent on [what is] other than God concerning it, then nothing of the reality of worshipping God and of the reality of relying on Him will remain with him. Nay, there is in this a portion of worshipping [what is] other than God and a portion of relying on [what is] other than God. This person is one of the most deserving of the Prophet's statement, 'May the worshipper of the dirham be wretched; may the worshipper of the dinar be wretched; may the worshipper of velvet cloth be wretched; may the worshipper of embroidered cloth be wretched.'[128] This person is certainly a worshipper of these objects, for even if he had sought them from God, he would have been pleased only if God had granted them to him [and] displeased if God had denied them to him. However, the worshipper of God is one who is pleased with that with which God is pleased, is displeased with that with which God is displeased, loves what God and His Messenger love, hates what God and His Messenger hate, makes alliances with God's saints and takes as enemies His enemies.

PERFECTING FAITH AND LOVE

This is the person who has perfected faith, as in the *ḥadīth*, 'Whoever loves for God, hates for God, gives for God and denies for God has indeed perfected faith.'[129] The Prophet said, 'The most reliable bonds of faith are love for the sake of God and hate for the sake of God.'[130] In the *Ṣaḥīḥ* it is reported from him (may God bless him and grant him peace), 'There are three qualities existing in the one who has attained the sweetness of faith: he is the one to whom God and His Messenger are dearer than all else; who loves a person only for the sake of God; and who abhors returning to disbelief after God has rescued him from it [as much] as he abhors being cast into fire.'[131]

This worshipper agrees with his Lord in what He loves and dislikes, for God and His Messenger are more beloved to him than anything else, and he loves a created being for the sake of God and not for the sake of any other,[132] for this is an aspect of the completion of his love for God. Indeed, the love for the beloved things [belonging to] the beloved one is an aspect of the completion of the love for the beloved one. When a worshipper loves God's prophets and saints because they uphold the beloved things of the True One and for no other reason, then he loves them for the sake of God and not for the sake of any other. He (Exalted is He) says, '...then God will bring forth a people whom He loves and who love Him, they being humble toward the believers and stern toward the disbelievers...' (Q.V.54), and, 'Say: If you love God then follow me, God will love you...' (Q.III.31).

The Messenger certainly commanded what God loves and forbade what He hates. He did what God loves and informed [others] about what God loves in all truthfulness. Therefore, whoever loves God must necessarily follow the Messenger; truthfully relate what he conveyed; obey him in what he commanded; and find solace in emulating what he did. Whoever does this is doing what God loves and so God (Exalted is He) will love him. God has established two signs for the people who love Him: following the Messenger and striving in His path. This is so because striving (*jihād*) is the reality of effort (*ḥaqīqat al-ijtihād*) that is given to obtain the faith and righteous deeds that God loves and to repulse the disbelief, rebellion and disobedience that God hates. He (Exalted is He) says, 'Say: If your fathers, your sons, your brothers, your wives, your kindred, the wealth that you have gained, the commerce in which you fear a decline, and the dwellings in which you delight are dearer to you than God and His Messenger and striving hard in His Cause, then wait until God brings about His command (of punishment); and God does not guide a rebellious people' (Q.IX.24).

Thus, with this punishment,[133] He threatens the one whose family and wealth are more beloved to him than God, His Messenger and striving in His Cause. Moreover, it is confirmed in the *Ṣaḥīḥ*[134] from him (may God bless him and grant him peace) that he said, 'By Him in whose Hand is my soul, none of you will truly believe until I have become more beloved to him than his children, his parents and all mankind together.' Also, it is reported in the *Ṣaḥīḥ*[135] that ᶜUmar b. al-Khaṭṭāb (may God be pleased with him) said to the Prophet, 'O Messenger of God,[136] you are more beloved to me than everything else except my own soul.' Then he replied, 'No! O ᶜUmar, not until I have become more beloved to you than your own soul.' ᶜUmar replied, 'Then, by God, you are more beloved to me than my own soul.' Then the Prophet said, 'Now, O ᶜUmar.'

LOVE AND HATE FOR THE SAKE OF GOD

Hence, the reality of love is only completed through friendship with the beloved, which is complying with Him in loving what He loves and hating what He hates. God loves faith and piety and hates <disbelief[137]>, rebellion and disobedience. Also, it is known that love stirs the will of a heart. The stronger love grows in a heart, the more it seeks to do beloved things. Then, when love becomes complete, it necessitates a decisive will toward obtaining beloved things. When a worshipper is capable of accomplishing them, he will achieve them, but if he is not capable of accomplishing them—[and] thus missing[138] [the beloved things] that have been determined for him—he will have the same reward as that of the one who accomplished them. It is just as the Prophet (may God bless him and grant him peace) said, 'Whoever invites to guidance will have a reward similar to the reward of those who follow him, without diminishing any of their reward; and whoever invites to misguidance will have a burden similar to the burdens of those who follow him, without diminishing any of their burden.'[139] Also, he said, 'Verily, there are men in Medina who never embarked on a journey nor passed through a valley, but they are with you.' They said, 'And they are still in Medina?' He said, 'They are still in Medina, for legitimate excuses prevented them (from travelling).'[140]

Striving is an exertion of effort and[141] an ability to achieve what the Truth loves and to reject what the Truth dislikes. Thus, if a worshipper has the capacity to strive but omits to do so, it is an indication of the weakness of love in his heart for God and His Messenger. It is known that beloved things are most often only attained by enduring hateful consequences, regardless of whether [or not] the love is righteous or corrupt. The lovers of leadership, wealth and images only attain their goals by bearing any harm that comes to them in this life, and in spite of any harm that might afflict them in this life and in the hereafter. Therefore, if those who love God and His Messenger do not endure [the type of harm that] sensible people endure in obtaining their beloved object, which they love instead of God, it indicates the weakness of their love for God. Furthermore, these [other] people follow a path that appears reasonable [to them].[142] But it is known that a believer is stronger [than others] in love for God as He (Exalted is He) says, 'Some people set up rivals of God; they love them as they love God. But those who believe love God more [than those others love their idols]...' (Q.II.165).

To be sure, a lover might follow a path by which he will not obtain the desired goal because of [the] weakness of his intellect and [the] corruptness of his imagination. Such a path is not praiseworthy even if [his] love itself were righteous and praiseworthy, [so] then how would it be if [his] love were corrupt and [his] path led nowhere—as [is the case] with reckless people who seek leadership, wealth and images, concerning [themselves with] a love of affairs that cause them harm and hinder the attainment of their goal.[143] However, the objective for any intelligent person[144] is to follow paths that lead to the attainment of their goal.

The Interaction of Love: Worship and Reliance

Now that this is clear, it follows that the more a heart increases [in] love for God, the more it increases [in its] worship of Him and [in its] freedom from everything other than Him;[145] and the more it increases [in its] worship of Him, the more it increases [in its] love of Him and [in] freedom from everything other than Him. A heart is <inherently[146]> in need of God in two respects: [firstly,] with respect to worship, which is the final cause (*al-ʿilla al-ghāʿiyya*), and, [secondly,] with respect to seeking help [from Him] and relying [on Him], which is the efficient cause (*al-ʿilla al-fāʿiliyya*). For a heart can become righteous, successful, rejoicing, delighted,[147] cheerful, peaceful and tranquil only by worshipping its Lord, loving Him and repenting to Him. Even if it were to obtain every created thing that delights it, a heart would never become tranquil and peaceful because there is an essential need in it for its Lord[148] in regard to His being its object of worship, love and longing. In this way, a heart obtains joy, contentment, delight, grace, peace and tranquillity. However, this happens to it only by the help of God, for only God is capable of providing this for it.[149] Thus, a heart is always in need of the reality of 'It is You alone we worship, and it is from You alone we seek help' (Q.I.5).

If a heart were helped to obtain whatever it loves, seeks, desires and wants while not obtaining acts of worship for God150 in regard to His being its ultimate desire and final intention— for as the beloved object, He is the heart's primary intention, [the heart] loving everything else because of Him, loving nothing for itself except

God—then, when it did not obtain [acts of worship], it would not have realised the reality of 'there is no deity except God,' nor the reality of the application of oneness, worship and love. This heart has a deficiency and a fault.[151] Furthermore, it has a proportional amount of pain, remorse and torment. If it were to work [to obtain] these sought after objects while not seeking help from God, relying on Him [or] being in need of Him to obtain them, then it would never obtain them. For what God wills, is and what He does not will, is not.

A heart[152] is in need of God in regard to His being the sought after goal, the beloved, the intended and the worshipped. Also, He is the One from whom things are requested, [from whom] help is sought and on whom is all reliance. Thus, He is [a heart's] deity, there being no deity for it but He and He is its Lord, there being no lord for it but He; and [a heart's] worship of God is only completed through these two aspects. Thus, when it is a lover of something other than God [because of the thing] itself, or turns to [that which is] other than God for help, then it is a worshipper of what it loves and a worshipper of that for which it hopes in accordance with the love and hope it has for that thing. But when [a heart] loves nothing for itself except God, loving another only for His sake and [when it] hopes for nothing except God and practises the means (*al-asbāb*) and obtains [worship] through them—witnessing that God is the One who created and determined them;[153] that whatever is in the Heavens and on earth has God as its Lord, Possessor and Creator;[154] and that he is in need of Him—then it has obtained a completeness in its worship for God according to what He destined for it.

ARROGANCE AND POLYTHEISM INHIBIT THE WILL TO WORSHIP

In this regard, people are on different levels and only God can count their paths.[155] Thus, from this point of view, the most perfect created beings, the most preferred, the highest and closest to God, the strongest and most guided, are those who are most complete in their worship of God. This is the reality of the religion of Islam with which God sent His messengers and revealed His books. [The reality is that] a worshipper should submit only to God and not to others. Thus, the one who submits to Him and to others is a polytheist (*mushrik*) and the one who refuses to submit to Him is arrogant (*mustakbir*). It is confirmed in the *Ṣaḥīḥ* from the Prophet (may God bless him and grant him peace) that he said, 'Whoever has in his heart an atom's weight of arrogance (*kibr*) will not enter Paradise. Likewise, whoever has in his heart an atom's weight of faith will not enter the Fire [eternally].'[156]

Thus, he has made arrogance the opposite of faith, for arrogance negates the reality of worship as [it] is confirmed in the *Ṣaḥīḥ*[157] from the Prophet (may God bless him and grant him peace) that he said, 'God says, "Majesty is My loincloth and grandeur (*kibriyā'*) is My garment. Thus, I shall punish whoever challenges Me concerning either of them."' Hence, majesty and grandeur are the particularities of Lordship and grandeur is higher than majesty, for He placed it in the rank of a garment just as He placed majesty in the rank of a loincloth. For this reason, the signal for prayer, for the call to prayer and for festivals is 'God is great' (*takbīr*). This *takbīr* is favoured [when it is given from] high places, such as on the hills of Ṣafā and Marwa, and when a person ascends to an elevated place or mounts an animal. Likewise, a fire may be extinguished by *takbīr*, no matter how big it might be. Also, Satan will run away when the call to prayer is made. God (Exalted is He) says, '...call on Me, and I shall respond to you. Those who are too proud to worship Me will surely enter Hell in humiliation' (Q.XL.60).

Whoever is too haughty to worship God must necessarily worship [what is] other than Him[158] because a person is naturally sensitive to being stirred by desire (*irāda*). It is confirmed in the *Ṣaḥīḥ*[159] from the Prophet (may God bless him and grant him peace) that he said, 'The most trustworthy names are Ḥārith and Hammām.' Ḥārith refers to an active earner and Hammām is a doer based on intention, for intention is the beginning of will (*irāda*). Thus, a person always has a will, and every will must necessarily have an object (*murād*) toward which it aims. Therefore, every worshipper necessarily has a beloved object that is the aim of his love and will. Hence, whoever does not have God as the object of his worship and [as] the aim of his love will—nay, [because] he is too haughty for this—he must necessarily have a beloved object besides God that subjugates him.[160] For he is a worshipper of that beloved object whether it is wealth, fame, or images; or whether it is anything he takes as a deity besides God such as the sun, the moon, the planets, idols and the graves of prophets and righteous people; or the angels and prophets[161] whom he takes as lords; or anything that he worships besides God. When a person is a worshipper of [what is] other than God, then he is surely a polytheist; and every arrogant person is a polytheist. For this reason, Pharaoh was one of the greatest of all [in his] arrogance in worshipping God and he was a polytheist.

God (Exalted is He) says, 'Indeed, We sent Moses with Our signs and a clear demonstration to Pharaoh, Hāmān and Qārūn, but they called him a sorcerer, a liar! But when he came to them with the truth from Us they said, "Kill the sons of those who believe with him and keep their women alive." But the plotting of the disbelievers is surely astray. And Pharaoh said, "Let me kill Moses while he calls on his Lord, I surely fear that he will change your religion or bring about corruption in the land." But Moses said, "I truly seek refuge with my Lord and your Lord from every arrogant one who does not believe in the day of reckoning"...Thus, God seals every arrogant, tyrannous heart' (Q.XL.23–27, 35), and, 'And [We destroyed] Qārūn, Pharaoh and Hāmān. Moses came to them with clear signs, but they were arrogant in the land, and yet they could not escape Us' (Q.XXIX.39), and, 'Pharaoh surely exalted himself on the earth and broke up its people into sects, oppressing a group among them, killing their sons and leaving their women alive; surely he was one of the corrupters' (Q.XXVIII.4), and, 'But when Our signs came openly to them, they said, "This is clearly magic." They denied them [those signs] wrongfully and arrogantly, though their souls were convinced by them. Then see what was the end of the corrupters' (Q.XXVII.13–14). There are many examples like this in the Qur'ān. Also, Pharaoh has been described as a polytheist in His verse, 'The chiefs of Pharaoh's people said [to him], "Will you allow Moses and his people to spread corruption in the land, and to abandon you and your gods?"...' (Q.VII.127).

Moreover, investigating this matter indicates that the greater a man's arrogance is as to worshipping God, the greater his polytheistic beliefs will be concerning God. This is so because the more he haughtily disdains worshipping God, the more his need and want increases for a beloved object, which then becomes the aim of his heart as [its] primary intention. Thus, by becoming subjugated to that object he becomes a polytheist. A heart will never dispense with all created beings until God becomes its only guardian, which it worships exclusively. This heart will seek help only from Him and rely only on Him. It will rejoice at only what He loves, and approve of and dislike only what the Lord hates and dislikes. This heart will befriend only those that God has befriended, and will take as enemies only those that God has taken as enemies. It will love only for the sake of God and hate only for the sake of God; give only for the sake of God and refrain from giving only for the sake of God. Thus, the stronger the sincerity of [the man's] religion[162] for God becomes, the more perfect his worship of God and his independence from created beings [will be]. The perfection of his worship of God frees him from arrogance and polytheism. Polytheism predominates among Christians and arrogance predominates among Jews. God (Exalted is He) says concerning the Christians, 'They took their priests and their monks, and the Messiah, the son of Mary, as lords besides God, but they were commanded to worship only one deity—there is no deity except He. Glorified is He above what they associate [with Him]' (Q.IX.31). He says concerning the Jews, '...Is it that whenever a messenger comes to you with what you yourselves do not desire, you become arrogant? Then some of them you deny and some you kill' (Q.II.87). He also says, 'I shall turn away from My signs those who behave arrogantly on the earth without right. Even if they see every sign, they will not believe in it; and if they see the way of righteousness, they will not take it as a way. But if they see the way of error, they will take it as a way…' (Q.VII.146).

Whereas arrogance necessitates polytheism—and polytheism is the opposite of Islam and the sin that God will never forgive—God (Exalted is He) says, 'God surely will not forgive that partners are associated with Him, but He forgives what is less than that for whom He wills; and whoever associates partners with God has strayed far away' (Q.IV.116).[163]

ABRAHAM AS THE MODEL FOR COMBATTING POLYTHEISM

From the first of them and the last of them, all of the prophets were sent with the religion of Islam, for it is the only religion that God accepts from humankind. Noah, peace be upon him, said, 'If you turn away, [then know that] I have not asked you for a reward, for my reward is only with God; and I have been commanded to be one of the Muslims' (Q.X.72). Concerning Abraham, the Exalted One says, 'Who dislikes the religion of Abraham except the one who fools himself? For We had chosen him in this world, and in the hereafter he will surely be one of the righteous. Remember when his Lord said to him, "Submit!" He said, "I submit to the Lord of the worlds." Abraham advised his sons and [so did] Jacob with this, "O my sons! God has chosen a religion for you, therefore, do not die except that you are Muslims"' (Q.II.130–132). Joseph (peace be upon him) said, '…take me as a Muslim and let me join the righteous' (Q.XII.101). Moses (peace be upon him) said, '… "O my people, if you believe in God, then rely on Him, if you are truly Muslims." Then they said, "We rely on God…"' (Q.X.84–85). The Exalted One says, 'We certainly revealed the Torah, in which [there] is guidance and light, and by which the prophets, who submitted, judged the Jews...' (Q.V.44). Bilqīs [the Queen of Sheba] said, '... "O my Lord, I have indeed been unjust to myself; now I submit myself with Solomon to God, the Lord of the worlds"' (Q.XXVII.44). The Exalted One says, 'When I inspired the disciples [of Jesus] to believe in Me and My Messenger, they said, "We believe, and so bear witness that we are Muslims"' (Q.V.111), and, 'The religion before God is Islam...' (Q.III.19), and, 'Whoever seeks other than Islam as a religion will not have it accepted from him...' (Q.III.85), and, 'Then do they seek other than the religion of God while all that is in the Heavens and on earth submits to Him, willingly or unwillingly, and they will be returned to Him' (Q.III.83).

Thus, He mentions the submission of existent beings as being willing or unwilling because all created beings are subjugated to Him by a universal subjugation (*al-taʿabbud al-ʿāmm*), whether one confirms it or denies it. They are under His authority and control,[164] for they submit to Him willingly or unwillingly. Not a single created being can evade what He has willed, determined and decreed, for there is no might and power except with Him. He is the Lord of the worlds and their Owner, managing them as He wills. He is the Creator of all of them, their Designer and Shaper. Anything other than Him is possessed, produced, brought forth, disposed of,[165] poor, wanting, subjugated and conquered while He is the One, the Conqueror, the Creator, the Designer and the Shaper.

Although God creates things through causes, He is the Creator and Determiner of each cause. [Every cause] is in need of Him just as the need of [any effect for a cause].[166] There is not a cause among created beings that is independent of action[167] or capable of deflecting harm. Rather, every cause is in need of another cause that helps it and repels any harm[168] opposing it and working against it. Only God (Glory be to Him) is fully free from what is other than He, there being no partner to help Him and no opposition to challenge Him or resist Him. The Exalted One says, '...Say: Do you think that the things you invoke besides God, if God intended some harm for me, could remove His harm, or if He intended some mercy for me, could stop His mercy? Say: God is sufficient for me! The trusting ones rely only on Him' (Q.XXXIX.38), and, 'If God touches you with harm, none can remove it but He, and if He touches you with good—but then He is able to do all things' (Q.VI.17).

The Exalted One says concerning [His] intimate friend (Abraham), '…"O my people, I am indeed innocent of what you associate [with God]. I have surely turned my face with sincerity toward the One who has created the Heavens and the earth, and I am not one of the polytheists." His people disputed with him. He said, "Do you dispute with me concerning God while He has guided me? I do not fear those whom you associate with Him, for only my Lord can will something. My Lord comprehends all things with full knowledge. Will you not be admonished? How should I fear what you have associated (with God) while you do not even fear that you are associating partners with God without any authority being sent down to you?" Thus, which of the two groups has more right to security, do you know? It is those who believe and do not obscure their faith with injustice. These are the ones who have security and are guided. This is Our evidence that We gave to Abraham against his people…' (Q.VI.78–83).

It is reported from ʿAbd Allāh b. Masʿūd (may God be pleased with him) in the two *Ṣaḥīḥs*[169] that when this verse came down, the Companions of the Prophet (may God bless him and grant him peace) trembled in fear of it and said to him, 'O Messenger of God! Which one of us does not obscure his faith with injustice?' He said, 'No, it is polytheism! Have you not heard the saying of the righteous worshipper: "Polytheism is surely a great injustice?"' (Q.XXXI.13).

Abraham, the intimate friend, the leader of sincere monotheists, was sent at a time when the earth was overwhelmed by the religion of the polytheists. God (Exalted is He) says, 'Remember when his Lord tested Abraham with certain commands which he fulfilled. He [God] said, "I am going to make you a leader for humankind." He said, "And from my offspring also?" He said, "My covenant does not include unjust people"' (Q.II.124). Thus, He made it clear that His covenant of leadership will not be extended to an unjust person, for He (Glory be to Him) never commanded that an unjust person should be a leader; and the greatest injustice is polytheism. The Exalted One says, 'Abraham was a model, obedient to God, a monotheist (*ḥanīf*), and, he was not one of the polytheists' (Q.XVI.120).

A model is <the teacher of good who is then imitated just as any good example is imitated[170]>. God established prophethood and scripture among Abraham's offspring and then sent prophets after him with his religion. The Exalted One says, 'Then We inspired you [Muḥammad, saying], "Follow the religion of Abraham with sincerity, and he was not one of the polytheists"' (Q.XVI.123), and, 'The people most deserving to be with Abraham are those who followed him, this Prophet, and those who believe; and God is the protecting helper of the believers' (Q.III.68), and, 'Abraham was neither a Jew nor a Christian, rather he was pure in faith, a Muslim, and he was not one of the polytheists' (Q.III.67), and, 'They say, "Be a Jew or a Christian, then you will be guided." Say [O Muḥammad]: No! [Follow] the religion of Abraham with sincerity, and he was not one of the polytheists. Say [O Muslims]: We believe in God and in what has been sent down to us and what was sent down to Abraham, Ishmael, Isaac, Jacob, and the Tribes, and what Moses and Jesus received, and what the prophets received from their Lord. We make no differences among them, and we have submitted ourselves (as Muslims) to Him' (Q.II.135–136).

INTIMATE LOVE AND INTIMATE FRIENDSHIP

It is confirmed in the *Ṣaḥīḥ*[171] from the Prophet (may God bless him and grant him peace) that 'Abraham is the best of creation.' Thus he is the most preferred prophet after the Prophet (may God bless him and grant him peace), and he is an intimate friend (*khalīl*) of God. It is also confirmed in the two *Ṣaḥīḥs*[172] from multiple reports that the Prophet (may God bless him and grant him peace) said, 'God has taken me as an intimate friend just as He took Abraham as an intimate friend.' He also said, 'If I were to take an intimate friend from the people of the earth, I would take Abū Bakr as an intimate friend. But your companion is an intimate friend of God.' He means himself. And he said, 'There shall be no open door in the mosque except the door of Abū Bakr.'[173] He also said, 'Those who came before you used to take graves as places of prostration (*masājid*). So do not take graves as places of prostration. I forbid you from doing that.'[174] Each of these *ḥadīth*s is reported in the *Ṣaḥīḥ*. It is also reported [there] that he made these statements a few days before his death. This is part of the perfection of his message.

This [message] contains the perfection of realising [the Prophet's] intimacy with God,[175] the origin of which is the love of God (Exalted be He) for a worshipper,[176] contrary to the claims of the Jahmiyya.[177] This [message] also contains the veritable oneness of God, and that nothing is to be worshipped but Him, refuting those who resemble the polytheists. In [this message] there is also a refutation of the Rāfiḍa who deprive Abū Bakr al-Ṣiddīq of his right and who are the most extreme of those facing the Qibla [Mecca] in the matter of polytheism.[178]

Intimacy (*khulla*) is the perfection of the love (*maḥabba*) required of a worshipper and the perfection of worship for God; and [intimacy coming] from the Lord (Glory be to Him) is the perfection of [His] Lordship toward His worshippers whom He loves, and who love Him. The term worship necessarily includes the perfection of humility and the perfection of love (*ḥubb*). Thus, they say that an enthralled heart (*qalb mutayyam*) is when a heart becomes enslaved (*mutaʿabbad*) by the beloved. Enthralment is enslavement, and the enthralled of God (*taym Allāh*) is the worshipper of Him (*ʿabduhu*). This highest level of perfection was attained by Abraham and Muḥammad (may God bless them and grant them peace). For this reason, he [Muḥammad] did not have an intimate friend among the people of the earth, for intimacy cannot bear association. This is similar in meaning to [the following line of poetry]: 'You penetrated the deepest recesses of the spirit in me, / And therefore the dear friend is now called an intimate.'[179]

[The meaning of this line] is contrary to basic love (*ḥubb*), for he (may God bless him and grant him peace) said in an authentic *ḥadīth* about Ḥasan and Usāma,[180] 'O God! I love them. May You love them and may You love whoever loves them!' ʿAmr b. al-ʿAs asked him, 'Who is the most beloved person[181] to you?' He replied, "ʿĀ'isha.' ʿAmr asked, 'Who among the men?' He said, 'Her father [Abū Bakr].'[182] Also, he said to ʿAlī (may God be pleased with him), 'I shall give the flag to a man who loves God and His Messenger and whom God and His Messenger love.'[183] There are many examples of this.

The Exalted One informs us that He loves the pious, the perfect devotees, the just, the penitent, the ones who purify themselves and the ones who fight in His Cause in close ranks as if they were a solid structure.[184] He says, '...then God will bring forth a people whom He loves and who love Him...' (Q.V.54). He has informed us about His love for His believing worshippers and the love of the believers for Him to the point that He says, '...but those who believe love God more...' (Q.II.165).

However, intimacy is very specific. Yet some people, imagining that love is above intimacy, say that Muḥammad is the beloved (*ḥabīb*) of God and Abraham is the intimate friend (*khalīl*) of God. But this statement is weak because Muḥammad is also the intimate friend of God, as is confirmed in many authentic *ḥadīths*. Furthermore, any narration stating that al-ʿAbbās [the Prophet's uncle] will be placed between a beloved and an intimate friend, and anything similar to this, is one of the fabricated *ḥadīths*[185] that are unsound and not to be relied on.

TASTING THE SWEETNESS OF FAITH

We mentioned previously that the love for God is <the love of Him and[186]> the love of what He loves just as it is narrated in the two

*Ṣaḥīḥ*s[187] from the Prophet (may God bless him and grant him peace) who said, 'There are three qualities existing in the one who has attained the sweetness of faith: [(1)] he is the one to whom God and His Messenger are dearer than all else, [(2)] who loves a person only for the sake of God, and [(3)] who abhors returning to disbelief after God has rescued him from it as he abhors being cast into fire.' He (may God bless him and grant him peace) informed us that the one possessing these three characteristics would find the sweetness of faith because the existence[188] of the sweetness of a thing follows the love of it. Thus, whoever loves and desires a thing will find the sweetness, delight and enjoyment of it only after obtaining his intended object. Delight is a matter occurring after obtaining the favoured object that is beloved or desired. Therefore, whoever says that delight is the actual attainment of the favoured object (as do some philosophisers and doctors[189]) has clearly erred in this matter, for attainment mediates between delight and love. For example, a person desires food. Delight will occur to him only after he eats it. Also, delight follows the sight of a thing. A person first sees a thing, then he delights in it. Delight follows the sight of a thing, it is not the same as sight itself, and it is not the vision of a thing. Rather, delight occurs after envisioning it. The Exalted One says, '...all that souls desire is in it (Paradise), and all that eyes delight in...' (Q.XLIII.71).

This is the case for all delights and pains that [are experienced by] a soul, such as enjoyment and sadness, for these occur by way of the perception of the beloved or disliked object. Perception itself is not the same as enjoyment or sadness. Thus, the sweetness of faith necessarily includes [a] delight in it and [an] enjoyment of what a believer finds as part of the sweetness of faith following the perfection of the worshipper's love for God. This has three components: perfecting this love, distinguishing it,[190] and repelling its opposite.

Perfecting this love means that God and His Messenger must be more beloved to a worshipper than all else. The love of God and His

Messenger is not satisfied by basic love (*aṣl al-ḥubb*); rather, it must necessarily be that God and His Messenger are more beloved to him than all else, as has already been mentioned. Distinguishing this love means that a worshipper must love a person only for the sake of God. Repelling the opposite of this love means that he detests [that which is] opposite of faith to a greater extent than [he hates] to be thrown into a fire. Consequently, love for the Messenger and the believers is an aspect of love for God. Thus, the Messenger of God (may God bless him and grant him peace) used to love the believers whom God loved because he was the most perfect person [in] loving God and the worthiest person, for he loved what God loves and hated what God hates.

LOVE IN BALANCE WITH HOPE AND FEAR

But no portion of intimacy may be for [what is] other than God. Thus, the Messenger said, 'If I were to take an intimate friend from among the people of the earth, I would take Abū Bakr as an intimate friend.'[191] He knew [that] intimacy holds [a] higher rank [than] unqualified love (*muṭlaq al-maḥabba*). The intended [meaning] of this *ḥadīth* is that intimacy and love for God are the veritable worship of Him (*taḥqīq ʿubūdiyyatihi*). Also, those who err in this matter do so in regards to imagining that worship is mere humility and submission without any love, and that love consists of extending or freeing passions, which [in truth] the concept of Lordship cannot bear.[192] For this reason, it is mentioned about Dhū al-Nūn that some people spoke about the problem of love in his presence and he said, 'Stay away from this matter. Souls should not hear of it, for they would curse it.'[193] Also, the people of cognizance and knowledge disliked attending the gatherings of those who spoke much about love without [any] apprehension. Some of the Righteous Predecessors said, 'Whoever worships God with love only is indeed a heretic (*zindīq*); and whoever worships Him with hope only is indeed a Murji'; and whoever worships Him with fear only is indeed a Harūrī.[194] But the one who worships Him with love, fear and hope is indeed a believer, an affirmer of the Divine Oneness (*muwaḥḥid*).'

For this reason there are some people of more recent generations who have extended the claim of love to the point [where it] led them to a certain type of foolishness and to a claim that precludes worship and leads the worshipper to [attribute to himself] a kind of lordship befitting only God. Some of these people make claims that exceed the limits set for the prophets and messengers. Or, they seek from God that which in all respects befits only Him—not even befitting the prophets and messengers.[195] Many shaykhs have stumbled concerning this topic.

The cause of this [error] is a weak [understanding] of the veritable worship that the messengers clarified, and which they accurately explained by means of the commandments and prohibitions that they brought. Furthermore, it is a weakness of the intellect by which a worshipper knows his true self. When the intellect is weak and knowledge of religion diminishes while love[196] remains in the soul, the soul entertains itself with its own foolishness in this matter. This is the same as with a person who entertains himself foolishly and ignorantly with the love of another person and who then says, 'I am a lover! Thus I cannot be blamed[197] for anything [that] I do which may be injurious and ignorant.' This is the source of error (*ʿayn al-ḍalāl*). It is similar to the statement of the Jews and the Christians who say, 'We are the sons of God and His beloved' (Q.V.18). But God (Exalted is He) says, '...Say: Then why does He punish you for your sins? But no! You are people from those whom He created. He forgives whom He wills and punishes whom He wills...' (Q.V.18).

LOVE IS UNITED WITH OBEDIENCE

Thus, His punishment of them for their sins necessarily [means] that they are not beloved and are not related to Him through the relation of sonship. Moreover, it necessarily [means] that they are subservient creatures. For the one whom God loves practices that which his <Beloved loves[198]> and he does not do anything that the True One hates or with which He is displeased, such as disbelief, corruption or disobedience. God hates the major sins that a person commits and continues to [commit] without repenting, just as He loves the good deeds that he does,[199] for His love toward a worshipper is commensurate with his faith and piety. The one who imagines that sins do not harm him because God loves him (even though he persists in doing them), is at the level of the one who claims that taking poison does not harm him even though he continues to take it without taking its antidote for the sound health of his constitution. Were this fool to reflect on the stories that God has narrated in His book about the prophets, about how they sought repentance and forgiveness, and about the kinds of trials to which they were subjected and by which they were cleansed and purified according to their circumstances, then he would know some of the harms that sins impart to sinners, even if they were those people who have the loftiest status. Indeed, if someone who loves a created being is not aware of his own welfare and is not wishing for it, but rather is acting in accordance with [that] love and is ignorant and oppressive, then this is a reason for the beloved to hate and shun him, [and] even to punish him.

Many seekers of the truth have followed various aspects of ignorance in religion with respect to the claim of loving God. Such ignorance includes exceeding the limits set by God, neglecting the rights of God, or assuming false claims that have no truth, such as the statement of one of them, 'I am innocent in regard to any novice[200] of mine who forsakes a person in the Fire.' Another has said, 'I am innocent in regard to any novice of mine who neglectfully allows a believer to enter the Fire.' The first one made his novice responsible for removing all those who are in the Fire and the second one made his novice responsible for preventing those believers who committed major sins from entering the Fire. Another says, 'On the day of resurrection I will extend my tent over Hell so that no one will enter it.'[201]

There are many similar sayings that are traceable to some famous shaykhs, but these are either lies told against them, or errors of theirs.

Such errors might stem from being in a state of intoxication (*sukr*), rapture (*ghalaba*), or annihilation (*fanā'*), during which a person's discernment vanishes or weakens so that he does not know what he is saying. Intoxication is actually delight without discernment. For this reason, whenever any of these people have regained consciousness, [they] sought forgiveness for such statements. But those shaykhs who listen profusely to poems that include love, passion, reproach, reproof and infatuation (*gharām*) have this as their original intention. For this reason, God has revealed a test for love through which He tests the lover. Thus He says, '...if you love God then follow me, God will love you...' (Q.III.31).

Therefore, the lover of God is only the one who follows His Messenger, for obeying the Messenger and following him is the verity of worship. Many of those who claim love stray from his law and his *Sunna*, and make claims of fantasies (*khayālāt*) that cannot be detailed here. Eventually, one of these people imagines that the commands have been lifted from him and the prohibitions have been made allowable for and other things that oppose the law of the Messenger, his *Sunna*, and obedience to him. On the contrary, however, He has made the love of God[202] and the love of His Messenger a struggle for His sake. This struggle necessarily includes the perfection of loving what God has commanded and the perfection of hating what God has prohibited. For this reason, He gives a description of those whom He loves and who love Him, '...humble toward the believers, unbending toward the unbelievers, and they struggle for the sake of God...' (Q.V.54).

THE CRITERIA OF LOVE

For this reason, the love of this religious community for God is more perfect than that of anyone before them, and their worship of Him is more perfect than that of anyone before them. The most perfect people of this community in this regard are the Companions of Muḥammad (may God bless him and grant him peace), and whoever more closely imitates them in this matter [of love] will move [closer] to perfection regarding it. Then how can this status compare to the claim of love by some people and to the statement of some shaykhs that 'love is a fire that burns everything in a heart except the intention of the beloved (*murād al-maḥbūb*)'?[203] They mean that God wills the existence of all being, and thus they imagine that the perfection of love is that a worshipper should love everything including disbelief, depravity and rebellion. But it is impossible for someone to love everything that exists; on the contrary, a person loves what suits him and benefits him and hates what is incompatible with him and harms him.[204] However, because of this error [those people] take advantage by following their passions,[205] for they love what they desire (such as images, leadership, excess wealth and mistaken innovations) all the while maintaining that these are included in the love of God,[206] but the love of God includes the hatred of what He and His Messenger hate and the striving of His people with soul and wealth.

The origin of their erring position is that they say, 'Love is a fire that burns everything in a heart except the intention of the beloved.' If [the one who said this] meant that the intention of God (Exalted is He) is[207] the religiously legislated will—which in itself means the love of Him and contentment with Him—then it is as if he says that it burns everything from a heart except what is beloved by God. This is a correct meaning; for he says that part of the completion of love[208] is to love only what God loves. For when I love <what He does not love[209]> this love is deficient. As for His predestining and determining what He hates, despises, detests and forbids, if I did not agree with Him in His hatred, despising and detesting, I would not be a lover of Him but a lover of what He hates.

Therefore, adhering to the law and striving to implement it are part of the major distinction between the people who love God, His saints, those whom He loves and who love Him, and those who claim love for God while observing only the universality of His Lordship or following certain innovations which contradict His law. Thus, the claim of [possessing] this love for God[210] is the sort of claim that the Jews and the Christians make about[211] love for God. Moreover, the claim of these people is surely worse than the claim of the Jews and the Christians, for these [people] are hypocrites and they will be [punished] in the lowest level of the Fire. Likewise, the claim of the Jews and the Christians would be worse than the claim [of these people] if they had not reached that sort of disbelief [through their claims].

There are [statements] about the love of God in the Torah and the Gospel[212] on which the Jews and the Christians agree. They even say that the love of God is one of the greatest commands of the law (*al-nāmūs*).[213] Thus, in the Gospel, the Messiah says[214] that one of his greatest commandments is that you love God with all your heart and all your mind and all your soul.[215] The Christians claim that they implement this love and that the asceticism and worshipping that they practice is part of this. However, they are dissociated from the love of God because they do not follow what He loves. Instead, they follow what angers God and they hate what pleases Him. Thus, He makes their deeds of no avail.

HOW TO APPROACH GOD THROUGH LOVE

God hates disbelievers; He abhors and curses them. However, He (Glory be to Him) loves those who love Him; it is not possible that a worshipper is a lover of God while God (Exalted is He) does not love him. On the contrary, the love of God for a worshipper is commensurate to the love of a worshipper for his Lord; but the reward of God for His worshipper is much greater, just as it is reported in an authentic divine *ḥadīth* from God (Exalted is He) who said, 'Whoever approaches Me by the span of a palm, I will approach him by the span of an arm; whoever approaches Me by the span of an arm, I will approach him by the span of his outspread arms; whoever comes to Me walking, I will hasten to him.'[216] He (Glory be to Him) has informed us that He loves those who are pious, perfectly devout and patient, and that He loves those who repent and purify themselves. Moreover, He loves the one who performs the obligatory and recommended deeds that He commanded just as it is narrated in an authentic *ḥadīth*, 'My worshipper continually approaches Me by performing voluntary deeds until I love him. Then once I love him, I become his hearing by which he hears and his sight by which he sees...'[217]

Many mistaken[218] people who follow <(certain) shaykhs[219]> in asceticism and acts of worship[220] have subscribed to some of that to which the Christians have subscribed, claiming love for God while contradicting His law, abandoning the struggle in His way, and other similar things. These people hold on to a religion by which they approach God[221] in the [same] way that the Christians are attached to ambiguous statements and stories in which the narrator's truthfulness is not known. Even if the narrator were truthful, he would not be infallible. Thus, these mistaken people make their leaders (*matbūʿīhim*)[222] legislators for them in religion just as the Christians made their priests and monks legislators for them in religion. Then they diminish worship by claiming that the elite can transgress it, just as the Christians claim concerning the Messiah.[223] They even affirm for their elite a certain association with God, similar to what the Christians affirm for the Messiah and his mother.[224] [Reviewing] the extent of the various claims would require a lengthy commentary at this point.

However, the religion of truth (*dīn al-ḥaqq*) is the veritable worship of God in every aspect and the veritable love for God at all levels. Commensurate with the perfection of worship are the perfection of the love of a worshipper for his Lord and the perfection of the love of the Lord for His worshipper. Likewise, commensurate with the diminishing of the former is the diminishing of the latter. Accordingly, whenever [there is] love in a heart for [what is] other than God, worship will exist in it for [what is] other than God. Whenever [there is] worship in a heart for [what is] other than God, love will exist in it for [what is] other than God.[225] Any love that is not devoted to God is false and any deed that is not intended for the Face of God is false.[226] Thus, the world is cursed, [in the sense that] everything in it is cursed except what is for the sake of God, and nothing is for the sake of God except what God and His Messenger love—which means that which is legislated. Any deed that is intended for [what is] other than God is not for God, and any deed that does not comply with God's legislation is not for God. Moreover, nothing is for God except what these two characteristics encompass: [(1)] an action must be for the sake of God and, [(2)] be in compliance with the love of God and His Messenger, which means all obligatory and recommended deeds, just as the Exalted One says, '...and so whoever hopes for the meeting with his Lord, let him do righteous deeds while associating none as a partner in the worship of his Lord' (Q.XVIII.110).

Therefore, it is necessary that [an accepted deed] is a righteous deed, which is obligatory or recommended; and it is necessary that it be purely and sincerely for the Face of God. The Exalted One says, 'No! Whoever submits himself entirely to God and is a perfect devotee, his reward is with his Lord; they shall have no fear nor shall they grieve' (Q.II.112). The Prophet (may God bless him and grant him peace) said, 'Whoever performs a deed that is not in accordance with our affairs has it rejected.'[227] He (may God bless him and grant him peace) also said, 'Deeds are based only on intentions. Each person shall be rewarded according to what he intends. Therefore, the one whose migration is to God and His Messenger shall have his migration be to God and His Messenger; and the one whose migration is to this world, to gain it, or to a woman, to marry her, shall have his migration be to that to which he migrated.'[228]

HIDDEN POLYTHEISM AND DESIRES

This principle is the fundamental principle of the religion of Islam to the extent that the realisation of it entails the realisation of the religion. God sent the messengers with this principle and revealed the Scriptures [based on it]. The Messenger (may God bless him and grant him peace) called to it, struggled for it, commanded by it and desired it. This principle is the pole of the religion around which its millstone turns. Polytheism (*shirk*), however, dominates souls, as is narrated in a *ḥadīth*, 'It [polytheism] is more hidden than the crawling of an ant.' In another *ḥadīth*, Abū Bakr said, 'O Messenger of God, how can we save ourselves from it while it is more hidden than the crawling of an ant?' The Prophet said, 'O Abū Bakr, shall I not teach you a word which you can say[229] to save yourself from both the smallest and greatest [aspects of it]. Say, "O God, I seek refuge with You from knowingly associating any partner with You, and I seek Your forgiveness for that which I do not know."'[230] Also, ʿUmar b. al-Khaṭṭāb used to say in his supplications, 'O God, make all my deeds righteous, and make them pure and sincere for Your Face, and do not allow any share of them to be for another.'

There are many hidden desires (*shahawāt*) that intermingle with souls,[231] corrupting them in the realisation of their love and worship for God and in the sincerity of their religion for Him. Shadād b. Aws said, 'O you Arabs! The things I fear the most for you are hypocrisy (*riyā'*) and hidden desire.' It was said to Abū Dāwud al-Sijistānī, 'What is hidden desire?' He replied, 'The love of leadership.' Kaʿb b. Mālik reported that the Prophet (may God bless him and grant him peace) said, 'The greed of a man for wealth and honour is more destructive to his religion than the damage of two hungry wolves among a flock[232] of sheep.' Tirmidhī said that this *ḥadīth* is authoritative [and] satisfactory (*ṣaḥīḥ ḥasan*).[233] The Prophet (may God bless him and grant him peace) explained that greed for wealth and honour is no less destructive of religion than the destruction of two hungry wolves for a flock of sheep. Likewise, he explained that the secure religion does not include this greed and that when a heart tastes the sweetness of its worship and love for God, nothing will be more beloved to it than that, and so he will prefer it. In this way, evil and blatant sin will be diverted from the people of sincerity to God, as the Exalted One says, '...[We did this so] that We might turn evil and blatant sin away from him. Surely he was one of Our chosen worshippers' (Q.XII.24).

The one who has sincerity for God has tasted the sweetness of his worship of God, which prevents him from the worship of others, and has tasted the sweetness of his love for God, which prevents him from loving others. For there is nothing sweeter, tastier, more delightful, more tender and more favourable to a heart[234] than the sweetness of faith, which necessarily includes its worship of God, its love for Him and the sincerity of religion for Him. This necessitates the attraction of a heart to God, for a heart becomes repentant to God and fearful of Him [with a balance of] hope and anxiety, just as the Exalted One says, 'The one who feared the Infinitely Merciful, unseen, and brought a repentant heart to Him' (Q.L.33). This is so because a lover fears either the cessation of that which he seeks, or the attainment of that which he dreads.[235] Thus, he could only be a worshipper and lover of God by having both fear and hope. The Exalted One says, 'Those on whom they call are themselves seeking a means of access to their Lord as to which of them is nearer. They hope for His mercy and fear His punishment; surely the punishment of your Lord is to be feared' (Q.XVII.57).

When a worshipper is sincere toward God, his Lord chooses him and revives his heart. He attracts his heart to Himself, thus diverting from it any evil and blatant sin that contradicts this attraction. [This heart] is then fearful of contradicting that attraction[236] in opposition to a heart that is not sincere to God, for it has an unqualified desire, will and love. Thus, an insincere heart desires whatever occurs to it and clings to whatever it desires, just as a branch bends in the direction[237] of the wind. Sometimes forbidden and non-forbidden images attract it, and it thus remains a captive slave to one who, were he to take it as a slave, would render it shameful, disgraceful and blameworthy. [At] other times [a desire for] nobility[238] and leadership attract an insincere heart, and thus one word pleases [the heart] and another word angers it. The one who praises an insincere heart—even if it is false praise—enslaves it; and the one who criticises it—even if it is the truth—becomes its enemy. Yet [at] other times dirhams, dinars and similar types of wealth are among the matters that enslave hearts, which in turn desire these things. Thus, [a worshipper with an insincere heart] takes his desire as his deity and follows his desire without any guidance from God. Whoever is not sincere to God and worshipping Him such that his heart is enslaved to its Lord [the One who has no partners] so that He is more beloved to him than anyone else and [so that] he is humble and submissive to Him—[well, then] if [he is] not, created beings enslave him and devils overwhelm his heart. He will be one of the tempters and the brethren of devils. Evil and blatant sin increases in him to an extent [that] only God knows. This is a necessary matter from which there is no escape. For if a heart is not a monotheist (*ḥanīf*), [that is,] turning to God and turning away from all others, it will be a polytheist. 'So set yourself entirely toward the religion with sincerity (*ḥanīf^an*), according to the true nature upon which He created all people—there is no altering the creation of God. That is the straight religion (*al-dīn al-qayyim*), but most people do not know it. Turn to Him, fear Him, be constant in prayer, and do not be one of the polytheists—one of those who split up their religion and become sects, each party rejoicing in what it has' (Q.XXX.30–32).

THE WAY OF ABRAHAM AND THE WAY OF PHARAOH

God (Glory be to Him) has made Abraham, and the progeny of Abraham, leaders for those pure worshippers who are sincerely devoted, the people of love and worship for God who have sincerity of religion for Him. In the same way, He has made Pharaoh, and the progeny of Pharaoh, leaders of the polytheists, who follow their own desires. God (Exalted is He) says concerning Abraham, 'We bestowed on him Isaac, and also Jacob as a grandson; We made each one righteous. We made them leaders, guiding others by Our command. We inspired them to do good deeds, to be constant in prayer, and to give charity; and they were Our worshippers' (Q.XXI.72–73).

He says concerning Pharaoh and his people, 'We made them leaders who invite to the Fire, and on the day of resurrection they will not be helped. We made a curse to follow them in this world, and on the day of resurrection they will be among the abhorred' (Q.XXVIII.41–42). For this reason, the followers of Pharaoh[239] are foremost among those who do not discriminate between what God loves and approves of, and what He determines and predestines. Moreover, they see only the comprehensive, unqualified will of God. Then, ultimately, they do not discriminate between the Creator and the created being. Rather, they make the existence of the former the same as the existence of the latter. Their people of realisation (*muḥaqqiqūhum*) say that the law contains obedience and disobedience, that reality (*ḥaqīqa*) contains disobedience without obedience, and that realisation (*taḥqīq*) contains neither obedience nor disobedience. This is the realisation of the path of Pharaoh and his people who denied the Creator and His speaking to His worshipper, Moses, and denied the commandments and prohibitions with which He sent him. But as for Abraham and his people, [and as for] the pure worshippers and the prophets, they know that there has to be a distinction between the Creator and the created, and between obedience and disobedience. They know that the more a worshipper increases in realisation,[240] the more his love for God increases, as well as his worship of Him, his obedience to Him and his avoidance of worshipping, loving and obeying anything else. However, these errant polytheists equate God with His creation, whereas Abraham said, '...Have you not looked at what you have been worshipping, you and your forefathers, they are surely enemies to me, save the Lord of the worlds' (Q.XXVI.75–77).

These people held on to the ambiguous statements of the shaykhs just as the Christians had done. An example of this is the term annihilation (*fanā'*), which is of three types:[241] [(1)] one type of *fanā'* is for the prophets and saints (*awliyā'*) who have reached perfection; [(2)] another type is for those who <aim to reach the level of> the saints and righteous people;[242] [and (3)] yet another type is for the apostatising hypocrites who spread confusion.

The Fanā' *of the Prophets and Saints*

THE *FANĀ'* OF THE WILL

As for the first type of *fanā'*, it is the annihilation of <the will for[243]> everything other than God to the extent that one loves only God, worships only God,[244] relies only on Him and seeks only Him. This is the meaning that must necessarily be the intention of the saying of Shaykh Abū Yazīd,[245] 'I want not to want other than what He wants.' That is the pleasing, beloved object, and that is the object of the religious will. The perfection of the worshipper is not to want, love and be contented [with] other than with what God wills, is pleased with and loves, and this is what He has ordered either as an obligatory act or a recommended act. [The worshipper] does not love [anything] other than what God loves, as do the angels, prophets and righteous people.[246] This is the meaning of what has been said about His verse, 'Except he who comes to God with a secure heart' (Q.XXVI.89).[247] It is said that it is secure from everything other than God, or from everything other than worshipping God, or from everything other than the will of God, or from everything other than the love of God. These expressions have one meaning: this meaning, whether you call it annihilation or not, is the beginning and end of Islam, it is the inner truth of religion (*bāṭin al-dīn*) and its outer appearance (*ẓāhiruhu*).

THE *FANĀ'* OF WITNESSING

As for the second meaning[248] of *fanā'*, it is <annihilation> of the witnessing of [what is] other <than God[249]>. This has occurred to many seekers (*sālikīn*) who have an attraction in their hearts that quickly proceeds toward the remembrance of God, the worship of Him and love of Him, while their hearts weaken in the matter of witnessing [that which is] other than what they worship or of seeing [that which is] other than what they intend. No thoughts other than [thoughts] of God come to their hearts; moreover, they are not aware of such things. It is as what is said about His verse, 'The heart of the mother of Moses became void, she would have exposed him had We not strengthened her heart so that she was one of the believers' (Q.XXVIII.10). They say that her heart was void (*fārigh*) of everything except of the remembrance of Moses. This often happens to the one for whom a matter becomes overwhelming,[250] whether it is related to love, fear, or hope. His heart remains diverted from everything except from what it loves, fears, or seeks, to the extent that, as it becomes absorbed in the thing, it perceives nothing else. As the experience becomes stronger for the one undergoing this annihilation, his self-existence becomes concealed due to its existence, his self-witnessing becomes concealed due to witnessing it, his self-remembrance becomes concealed due to the remembrance of it, and his self-knowledge becomes concealed due to the knowledge of it.[251] Thus, the one who does not exist, perishes [that is, the other subjugated created beings], while He who does not cease to exist, remains [that is, the Exalted Lord]. The intended meaning is that [created beings] are annihilated in [the capacity of] the worshipper to witness and remember them, and he is annihilated [in the sense that] he cannot comprehend or witness them. When this [process] grows stronger, the lover becomes weaker until he becomes confused in his discernment; then he thinks that he is his beloved. This is just as is mentioned about a man who throws himself into a river, and then his lover throws himself after him. Then the man says, 'I fell in, but what caused you to fall in after me?' He says, 'I disappeared into you so that I thought you were I.'

Many people have slipped[252] concerning this topic, for they thought that this was unity (*ittiḥād*) and that the lover so unites with the beloved that there is no difference between them in the selfsame existence of the two. But this is a mistake.[253] For surely nothing at all ever unites with the Creator.[254] Moreover, a thing does not unite with another thing except when there is alteration, corruption, or the occurrence of a third thing from the union of the two, which is neither this nor that. This happens, for example, when water unites with milk or wine. However, there is union in objects of will, [both] beloved things and hated things, the two agreeing in the type of will (*irāda*) and [type of] aversion (*karāha*). This one loves and hates what that one loves and hates, is pleased with what the other is pleased with, displeased with what the other is displeased with, detests what the other detests, allies himself with [the one with] whom the other allies himself, and has enmity for [the one for] whom the other has enmity. However, all this [kind of] annihilation has a deficiency in it.[255]

THE STRUGGLE TO REMAIN CONSCIOUS IN WORSHIP

The greatest saints, such as Abū Bakr and ʿUmar (may God be pleased with them), and the outstanding leaders of the Emigrants (*al-muhājirūn*) and the Helpers (*al-anṣār*),[256] did not experience this annihilation—not to mention those prophets who were above them in rank. However, something [like] this did occur after [the time of] the Companions. Likewise, all aspects of this manner [of annihilation], in which there is a loss of intelligence and discernment in the stages of faith (*aḥwāl al-īmān*)[257] that occur to a heart, [did not affect] the Companions, who were more perfect, stronger[258] and firmer in the stages of faith than to undergo a loss of their intellect or to experience fainting, weakness,[259] intoxication, annihilation, rapture, or madness. But the appearance of these [experiences] first occurred among the Followers of the Companions who were worshipping in Basra, for there were some of them who fainted when listening to the Qur'ān, and some who died, such as Abū Juhayr al-Darīr and Zurāra b. Abī Awfā, the judge of Basra.[260]

Likewise, annihilation and intoxication were experienced by some Ṣūfī shaykhs, weakening their discernment to the point that, [while] in this state, they said things [which] they [then] recognised as being wrong when they recovered. Such stories have been related about Abū Yazīd, Abū al-Ḥasan al-Nūrī,[261] Abū Bakr al-Shiblī and others. This is contrary to those who remained [the] master of their intellect[s] and discernment in their states, such as Abū Sulaymān al-Dārānī, Maʿrūf al-Karkhī,[262] Fuḍayl b. ʿIyād and, especially, al-Junayd.[263] They did not succumb to states such as annihilation and intoxication. Moreover, the entire [experience of][264] their <hearts[265]> is that they are concerned with nothing other than the love of God, His will and His worship, while maintaining a capacity for knowledge and discernment by which they witness affairs as they actually are. Indeed, they witness created beings as existing by God's command, controlled by His will, <complying with Him[266]>, and devoted to Him, for they [maintain a capacity for] vision and remembrance. They witness this as being a confirmation of, and support for, the purity of religion in their hearts, the abstraction of oneness,[267] and the worship of Him alone, Who has no partners. This is the truth to which the Qur'ān invites, and with which the people of veritable faith and all of the people of knowledge stand, and our Prophet is the leader of them and the most perfect of them. For this reason, when he was taken up to the Heavens and viewed the signs (*al-ayāt*) that are there, and his Lord revealed to him various confidential matters, he returned to them [the people on earth] in the morning with his state unaltered, and that event did not overwhelm him. This is contrary to the unconsciousness that had overwhelmed Moses.[268]

Part II

THE *FANĀ'* OF EXISTENCE

As for the third type of what is called annihilation, it is to witness that there is no existence except God and that the being of the Creator is the [same as] the being of the created beings, without any difference between the Lord and the slave. This is the annihilation of the people of <disbelief[269]> misguidance and heresy (*ilḥād*), those who have succumbed to [beliefs of] incarnation and unity with the divinity (*al-ḥulūl wa'l-ittiḥād*).[270] When one of the shaykhs of the straight path[271] says something such as, 'I do not see [anything] other than God,' or 'I do not look at [anything] other than God,' then the intention of that is, 'I do not see a Lord other than Him, nor a Creator or Controller other than Him, and there is no deity other than Him, and I do not look at [anything] other than Him, [neither] loving it, fearing it, [nor] hoping in it.' The eye looks toward that to which [the] heart is attached. Thus, whoever loves a thing or hopes in it, or fears a thing, will [either] turn toward it [or turn away from it].[272] But when one has no love for it in his heart—no hope in it, no fear of it, no hatred for it, or any attachment of the heart for it, then his heart does not intend to turn toward it, look at it, or see it. But if by chance he saw something briefly, it would be as if he had seen a wall.[273] And so it is with whatever is not attached to his heart.

The righteous shaykhs (may God be pleased with them) mention something about the abstraction of oneness and the real purity of the whole religion (*taḥqīq ikhlāṣ al-dīn kullihi*) in the sense that the worshipper does not turn toward [anything] other than God and does not look at [anything] other than Him, having no love for it, no fear of it, nor hope in it. Moreover, a heart will be void of created beings, isolated from them, not looking at them except by the light of God. Thus, he hears by the truth, he sees by the truth, he grasps by the truth, and he walks by the truth. Then he loves those created beings whom God loves and hates those of them whom God hates, and he allies himself with those whom God has protected and has enmity for those whom God holds as enemies, and he fears God concerning them and does not fear them concerning God.[274] This is the pure, secure heart that applies oneness; the submitting, believing heart that is cognizant and applies oneness according to the knowledge of the prophets and messengers, based on their realisation and application of oneness.[275]

As for the third type, which is the annihilation in being (*al-fanā' fī al-wujūd*), this is the very essence of the people of Pharaoh, their application of oneness and their knowledge. They are similar to the Karmathians (*al-Qarāmiṭa*[276]) and others like them.[277] However, those who follow the prophets [experience] only a praiseworthy type of annihilation[278] and these are the people whom God extols; His pious saints, His successful party and His victorious army.

In using these statements [mentioned above], it is not the intention of the shaykhs and righteous people to say that [any of] the created beings [that] I see with my own eyes is [itself] the Lord of the earth and the Heavens. No one would say this except one who is in [a state of] extreme error and corruption—either corruption of the intellect or corruption of conviction. Thus, he wavers between insanity and heresy.[279] Every shaykh who emulates them [the righteous shaykhs] in religion is in agreement with that on which the Righteous Predecessors and leading scholars of this religious community agree; that is, that the Creator (Glory be to Him) is set apart (*mubāyin*) from created beings, that nothing of His essence (*dhāt*) is in His created beings, and nothing of His created beings is in His essence,[280] and that it is necessary to separate the Eternal One (*al-qadīm*) from the temporal one (*al-ḥādith*) and to distinguish the Creator from the created. Their statements concerning this are more numerous than it is possible to mention here.[281]

THE MEANING OF *FARQ* AND *JAMᶜ*

They [the shaykhs] have spoken about the illnesses and doubts that hearts experience and [have said] that a certain person might witness the existence of created beings and think [that] it was the Creator of the earth and Heavens because there is no discernment [or] criterion [for judgement] in his heart. Such a person is on the same level as one who sees the rays of the sun, thinking that it is the sun in the sky. [The shaykhs] have also spoken about 'separation' (*farq*) and 'joining' (*jamʿ*),[282] and the various explanations[283] [that they use] are similar to what is used for annihilation. When a worshipper witnesses separation and multiplicity (*kathra*) among created beings, his heart remains attached (*mutaʿalliq*)[284] to them, observing them in [their] diversity,[285] and [remains] attached to them with love, fear and hope. But when he moves toward joining, his heart concentrates on (*mujtamiʿ ʿalā*) the oneness of God and the worshipping of Him alone without partners, [and] his heart turns toward God after being turned toward created beings. Thus, his love comes to be for his Lord, his fear is of his Lord, his hope is in his Lord, and his seeking help is from his Lord. In this state his heart may not have the capacity to view the created being in order to separate the Creator and the created; as he concentrates on the Truth, [his] vision and intention are diverted from creation. This is similar to the second type of annihilation.

However, after that there is the second separation (*al-farq al-thānī*), which is that [in which] he witnesses that the created beings are dependent on God (*qā'ima bi'Llāh*) and are controlled by His command. He witnesses that their multiplicity is absent from the oneness of God (*maʿdūma bi-waḥdāniyyat Allāh*) (Glory be to Him and Exalted is He) and that He (Glory be to Him) is the Lord of produced beings (*rabb al-maṣnūʿāt*), their Deity, Creator and Owner.[286] Thus, he views the difference between the Creator and the created, distinguishing between this and that, while his heart concentrates on God with purity, love, fear, hope, request for help, reliance on God, making alliances for His sake, making enemies for His sake and all such examples of that. He witnesses the separation of created beings and their multiplicity while testifying that God is the Lord, Owner and Creator of everything, and that He is God, there being no god other than He. This is the soundly established witnessing (*al-shuhūd al-ṣaḥīḥ al-mustaqīm*) and this is obligatory for the knowledge of a heart—in its testimony, remembrance and cognition, and in the state of a heart—[in] its worshipping, intending, willing, loving, alliance-making and obedience.

This is the essence of the testimony that there is no deity except God, for this negates the divinity of everything other than the True One in a worshipper's heart and confirms the divinity of the True One in his heart. Thus, he will negate[287] the divinity of every created being and confirm the divinity of the Lord of the worlds, the Lord of the earth and the Heavens. This necessarily includes the concentration of a heart on God and its forsaking everything other than Him, for then a worshipper will be separating the Creator and the created in his knowledge and his intention, in his testimony and his will, and in his cognizance and his love, so as to be a knower of God, a rememberer of Him, and a cogniser of Him. With all of this he will [then] know the dissimilarity of God from His creation, His isolation from them and His uniqueness over them (*tawaḥḥuduhu dūnahum*). He will be a lover of God, a glorifier of Him, a worshipper of Him, hoping in Him, fearing Him, loving for His sake,[288] making alliances and enemies for His sake, seeking help from Him and relying on Him. He will avoid worshipping [anything] other than Him, relying on [any] other, seeking help from another, fearing him, hoping in him, making alliances and enemies by him, being obedient to his command, or doing anything [concerning another] that is specific to the divinity of God (Glory be to Him and Exalted is He). His confirmation of the divinity of God over anything other than Him necessarily includes separating[289] Him [from the other] in His Lordship, for He is the Lord of everything, its Owner, Creator and Controller. At that time he will become a [true] believer in God's Oneness.

THE GRAMMAR OF *DHIKR*

It is clear that the preferred remembrance is 'there is no deity except God' just as Tirmidhī, Ibn Abī al-Dunyā[290] and others have reported as attributable to the Prophet (may God bless him and grant him peace), who said, 'The preferred remembrance is "There is no deity except God," and the preferred supplication is "All praise belongs to God."'[291] In the *Muwaṭṭa'* and elsewhere it is reported from Talḥa b. ʿUbayd Allāh[292] that the Prophet (may God bless him and grant him peace) said, 'The preferred statement that I and the prophets before me have said is "There is no deity except God, alone and without partners, to Him belongs all dominion and praise, and He has power over all things."'

Whoever maintains that this is a remembrance for the masses, that the remembrance of the elite is a single name, and [that] the remembrance of the very special elite is a pronoun, are erring and mistaken.[293] The argument of some of them concerning this is His statement, '...Say: God! Then leave them playing in their vain discourse' (Q.VI.91). This argument is a clear error on their part,[294] for the noun ['God'] that is mentioned in this matter is [given] in answer to a question in His previous verse, 'Say: Who has sent down the book that Moses brought as a light and guidance for people?' <That is, God has sent down the book that Moses brought.[295]> Thus, the noun ['God'] is the subject of a nominal sentence and its predicate has been indicated by the question. This is similar to being asked 'Who is coming?' and you answer 'Zayd.'[296]

A single noun, whether substantive or pronoun, is not a complete statement or a meaningful sentence. Faith, disbelief, commandment, or prohibition are not attached to a single noun. None of the predecessors of this religious community (*salaf al-umma*) has mentioned this; the Messenger (may God bless him and grant him peace) did not legislate this; and a heart does not receive in itself any meaningful cognizance or beneficial state (*ḥāl*) from this. However, a single noun presents an unqualified concept[297] to [a heart] on which no judgement of negation or of confirmation can be based. For if the cognition and condition of a heart is not attached to what is meaningful in itself, then there is nothing meaningful in that heart.[298] The law only legislates sayings of remembrance that are meaningful in themselves, and not what obtains meaning through something else. Certain people who persist in this remembrance[299] have succumbed to various kinds of heresy and types of unification, as has been mentioned elsewhere.

It is mentioned that a certain shaykh said, 'I fear dying between the negation and the affirmation, the one whose condition being such is not to be imitated.'[300] However, this statement is wrong, for it is obvious that if a worshipper were to die in this condition, he would die based on his aim and intention, for deeds are based on intentions. It is confirmed that the Prophet (may God bless him and grant him peace) ordered that what should be said to a dying person is, 'There is no deity except God,' and he said, 'He whose last statement is "There is no deity except God" will enter Paradise.' Now, if what he had mentioned were dangerous,[301] he would not have instructed a dying person to use [such] a statement, out of fear that he would die during it in other than a praiseworthy state of death. Rather, he would have instructed him to utter a remembrance consisting of a single noun.

The remembrance by way of a single noun or pronoun[302] is far from the *Sunna*, [and instead] nearer to innovation and near to the misguidance of Satan. For whoever says, 'O he, O he (*yā huwa, yā huwa*),' or 'he, he (*huwa, huwa*),' or anything like this, has used a pronoun that refers to only what his heart has conceptualised, but a heart may be guided or misguided—yet, the author of *al-Fuṣūṣ* [*al-Ḥikam*] wrote a book that he called *Kitāb al-huwa*.[303] Now, some of them maintain that His statement, '…And none knows its interpretation (*ta'wīlahu*) except God…' (Q.III.7), means, 'And none knows the interpretation of this noun that is (the pronoun) 'he' (*al-huwa*).' They say this even though the Muslims—and for that matter all intelligent people—agree that it is clearly false. But they will think this way, though I once said to one of them who spoke about this, 'If it were as you say it is, then the verse would be "and none knows the interpretation of 'he' (*ta'wīl huwa*)," with a disconnected pronoun.'

Then a certain shaykh often mentions in argument the statement, 'God', in His verse, 'Say God! Then leave them,' thinking that God ordered his Prophet to say a single noun. But this is a mistake[304] as is agreed on by the people of knowledge. For His statement, 'Say God,' means God is the One who has sent down the book that Moses brought. This is in answer to His verse, 'Say! Who has sent down the book that Moses brought as a light and guidance for people? But you make it into separate sheets to show while hiding much of it, and yet you were taught what you and your fathers did not know. Say God!' That is, God is the One who sent down the book that Moses brought, thereby refuting the statement of the one[305] who said, 'God does not send anything down to man.' Thus He asks, 'Who has sent down the book that Moses brought?' Then He Himself answers with, 'Say God' sent it, then let those who deny revelation play in their vain discourse.

MEANINGFUL STATEMENTS IN THE ARABIC LANGUAGE

A further explanation of the aforementioned passage is what Sībawayh and other leading grammarians have said about the fact that the Arabs speak in terms of phrases (*yaḥkūna bi'l-qawl*) so long as [those phrases] are complete utterances (*kalām*). They do not speak in such terms when [those phrases] are [merely] phrases (*qawl*), for phrases are not used in speaking unless they are complete utterances (*kalām tāmm*), either nominal or verbal sentences. For this reason they say *inna*[306] [with an 'i' vowel point (*kasra*), not an 'a' vowel point (*anna*)] when it occurs after the verb *qāla*, for a phrase cannot be spoken as a single noun.[307] Also, God (Exalted is He) does not command anyone by mentioning a single noun, and He does not legislate for the Muslims[308] [by using] an isolated, single noun, for by agreement of the Muslims, such a noun cannot benefit faith,[309] and no act of worship or proclamation has been ordered by way of a single noun.

Similar to the one who restricts himself to a single noun is what has been mentioned about an Arab who passed by a man calling [people] to pray by saying, 'I bear witness that Muḥammad, Messenger of God.' He placed both nouns in the accusative state, and thus the Arab said, 'What is this he is saying? Here is the noun, but where is its predicate that will complete the sentence?'[310] In the Qur'ān, there are other examples [of using complete sentences] such as, 'Mention the Name of your Lord, and devote yourself to Him completely' (Q.LXXIII.8), and, 'Glorify the Name of your Lord, the Most High' (Q.LXXXVII.1), and, 'But the successful one is he who purifies himself, and mentions the Name of his Lord, and prays' (Q.LXXXVII.14–15), and, 'Then glorify the Name of your Lord, the Supreme' (Q.LVI.74). These verses preclude remembering Him by a single noun. Moreover, it is recorded in the *Sunan*[311] that when the verse, 'Then glorify the Name of your Lord, the Supreme,' was sent down, the Prophet said, 'Put this in your bowing [during the prayer].' And when the verse, 'Glorify the Name of your Lord, the Most High,' was sent down, he said, 'Put this in your prostration.' Thus, he legislated for them that they should say 'Glory be to my Lord, the Supreme,' in bowing and say, 'Glory be to my Lord, the Most High,' in prostration. In the *Ṣaḥīḥ*[312] it is recorded that he used to say, 'Glory be to my Lord, the Supreme,' in his bowing and, 'Glory be to my Lord, the Most High,' in his prostration. This is the meaning of his statement, 'put this in your bowing and in your prostration,' according to the agreement of the Muslims.

Thus, glorifying the Name of his Lord, the Most High, and mentioning the Name of his Lord, and all such statements, are expressed in complete, meaningful sentences as it is recorded in the *Ṣaḥīḥ*[313] that the Prophet (may God bless him and grant him peace) said, 'The four preferred statements after [the recitation of] the Qur'ān are taken from the Qur'ān, "Glory be to God," "All praise is for God," "There is no deity except God," and "God is the Greatest."' In the *Ṣaḥīḥ*[314] it is recorded that he (may God bless him and grant him peace) said, 'There are two statements light on the tongue, heavy on the scale [of judgement], and beloved to God, "Glory and praise be to God," and, "Glory be to God, the Supreme."' In the two *Ṣaḥīḥs*[315] it is recorded that he (may God bless him and grant him peace) said, 'As for the one who says one hundred times during the course of his day, "There is no deity except God, alone and without partners, to Him belongs dominion and praise, and He has power over all things," God has granted him protection from Satan during this day until the evening. No one has brought anything more preferable than this except a man who says what the other said and then adds more to it. As for the one who says one hundred times during the course of his day, "Glory and praise be to God, glory be to God, the Supreme," his sins will be taken from him, even if they were like the foam on the ocean.' In the *Muwaṭṭa'*[316] and other books, it is recorded that he (may God bless him and grant him peace) said, 'The most preferred statement that I and the prophets before me have said is, "There is no deity except God, alone and without partners, to Him belongs all dominion and praise, and He has power over all things."' In the *Sunan* of Ibn Mājah[317] and other books, it is recorded that he (may God bless him and grant him peace) said, 'The most preferred remembrance is "There is no deity except God," and the most preferred supplication is, "All praise is due to God."' There are many examples similar to these *ḥadīth*s about the [different] kinds of statements concerning remembrance and supplication. Further examples are in the Qur'ān, [such as,] 'Do not eat from that on which the Name of God has not been mentioned...' (Q.VI.121), and, '...Then eat from that which they catch for you and mention the Name of God on it...' (Q.V.4).

However, as for His statement, 'In the Name of God,' it is a complete sentence in accordance with the two most distinct statements of the grammarians, for it is either a nominal sentence or a verbal sentence. The reconstruction [of the missing sentence element here] is either, 'My sacrifice is in the Name of God,' or, 'I sacrifice in the Name of God.'[318] This is similar to the Qur'ān reciters saying, 'In the Name of God, the Infinitely Merciful, the Compassionate,' for the reconstruction is, 'My recitation is in the Name of God,' or, 'I recite in the Name of God.' Concerning this example, people suppress [the complete sentence], which is, 'My initiation [of an action] is in the Name of God,' or, 'I initiate [an action] in the Name of God.' The former is better because the whole action is the object of, 'In the Name of God,' not just the onset of it. This same [grammatical rule] applies to the pronoun (*al-muḍmar*) in His statements, 'Read! In the Name of your Lord who created' (Q.XCVI.1), and, '…In the Name of God [will be] its moving and its anchoring…' (Q.XI.41). This also occurs in the statement of the Prophet (may God bless him and grant him peace), 'Whoever had slaughtered before the prayer, let him slaughter another in its place, and whoever has not slaughtered, let him slaughter in the Name of God.'[319] Also related to this topic is the statement of the Prophet (may God bless him and grant him peace) to his stepson, ʿUmar b. Abī Salama, in an authentic *ḥadīth*, 'Pronounce the Name of God (*sammi Allāh*), eat with your right hand and eat from what is nearest to you.'[320] The intention here is to say, 'In the Name of God,' it is not merely to mention a single noun. Likewise, there is a statement from him (may God bless him and grant him peace) to ʿAdī b. Ḥātim in an authentic *ḥadīth*, 'When you send your hunting dog, mention the Name of God, and then eat.'[321] Also, there is a statement from him (may God bless him and grant him peace), 'When a man enters his house and mentions the Name of God upon entering, upon leaving, and upon eating, Satan says, "There is no overnight stay with you, nor any dinner."'[322] There are many examples of this.

Likewise, the legislated means of mentioning God (Exalted is He) for the Muslims in their prayer, their call to prayer, their pilgrimage and their celebrations is only by way of a complete sentence. For example, the saying of the caller to prayer is, 'God is the Greatest, God is the Greatest, I testify that there is no deity except God, and I testify that Muḥammad is the Messenger of God.' The sayings of those who pray are, 'God is the Greatest; Glory be to my Lord, the Supreme; Glory be to my Lord, the Most High; God hears those who praise Him; My salutations are for God.' The saying of a pilgrim[323] is, 'Here I am at Your service, O God, here I am at Your service.' Again, there are many examples of this. Thus all of the sayings of remembrance that God has legislated are in the form of complete sentences, not single nouns—whether explicit or pronoun. This is what is called a [meaningful] statement (*kalima*) according to the Arabic language as in his saying, 'There are two statements (*kalimatāni*) light on the tongue, heavy on the scale [of judgement], and beloved to the Infinitely Merciful, <"Glory and praise be to God," and, "Glory be to God, the Supreme">.'[324] There is also his saying, 'The most preferred statement spoken by a poet is the statement of Labīd, "Is not everything other than God false."'[325] Also the verses of God (Exalted is He) are part of this topic, '...Dreadful is the word (*kalima*) that comes out of their mouths...' (Q.XVIII.5), and, 'Perfected is the word (*kalima*) of your Lord in truth and justice...' (Q.VI.115).

There are many examples of the use of the term 'word' (*kalima*) in the Qur'ān, the *Sunna* and the rest of the speech of the Arabs; however, the only thing meant by it is a complete sentence.[326] Similarly, the term 'letter' (*ḥarf*) used to be used for a noun, for it is said, 'This is a strange word (*ḥarf gharīb*);' that is, the expression of the noun is strange.

Sībawayh divided the sentence into nouns, verbs and particles (*ḥarf*) that convey a meaning, not being a noun or verb.[327] He named each of these divisions a part of speech (*ḥarf*), but the particularity of the third is that it is a particle, 'which conveys a meaning, not being a noun or verb.' He also used the term, *ḥarf*, for the letters of the alphabet, but that refers to the names [of the letters], and the expression of these letters includes these names as well as others. This is similar to what the Prophet (may God bless him and grant him peace) said, 'Whoever reads the Qur'ān with proper pronunciation (*aʿrabahu*) will have ten good deeds for each letter (*ḥarf*). But I am not saying that [the letters] *alif*, *lām*, *mīm* is one *ḥarf*; rather, *alif* is a *ḥarf*, *lām* is a *ḥarf* and *mīm* is a *ḥarf*.'[328] Also, Khalīl <b. Aḥmad[329]> asked his companions about the pronunciation of the letter (*ḥarf*) 'zāy' in the word 'Zayd.' They said, 'zāy,' but he said, 'You gave me the name, however, the letter is pronounced "z."'

Thus, the grammarians are agreed that this expression [which is] referred to in language as a *ḥarf*, is also called a 'word' (*kalima*), and [they are agreed] that the term 'particle' (*ḥarf*) is specifically used for a term, 'which conveys a meaning, not being a noun or verb,' such as prepositions. As for the terms for the letters of the alphabet, sometimes they are designated as the sound of that particular letter (*ḥarf*) and sometimes as the name of that letter. As this technical usage became preponderant, it is easily imaginable that people became accustomed to this [as the standard usage] in the language of the Arabs. Some people have made the linguistic expression, 'word' (*kalima*), into a collective term (*mushtarak*) referring to either a noun or a sentence (*jumla*). But the only known use of the term *kalima* in the pure language is as a complete sentence (*jumla tāmma*).

The intention here is that the legislated [ways of] remembering God is the remembrance of Him by way of a complete sentence, which is called [meaningful] speech (*kalām*)—the unit of which is a sentence (*kalima*). This *kalima* is that which benefits hearts and by which reward and recompense, nearness to God,[330] cognizance of Him, love for Him and apprehension of Him are obtained. These are some of the exalted goals and lofty intentions obtained through this *kalima*. However, restricting remembrance to a single noun, whether explicit or pronoun, has no basis, particularly [with its] being the form of remembrance of the elite and the gnostics (*al-khāṣṣa wa'l-ʿārifīn*). Rather, this is a means toward various forms of innovations and types of error, and it is an expedient toward concepts of corrupt states that are the states of the heretics (*Ahl al-Ilḥād*) and of the monists (*Ahl al-Ittiḥād*), as has been mentioned elsewhere.

The Summation of Correct Worship

The entire religion is based on two principles: [(1)] that nothing is worshipped except God, and [(2)] that He is only worshipped[331] according to what He has legislated; He is not worshipped according to innovations. The Exalted One says, '...Thus, whoever hopes on the meeting with his Lord, let him do righteous deeds and not associate anyone in worshipping his Lord' (Q.XVIII.110). This is the essential truth of the two testimonies of faith: the testimony that there is no deity except God, and the testimony that Muḥammad is the Messenger of God. The first one confirms that we worship only Him, and the second one confirms that Muḥammad is His Messenger, the bearer of news from Him. Thus, it is incumbent on us to affirm his message and to obey his command, for he has explained to us the way in which we [should] worship God and has prohibited us from inventing matters, informing us that they are errors. God (Exalted is He) says, 'No! But whoever submits himself fully to God while doing good has his reward with his Lord; there shall be no fear upon them and they shall not grieve' (Q.II.112).

Similarly, we have been ordered to fear only God, to rely only on Him, to direct our wishes toward only Him, to seek help from only Him, and to make our worship for only Him. Likewise, we have been ordered to follow the Messenger, to obey him and to imitate him, for the allowable is what he allowed, the forbidden is what he forbade, and the religion is what he legislated. God (Exalted is He) says, 'But if they had only been pleased with what God and His Messenger gave them and had said, "God suffices for us; God and His Messenger will give us from His bounty; we are surely directing our wishes toward God"' (Q.IX.59).

Thus, He made the dispersing of goods a right of God and His Messenger, just as God (Exalted is He) says, '...whatever the

Messenger gives you, take it; and from whatever he prohibits you, avoid it…' (Q.LIX.7). He made reliance on God a right of God alone by His statement, 'and had they said: God suffices for us,' for He did not say, 'and His Messenger.' He also says,[332] '(The believers are) those to whom people said, "Men are surely gathering against you, so fear them." But this increased them in faith and they said, "God suffices for us, and how perfect a protector He is"' (Q.III.173). A verse similar to this is, 'O Prophet! God suffices for you and for any believers who follow you' (Q.VIII.64). That is, He suffices for you and He suffices for the believers just as the Exalted One says, 'Is not God sufficient for His worshipper…' (Q.XXXIX.36) and '…God and His Messenger will give us from His bounty…' (Q.IX.59).

Thus, He made the dispersing of goods a right of God and His Messenger, but He gave precedence to mentioning bounty because bounty is in God's Hand and He gives it to whomever He wills, for God is the Possessor of great bounty. His bounty comes to His Messenger and to the believers. He also says, '…we are surely directing our wishes toward God.' Thus, He established that the act of wishing must be directed toward God alone, just as in His verse, 'And so when you are relieved, still toil; and to your Lord direct your wishes' (Q.XCIV.7–8).

The Prophet (may God bless him and grant him peace) said to Ibn ʿAbbās, 'When you ask, ask of God, and when you seek help, seek it from God.'[333] The Qur'ān gives many examples of this and it is mentioned in other places. Thus, He established that worshipping, fearing and pious acts must be for God alone, but He established that obedience and love are for both God and His Messenger. This is similar to what Noah said, 'That you worship God and act piously toward Him, and that you obey me' (Q.LXXI.3), and, 'As for whoever obeys God and His Messenger, and fears God and acts piously toward Him, these are the successful' (Q.XXIV.52).

There are many examples of this. Thus, the messengers ordered the worshipping of Him alone, the directing of wishes to Him, reliance on Him, but obedience <to Him[334]> and themselves. Satan then led the Christians and others like them astray, for they associated partners with God and disobeyed the messengers. Thus, they took their priests and monks, and the Messiah, the son of Mary, as rivals besides God. They began directing their wishes to them, relying on them and asking of them while [simultaneously] disobeying their commands and opposing their customs.

God has guided the believers, the sincere worshippers of God, the people of the straight path, those who know the truth and follow it. Thus, they are not the ones who have earned His wrath, nor the ones who are astray. They have purified their religion for God, submitted themselves fully to Him, and turned repentantly to their Lord. They love God, hope in Him, fear Him, ask of Him, direct their wishes toward Him, entrust their affairs to Him and rely on Him. They obey His messengers, support them, respect them, love them, ally themselves to them and follow them. They adhere to their teachings and are guided by their light. This is the religion of Islam with which God has sent the former and latter messengers. It is the only religion that God will accept from anyone and it is the [only] true worship of the Lord of the worlds.

Thus, we ask God, the Majestic, to make us and all our brother Muslims firm in Islam, to perfect it for us and to let us die in it. All praise is for God, the Lord of the worlds. May His blessing and peace be upon our master, Muḥammad, the seal of the prophets, and upon his family and companions.

NOTES TO TRANSLATION

1 The texts give various honorifics describing Ibn Taymiyya, which need not be listed here.

2 For the purpose of this translation, the use of three dots (...) in Qur'ānic quotations indicates that an incomplete verse has been quoted, or that whole verses were omitted from lengthier passages. Edition 1 does not always indicate which parts of verses are quoted. However, some lengthy Qur'ānic quotations are broken up by the phrases, 'to His statement' (*ilā qawlihi*) and 'to the verse' (*ilā al-aya*), or with the phrase 'to the end of the sura' (*ilā akhir al-sūra*).

3 Literally: '*wa'l-mamlūk min al-adamiyyīn wa'l-bahā'im*' (human and animal possessions). Editions 3 and 4 insert *wa-ibn al-sabīl* ('wayfarers') before 'slaves and animals.'

4 There are two main points that Sunnī exegetes raised concerning this verse. The first was that God had created humans and *jinn* for the purpose of worshipping Him, not out of any need that He had for that. The second point was that the test of their worship was whether they did it willingly or unwillingly. Ibn Taymiyya was implying that people were not coerced by God to worship only Him. See Ibn Kathīr, ibid., vol. III, p. 387.

5 Ibn Taymiyya gave the standard Sunnī interpretation of the word *yaqīn* in this verse as meaning death. He discusses this point below in his refutation of some Ṣūfī interpretations of *yaqīn* as meaning the attainment of certainty in knowing the truth and thus also obtaining a waiver from performing religious obligations. For a review of the Sunnī exegesis of this verse, see Ibn Kathīr, ibid., vol. II, p. 320.

6 Although the term 'son' is used, the immediate reference here concerns the claim of pagan Arabs that the angels were the daughters of God. The interpretation was that the attribute of worship ascribed to the angels negated the attribute of sonship; see Ibn Kathīr, ibid., vol. II, p. 505.

7 Editions 2 and 4 have *al-nubuwwa* (prophethood) instead of *al-bunuwwa* (sonship).

8 Bukhārī, *anbiyā'* 48; Dārimī, *raqāq* 68; Aḥmad, 1:23, 24, 47, 55, 60. All references to *ḥadīth*s, unless otherwise noted, are taken directly from Arent Jan Wensinck, *Concordance et indices de la tradition musulmane*, 8 vols., repr., Istanbul: Çağri Yayinlari & Tunis: Maison Souhnoun, 1988. Although I have cross-checked each *ḥadīth* by searching various key words, I cannot guarantee that all listings are given.

9 The referents of the pronouns are not specified. This interpretation is taken from Jalāl al-Dīn ʿAbd al-Raḥmān al-Suyūṭī and Jalāl al-Dīn Muḥammad

al-Maḥallī, *al-Qurān al-karīm bi-tafsīr al-imāmayn al-Jalālayn*, Beirut: Dār al-ᶜIlm li'l-Jamīᶜ, [no date], p. 697. An equally acceptable interpretation would be: 'Thus he [Gabriel] revealed to His worshipper [Muḥammad] what He [God] had revealed;' see Muḥammad Shawkānī, *al-Qur'ān al-karīm wa-bi'l-hāmish zubdat al-tafsīr min fatḥ al-qadīr*, ed. Muḥammad Sulaymān ᶜAbd Allāh al-Ashqar, Kuwait: Wizārat al-Awqāf wa'l-Shu'ūn al-Islāmiyya, 1406/1985, p. 700 and Ibn Kathīr, ibid., vol. III, p. 398.

10 Two interpretations were given for this verse: (1) some jinn gathered around Muḥammad to hear the recitation, and (2) some jinn and people jostled the Prophet to try to stop him; see Shawkānī, ibid., p. 772 and Ibn Kathīr, ibid., vol. III, p. 559.

11 Bukhārī, *īmān* 37, *tafsīr sūra* 31: *bāb* 2.

12 Edition 4 has only *islām*.

13 Ibn Manẓūr, ibid., s.v. '*ḥsn*', defined the term *iḥsān* within the context of this *ḥadīth* as sincerity (*ikhlās*). He stated, '*Iḥsān* is a condition for the soundness of both faith and submission because one can express a statement and perform an action without sincerity.' On the issue of *iḥsān* as a theological concept in relation to *islām* and *īmān*, Izutsu states that *iḥsān* was never 'elaborated theoretically by the theologians;' ibid., pp. 58–59.

14 Ibn Taymiyya presents a slightly more detailed discussion below concerning various concepts of love in relation to states of psychological and emotional dependence. In contrast to Ibn Taymiyya, Ibn al-Qayyim wrote extensively on the terms and concepts related to love theory in his work, *Rawdat al-muḥibbīn wa-nuzhat al-mushtāqīn*, and he discussed over 60 terms related to the category of love (see pp. 23–55); *Rawdat al-muḥibbīn wa-nuzhat al-mushtāqīn*, Beirut: al-Mu'assasat al-Jāmiᶜiyya li'l-Dirāsāt wa'l-Nashr wa'l-Tawzīᶜ, 1402/1982. For a detailed discussion of Ibn Taymiyya's beliefs on love theory within the context of Ḥanbalī thinking on this topic, see Bell, *Love Theory*, pp. 54–89.

15 Lane, ibid., s.v. '*tym*', defines *taym* as enslavement because of love and as a vehement love that deprives one of reason.

16 This same schematic view of love is found in '*al-Tuḥfa al-ᶜirāqiyya fī al-aᶜmāl al-qalbiyya*,' in *Majmūᶜ fatāwā*, vol. x: *Kitāb ᶜilm al-sulūk*, pp. 70–71. Ibn Taymiyya also included a lengthy discussion on *ᶜishq* in '*Amrād al-qulūb wa-shifā'uhā*,' in *Majmūᶜ fatāwā*, vol. x, pp. 131–132.

17 Edition 5 has *al-khudūᶜ* instead of *al-dhull*.

18 This insertion is from Edition 3.

19 The only other reference to this verse that I have been able to find is in '*Qā'ida fī al-tawassul wa'l-wasīla*' in *Majmūᶜ Fatāwā*, vol. I, p. 306, which also does not go into details. Ibn Taymiyya was interpreting Q.VIII.64 within the limits of his theological position concerning the concept of sufficiency, which he categorized as one of the duties which are only for God. He rejected the notion that the believers suffice for Muḥammad. A fuller explanation of this stance was given

by Ibn al-Qayyim in *Zād al-maʿād* in which he gave four interpretations of the verse based on the usages of the conjunction '*wa-*' in the phrase *ḥasbuka Allāhu wa-man ittabaʿaka*. Three of them, he stated, were acceptable: (1) if *wa* links *man* to the *ka* in a genitive construction; (2) if *wa* has the meaning of *maʿa* and *man* is in the accusative case, as in the statement *ḥasbuka wa zaydan dirhamun*; and, (3) if *man* is the subject of a nominal sentence (*mubtadaʾ*) and is predicated by reconstruction (*taqdīr*) with *fa-ḥasbuhum Allāhu*. The fourth possibility was rejected, according to Ibn al-Qayyim, because the meaning would be pure error if *man* were in the nominative case and linked to the noun *Allāhu*; see *Zād al-maʿād*, 5 vols, Beirut: Mu'assasat al-Risāla & Kuwait: Maktabat al-Manār al-Islāmiyya, 1407/1987, vol. I, pp. 35–36. In support of this interpretation, Ibn Kathīr also stated that this was the position of Ibn Abī Ḥātim, who reported it from al-Shuʿbī (d. 104/722–3 or 107/725–6); ibid., vol. II, p. 117. However, other exegetes accepted the interpretation which was rejected by Ibn Taymiyya. Ṭabarī and Fakhr al-Dīn al-Rāzī explained that one could say that the believers were sufficient for Muḥammad so long as it was understood that they were a means by which God granted victory to him; see Ṭabarī, ibid., vol. IV, p. 48–49 and Fakhr al-Dīn al-Rāzī, *al-Tafsīr al-kabīr li'l-imām al-Fakhr al-Rāzī*, Beirut: Dār Iḥyā' al-Turāth al-ʿArabī, no date, vol. XV, pp. 191–192,. This interpretation is also mentioned by Suyūṭī and Maḥallī, ibid., p. 244 and Shawkānī, ibid., p. 236.

20 Editions 3 and 4 have *qudratihi* instead of *qadarihi*.

21 Edition 3 inserts *li-kulli shay'in wa-mudabbiruhu wa-musakhkhiruhu*.

22 Editions 2, 3 and 4 have *ʿalimū* instead of *ʿarafū*.

23 Edition 3 has *āmanū* instead of *iʿtarafū* and then inserts *wa-shakarūhu bi-ʿubūdiyyati al-ālihiyya raghaban wa-rahaban*.

24 In this passage, knowledge is being contrasted with ignorance and cognizance is being contrasted with denial. The terms being used are translated as follows: *ʿalima* means to know, *ʿarafa* means to cognize, *iʿtarafa* means to acknowledge, *maʿrifa* means cognizance, *ankara* means to deny, *jaḥada* means to disavow and *jahala* means to be ignorant of something. These translations will be maintained throughout the text. In his classification of human beings and his description of the development of a worshipper, Ibn Taymiyya maintained a constant tension between ignorance and knowledge, and between cognizance and denial. Intricately linked to ignorance and denial was the concept of arrogance.

25 Editions 3, 4 and 5 have *iʿtarafa* instead of *ʿarafa*.

26 The term *ḥaqīqa* in a theological and philosophical context has been translated as truth, reality and essence. In reference to Ibn Taymiyya's empirical view of particulars in the external world, Hallaq states that individuals exist '...in the context of a reality (*ḥaqīqa*) that is different from other realities;' *Ibn Taymiyya against the Greek Logicians*, p. xxii. Elsewhere (p. 87), concerning Ibn Taymiyya's discussion of the conditional hypothetical syllogism, Hallaq refers to the essence (*ḥaqīqa*) of an inference remaining unchanged. Seyyed Hossein Nasr discusses

ḥaqīqa in terms of an inner truth that lies at the heart of the Qur'ān, in opposition to its external dimension which is related to Islamic law; see 'The Qur'ān and *Ḥadīth* as source and inspiration of Islamic philosophy,' in *History of Islamic Philosophy,* Part I, New York: Routledge, 1996, p. 29. Chittick translates *ḥaqīqa* as 'reality' in reference to Ibn ʿArabī's conception of '...the Divine Essence considered in respect of a particular relationship which It assumes with the creatures,' and *ḥaqīqa* is the descriptive term for this relationship; ibid., p. 37. As for my purposes, I translate *ḥaqīqa* as 'reality' unless otherwise noted.

27 For this translation of *la-aḥtanikanna dhurriyyatahu*, see J. Penrice, *A Dictionary and Glossary of the Korān*, repr., Karachi: Rahim Brothers, 1987, p. 39.

28 The Arabic term is *Ahl al-Maʿrifa wa'l-Taḥqīq*, which refers to the well-known Ṣūfī concepts of gnosis and realization. Throughout the translation, I use English terms related to the root meaning of 'to cognize' for all Arabic words derived from the root *ʿ-r-f*. In classical Ṣūfī understanding, as explained by Chittick, *maʿrifa* was a 'gnostic science' that was at a higher level than knowledge (*ʿilm*); see ibid., pp. 148–149. He states that the term may be rendered as 'true knowledge' or 'to recognize'. My use of 'realization' for *taḥqīq* is based on its use by Ernst; ibid., p. 59. The Ṣūfī concept of *taḥqīq* (for which Chittick prefers 'verification') was a 'station of the great gnostics, those who have verified the truth of their knowledge through unveiling and direct vision;' Chittick, ibid., pp. 166–168.

29 Khaḍir or Khiḍr is the name of the servant whom Moses accompanied as mentioned in Q.XVIII.60–82. Although unnamed in the Qur'ān, the Prophet spoke of Khaḍir at length as reported in authentic *ḥadīth*s, giving his name along with other details of his encounter with Moses. A full discussion of him would be much too lengthy to go into here, especially if one attempts to determine the authentic reports among the numerous fabricated stories. For a review of the information concerning Khaḍir, see Wensinck, *EI2*, vol. IV, s.v. '*al-Khaḍir*.' Ibn Ḥajar has a lengthy discussion of the authenticity of the reports related to Khaḍir in his *Fatḥ al-bārī*; see vol. VIII, pp. 409–425). For our purposes, several important issues concerning his status must be discussed. Ibn Taymiyya mentioned Khaḍir because the latter featured prominently in the belief system of many Ṣūfī mystics as an example of a man who had attained 'cognizance'; see Schimmel, ibid., passim. Thus, he became the basis of, and justification for, their claims of mystical knowledge. In this context, the statements of Ibn Ḥajar concerning Khaḍir's status and the level of his knowledge help to explain the various opinions about him. In his *Fatḥ al-bārī*, Ibn Ḥajar discussed Khaḍir in the context of refuting many of the Ṣūfī claims concerning him. In summary, he argued that: (1) Khaḍir was a prophet but not a messenger, and only the people of falsehood called him God's saint (*walī*); (2) Khaḍir did not have complete knowledge of the unseen (*ghayb*), because prophets only receive limited knowledge; (3) human intelligence is deficient and incapable of comprehending the secrets of Lordship (*asrār al-rubūbiyya*); and (4) it is an act of disbelief to claim secret knowledge by

making statements such as: (a) there is a path of knowledge which necessitates abandonment of the law; (b) the judgments of the law are for the masses, but God's saints have no need for revealed texts, for they can judge according to their hearts and minds (*khawāṭir*) because their purification and renunciation brings them divine knowledge (*al-ʿulūm al-ilāhiyya*) and divine truths (*al-ḥaqā'iq al-rabbāniyya*); and (c) one should not obtain knowledge from the dead (i.e., from transmitted sources), but obtain it directly from the Living One who never dies. These points and others that Ibn Ḥajar discussed reflected Ibn Taymiyya's stance on Khaḍir; see Ibn Ḥajar, *Fatḥ al-bārī*, vol. 1, pp. 217–220.

30 Edition 3 inserts *al-kāfirīn wa'l-fāsiqīn*.

31 For Ibn Taymiyya, the concept of oneness consists of two aspects which he refers to as *tawḥīd qawlī* and *tawḥīd ʿamalī*; see '*Qā'ida fī al-tawassul wa'l-wasīla*,' in *Majmūʿ Fatāwā*, vol. 1, p. 367. In this translation, I shall only distinguish between these two different aspects of *tawḥīd* when necessitated by the context of particular passages. In such cases, the concept of *tawḥīd qawlī* will be rendered as 'the declaration of oneness', and the concept of *tawḥīd ʿamalī* will be rendered as 'the application of oneness.'

32 Ibn Taymiyya's statement reads, *fa'l-ilāh alladhī yu'allihuhu al-qalb*. He explains below that a heart must worship something; that is, it must direct its love, hope and fear toward something. False deities are created by people when they direct their worship toward a thing that is in itself unworthy of that worship.

33 Editions 3, 4 and 5 have *yukrimuhum bi-jannatihi* instead of *bi-ḥasabihi*.

34 Editions 3 and 4 have *al-muddaʿīn* instead of *al-muntasibīn*.

35 The word *ʿirfān* is usually translated as gnosis, which in Ṣūfī terminology means 'a form of knowledge which can be achieved only through spiritual practice, not by book learning or study with a teacher;' Chittick, ibid., p. 149.

36 ʿAbd al-Qādir al-Jilānī was born c. 470/1077 and died in 561/1166. He was a leading Ḥanbalī scholar who followed the Ṣūfī path. For a review of the biographical material about him, see D. S. Margoliouth, 'Contribution to the Biography of ʿAbd al-Kadir of Jilan,' *Journal of the Royal Asiatic Society*, April, 1907, pp. 267–310.

37 The last two sentences of this quotation read: *fa-nāzaʿtu aqdāra al-ḥaqq bi'l-ḥaqq li'l-ḥaqq wa'l-rajul man yukūnu munāziʿan li'l-qadar lā man yakūnu muwāfiqan li'l-qadar*. I have not found any instance of this quotation attributed to ʿAbd al-Qādir. There is a similar statement in Kalābādhī, which reads: *al-tawāḍuʿ qabūlu al-ḥaqq min al-ḥaqq li'l-ḥaqq*; ibid., p. 116. See also Arberry's translation, ibid., p. 88. Thomas Michel, in his review of Ibn Taymiyya's *Sharḥ futūḥ al-ghayb* (which is a commentary on ʿAbd al-Qādir's famous work), indicates that ʿAbd al-Qādir taught an antivoluntarist view of religion; 'Ibn Taymiyya's *Sharḥ* on the *Futūḥ al-ghayb* of ʿAbd al-Qādir al-Jīlānī,' *Hamdard Islamicus,* vol. IV, no. 2, 1981, pp. 6–7. That is, ʿAbd al-Qādir spoke '...of annihilation of the will and surrendering to the predetermined decrees of God rather than to His command to active obedience...' However, this statement does not do justice to ʿAbd al-Qādir's

insistence on obedience to Islamic law, for as Walther Braune points out, ʿAbd al-Q̲ādir maintained the traditional Ḥanbalī position with regard to religious duties. Braune also argues that ʿAbd al-Q̲ādir intentionally stressed obedience to the law in opposition to the widespread antinomian beliefs of many Ṣūfīs; see *Die Futūḥ al-Ġaib des ʿAbd Q̲ādir*, Berlin & Leipzig: Walter De Gruyter & Co., 1933, pp. 38–40. Thus, Ibn Taymiyya's view that it was impossible to cease willing at any state, and that patience and resignation must be balanced with an active embrace of commanding good and forbidding evil, coincided with the position of earlier Ḥanbalī Ṣūfīs such as ʿAbd al-Q̲ādir.

38 Bukhārī, *anbiyā'* 31, *tawḥīd* 37; Muslim, *qadar* 13, 15.

39 Editions 3 and 4 have *fa-inna Ādama qad tāba ilā rabbihi* instead of *fa-inna Ādama tāba Allahu ʿalayhi*.

40 The Arabic expression for 'until he reaches the point that' is *ḥattā yu'awwila bihi al-amra ilā an*. Edition 3 has *hādhihi al-taswiya* instead of *al-amra*. The verb *awwala* in its original meaning, as per Lane, is 'to cause a thing to come to such a state or condition, to bring or reduce it thereto;' Lane, ibid., s.v. *'-w-l*.

41 I am reading *ʿubbād* as the plural of *ʿabd* instead of *ʿibād*, which has the meaning of worshipper. Edition 3 has *al-ʿālamīn*.

42 Although he often mentioned the various Ṣūfī shaykhs collectively, Ibn Taymiyya clearly recognized the differences between them. This was made clear in his *Risāla ilā Naṣr al-Manbijī*, in which he also credited Ibn ʿArabī for insisting on obedience to the law and stated that many people benefited from him because of this; '*Risāla ilā Naṣr al-Manbijī*,' in *Majmūʿ fatāwā*, vol. II: *Kitāb tawḥīd al-ulūhiyya*, p. 470. The antinomianism related to the concept of the unity of being was more directly attributed to the followers of Ibn ʿArabī. For instance, Hermann Landolt informs us that ʿIzz al-Dīn Maḥmūd Kāshānī (d. 735/1334) claimed that when one cognizes ('erfährt') that all acts come from God, then the difference between good and evil becomes baseless; 'Der Briefwechsel zwischen Kāshānī und Simnānī über Waḥdat al-Wuǧūd,' *Der Islam*, vol. L, no. 1, 1973, p. 51.

43 Ibn Mājah, *muqaddima* 12; al-Dārimī, *faḍā'il al-qur'ān* 1; Aḥmad, III:167, 168, 242.

44 The phrase Ibn Taymiyya uses here is *laysa huwa ḥālan fīhā* ('He does not have a mode of existence in them'). I understand *ḥāl* in this context to indicate its lexical meaning of 'changing or moving from one state or condition to another;' see Lane, ibid., s.v. '*ḥ-w-l*.' That is, neither God nor any aspects of His names and attributes reside in the creation in any possible way. This is just one of the ways in which Ibn Taymiyya expressed a complete distinction between God and the creation. In some respects, his words echoed statements made by Ibn ʿArabī concerning his understanding of the relationship between God and the cosmos in the *barzakh*, or what Ibn ʿArabī called the realm of 'Nondelimited Imagination,' where, according to his interpretation of the concept, God comes to be (*kāna*); see Chittick, ibid., p. 125. The *barzakh* is also

considered by Ibn ʿArabī to be the ontological locus for anthropomorphism where '...the Real [*al-haqq*] undergoes fluctuation in states to make manifest our entities...;' see Chittick, ibid., pp. 181–186.

45 The subject of the verb *yaʿlamūna* is not clearly identifiable here. The beginning of the sentence reads *wa-yaʿlamūna maʿa dhālika anna Allāha*. In Edition 3, the compound noun *khāṣṣatu Allāh* ('the elite of God') appears before the verb, thus referring back to 'the people of the Qur'ān.'

46 Tirmidhī, *ṭibb* 21, *qadar* 12; Ibn Mājah, 1.

47 I have not found any *ḥadīth* in Wensinck's *Concordance* with this wording. However, there is a similar *ḥadīth* reported by Tirmidhī which reads, 'A supplication is suspended between heaven and earth, and nothing of it ascends any further until you perform prayers for your Prophet (may God bless him and grant him peace);' Tirmidhī, *ṣalāh* 482, *witr* 21.

48 Edition 4 has *lā yufarriqūn*, which does not make sense because Ibn Taymiyya was pointing out how certain antinomian groups distinguished between the common folk and the elite.

49 Edition 3 has *mudabbir* and Edition 4 has *yudabbir* instead of *murīd*.

50 The Arabic reads: *man yarāhu shuhūdan*. One of the definitions given by Lane, ibid., for the root *r-'-y* is to experience something, which fits in with the concept of a profound state of knowledge beyond intellectual understanding.

51 Editions 3, 4 and 5 have *lā yajʿalūna al-jabr*, which contradicts the point of the previous statement.

52 Edition 3 has *al-islām* instead of *al-tawḥīd*.

53 Editions 3 and 4 have *dūna* instead of *wa-raddat*.

54 Ghazālī made the same judgment concerning the Ṣūfī who claims that 'he has attained a state of intimacy with God Most High which dispenses him from the canonical Prayer and permits him to drink wine and to commit sins and to accept the largesse of the Sultan.' His opinion is that such a one 'ought to be killed [*lā shakka fī wujūbi qatlihi*], even though his status regarding eternity in the Fire may be debatable;' *Fayṣal al-tafriqa*, p. 28. The translation of Ghazālī is from McCarthy, ibid., p. 163; and the Arabic transliteration in square brackets is my addition.

55 Edition 3 has the following insertion: *fī qalbihi al-ḍāll al-ghāfil min Allāh* (in his heart is error, being neglectful of God); and edition 5 inserts *fī qalbihi maʿan mā fīhi min ghafla ʿan Allāh jalā wa-ʿalā* ('in his heart, along with what else is in it, is negligence of God, glorious and exalted').

56 In this paragraph, Ibn Taymiyya contrasted the two branches of knowledge recognized by medieval Muslim scholars; namely, reason and revelation. He maintained that favoring reason over revelation, when that reasoning contradicts the clear statements of revelation, leads to misguidance. Gardet states that traces of the term *ʿaqliyyāt* can be found in Muʿtazilī disputations over religious knowledge (*ʿilm dīnī*); *EI2*, s.v. '*ʿAḳliyyāt*' and '*al-Ḳaḍā' wa'l-*

Ḳadar.' The Muʿtazilī divided religious knowledge into knowledge drawn from reason (*ʿilm ʿaqlī*) and knowledge drawn from revelation (*ʿilm sharʿī*). In the terminology of *kalām* the term *ʿaqliyyāt* refers to all subjects amenable to reason even if transmitted by revelation.

57 Bukhārī, *īmān* 9, 14, *ikrāh* 1; Muslim, *īmān* 66, 67; Abū Dāwud, *zakāh* 5; Tirmidhī, *ʿilm* 10; Nasā'ī, *īmān* 2 and 3; Ibn Mājah, *fitan* 23; Aḥmad, II:298, 560.

58 Muslim, *īmān* 56; Tirmidhī, *īmān* 10; Aḥmad, I:208.

59 Sufyān b. ʿUyayna (107/726–198/814) was originally from Kufa but lived and died in Mecca. He was a famous traditionist and ascetic; see Reinert, *Die Lehre vom* tawakkul *in der klassischen Sufik*, Berlin: Walter De Gruyter & Co., 1968, p. 322.

60 Editions 3 and 5 insert *wa-yughramūna bi-* between *yamīlu hā'ulā'i ilā* and *samāʿi al-shiʿr*.

61 Edition 3 inserts *wa'l-ālāt al-mūsiqiyya* after *al-aswāt*.

62 Edition 3 has *mustamsikūna bi-mā ikhtārū bi-hawāhum min al-dīn* instead of *mustamsikūna bi'l-dīn*.

63 Reinert discusses the relationship between the means and reliance in Ṣūfī thinking; ibid., pp. 141–162. In classical Ṣūfī doctrine, the *asbāb* are set in opposition to *tawakkul*, which is to live with God without obligation. Ibn Taymiyya is arguing that *tawakkul* is to live in conformity with the means that God revealed.

64 Muslim, *qadar* 31; Abū Dāwud, *sunna* 17; Nasā'ī, *janā'iz* 58; Ibn Mājah, *muqaddima* 10; Aḥmad, VI:41, 208. The second half of the *ḥadīth* is omitted from Editions 3 and 4.

65 Bukhārī, *qadar* 4.

66 This reference is to certain Ṣūfī beliefs related to the mystical experience. The concept of unveiling is the basis for the gnosticism of the Ṣūfīs. The term *kashf*, from which is derived *mukāshafa*, is translated into terms such as 'revelation,' 'uncovering' or 'disclosure,' and is synonymous with other Ṣūfī terms such as *fatḥ*, *futūḥ* or *ʿilm al-futūḥ*; see Ernst, ibid., pp. 139 and 151. In describing the difference between unveiling and reflection (*fikr* or *tafakkur*) in Ibn ʿArabī's critique of the intellect, Chittick explains that reflection is '...a peculiar mental process...which is the domain of the proponents of Kalām and the philosophers;' ibid., p. 63. As for unveiling, he explains that the position of Ibn ʿArabī and the great Ṣūfīs was that *kashf* refers to '...knowledge given to them by God without the interference of that rational or considerative faculty known as reflection.' Ibn Taymiyya held an intermediary position concerning the intellect. He rejected the role of the intellect as described by the speculative theologians, while upholding the need for the intellect in opposition to a mystical knowledge that he claimed was mere deception.

67 For Ṣūfī gnostics, religious law leads one away from knowing God. Nicholson, ibid., p. 72, in discussing the teachings of the fourth-/tenth-century Egyptian mystic Niffarī, explains that 'Niffarī bids the gnostic perform only such acts of

worship as are in accordance with his vision of God, though in doing so he will necessarily disobey the religious law which was made for the vulgar.'

68 *Sulūk* and *tawajjuh* are technical terms used by the Ṣūfīs to describe their passage from one state or station to another. I have adopted these translations from Ernst, who does not refer to them in combination; ibid., pp. 3, 58. *Sulūk* is the wayfaring of the Ṣūfī in pursuit of cognizance of the Divine Reality, whereas *tawajjuh* is the concentration on, or attentiveness to, a particular thing. In Ibn ʿArabī's metaphysics, *tawajjuh* is God's attentiveness directed 'toward someone [meaning] that He manifests His reality to that person through self-disclosure;' see Chittick, ibid., p. 280.

69 Ibn Taymiyya used the expression *fī kulli waqt*, which simply means 'in each moment.' However, in the present context it suggests further allusion to Ṣūfī terminology. For instance, Ibn ʿArabī used the term *waqt* in reference to a servant's nearness to certain names of God. Concerning his metaphysical doctrine on this matter, he stated that 'in each moment [a] ...servant must be the possessor of nearness to one divine name and the possessor of distance from another name which, at that moment, has no ruling property over him;' see Chittick, ibid., p. 151. Ibn Taymiyya indicated that the authentically transmitted *Sunna* must guide a worshipper in every apparent deed and inner state.

70 Edition 3 inserts *wa'l-ẓunūn* ('opinions'), and Edition 4 mentions only *al-bidaʿ* ('innovations').

71 Edition 3 inserts *laysat fī'l-kitāb wa-lā fī ṣaḥīḥi al-sunna fa-innahā wa-in qāla man qālahā wa-ʿamila bihā man ʿamila* (meaning, acts which 'are not in the Book or in the authenticated *Sunna*—even if someone has spoken of them and practised them').

72 Editions 3, 4 and 5 have *man yaʿmalu mā lā yajūz* instead of *mā yuʿlamu annahu fujūr*.

73 Abū ʿAlī al-Fuḍayl b. ʿIyād b. Masʿūd b. Bishr al-Tamīmī al-Yarbūʿī was from the tribe of Tamīm and was born in Samarqand in 105/723. It is said that in his early years he was a brigand but was converted to a religious life. He became a disciple of Sufyān al-Thawrī, studied *ḥadīth* in Kufa and lectured at the court of the Abbasid Caliph Ḥārūn al-Rashīd. He died in Mecca in 187/803. See Reinert, ibid., p. 302, and Brockelmann, *GAL*, vol. 1, p. 636.

74 Edition 3 inserts *wa'l-ʿamal bihi* ('and acting according to it').

75 Aḥmad, II:50, 96.

76 Edition 3 inserts *al-sayyi'āt allatī zayyanahā al-shayṭān*, and Edition 4 has *al-sayyi'āt* instead of *al-shayṭān*.

77 Edition 4 is missing *al-nās*.

78 Editions 3 and 5 have *ʿulūhiyya* instead of *rubūbiyya*.

79 Editions 1 and 2 have *wa-durūb* after *ʿumūm wa-khusūs*.

80 This example is taken from a *ḥadīth* reported by Aḥmad, I:307; II:325, 430; IV:402, 403.

81 Bukhārī, *jihād* 70; *raqāq* 10.

82 The next few paragraphs address the issue of seeking wealth as it relates to

reliance on God. Ibn Taymiyya touched on the question of working for provisions as opposed to begging, which had become a major tenet of some Ṣūfī groups. Ibn Taymiyya's basic position was that working did not contradict the idea of relying on God. The issue of reliance (*tawakkul*) in Ṣūfī thinking has been dealt with in detail by Reinert, ibid., pp. 170–190, who identifies Shaqīq al-Balkhī as the classical representative of the concept of abandoning work (p. 170). He also notes that Ibn Ḥanbal emphasized the need for both *tawakkul* and work, and ʿAbd Allah b. al-Mubārak's position was that working does not hinder a Muslim from *tawakkul*, but that there is a risk that he might corrupt it (p. 220).

83 These terms refer to the common types of *ḥadīth* collections. *Ṣiḥāḥ* is the plural of *Ṣaḥīḥ* and refers to collections such as *Ṣaḥīḥ al-Bukhārī*. *Sunan* is the plural of *Sunna* and refers to collections such as *Sunan Abī Dāwud*. *Masānīd* is the plural of *Musnad* and refers to collections such as *Musnad Aḥmad*.

84 Bukhārī, *zakā* 52; Nasā'ī, *zakā* 83; Aḥmad, II:15, 88.

85 Tirmidhī, *zakā* 22, 23; Ibn Mājah, *zakā* 16, 26; Abū Dāwūd, *zakā* 24; Dārimī, *zakā* 15; Aḥmad, I:388, 441.

86 Abū Dāwūd, *zakā* 26; Tirmidhī, *zakā* 23; Ibn Mājah, *tijārāt* 25; Aḥmad, III:114, 127.

87 Bukhārī, *zakā* 50, 53, *buyūʿ* 15, *musāqā* 13; Tirmidhī, *zakā* 38; Nasā'ī, *zakā* 85; Aḥmad, I:124, II:243, 257, 300, 395, 418, 475, 496.

88 Bukhārī, *zakā* 51; Muslim, *zakā* 110, 111; Dārimī, *zakā* 19; Nasā'ī, *zakā* 94; Aḥmad, II:99.

89 Bukhārī, *zakā* 18, 50, *raqāq* 20; Muslim, *zakā* 124; Abū Dāwūd, *zakā* 28; Tirmidhī, *birr* 77; Dārimī, *zakā* 18; *Muwaṭṭa'*, *ṣadaqa* 7; Nasā'ī, *zakā* 85; Aḥmad, III:12, 44, 47, 93, 403, 434.

90 The word *al-sawṭ* is missing from edition 1.

91 I have not found specific references to these two *ḥadīth*s in the *Musnad* and *Ṣaḥīḥ Muslim*.

92 Tirmidhī, *qiyāma* 59; Aḥmad, I:293, 303, 307.

93 The issue here refers to the Arabic syntax of the verse in question: *fa'btaghū ʿind Allāh al-rizq*. Ibn Taymiyya was saying that changing the normal word order (i.e., verb-object-adverb) by pre-positioning the adverb (*taqdīm al-ẓarf*) brought additional meanings of particularization (*ikhtiṣāṣ*) and restriction (*ḥaṣr*) to a sentence.

94 Edition 3 has *fa-lā yas'alu rizqahu illā min Allāh wa-lā yashtakī illā ilayhi*.

95 These references are to *hajr jamīl* in Q.LXXIII.10, *ṣabr jamīl* in Q.XII.18 and 83, and *ṣafḥ jamīl* in Q.XV.85 respectively. Ibn Taymiyya also discussed these terms in a separate essay that is included in *Majmūʿat al-rasā'il wa'l-masā'il*, vol. 1, pp. 2–9.

96 Abū ʿAbd al-Raḥmān Ṭāwūs b. Kaysān (d. 106/725) was a Follower of the Prophet who was known for excessive acts of worship and an asceticism based on the fear of Hellfire; see Reinert, ibid., p. 323.

97 Editions 3 and 4 insert *fī qirā'athi*.

98 Edition 3 has *tashannujuhu* for *nashījuhu*.

99 I have not found any reference for this supplication.

100 I have not found this *ḥadīth* in the *Concordance*. However, Ibn Kathīr mentions it in his report on the Prophet's mission to Ṭā'if; *Bidāya*, vol. III, p. 134.

101 Edition 4 has *min ghayri Allāh* instead of *min Allāh*, which does not make sense in the context of making it necessary for a heart to turn away from worshipping God.

102 Editions 1 and 5 have *mudīran lahum*; Edition 3 has *mudabbiran li-umūrihim*; and Editions 2 and 4 have *mudabbiran lahum*.

103 Edition 3 has *tataḥakkamu fīhi* instead of *taḥkumu fīhi*. The former verb form is more appropriately used with the preposition *fī*, whereas *taḥkumu* should be used with *ʿalā*.

104 Edition 3 inserts *aw mālikuhu*.

105 Edition 3 has *ʿalimat* for *darat*.

106 This insertion is from Editions 3, 4 and 5, which have *badanahu*. The term *bi-dūnihi* found in Editions 1 and 2 does not make sense here.

107 Only Editions 1 and 2 have *wa-'asara*.

108 Edition 3 has *mā dāma* instead of *idhā kāna*.

109 This insertion is from edition 3, which has *malik al-jasad*.

110 In Edition 3 the adjective *al-dhalīla* is added to *al-ʿubūdiyya*.

111 Edition 3 inserts *kullu al-ḍarar*.

112 Bukhārī, *raqāq* 15; Muslim, *zakā* 120; Tirmidhī, *zuhd* 40; Ibn Mājah, *zuhd* 9; Aḥmad, II:243, 261, 315, 390, 438, 443, 539, 540.

113 Edition 3 has '*la-ʿamru 'Llāhi*' instead of '*la-ʿamrī*'.

114 Editions 3 and 4 have *lā yudānīhi ʿadhāb* instead of *lā thawāb fīhi*.

115 For Ibn Taymiyya's views on *ʿishq*, see '*Amrāḍ al-qulūb wa-shifā'uhā*,' pp. 131–133. He wrote that *ʿishq* is an excessive love (*maḥabba mufriṭa*) that surpasses limits without itself being limitless, and thus cannot refer to God whose love has no limits. Also, he stated that *ʿishq* was related to willful actions (*min bāb al-irādāt*) and imagination (*min bāb al-taṣawwurāt*). Thus, *ʿishq* becomes a corruption in forming ideas, for one imagines the object of passionate love to be something other than what it actually is. By maintaining a distinction between *ḥubb* and *ʿishq*, Ibn Taymiyya followed the Ḥanbalī tradition of censuring passionate love; see Giffen, ibid., pp. 15–29, and Bell, *Hanbalite Teaching on Love*, pp. 52–58. Jāḥiẓ, who was one of the earliest scholars to speak in detail about this topic, explained that *ʿishq* was more than simple love, for '*ʿishq* is the name for what exceeds that which is called *ḥubb* and every *ḥubb* is not called *ʿishq*, for *ʿishq* is the name for what exceeds that degree...;' Giffen, ibid., p. 85. Jāḥiẓ also saw passionate love as a disease, which was another concept echoed by the Ḥanbalīs. In his *Risālat al-qiyān* he wrote in reference to profane love, 'Now I will describe for you the definition of passion of love, so that you may understand what exactly it is. It is a malady which smites the spirit (*rūḥ*), and affects the body as well by contagion...Passion is compounded of love and infatuation (*hawā*) and natural affinity (*mushākala*) and

habitude of association (*ilf*). It begins with a growing intensity, reaches a climax, and then falls off by natural progression to the stage of complete dissolution and the point of positive revulsion... "Love" (*ḥubb*) is a term applied to the concept which [linguistic] convention prescribes [as its meaning], and there is no other descriptive term for this. One can say, "a man loves God", "God loves the believer", "a man loves his child", "a boy loves his father" or "loves his friend" or "his country" or "his people", and his love can tend in any direction he likes; but none of this can be called passion. One understands therefore that the term "love" is not adequate to express the idea of "passion"; the latter needs the addition of the other factors...;' A. F. L. Beeston, *The Epistle on Singing-Girls of Jāhiz*, Warminster, Wilts.: Aris & Phillips Ltd., 1980, pp. 28–30. The Ḥanbalīs used these same arguments in a moral context to refute the Ṣūfī concept of experiencing *ᶜishq* in relation to God.

116 Editions 3 and 4 change the subject of the verb to *qalbuhu*.

117 Edition 3 inserts *wa'l-khasrān*.

118 Edition 4 inserts *asbāb*; thus the translation reads, 'One of the greatest causes of this affliction...'

119 Edition 3 inserts *wa-amtaᶜ*; Edition 4 reverses *lā aṭyab wa-lā adhall*.

120 Editions 1 and 2 have *bi-ghalabati nafsihi*, and Editions 3, 4 and 5 have *taghlībuhu nafsuhu*.

121 Edition 3 has *li-khayri al-maḥbūb* instead of only *al-maḥbūb*.

122 Editions 3 and 4 have *fa-inna dhikr Allāh ᶜibādat Allāh wa-ᶜibādat al-qalb li'Llāh*.

123 Edition 3 has *aqwā tazkiya* instead of *azkā li'l-nafs*.

124 Edition 3 has *yaᶜfū ᶜammā yajtarihūnahu* instead of *yaᶜfū ᶜanhum*.

125 After *istaᶜbadahu*, Edition 4 inserts *yastaᶜbiduhu li'l-ākhar* and Edition 3 inserts *mustaᶜbid li'l-ākhar*.

126 Edition 3 inserts *al-māl*.

127 This is a paraphrase of Q.LXX.19–21. Editions 1 and 3 state *fa-yakūnu halūᶜan idhā massahu al-khayr manūᶜan*. Editions 2, 4 and 5 state *fa-yakūnu halūᶜan idhā massahu al-sharr jazūᶜan wa-idhā massahu al-khayr manūᶜan*.

128 Bukhārī, *jihād* 70, *raqāq* 10.

129 Abū Dāwūd, *sunna* 15; Tirmidhī, *qiyāma* 60; Aḥmad, III:438, 440.

130 The exact wording of this *ḥadīth* appears in Ibn Hajar, *Fatḥ al-Bārī*, vol. 1, p. 47. Cf. similar *ḥadīths* in Abū Dāwud, *sunna* 2; Aḥmad, IV:286, V:146.

131 Bukhārī, *īmān* 9, 14, *ikrāh* 1; Muslim, *īmān* 66, 67; Abū Dāwud, *zakāh* 5; Tirmidhī *ᶜilm* 10; Nasā'ī, *īmān* 2 and 3; Ibn Mājah, *fitan* 23; Aḥmad, II:298, 560.

132 Editions 3 and 4 have *lā li-gharadi ākhar* instead of *lā li-wajhi ākhar*.

133 Edition 3 has *bi-hādhā al-waᶜīd al-shadīd* instead of only *hādhā al-waᶜīd*.

134 Bukhārī, *īmān* 8; Muslim, *īmān* 70; Nasā'ī, *īmān* 19; Ibn Mājah, *muqaddima* 9; Dārimī, *raqāq* 29.

135 Bukhārī, *aymān* 3. On the relation of this *ḥadīth* to the previous one, see Ibn Ḥajar, ibid., vol. 1, p. 59.

136 Editions 2 and 4 insert *wa'Llāhi* here, which does not appear in the version reported by Bukhārī.

137 Editions 3, 4 and 5 add *al-kufr* to *al-fusūq wa'l-ʿisyān*.

138 Editions 1, 2 and 3 have *fa-faqada mā yuqdaru ʿalayhi*, and Editions 4 and 5 have *fa-faʿala*. This latter wording with *fa-faʿala* appears to be a mistake because it would mean that he does what he is incapable of doing. The point Ibn Taymiyya was making is that a worshipper will be rewarded according to his intention so long as he exerts all efforts to complete his action even if he fails in doing so.

139 Muslim, *zakā* 70, *ʿilm* 15; Tirmidhī, *ʿilm* 16; Ibn Mājah, *muqaddima* 14, 15; Dārimī, *muqaddima* 44; *Muwaṭṭa'*, *Qur'ān* 41; Aḥmad, II:505, 521, III:357, 359–362, V:378.

140 Bukhārī, *jihād* 35; Abū Dāwūd, *jihād* 19; Ibn Mājah, *jihād* 6; Aḥmad, III:103, 160, 214, 341.

141 Edition 3 inserts *huwa kullu mā yamliku min*.

142 Editions 1, 2 and 5 have *idhan kāna mā salakahu ūlā'ika huwa al-ṭarīq alladhī yasīru bihi al-ʿāqil*. Edition 4 reads *idhan kāna mā yaslukuhu ūlā'ika huwa al-ṭarīq alladhī yushīru bihi al-ʿaql*. Edition 3 reads the same as 4 except that it has *idh* for *idhan* and inserts *fī naẓarihim* after *ūlā'ika*.

143 Editions 3 and 4 have *maṭlūb* instead of *maqṣūd*.

144 Editions 1 and 5 have *al-ʿāqil*, Editions 2 and 4 have *al-ʿaql*, and Edition 3 has *dhū'l-ʿaql al-salīm*.

145 The statement 'and the freedom...Him' is missing from Editions 3 and 4.

146 Editions 1, 2 and 5 have *al-qalb faqīr bi'l-dhull ilā Allāh*. I prefer the reading in editions 3 and 4, which have *bi'l-dhāt* for *bi'l-dhull*. One of Ibn Taymiyya's most fundamental beliefs was that the soul and all creation are dependent on God.

147 Edition 3 has *yanʿamu* instead of *yaltadhdhu*; and edition 4 reverses *yasurru* ('rejoicing') and *yaltadhdhu* ('delighted').

148 Edition 3 has *bi'l-fiṭra* inserted after *ilā rabbihi*.

149 Edition 3 has *al-surūr wa'l-sukūn* instead of *dhālika lahu*.

150 Edition 3 inserts *fa-lan yaḥsula illā al-alam wa'l-ḥasra wa'l-ʿadhāb wa-lan yakhluṣa min ālāmi al-dunyā wa-nakadi ʿīshihā illā bi-ikhlāṣi al-ḥubb li'Llāh* ('therefore, it will obtain only pain, grief and punishment, and it will only free itself from the torments of this world and the misfortune of this life by the sincerity of love for God').

151 Edition 3 has *naqṣu al-tawḥīd wa'l-īmān* instead of *al-naqṣ wa'l-ʿayb*.

152 There is a difference in the Arabic editions concerning the subject of this sentence which affects the translation of this paragraph. Editions 1, 2, 4 and 5 begin the sentence with *fa-huwa*, which refers back to *al-qalb*; however, edition 3 begins the sentence with *fa'l-ʿabd*, which would change the reference of the pronouns. For the sake of continuity, I have kept *al-qalb* as the subject. The additions of 'heart' in square brackets in this paragraph appear as the pronouns '*huwa*' or '*-hu*' in the Arabic editions.

153 Edition 3 inserts *wa-sakhkharahā lahu*.

154 Edition 3 has *musakhkhiruhu* instead of *khāliquhu*.

155 Editions 3 and 4 have *tarafayhā* instead of *ṭuruqahā*.

156 Bukhārī, *īmān* 33, *manāqib* 28, *tawḥīd* 19, 24, *raqāq* 35, 51. Edition 3 has *lā yakhludu fīhā* instead of *lā yadkhuluhā* in reference to entering the fire. There are many *ḥadīths* which convey this meaning through various terms and expressions; see Tirmidhī, *jahannam* 9, 10; Ibn Mājah, *muqaddima* 9, *zuhd* 37; Aḥmad, I:416, 458, III:116, 173, 248, 276, IV:118. For a discussion of the *ḥadīths* related to the Prophet's intercession and the order in which the sinful believers will be removed from hellfire, see Ibn Hajar, ibid., vol. XIV, pp. 392–399, 419–434.

157 I have found no references to this *ḥadīth* in Bukhārī. See Abū Dāwud, *libās* 25; Ibn Mājah, *zuhd* 16; Aḥmad, II: 376, 414, 427, 442.

158 Edition 3 inserts *wa-dhillu lahu*.

159 I have found no references to this *ḥadīth* in Bukhārī. See Abū Dāwud, *adab* 61; Aḥmad, II:345.

160 Edition 3 inserts *wa-yastadhillu lahu*.

161 Edition 3 inserts *wa'l-awliyā'*.

162 Edition 3 inserts *wa-ḥubbuhu*.

163 Editions 2, 3, 4 and 5 also include Q.IV.48.

164 Editions 1, 2, 4 and 5 have *wa-hum madīnūna mudabbarūn*. Edition 3 has *mamlūk lahu* instead of *madīnūn*. The term *madīnūn* appears twice in the Qur'ān: Q.XXXVII.53 and Q.LVI.86.

165 Edition 4 is missing *ma'thūr*.

166 Editions 1, 2 and 4 have *fa-huwa khāliq al-sabab wa'l-muqaddir lahu wa-hādhā muftaqir ilayhi ka-iftiqār hādha*. Edition 3 has an insertion in the latter part of the sentence with the result that the meaning is more explicit:...*wa-hādhā al-sabab muftaqir ilayhi ka-iftiqār al-musabbab*. Edition 5 has the insertion *al-sabab* but not *al-musabbab*.

167 Edition 3 has *bi-fiʿl khayr* instead of only *bi-fiʿl*.

168 Editions 3 and 4 have *al-ḍidd* instead of *al-ḍarar*.

169 Bukhārī, *anbiyā'* 41, *tafsīr* 31: *bāb* 13, *istitāba* 1. I have not found this *ḥadīth* in *Ṣaḥīḥ Muslim*.

170 This version is from Editions 3 and 4 which reads *al-umma huwa muʿallimu al-khayr alladhī yu'tammu bihi kamā anna al-qudwa alladhī yaqtadī bihi*. Editions 1, 2 and 5 have *al-umma huwa al-qudwa bi'l-fiʿli al-khayr alladhī yatimmu bihi kamālu al-qudwa alladhī yaqtadī bihi* ('a model is the example for good action by which the perfection of the example is completed, itself [then] being imitated'). This wording is altered slightly in Edition 2, which has *ka-mā al-qudwa* instead of *kamālu al-qudwa*. In this case, the version in Editions 3 and 4 seems more precise.

171 I have not found this in Bukhārī or elsewhere.

172 Editions 2, 3 and 4 have *Ṣaḥīḥ* instead of *Ṣaḥīḥayn*. I have not found this *ḥadīth* in either Bukhārī or Muslim. However, it does appear in Ibn Mājah, *muqaddima* 11. Ibn Ḥajar, ibid., vol. VII, pp.14, 23, mentions this *ḥadīth* in connection with the

two that follow in Ibn Taymiyya's text and these do appear in Bukhārī.

173 This narration and the previous one are part of one *ḥadīth*; see Bukhārī, *ṣalā* 80, *faḍā'il al-ṣaḥaba* 3, 5, *farā'iḍ* 9; Muslim, *masājid* 28, *faḍā'il al-ṣaḥaba* 6, 7; Tirmidhī, *manāqib* 14–16; Dārimī, *farā'iḍ* 11; Aḥmad, I: 270, 359, III: 18, 478, IV: 4, 5, 212.

174 Although Ibn Taymiyya's wording was not exactly as it appears in the *ḥadīth*, see Bukhārī, *janā'iz* 62, 96, *anbiyā'* 50; Muslim, *masājid* 13, *janā'iz* 106; *Muwaṭṭa'*, *safar* 85, *madīna* 17; Aḥmad, V: 204.

175 The Arabic reads: *tamām taḥqīq mukhāllatihi li'Llāh*. Edition 4 reverses *tamām* and *taḥqīq*.

176 Editions 3 and 4 insert *wa-maḥabbat al-ʿabd li'Llāh* ('and the love of a worshipper for God').

177 I interpret Ibn Taymiyya's use of the term '*jahmiyya*' to be a reference to the beliefs of the Muʿtazila, since he uses the terms interchangeably; see his '*Risālat al-jahmiyya*,' in *Majmūʿ fatāwā*, pp. 61–72, where he explains that they deny the reality of love because they say that 'love cannot exist except by affinity (*li-munāsaba*) between the lover and the beloved, and that there is no affinity between the Eternal One and the temporal one which could necessitate love.' On the Muʿtazilī theory of love, see Bell, *Love Theory*, p. 74. On the Muʿtazila in general, see Goldziher, ibid., pp. 87–111, and *EI2*, vol. III, s.v. '*al-Muʿtazila*.'

178 The Arabic reads: *ishrākan bi'l-bashar*; and edition 3 has *ishrākan bi-ʿibādat wa-ghayrihi min al-bashar*. Ibn Taymiyya's statement seems to be a generalization incorporating two aspects of Shiism. Firstly, the label, *Rāfiḍa*, was a common Sunnī term for the Shīʿa, who are those Muslims who claim that ʿAlī was divinely designated as the successor to the Prophet. Secondly, the reference to *ishrākan bi'l-bashar* could mean either the belief of various extremist (*ghulūw*) groups who believed in the divinity of ʿAlī, or it could mean the belief in the occultation of the Twelfth Imam. On the early history of the Shīʿa, see Madelung, ibid., pp. 77–92 and Arjomand, ibid., pp. 25–61.

179 All the editions of Ibn Taymiyya's text have the same wording for this verse of poetry: *qad takhallalta maslaka al-rūḥi minnī wa-bi-dhā summiya al-khalīlu khalīlan*. This verse was also quoted by Ibn ʿArabī in his *Fuṣūṣ al-Ḥikam*, the only difference being *bihi* instead of *bi-dhā*; see Ibn ʿArabī, *Fuṣūṣ al-Ḥikam*, ed. Abū al-ʿAlā ʿAfīfī, Beirut: Dar al-Kitāb al-ʿArabī, 1966, p. 80. Both scholars used the verse in reference to their respective views on the importance of Abraham in Islamic tradition. Although the verse appears in Ibn Taymiyya's and Ibn ʿArabī's text without vowel marks, the only word which could be read in multiple ways is *takhallalta*, which is the reading that I am using. By contrast, Austin has read *takhallaltu* in his translation of the *Fuṣūṣ al-Ḥikam* and translates the verse as, 'I have penetrated the course of the spirit within me, / And thus was the Intimate [of God] so called;' see Ibn ʿArabī, *Fuṣūṣ al-Ḥikam*, trans. R. W. J. Austin as *Ibn al-Arabi: The Bezels of Wisdom*, New York: Paulist Press, 1980, p. 90 (the square brackets are Austin's). The different translations clearly highlight the opposing theologies of

Ibn Taymiyya and Ibn ʿArabī: whereas Ibn Taymiyya has used this verse in the context of his belief in the ultimate distinction between God and creation, Ibn ʿArabī was writing from his perspective of the unity of being and he prefaced his quotation of the verse with the statement, *li-takhallalahu wa-ḥasarahu jamīʿa mā ittasafat bihi al-dhātu al-ilāhiyya*. Regarding this, Austin writes that Abraham was the Intimate of God 'because he had embraced [takhallala] and penetrated all the Attributes of the Divine Essence' (the square brackets are Austin's).

180 This *ḥadīth* refers to al-Ḥasan b. ʿAlī (d. 50/670) and Usāma b. Zayd (d. 54/674). The *ḥadīth* is reported by al-Bukhārī in his *Ṣaḥīḥ* in the chapter '*Bāb manāqibi al-Ḥasan wa'l-Ḥusayn*;' see Ibn Ḥajar, ibid., vol. VII, pp. 94–99. Ibn Taymiyya cited this *ḥadīth* to highlight the difference between *khulla* and *ḥubb*: whereas a person's *ḥubb* can be associated with many people at varying levels of intensity, *khulla* can only be associated with one other and, from a religious point of view, this other must, of course, be God.

181 Edition 3 has *al-nisā'* for *al-nās*.

182 Bukhārī, *faḍā'il al-ṣaḥāba* 5.

183 Ibn Mājah, *muqaddima* 11.

184 This list of the types of people whom God loves is taken from various verses of the Qur'ān, for example: 'the pious' (*al-muttaqūn*) in Q.III.76; 'the perfect devotees' (*al-muḥsinūn*) in Q.II.195 and Q.V.13; 'the just' (*al-muqsiṭūn*) in Q.XLIX.9 and Q.LX.8; 'the penitent' (*al-tawwābūn*) and 'the ones who purify themselves' (*al-mutaṭahhirūn*) in Q.II.222; and 'the ones who fight in His cause in close ranks as if they were a solid structure' in Q.LXI.4.

185 The technical term is *aḥādīth mawḍūʿa*, which was used by the *Ahl al-Ḥadīth* to designate the lowest level of weak *ḥadīth*s; see Ṣāliḥ, ibid., pp. 305–322 and Ibn al-Jawzī's introduction to his *Kitāb al- Mawḍūʿāt*. Ibn al-Jawzī mentioned several fabricated (*mawḍūʿ*) *ḥadīth*s which said that al-ʿAbbās would be placed between Muḥammad and Abraham in paradise; see *Kitāb al- Mawḍūʿāt*, vol. II, pp. 30–37.

186 This insertion is from Edition 3.

187 Bukhārī, *īmān* 9, 14, *ikrāh* 1; Muslim, *īmān* 66, 67; Abū Dāwud, *zakāh* 5; Tirmidhī *ʿilm* 10; Nasā'ī, *īmān* 2 and 3; Ibn Mājah, *fitan* 23; Aḥmad, II:298, 560.

188 Instead of *wujūd*, Edition 3 has *wijdān*, and Editions 2 and 4 have *wajd*. These two alternative words convey the meaning of a 'passion or ardor for the sweetness of a thing.'

189 The Arabic terms are *al-mutafalsifa wa'l-aṭibbā'*. I have not been able to identify the specific groups or persons who make such claims.

190 Edition 3 has *tafrīgh* for *tafrī'*. The same reading occurs in the next paragraph.

191 Bukhārī, *ṣalā* 80, *faḍā'il al-ṣaḥaba* 3, 5, *farā'iḍ* 9; Muslim, *masājid* 28, *faḍā'il al-ṣaḥaba* 6, 7; Tirmidhī, *manāqib* 14–16; Dārimī, *farā'iḍ* 11; Aḥmad, I: 270, 359, III: 18, 478, IV: 4, 5, 212.

192 The Arabic in editions 1, 2, 4 and 5 reads, *wa-anna al-maḥabba fīhā inbisāṭun fī al-ahwā aw idlālun lā taḥtamiluhu al-rubūbiyya*. Edition 3 has *idhlāl* for *idlāl*.

193 This is the famous Ṣūfī Abū al-Fayḍ b. Ibrāhīm al-Ikhmīmī Dhū al-Nūn al-Miṣrī (d. 245/860); see Reinert, ibid., p. 301. This quotation was cited almost verbatim by Qushayrī, the only difference being that Ibn Taymiyya began with *amsikū* instead of *kaffū*; see Qushayrī, ibid., p. 253.

194 For an explanation of this terminology, see Marshall Hodgson, *The Venture of Islam: Conscience and History in a World Civilization,* vol. 1, Chicago: Chicago University Press, 1974. He states that the term *zindīq* referred to 'anyone suspected of cloaking an esoteric faith beneath his profession of Islam' (p. 291); *murji'* referred to one who allowed Muslims the 'benefit of a doubt' concerning sinful deeds and 'insisted that what counted was the inner conscience, which only God could judge' (p. 264); and *ḥarūrī* referred to some of the earliest defectors from ʿAlī's supporters who first gathered at Ḥarūrā near Kufa and later became known as the Khawārij (p. 215).

195 Edition 3 inserts *faḍlan ʿan-man hum dūnahum.*

196 Edition 3 has *maḥabba tā'isha jāhila* instead of only *maḥabba.*

197 Editions 1, 2 and 5 have *fa-lā ūkhadhu*; the other editions have *fa-lā u'ākhadhu.*

198 Edition 1 reads, *fa-man kāna Allāhu yuḥibbuhu istaʿmalahu fīmā yuḥibbuhu wa-maḥbūbuhu lā yafʿalu.* The *wa* before *maḥbūbuhu*—which does not appear in the other editions—does not make sense here because it forces *maḥbūbuhu* to be the subject of *lā yafʿalu.* Thus, I am following the reading found in the majority of the editions.

199 Edition 3 has two insertions indicating that God not only hates the sins of a sinner and loves the good deeds of a worshipper, but that He also hates the sinner and loves the worshipper. The text reads as follows with the insertions of Edition 3 between angle brackets: *wa-man faʿala al-kabā'ir wa-aṣarra ʿalayhā wa-lam yatub minhā fa-inna Allāha <yabghuḍuhu wa->yabghuḍu minhu dhālika kamā yuḥibbu <ʿabdahu al-mu'min wa-yuḥibbu> minhu mā yafʿaluhu min al-khayr.*

200 The term is *murīd*, which is also translated as 'adept' or 'disciple'; see Schimmel, ibid., pp. 100–104. It refers to the special relationship between a Ṣūfī master and his student.

201 I have been unable to find a source for the three quotations mentioned in this paragraph, although Nicholson reports a similar claim attributed to the Persian Ṣūfī Abū al-Ḥasan al-Khurqānī (or Kharaqānī) (d. 424/1033), through whom ʿAbd Allāh al-Anṣārī al-Harawī entered the Ṣūfī path. He said, 'If any one does not believe that I shall stand up at the Resurrection and that he shall not enter Paradise until I lead him forward, let him not come here to salute me;' Nicholson, ibid., p. 137. Khurqānī's alleged power of intercession stemmed from his belief that he would be resurrected as a martyr, for he asserted that he has been 'killed by the sword of longing' for God; Schimmel, ibid., p. 90.

202 Edition 3 has *asās maḥabbatihi* instead of *maḥabbata Allāh.*

203 Schimmel discusses several statements with very similar meanings; ibid.,

pp. 134–135, 178. She explains that in this common Ṣūfī metaphor, the 'fire of love' was symbolic of the spiritual purification needed to approach the beloved. In this paragraph, Ibn Taymiyya mentioned what he understood to be the incorrect interpretation of this statement and in the following paragraph he mentioned what he understood to be its correct interpretation.

204 Edition 3 has *yabghuḍu mā fīhi darrarahu* instead of *yabghuḍu mā yunāfīhi wa yadurruhu*.

205 Edition 3 inserts *thumma zādahum inghimāsan fī ahwā'ihim wa-shahawātihim*.

206 Edition 3 inserts *wa-kadhdhabū wa-ḍallū fa-inna*.

207 This passage poses some difficulties. Editions 1, 2, 4 and 5 read, *aṣl ḍalālihim anna hādhā al-qā'il alladhī qāl anna al-maḥabba nār tuḥarriq mā sawā murādi al-maḥbūb qaṣada bi-murādi Allāh taʿālā*... However, what follows is a description of what Ibn Taymiyya considered to be correct love; not an error. I have inserted the conjunction, 'if,' in order to coordinate the statement that follows with the presumed conditional clause, *fa-ka-annahu qāl*... ('then it is as if he says...'). Edition 3 avoids this difficulty with the following insertion after *mā sawā murādi al-maḥbūb*: *qaṣada bi-murādi Allāh taʿālā al-irādat al-kawniyya fī kulli al-mawjūdāt amma law qāl mu'min bi'Llāh wa-kutubihi wa-rusulihi min ghayri hā'ulā' al-ṣūfiyya mithla hādhihi al-maqāla fa-innahu yaqṣidu*.... The full translation now reads: 'The origin of their erring position is that they say, "Love is a fire that burns everything in a heart except the intention of the beloved," meaning that the intention of God (Exalted be He) is the existential will, which affects all existing things. But were a believer in God, His Books and His Messengers, who is not one of these Ṣūfīs, to say a similar statement he would mean...'

208 Edition 3 inserts *li'Llāh*.

209 Editions 2, 3 and 4 have *mā lā yuḥibbu* instead of *al-maḥbūb*, which accords better with the sense of the statement.

210 Edition 3 has *hādhihi al-maḥabba kalima* instead of *hādhihi al-maḥabba li'Llāh*.

211 Edition 3 inserts *al-bunuwwa wa-*.

212 Edition 3 inserts *al-targhīb fī*.

213 According to Lane, the word *nāmūs* refers originally to a secret message told to someone. From this meaning, it is related to revelation in the sense of a secret told by God to a prophet; thus, it also means 'the law of God.' The expression *al-nāmūs al-akbar* refers to Gabriel as the deliverer of the secret message; ibid., s.v. '*n-m-s*.' However, Lane rejects the connection of *nāmūs* with the Greek *nomos*. On the other hand, M. Plessner mentions several early Muslim sources that accept the origin of the term from the Greek; *EI2*, s.v. '*Nāmūs*.' Ibn Taymiyya recognized *nāmūs* as a Greek loan word, which he said the Greek philosophers, such as Aristotle, had defined as 'a complete political system for the city states' (*al-siyāsa al-kulliyya li'l-madā'in*). See Ibn Taymiyya, *Tafsīr ṣūrat al-ikhlāṣ*, p. 79.

214 In Edition 3, the reference to the Messiah is missing.

215 This biblical reference is to Mark 12:29–30; see also Deuteronomy 6:4–5.

216 Bukhārī, *tawḥīd* 15, 50; Muslim, *dhikr* 2, 3, 20–22, *tawba* 1; Tirmidhī, *daʿawāt* 131, Ibn Mājah, *adab* 58; Aḥmad, II: 251, 316, 413, 435, 480, 482, 500, 509, 524, 534, 535, III: 40, 122, 127, 130, 138, 272, 383, V: 153, 155, 169.

217 This is the first part of a longer *ḥadīth*; see Bukhārī, *raqāq* 38; Aḥmad, IV:256.

218 Edition 3 has *al-ḍāllīn* for *al-mukhṭiʿīn*.

219 This insertion is from Editions 4 and 5, which have *ashyākhan*. In the context of Ibn Taymiyya's ensuing discussion of mistaken leaders, this variant is more appropriate than the *ashyā'* found in Editions 1 and 2, or *ashyā'a al-mubtadaʿa* found in Edition 3.

220 Edition 3 inserts *ʿalā ghayri ʿilm wa-lā hudan wa-lā nūr min al-kitāb wa'l-sunna*.

221 Edition 3 has *rabbihim* instead of *Allāh*.

222 Edition 3 inserts *wa-shuyūkhahum*.

223 Edition 3 inserts *wa'l-qasāwisa*.

224 Edition 3 inserts *wa'l-qasīsīn wa'l-ruhbān*.

225 This sentence is missing from Edition 3.

226 Edition 3 inserts *kamā anna kulla ʿamal lā yakūnu ʿalā al-ṣaḥīḥi al-ṣarīḥ min hadyi rasūli Allāh fa-huwa bāṭil*.

227 Bukhārī, *bad' al-waḥy* 1, *īmān* 41, *nikāḥ* 5, *talāq* 11, *manāqib al-ansār* 45, *ʿatiq* 6, *aymān* 23, *ḥiyal* 1; Muslim, *imāra* 155; Abū Dāwud, *talāq* 11; Tirmidhī, *faḍā'il al-jihād* 16; Nasā'ī, *tahāra* 59, *talāq* 24, *aymān* 19; Ibn Mājah, *zuhd* 26; Aḥmad, I: 25, 43.

228 Bukhārī, *iʿtisām* 20, *buyūʿ* 60, *ṣulḥ* 5; Muslim, *aqdiyya* 17, 18; Abū Dāwud, *sunna* 5; Ibn Mājah, *muqaddima* 2; Aḥmad, VI:146, 180, 256.

229 Edition 3 has *qabaltahā* for *qultahā*.

230 These two *ḥadīth*s are reported by Aḥmad, I:307, II:325, 430, IV: 402, 403.

231 Edition 3 adds the adjective *al-jāhila* to *al-nufūs*.

232 Editions 3 and 4 have *zarība* instead of *ḥaẓīra*.

233 Tirmidhī, *zuhd* 43; Dārimī, *raqāq* 61; Aḥmad, III:456, 460.

234 Edition 3 adds the adjective *al-salīm* to *al-qalb*.

235 Editions 3, 4 and 5 have *wa-ḥuṣūl marghūbihi* instead of *aw ḥuṣūl marḥūbihi*.

236 Editions 3 and 4 have *yakhāfu min ḥuṣūli diḍḍi dhālika* instead of *yakhāfu min diḍḍi dhālika*.

237 Edition 3 has *ayyu nasīmin marra bihi ʿazma* instead of *marra bi-ʿaṭfihi*.

238 Edition 2 has *shawq* instead of *sharaf*.

239 Edition 3 inserts *shuyūkh al-ṣūfiyya* before *atbāʿ firʿawn*.

240 Edition 3 inserts *li-hādhā al-farq*.

241 The editor of Edition 3, Muḥammad Ḥāmid al-Faqī, states that Ibn Taymiyya erred in the matter of defining *fanā'* and classifying it into three types. This is one of two such statements by Faqī (see below, p. 66). Other than al-Faqī's harsh stance against Sufism, there is no reason to claim that Ibn Tayimyya erred in the matter of defining fanā' or failed to fully understand the origin and nature of Sufism.

242 The insertion is from Editions 3, 4 and 5, which have *li'l-qāṣidīn min al-awliyā' wa'l-ṣāliḥīn*. Editions 1 and 2 have *li'l-qāṣirīn...*, for which the translation is 'fall short of the level of....'

243 Editions 3, 4 and 5 have *ʿan irādat mā* instead of *ʿan-mā*.

244 Editions 3 and 4 have *iyyāhu* instead of *Allāh*.

245 This is the well-known Ṣūfī Tayfūr b. ʿIsā b. Surūshān al-Bisṭāmī (or al-Basṭāmī), d. 261/875.

246 Cf. this description with that of al-Qushayrī in his section on *fanā'* and *baqā'*; ibid., pp. 61–63. See also Richard Gramlich, *Das Sendschreiben al-Qushayrīs*, pp. 121–123.

247 Abū Naṣr al-Sarrāj discussed this verse in his *Kitb al-lumāʿ fī al-taṣawwuf*; see Gramlich's edition, *Schlaglichter über das Sufitum*, pp. 132 and 152.

248 Editions 1, 2 and 5 have *maʿnā* and the others have *nawʿ*.

249 The insertion is from Editions 3, 4 and 5, which have *al-fanā' ʿan shuhūdi al-siwā* instead of *al-ghinā ʿan shuhūdi al-siwā*.

250 Editions 1, 2 and 3 have *dahimahu* and the others have *faqimahu*.

251 The Arabic of all the text editions reads: *fa-idhā qawiya ʿalā ṣāḥibi al-fanā' hādhā fa-innahu yaghību bi-mawjūdihi ʿan wujūdihi wa-bi-mashhūdihi ʿan shuhūdihi wa-bi-madhkūrihi ʿan dhikrihi wa-bi-maʿrūfihi ʿan maʿrifatihi*. In his *Risāla ilā Naṣr al-Manbijī*, Ibn Taymiyya explained this experience as 'an annihilation of comprehending the other' (*fanā' ʿan idrāki al-siwā*; p. 459) and did so in the context of its relation to the meaning of oneness, referring to it as the 'annihilation of the incapable ones' (*fanā' al-qāṣirīn*). Ibn al-Qayyim described the same process in his *Madārij al-Sālikīn*; see vol. 1, p. 169. In reference to knowledge (*maʿrifa*), he said that one's knowledge disappears and vanishes into the thing that has become known, and went on to say that this occurs to all qualities of a person, such as witnessing, remembering, loving, etc. Ibn al-Qayyim then clearly stated that this annihilation is defective and in no way leads to perfection, which is exemplified by Abraham and Muḥammad. He also placed this kind of annihilation prior to the rank (*al-daraja*) of annihilation of the witnessing of annihilation, which was for him an even more erring rank. Ibn Taymiyya made no mention here of the annihilation of the witnessing of annihilation, but it was mentioned by al-Qushayrī, ibid., pp. 61–63; see also Gramlich, *Das Sendschreiben al-Qushayrīs*, pp. 121–123.

252 Editions 1, 2 and 4 have *zalla fīhi aqwām* and Editions 3 and 5 have *zallat fīhi aqdām*.

253 Edition 3 has *ḍalāl baʿīd* instead of *ghalaṭ*.

254 Cf. the statement attributed to al-Junayd in Gramlich, ibid., p. 30. Edition 3 has the following insertion: *li-anna laysa ka-mithlihi shay'un wa huwa al-samīʿu al-basīr wa-huwa al-aḥadu al-ṣamad alladhī lam yalid wa-lam yūlad wa-lam yakun lahu kufuwan aḥad*, which is a paraphrase of Q.XLII.11 and Q.CXII.1–4.

255 Although the unity of objectives and will mentioned here is similar to the annihilation of the will in the first type of *fanā'*, there is an important difference

in this context because Ibn Taymiyya was talking about a union of wills which includes a level of unconsciousness or unawareness of the union. The annihilation of witnessing was considered to be a deficiency or shortcoming on the part of the worshipper and he explains below that maintaining awareness in every state of worship was a mark of the best worshippers; see section, 'The Struggle To Remain Conscious In Worship,' in this translation. This view was echoed by Ibn al-Qayyim in his *Madārij al-sālikīn*; see vol. 1, p. 169.

256 The two groups of the Companions were the Emigrants from Mecca and the Helpers from Medina.

257 Edition 3 has only *aḥwāl*.

258 Edition 3 inserts *ʿuqūlan* and thus the translation would read: 'more perfect, stronger as to rational faculties and firmer…'

259 Editions 1, 2 and 5 have *ḍuʿf* and Editions 3 and 4 have *ṣaʿq*.

260 This report was also mentioned by Ibn Taymiyya in *al-Ṣūfiyya wa'l-fuqarā'*. I have not found any information about Abū Juhayr al-Darīr. As for Zurāra b. Abī Awfā (Editions 4 and 5 have Ibn Awfā), Ibn Ḥajar reported the same story and gave his name as Zurāra b. Awfā and his death date as 93/712; *Tahdhīb al-tahdhīb*, 12 vols., Beirut: Dār al-Ṣādir, 1325/1907, vol. III, p. 322.

261 All the text editions have Abū al-Ḥasan; however, his name was more commonly given as Abū al-Ḥusayn; see Kalābādhī, ibid., p. 42 and Reinert, ibid., p. 317. He was also known as Ibn al-Baghawī and died in 295/908.

262 This is the common name used to refer to Abū Maḥfūẓ b. Fayrūz (or Fayrūzān); see Reinert, ibid., p. 313. He was also referred to as Abū Saʿīd; see Kalābādhī, ibid., p. 40. He died in 200/816.

263 This is the famous Ṣūfī Abū al-Qāsim b. Muḥammad, who died in 297/910 or 298/911; see Reinert, ibid., p. 303. In Edition 3, Faqī adds a footnote in which he denounces all the Ṣūfīs and states that Ibn Taymiyya did not understand the truth about Sufism and its relation to Indian, Persian and Greek thought (p. 67).

264 Edition 3 inserts *min al-muslimīna alladhīna lā yahtadūna illā bi-hadyi al-kitāb wa'l-sunna*.

265 Editions 1 and 2 have *ʿuqūlihim* and the other editions have *qulūbihim*.

266 Editions 1 and 2 have the spelling *m-s-b-h-h*, which appears to be an error. The other editions have *mustajība lahu*.

267 Ibn Taymiyya's term was *tajrīd al-tawḥīd*. I have chosen to translate *tajrīd* as 'abstraction' in the sense that the active oneness (*tawḥīd ʿamalī*) is a process of removing false deities from one's heart and worshipping only God. The term *tajrīd* and its passive participle *mujarrad* have been translated by others in various ways, depending on the context. For instance, Hallaq uses 'abstraction' in the context of philosophy and logic (ibid., p. 147); Chittick uses 'disengagement' in reference to Ibn ʿArabī's discussion of imagination and dreams (ibid., pp. 115, 120); and Gully uses 'absolution' in a grammatical context (ibid., p. 162).

268 This is a reference to Q.VII.143.

269 Edition 3 inserts *wa'l-kufr*.

270 Edition 3 inserts *wa-yabra'u ʿanhu*.

271 Edition 3 inserts *ʿalā hadyi al-kitāb wa'l-sunna ka'l-ṣaḥāba wa'l-a'immati al-muhtadīn*.

272 The Arabic sentence reads: *fa-man aḥabba shay'an aw rajāhu aw khāfahu iltafata ilayhi*.

273 This passage is very similar to statements reported by Kalābādhī; ibid., p. 147–148. The latter described *fanā'* as an experience in which one has '...no feelings towards anything whatsoever...' In this context, he reported that ʿAmir b. ʿAbd Allāh, who died during the caliphate of Muʿāwiya (r. 41/661–60/680), had said, 'I do not care whether I saw a woman or a wall.' Kalābādhī stated that for the worshipper all things become one, but that this 'does not imply that disaccord is in him accord, or that prohibition is for him the same as commandment...;' translation from Arberry, ibid., pp. 120–121.

274 Editions 3 and 4 have the following insertion: *wa-yarjū Allāha fīhā wa-lā yarjūhā fī Allāh*.

275 The word order varies slightly in some of the editions. The only major differences are in Edition 3, which inserts *al-muḥaqqiq al-muwaḥḥid* after *al-mu'min* ('believing heart') and in Edition 4, which inserts *al-muḥaqqiq* after *al-ʿārif* ('cognizant'). Also, both these editions have *bi-ḥaqīqatihim* for *taḥqīqihim*, which I have translated as 'their realization.'

276 Ibn Taymiyya uses the term, *al-qarāmiṭa*, as a general reference to the Ismāʿīlīs, whom he considered to be hypocrites. The Karmathians were actually a sect that broke away from the main branch of the Ismāʿīlī Fāṭmids in the early fourth/tenth century. See Tariq al-Jamil, 'Ibn Taymiyya and Ibn al-Muṭahhar al-Ḥillī: Shiʿi Polemics and the Struggle for Religious Authority in Medieval Islam,' in *Ibn Taymiyya and his Times*, pp. 236 and 244, n. 29.

277 Edition 3 inserts *min kulli man yadīnu bi-waḥdati al-wujūd alladhīna naṭaqa ʿanhum al-Hallāj wa-Ibn ʿArabī wa-Ibn al-Fārid wa-Ibn Sabʿīn wa'l-ʿAfīf al-Tilimsānī*.

278 Edition 3 has *al-taḥqīq al-maḥmūd* instead of *al-fanā' al-maḥmūd*.

279 This is an important point which Ibn Taymiyya upholds in line with traditional Ḥanbalī thinking. A Muslim's knowledge of God and his understanding of his relationship to God must be based on the sound knowledge of revelation as it appears in the Qur'ān and the authentic *Sunna*. This revealed knowledge then becomes the criterion by which internal experiences can be judged. On this topic see *Madārij al-Sālikīn*, vol. I, p. 531, where Ibn al-Qayyim states that tastes, states and passions cannot be the judge (*ḥākim*) but must be judged (*maḥkūm ʿalayhi*) by God's revelation.

280 Ibn Taymiyya refers to the same statement in his *Istiqāma*, vol. I, p. 115, where he mentions that it is from Abū Ṭālib al-Makkī. The following quote appears in Makkī's *Qūt al-Qulūb*, 4 vols., Cairo: al-Maktaba al-Ḥusayniyya, 1351/1932, vol. III, p. 122, *laysa fī dhātihi siwāhu wa-lā fī siwāhu min dhātihi shay' laysa fī al-khalq illā*

al-khalq wa-lā fī al-dhāti illā al-khāliq. See also Richard Gramlich, *Die Nahrurug der Herzen: Abū Ṭālib al-Makkīs Qūt al-Qulūb,* 4 vols., Stuttgart: Franz Steiner Verlag, 1992, vol. III, p. 10.

281 The necessity of maintaining God's distinction from His creation is the foundation of the belief of the *Ahl al-Sunna wa'l-Jamāʿa*. This point is clearly explained by Ibn Ḥajar in *Fatḥ al-Bārī*, vol. XIII, p. 344, where he defines God's Oneness in terms of repudiating anthropomorphism (*tashbīh*) and negation (*taʿṭīl*) in reference to the names and attributes of God. He then quotes from Qushayrī that Junayd defined *tawḥīd* as separating the Eternal One from the temporal one (*muḥdath*). The terms Qushayrī, ibid., pp. 5, 233, uses are *qidam* and *ḥadath*, see also Gramlich, *Das Sendschreiben al-Qushayrīs*, pp. 25, 414. Similar statements are found in Kalābādhī, ibid., p. 25; the following quote is from Arberry, ibid., p. 1, 'Whose essence, being unique, does not resemble the essence of created beings, and whose qualities are far removed from the qualities of creatures born in time.'

282 The terms *farq*, or *tafriqa*, and *jamʿ* have been translated as 'separation' and 'concentration,' respectively, by Arberry, ibid., p. 114. Gramlich translates them as 'Trennung' and 'Vereinigung'; *Das Sendschreiben al-Qushayrīs*, p. 118. The particular context in which they are used allows for a variety of English terms. For the purpose of this translation, I shall render *farq* as 'separation' and *jamʿ* as 'joining.'

283 Editions 1 and 3 have *al-ʿibārāt al-mukhtalifa*, and Editions 4 and 5 have *al-ʿibārāt al-mulaffata*. Edition 2 has *al-ʿibādāt* instead of *al-ʿibārāt*.

284 Edition 2 has *mutafarriq*.

285 Edition 1 has *mushattitan naẓaran ilayhā*; the other editions have *mutashattitan nāẓiran ilayhā*, with Edition 2 having *naẓaran* instead of *nāẓiran*.

286 In this passage, Ibn Taymiyya explained the experience of *farq* and *jamʿ* while maintaining the ontological difference between God and the creation. The experience of joining that creates a sense of unity in creation is the realisation that all things exist by God's act of creation. If one becomes lost in this state, he will believe that this vision of unity in the act of creation is the same as the unity of the Creator's essence. The second separation is what saves the worshipper from ontological confusion and thus from polytheism. In his *Risāla ilā Naṣr al-Manbijī*, p. 459, Ibn Taymiyya summarized this point as follows: 'It is witnessing separation in joining and multiplicity in oneness, for he witnesses the existence of beings (*qiyām al-kā'ināt*) with their differences as occurring through the existence of God (*bi-iqāmat Allāh*), alone (Exalted is He) and His Lordship.'

287 Edition 2 has *fanā'* instead of *nāfiyan*.

288 This attribute appears in only Edition 1, which reads *muḥibban fīhi*.

289 Editions 1 and 2 have *mutadammin li-ifrādihi*; the other editions have *yatadammanu iqrārahu*.

290 Abū Bakr ʿAbd Allāh b. Abī al-Dunyā (d. 281/894) was a traditionist best known for his collections of *ḥadīths* on ethical and moral behavior; see Reinert, ibid., p. 306.

291 In the *Concordance*, Wensinck lists only Ibn Mājah, *adab* 55, but Khaṭīb Tibrīzī reported that it was also narrated by Tirmidhī; *Mishkāt al-Maṣābīḥ,* vol. II, p. 9.

292 This is the name which appears in Editions 1 and 2. Editions 3, 4 and 5 have Talḥa b. ʿAbd Allāh b. Kathīr, with Edition 2 also listing Ibn Kathīr. He was a famous Companion who died in 36/656. The *ḥadīth* appears twice in the *Muwaṭṭa'* of Mālik b. Anas and in both cases the name appears as Talḥah b. ʿUbayd Allāh b. Karīz; see '*Mass al-qur'ān*,' in *al-Muwaṭṭa',* ed. by Muḥammad ʿAbd al-Bāqī, 2 vols., Cairo: Dār Iḥyā' al-Kutub al-ʿArabiyya, 1986, *ḥadīth* no. 32 and *hajj* no. 246.

293 Edition 3 has *ḍāllūn muḍill* instead of *ḍāllūn ghālitūn*. On the various forms of Ṣūfī remembrance (*dhikr*) using a single noun or pronoun, see Schimmel, ibid., pp. 72, 172, 270, 385, 420 and 422.

294 Edition 3 inserts *bal min taḥrīfihim li'l-kalim ʿan mawāḍiʿihi*.

295 This sentence is from Editions 3, 4 and 5. I have included it here in order to clarify the argument.

296 Editions 1 and 2 have *man jā'*, which is not a nominal sentence. Editions 3, 4 and 5 have *man jāruhu*. Ibn Taymiyya digressed from his explanation of Q.VI.91 by discussing the topics of legitimate supplications and Arabic grammar. The explanation of Q.VI.91 resumes below.

297 Edition 2 has *quṣūr* instead of *taṣawwur*.

298 Ibn Taymiyya was in effect denouncing a common practice found in all forms of mysticism, namely, meditating while repeating a simple word or phrase in order to empty one's heart or soul of all meaning so that the ultimate reality may enter into the mystic, in other words, the mystic strives to become devoid of conscious thought in order to unite with the ultimate reality. An example of this are the kōans used in Zen Buddhism, which are riddles or meaningless expressions intended to bring about spiritual insight; see Robert S. Ellwood, *Mysticism and Religion*, Englewood Cliffs, NJ: Prentice-Hall Inc., 1980, p. 3. Ibn Taymiyya's argument was that although the mystic experiences an emptiness that seems to lead to a union with ultimate reality (i.e., a union with God), the meaninglessness in his heart simply allows his preexisting desires to dictate his interpretation of the experience. In his criticism of the mystical experience, W. T. Stace raises a similar objection, 'Theistic mystics, having reached the experience of the undifferentiated unity and the merging of their own individualities in that unity, jump without further ado to the conclusion that what they have experienced is "union with God." We do not here question the use of the word "union." But it seems important to raise the question whether the word "God" is appropriate.' See *Mysticism and Philosophy*, Philadelphia and New York: J. Ibn Lippincott Co., 1960, p. 178.

299 Edition 3 inserts *bi'l-ismi al-mufrad wa-bi-huwa*.

300 This refers to dying between the utterance of 'there is no deity' and 'except God.' The implication is that one would die negating God's existence.

301 Edition 3 has *maḥẓūr* instead of *maḥdhūr*.

302 Edition 1 has *bi'l-ismi al-mufrad aw al-muḍmar*; Edition 2 has *bi'l-ismi al-mufradi al-muḍmar*; the other editions have *bi'l-ismi al-muḍmari al-mufrad*.

303 According to Yahya Osman, Ibn ʿArabī composed a book entitled *Kitāb al-hūwa huwa kitāb al-yā* and Osman lists the work's alternative titles as *Kitāb al-yā' wa-huwa kitāb al-hū*, *Kitāb al-hū* and *Kitāb al-yā'*. He also mentions a *Kitāb al-huwiyya*. See Yahya Osman, *Histoire et classification de l'oeuvre d'Ibn ʿArabī*, 2 vols., Damascus: Centre National de la Recherche Scientifique, 1964, vol.1, pp. 178–179. Brockelmann also mentions a *Kitāb al-yā' wa huwa kitāb al-huwa*; *GAL*, vol. 1, p. 578.

304 Edition 3 inserts *bal taḥrīf*.

305 Edition 3 inserts *min al-mukadhdhibīna li-rasūl Allāh*.

306 The statement reads: *wa-yaksirūna inna*.

307 Ibn Taymiyya was describing the distinction between *kalām* (sentence) and *qawl* (phrase), which was accepted by most grammarians. The reference to Sībawayh, although not an exact quotation, seems to refer to his *Kitāb*; see ʿAmr b. ʿUthmān Sībawayh, *Kitāb Sībawayh: Le livre de Sībawayh, traite de grammaire arabe par Sībouya, dit Sībawayh*, ed. Hartwig Derenbourg, 2 vols., Paris: Imprimerie nationale, 1881, vol. 1, pp. 50 and 419–420. In reference to these pages in Sībawayh's *Kitāb*, Rafael Talmon has argued that later grammarians misunderstood him, thinking that he was using *kalām* as a technical term; '"*Al-kalām mā kāna muktafiyan bi-nafsihī wa-huwa ğumla*": A Study in the History of Sentence-Concept and the Sībawaihian Legacy in Arabic Grammar,' *ZDMG*, vol. CXXXVIII, 1988, pp. 74–79. Talmon attributes the origin of this misunderstanding to al-Mubarrad (d. 285/898). The later grammarians' understanding of the *kalām/qawl* distinction has been clarified by C. H. M. Versteegh who quoted the explanation of Ibn Jinnī (d. 392/1002) that '...*kalām* means every autonomous and meaningful expression...and *qawl* means in principle every utterance that is produced by the tongue;' *Arabic Grammar and Qur'anic Exegesis in Early Islam*, New York: E. J. Brill, 1993, p. 100.

308 Edition 3 inserts *dhikran bi*....

309 Edition 3 has *shay'an min al-īmān* instead of *al-īmān*.

310 The reader's understanding of this sentence in the original text is dependent on the particularities of Arabic grammar. The Arabic text reads, *anna baʿḍa al-aʿrāb marra bi-mu'adhdhin yaqūlu ashhadu anna muḥammadan rasūla Allāh bi'l-naṣb*. By putting a *fatḥa* (the vowel point 'a') at the end of the word *rasūl*, he made both nouns the subject of *anna*, thus rendering the statement meaningless. His response was, *mādhā yaqūl hādhā hādhā huwa al-ism fa-ayna al-khabar ʿanhu alladhī bihi yatimmu al-kalām*.

311 Abū Dāwud, *ṣalāh* 147; Ibn Mājah, *iqāma* 20; Dārimī, *ṣalāh* 69; Aḥmad, IV:155.

312 I have not found this *ḥadīth* in Bukhārī. See Abū Dāwud, *ṣalāh* 147, 149, 150; Ibn Mājah, *iqāma* 20; Dārimī, *ṣalāh* 69; Aḥmad, I:232, 371, V:382, 384, 389, 394, 397, 398, 400.

313 Bukhārī, *aymān* 19; Aḥmad, V:20.

314 Bukhārī, *tawḥīd* 58, *daʿawāt* 66, *aymān* 19; Muslim, *dhikr* 30; Tirmidhī, *daʿawāt* 59; Ibn Mājah, *adab* 56; Aḥmad, II:232.

315 Bukkārī, *bad' al-khalq* 11, *daʿawāt* 65; Muslim, *dhikr* 27; Tirmidhī, *daʿawāt* 59, 62; Ibn Mājah, *duʿā'* 14; *Muwaṭṭa'*, *Qur'ān* 20; Aḥmad, II:2, 3, 375, IV:227.

316 *Muwaṭṭa'*, *mass al-Qur'ān* 32, *ḥajj* 246.

317 Ibn Mājah, *adab* 55.

318 Ibn Taymiyya was clarifying that phrases such as '*bism Allāh*,' which are legislated in the Qur'ān and *Sunna*, are actually complete sentences by way of reconstruction (*taqdīr*); on the use of this term, see Gully, ibid., p. 18. Ibn Taymiyya's reasons for mentioning this were probably to forestall the counter argument that incomplete sentences (and therefore single nouns) were permitted as a form of remembrance.

319 Bukhārī, *ʿīdayn* 5, 10, 17, 23, *dhaba'iḥ* 17, *aḍāḥī* 1, 4, 8, 11, 12; Muslim, *aḍāḥī* 1–4, 10, 11; Nasā'ī, *ʿīdayn* 8, 30, *ḍaḥāyā* 4, 17, Ibn Mājah, *aḍāḥī* 12; Aḥmad, III:113, 117, 364, 385.

320 Bukhārī, *aṭʿima* 2; Muslim, *ashriba* 107–109; Abū Dāwud, *aṭʿima* 19; Tirmidhī, *aṭʿima* 2, 47; Ibn Mājah, *aṭʿima* 8; Dārimī, *aṭʿima* 1, 8, 15; *Muwaṭṭa'*, *ṣifāt al-nabī* 32.

321 Bukhārī, *wuḍū'* 33, *buyūʿ* 3, *dhabā'iḥ* 2, 3, 7–10, *tawḥīd* 13; Muslim, *ṣayd* 1–3; Abū Dāwud, *aḍāḥī* 22; Tirmidhī *ṣayd* 1, 6; Nasā'ī, *ṣayd* 1–3, 5–8, 18, 20, 21, *ḍaḥāyā* 19; Ibn Mājah, *ṣayd* 3; Aḥmad, I:231.

322 Muslim, *ashriba* 103; Abū Dāwud, *aṭʿima* 15; Ibn Mājah, *duʿā'* 19; Aḥmad, III:346, 383.

323 The term used is *al-mulabbī*; however, Edition 3 has *al-nabī*.

324 This insertion of the complete *ḥadīth* is from Editions 3, 4 and 5.

325 Bukhārī, *raqāq* 29.

326 In this statement and in the two following paragraphs, Ibn Taymiyya was presenting (in a very summarized manner) the general conclusions of Arab grammarians concerning the definition of a complete sentence and the technical terms for the parts of a sentence. The discussion revolves around the terms *jumla*, *kalima* and *ḥarf*. *Jumla* ('sentence') first appeared as a technical term in the works of al-Mubarrad (d. 285/898); see Versteegh, ibid., p. 102. In the works of the grammarians of the second/eighth and early third/ninth centuries, *kalima* was used for 'sentence' and 'word', while *ḥarf* was used for 'word' and 'letter'. Versteegh stresses that Sībawayh attempted to establish a distinction between *kalima* as 'sentence' and *ḥarf* as 'particle'; ibid., pp. 103–104. For a more detailed discussion of these terms, see Wolfdietrich Fischer,

'Zur Herkunft des grammatischen Terminus *Harf,*' *Jerusalem Studies in Arabic and Islam,* vol. xii, 1989, pp. 135–145.

327 This division is from the opening sentence in Sībawayh, ibid., vol. 1, p. 1. The definition of a particle reads: *ḥarfun jā' li-maʿnan laysa bi-ism wa-lā fiʿl.* Michael G. Carter translates this definition as 'a bit which comes for a meaning'; *Arabic Linguistics: An Introductory Classical Text with Translation and Notes*, Studies in the History of Linguistics, vol. xxiv, Amsterdam: John Benjamins, 1981, p. 15, n. 1.25. Gully also uses the same translation; ibid., pp. 116–118. Fischer translates this as 'das sprachliche Element, "das Bedeutung hat, das aber weder Nomen noch Verbum ist...."'; ibid., p. 137.

328 Dārimī, *faḍā'il al-Qur'ān* 1.

329 This insertion is from Edition 3.

330 Edition 3 has *tajdhīb al-qulūb ilā Allāh* instead of *al-qurb ilā Allāh.*

331 Editions 3, 4 and 5 have *an lā naʿbudu illā Allāh wa-an lā naʿbuduhu illā...*, whereas Editions 1 and 2 expresses this with the passive *yuʿbadu.*

332 Edition 3 inserts *fī waṣfi al-ṣaḥāba raḍiya Allāhu ʿanhum.*

333 Tirmidhī, *qiyāma* 59; Aḥmad, 1:293, 303, 307.

334 This insertion is from Edition 3.

BIBLIOGRAPHY

IBN TAYMIYYA

Dar' taʿāruḍ al-ʿaql wa'l-naql, ed. Muḥammad Rashād Sālim, Riyadh: Jāmiʿat al-Imām Muḥammad b. Saʿūd al-Islāmiyya, 1399/1979.

Al-Istiqāma, ed. Muḥammad Rashād Sālim, 2 vols., Cairo: Maktabat al-Sunna, 1409/1989.

'*Kitāb bughyat al-murtād*,' in *Majmūʿat fatāwā Ibn Taymiyya al-kubrā*, vol. v, Cairo: Dār al-Manār, 1408/1988, pp. 291–430.

Kitāb al-īmān, Beirut: Dār al-Kutub al-ʿIlmiyya, 1412/1991.

Kitāb al-nubuwwāt, Lebanon: Dār al-Qalam, [no date].

Majmūʿ fatāwā shaykh al-islām Aḥmad b. Taymiyya, 37 vols., Riyadh: Maṭbaʿat al-Ḥukūma, 1386/1966.

Particular use has been made of the following volumes of the *Majmūʿ fatāwā*:

'*Amrāḍ al-qulūb wa-shifā'uhā*,' in *Majmūʿ fatāwā shaykh al-islām Aḥmad b. Taymiyya*, vol. x: *Kitab ʿilm al-sulūk*, pp. 91–137.

'*Al-Farq bayn awliyā' al-raḥmān wa-awliyā' al-shayṭān*,' in *Majmūʿ fatāwā shaykh al-islām Aḥmad b. Taymiyya*, vol. xi: *Kitāb al-taṣawwuf*, pp. 157–311.

'*Al-Furqān bayn al-ḥaqq wa'l-bāṭil*,' in *Majmūʿ fatāwā shaykh al-islām Aḥmad b. Taymiyya*, vol. xiii: *Kitāb muqaddimat al-tafsīr*, pp. 5–230.

'*Al-Kaylāniyya*,' in *Majmūʿ fatāwā Shaykh al-Islām Aḥmad b. Taymiyya*, vol. xii: *Kitāb al-Qur'ān*, pp. 323–502.

'*Mas'alat al-aḥruf allatī anzala Allāh ʿalā Ādam*,' in *Majmūʿ fatāwā shaykh al-islām Aḥmad b. Taymiyya*, vol. xii: *Kitāb al-Qur'ān*, pp. 37–117.

'*Muqaddima fī uṣūl al-tafsīr*,' in *Majmūʿ fatāwā shaykh al-islām Aḥmad b. Taymiyya*, vol. xiii: *Kitāb muqaddimat al-tafsīr*, pp. 329–375.

'*Qā'ida fī'l-tawassul wa'l-wasīla*,' in *Majmūʿ fatāwā shaykh al-islām Aḥmad b. Taymiyya*, vol. i: *Kitāb al-rubūbiyya*, pp. 142–368.

'*Risāla ilā Naṣr al-Manbijī*,' in *Majmūʿ fatāwā shaykh al-islām Aḥmad b. Taymiyya*, vol. ii: *Kitāb tawḥīd al-ulūhiyya*, pp. 452–479.

'*Risālat al-jahmiyya*,' in *Majmūᶜ fatāwā shaykh al-islām Aḥmad b. Taymiyya*, vol. x: *Kitāb ᶜilm al-sulūk*, pp. 61–72.

'*Al-Tuḥfa al-ᶜirāqiyya fī al-aᶜmāl al-qalbiyya*,' in *Majmūᶜ fatāwā shaykh al-islām Aḥmad b. Taymiyya*, vol. x: *Kitāb ᶜilm al-sulūk*, pp. 5–90.

'*Al-ᶜUbūdiyya fī al-islām*,' in *Majmūᶜ fatāwā shaykh al-islām Aḥmad b. Taymiyya*, vol. x: *Kitāb ᶜilm al-sulūk*, pp. 149–237.

Majmū'at al-rasā'il wa'l-masā'il, ed. Muḥammad Rashīd Riḍā, 5 vols., Cairo: al-Turāth al-ᶜArabī, 1976.

Particular use has been made of the following volumes of the *Majmū'at al-rasā'il*:

'*Ibṭāl waḥdat al-wujūd*,' in *Majmū'at al-rasā'il wa'l-masā'il*, vol. 1, pp. 61–120.

'*Risāla ilā Naṣr al-Manbijī*,' in *Majmū'at al-rasā'il wa'l-masā'il*, vol. 1, pp. 161–183.

Al-Risāla al-tadmuriyya, Cairo: al-Maṭbaᶜa al-Salafiyya, 1387/1968.

'*Risālat al-ᶜubūdiyya fī tafsīr qawlihi taᶜālā yā ayyuhā al-nās uᶜbudū rabbakum*,' in *Majmūᶜ Rasā'il*, ed. Muḥammad Badr al-Dīn Abū Firās al-Naᶜsānī al-Ḥalabī, Cairo: al-Maṭbaᶜa al-Ḥusayniyya al-Miṣriyya, 1323/1905, pp. 2–44.

Al-Ṣārim al-maslūl ᶜalā shātim al-rasūl, ed. Muḥammad Muḥyī al-Dīn ᶜAbd al-Ḥamīd, Tanta: Maktabat Tāj, 1379/1960.

Ṣiḥḥat uṣūl madhhab ahl al-Madīna, ed. Aḥmad Ḥijāzī Aḥmad al-Saqā, Cairo: Maktabat al-Thaqāfa al-Dīniyya, 1988.

Al-Ṣūfiyya wa'l-fuqarā', ed. Muḥammad Jamīl Ghāzī, Jeddah: Sūq al-Nādā, [no date].

Tafsīr ṣūrat al-ikhlāṣ, ed. Ṭaha Yūsuf Shāhīn, Cairo: Dār al-Ṭibāᶜa al-Muḥammadiyya, [no date].

Al-ᶜUbūdiyya, ed. ᶜAbd al-Raḥmān al-Bānī, Beirut: al-Maktab al-Islāmī, 1399/1979.

Al-ᶜUbūdiyya, ed. Muḥammad Ḥāmid al-Faqī, Cairo: Maṭbaᶜat al-Sunna al-Muḥammadiyya, 1367/1947.

Al-ᶜUbūdiyya fī al-islām, Cairo: al-Maṭbaᶜa al-Salafiyya, 1387/1967.

REFERENCE WORKS

Abū Zahra, Muḥammad, *Ibn Taymiyya: hayyātuhu wa-ᶜaṣruhu ārā'uhu wa-fiqhuhu*, Cairo: Dār al-Fikr al-ᶜArabī, [no date].

Ali, Abdullah Yusuf, *The Holy Qur-ān: English Translation of the Meanings and Commentary*, rev. trans., Medina: King Fahd Holy Qur-ān Printing Complex, 1410/1989.

Bibliography

Arjomand, Said Amir, *The Shadow of God and the Hidden Imam: Religion, Political Order, and Societal Change in Shiite Iran from the Beginning to 1890*, Chicago & London: University of Chicago Press, 1988.

Ayoub, Mahmoud, *The Qur'ān and its Interpreters*, 2 vols., Albany: State University of New York Press, 1984.

Azami, Mohammad Mustafa, *On Schacht's Origins of Muhammadan Jurisprudence*, Riyadh: King Saud University & New York: John Wiley & Sons Inc., 1985.

———, *Studies in Early Ḥadīth Literature*, Indianapolis: American Trust Publications, 1978.

Baghdādī, Abū Manṣūr ʿAbd al-Qāhir al-, *al-Farq bayn al-firaq*, Beirut: Dār al-Āfāq al-Jadīda, 1408/1987.

———, *al-Farq bayn al-firaq*, trans. Kate Chambers Seelye as *Moslem Schisms and Sects:* (al-Fark bain al-firak) *being the history of the various philosophic systems developed in Islam, by abū-Mansūr ʿabd-al-Kāhir ibn-Tāhir al-Baghdādi*, New York: AMC Press Inc., 1966.

Bazzār, Abū Ḥafs ʿUmar b. ʿAlī al-, *al-Aʿlām al-ʿaliyya fī manāqib Shaykh al-Islām Ibn Taymiyya*, ed. Ṣalāḥ al-Dīn al-Munajjid, Beirut: Dār al-Kitāb al-Jadīd, 1396/1976.

Beeston, A. F. L., *The Epistle on Singing-Girls of Jāhiz*, Warminster, Wilts.: Aris & Phillips Ltd., 1980.

Bell, Joseph N., 'The Hanbalite Teaching on Love,' Ph.D. dissertation, Princeton University, 1971.

———, *Love Theory in Later Hanbalite Islam*, Albany: State University of New York Press, 1979.

Bernards, Monique, *Changing Traditions: Al-Mubarrad's Refutation of Sībawayh and the Subsequent Reception of the* Kitāb, Leiden & New York: E. J. Brill, 1997.

Bori, Caterina, 'Ibn Taymiyya *wa-Jamāʿatuhu*: Authority, Conflict and Consensus in Ibn Taymiyya's Circle,' in *Ibn Taymiyya and His Times*, ed. Yossef Rapoport and Shahab Ahmed, New York: Oxford University Press, 2010, pp. 23–52.

Braune, Walther, *Die Futūḥ al-Ġaib des ʿAbd al-Qādir*, Berlin & Leipzig: Walter De Gruyter & Co., 1933.

———, 'Ibn al-Ǧauzīs Streitschrift gegen den Sufismus,' *Annali dell'Istituto Universitario Orientale di Napoli*, Nuova Serie, vol. 1, 1940, pp. 305–313.

Brockelmann, Carl, *Geschichte der arabischen Litteratur* (*GAL*), 2 vols. and 3 supplements, Leiden: E. J. Brill, 1937–49.

Brockett, Adrian, 'The Value of the Hafs and Warsh Transmissions for the Textual History of the Qur'ān,' in *Approaches to the History of the Interpretation of the Qur'ān*, ed. Andrew Rippin, Oxford: Clarendon Press, 1988, pp. 31–45.

Burrell, David B., *Freedom and Creation in Three Traditions*, Notre Dame: University of Notre Dame Press, 1993.

Calder, Norman, 'Tafsīr from Ṭabarī to Ibn Kathīr: Problems in the Description of a Genre, Illustrated with Reference to the Story of Abraham,' in *Approaches to the Qur'ān*, ed. G. R. Hawting and Abdul-Kader A. Shareef, London & New York: Routledge, 1993, pp. 101–139.

Carter, Michael G., ed., *Arabic Linguistics: An Introductory Classical Text with Translation and Notes*, Studies in the History of Linguistics, vol. XXIV, Amsterdam: John Benjamins, 1981.

———, 'Language Control as People Control in Medieval Islam: the Aims of the Grammarians in their Cultural Context,' *al-Abhath: Journal of the Faculty of Arts and Sciences, American University of Beirut*, vol. XXXI, 1983, pp. 65–83.

Chittick, William, *The Sufi Path of Knowledge: Ibn al-ʿArabi's Metaphysics of Imagination*, Albany, NY: State University of New York Press, 1989.

Curtis, Roy Young Muhammad Mukhtar, 'Authentic Interpretation of Classical Islamic Texts: An Analysis of the Introduction of Ibn Kathīr's *Tafsīr al-Qur'ān al-ʿAẓīm*,' Ph.D. dissertation, University of Michigan, 1989.

Dhahabī, Muḥammad Ḥusayn al-, *al-Tafsīr wa'l-mufassirūn*, 3 vols., Cairo: Dār al-Kutub al-Ḥadītha, 1396/1976.

Ellwood, Robert S., *Mysticism and Religion*, Englewood Cliffs, NJ: Prentice-Hall Inc., 1980.

Ernst, Carl, *Words of Ecstasy in Sufism*, Albany, NY: State University of New York Press, 1985.

Fakhry, Majid, *A History of Islamic Philosophy*, New York: Columbia University Press, 1983.

Farhadi, A. G. Ravan, *ʿAbdullah Ansārī of Herat (1006–1089 C.E.): An Early Sūfī Master*, Richmond, Surrey: Curzon Press, 1996.

Fischer, Wolfdietrich, 'Zur Herkunft des grammatischen Terminus *ḥarf*,' *Jerusalem Studies in Arabic and Islam*, vol. XII, 1989, pp. 135–145.

Gardet, Louis and Anawati, M. M., *Introduction à la théologie musulmane: essai de théologie comparée*, Études de philosophie médiévale, 37, Paris: J. Vrin, 1970.

Ghazālī, Abū Ḥāmid al-, *Iḥyā' ʿulūm al-dīn*, 4 vols., Cairo: al-Matbaʿa al-Azhariyya al-Miṣriyya, 1316/1899.

———, *Fayṣal al-tafriqa bayna al-islām wa'l-zandaqa*, ed. Hogga Mustapha, Casablanca: Dār al-Naṣr al-Maghribiyya, 1983.

Gilbert, J. E., 'Institutionalisation of Muslim Scholarship and Professionalization of the *ʿUlamā'* in Medieval Damascus,' *Studia Islamica*, vol. LII, 1980, pp. 105–134.

Giffen, Lois Anita, *Theory of Profane Love Among the Arabs: the Development of the Genre*, New York: New York University Press, 1971.

Goldziher, Ignaz, *Vorlesungen über den Islam,* Heidelberg: Carl Winter's Universitätsbuchhandlung, 1910.

Gramlich, Richard, *Das Sendschreiben al-Qushayrīs über das Sufitum*, Wiesbaden: Franz Steiner Verlag, 1989.

———, *Die Nahrung der Herzen: Abū Ṭālib al-Makkīs* Qūt al-Qulūb, 4 vols., Stuttgart: Franz Steiner Verlag, 1992.

———, *Schlaglichter über das Sufitum: Abū Naṣr as-Sarrāǧs* Kitāb al-lumaʿ, Stuttgart: Franz Steiner Verlag, 1990.

Grousset, René, *The Empire of the Steppes: A History of Central Asia*, tr. Naomi Walford, New Brunswick, NJ: Rutgers University Press, 1970.

Gully, Adrian, *Grammar and Semantics in Medieval Arabic: A Study of Ibn-Hisham's 'Mughni l-Labib'*, Richmond, Surrey: Curzon Press, 1995.

Hallaq, Wael B., *Ibn Taymiyya Against the Greek Logicians*, New York: Oxford University Press, 1993.

———, 'Ibn Taymiyya on the Existence of God,' *Acta Orientalia*, vol. LII, 1991, pp. 49–69.

Harawī, Abū Ismā'īl ʿAbd-Allāh al-Anṣārī al-, *Kitāb manāzil al-sā'irīn*, French tr. S. de Laugier de Beaurecueil, Cairo: Institut français d'archéologie orientale, 1962.

Heinrichs, Wolfhart, 'On the Genesis of the *Ḥaqīqah-Majāz* Dichotomy,' *Studia Islamica*, vol. LIX, 1984, pp. 111–140.

Hodgson, Marshall G. S., *The Venture of Islam: Conscience and History in a World Civilization*, 3 vols., Chicago: Chicago University Press, 1974.

Holtzman, Livnat, 'Human Choice, Divine Guidance and the *Fiṭra*

Tradition: The Use of Hadith in Theological Treatises by Ibn Taymiyya and Ibn Qayyim al-Jawziyya,' in *Ibn Taymiyya and His Times*, ed. Yossef Rapoport and Shahab Ahmed, New York: Oxford University Press, 2010, pp. 163–188.

Hoover, Jon, 'God Acts by His Will and Power: Ibn Taymiyya's Theology of a Personal God in his Treatise on the Voluntary Attributes,' in *Ibn Taymiyya and His Times*, ed. Yossef Rapoport and Shahab Ahmed, New York: Oxford University Press, 2010, pp. 55–77.

Houtsma, M., et al., eds., *Encyclopaedia of Islam*, 9 vols., 1st edn. (*EI*[1]), Leiden: E. J. Brill, 1913–1936.

Hujwīrī, ʿAlī b. ʿUthmān al-, *Kashf al-maḥjūb*, tr. Reynold Nicholson as *The Kashf al-Maḥjūb: The Oldest Persian Treatise on Sufism*, London: Luzac, 1976.

Ibn ʿAbd al-Hādī, Muḥammad, *al-ʿUqūd al-durriya*, Beirut: Dār al-Kutub al-ʿIlmiyya, 1975.

Ibn ʿArabī, Muḥyī al-Dīn, *Fuṣūṣ al-ḥikam*, ed. Abū al-ʿAlā ʿAfīfī, Beirut: Dar al-Kitāb al-ʿArabī, 1966.

———, *Fuṣūṣ al-ḥikam*, trans. R. W. J. Austin as *Ibn al-Arabi: The Bezels of Wisdom*, New York: Paulist Press, 1980.

Ibn ʿAṭiyya, Abū Muḥammad ʿAbd al-Haqq b. Ghālib, *al-Muḥarrar al-wajīz fī tafsīr al-kitāb al-ʿazīz*, ed. ʿAbd al-Salām ʿAbd al-Shāfī Muḥammad, Beirut: Dār al-Kutub al-ʿIlmiyya, 1413/1993.

Ibn Ḥajar al-ʿAsqalānī, Aḥmad b. ʿAlī, *al-Durar al-kāmina fī aʿyān al-mi'at al-thāmina*, 5 vols., Cairo: Dār al-Kutub al-Ḥadītha, [no date].

———, *Fatḥ al-bārī sharḥ Saḥīḥ al-Bukhārī*, 13 vols. and introduction, Beirut: Dār al-Maʿrifa, [no date].

———, *Tahdhīb al-tahdhīb*, 12 vols., Beirut: Dār al-Ṣādir, 1325/1907.

Ibn Ḥanbal, Aḥmad, *ʿAqīdat Aḥmad b. Ḥanbal bi-riwāyat Abī Bakr al-Khallāl*, ed. ʿAbd al-ʿAzīz ʿIzz al-Dīn al-Shīrawān, Damascus: Dār Quṭaybiyya, 1408/1988.

Ibn ʿImād al-Ḥanbalī, Abū al-Falāḥ ʿAbd al-Ḥayy, *Shadharāt al-dhahab fī akhbār man dhahaba*, 8 vols., Beirut: Dār al-Fikr, 1414/1994.

Ibn al-Jawzī, Abū al-Faraj ʿAbd al-Raḥmān, *Kitāb al-mawḍūʿāt*, 3 vols., Beirut: Dar al-Fikr, 1403/1983.

Ibn Kathīr, ʿImād al-Dīn Abū al-Fidā' Ismāʿīl, *al-Bidāya wa'l-nihāya*, ed. Aḥmad Abū Māhim et al., 14 vols., Beirut: Dār al-Kutub al-ʿIlmiyya, 1407/1987.

———, *Mukhtaṣar tafsīr Ibn Kathīr*, ed. Muḥammad ʿAlī al-Ṣābūnī, 3 vols., Beirut: Dār al-Qur'ān al-Karīm, 1402/1981.

Ibn Khallikān, *Ibn Khallikan's Biographical Dictionary*, tr. W. Mac Guckin de Slane, 4 vols., repr., New York & London: Johnson Reprint Corporation, 1961.

Ibn Manẓūr, Abū Faḍl Jamāl al-Dīn Muḥammad, *Lisān al-ʿArab*, 15 vols., Beirut: Dār Ṣādir, [no date].

Ibn al-Qayyim al-Jawziyya, Muḥammad b. Abī Bakr, *Asmāʾ muʾallafāt Ibn Taymiyya*, ed. Ṣalāḥ al-Dīn al-Munajjid, 2nd ed., Damascus: Maṭbūʿāt al-Majmaʿ al-ʿIlmī al-ʿArabī, 1372/1953.

———, *Madārij al-sālikīn bayna manāzil iyyāka naʿbudu wa-iyyāka nastaʿīn*, 3 vols., Cairo: Dār al-Ḥadīth, [no date].

———, *Rawḍat al-muḥibbīn wa-nuzhat al-mushtāqīn*, Beirut: al-Mu'assasa al-Jāmiʿiyya li'l-Dirāsāt wa'l-Nashr wa'l-Tawzīʿ, 1402/1982.

———, *Zād al-maʿād*, 5 vols., Beirut: Mu'assasat al-Risāla & Kuwait: Maktabat al-Manār al-Islāmiyya, 1407/1987.

Ibn Rajab, Zayn al-Dīn ʿAbd al-Raḥmān, *Kitāb al-dhayl ʿalā ṭabaqāt al-ḥanābila*, 2 vols., Beirut: Dār al-Maʿrifa, [no date].

Ibn Sīnā, Abū ʿAlī al-Ḥusayn, '*Fī ithbāt al-nubuwwa*,' in *Tisʿ rāsāʾil fī al-ḥikma wa'l-ṭabīʿiyyāt*, Cairo: al-Maṭbaʿa al-Hindiyya, 1327/1908, pp. 120–132.

Ibn Taymiyya, Majd al-Dīn ʿAbd al-Salām, *al-Muḥarrar fī al-fiqh ʿalā madhhab al-imām Aḥmad b. Ḥanbal wa-maʿahu al-nukat wa'l-fawāʾid al-saniyya ʿalā mushkil al-muḥarrar li-Majd al-Dīn Ibn Taymiyya taʾlīf Shams al-Dīn Ibn Mufliḥ al-Ḥanbalī al-Maqdisī (713/1313–763/1360)*, ed. Muḥammad Ḥāmid al-Faqī, 2 vols., Cairo: Maṭbaʿat al-Sunna al-Muḥammadiyya, 1369/1950.

———, *al-Muntaqā min aḥādīth al-aḥkām*, Cairo: al-Maktaba al-Salafiyya, [no date].

Irwin, R., *The Middle East in the Middle Ages: The Early Mamluk Sultanate, 1250–1382*, Carbondale & Edwardsville, IL: Southern Illinois University Press, 1986.

Izutsu, Toshihiko, *The Concept of Belief in Islamic Theology: A Semantic Analysis of Imān and Islām*, Yokohama: Yurindo Publishing Co. Ltd., 1965.

Jackson, Sherman A., 'Ibn Taymiyyah on Trial in Damascus,' *Journal of Semitic Studies*, vol. XXXIX, no. 1, 1994, pp. 41–85.

Jamil, Tariq al-, 'Ibn Taymiyya and Ibn al-Muṭahhar al-Ḥillī: Shiʿi Polemics and the Struggle for Religious Authority in Medieval Islam,' in *Ibn Taymiyya and His Times*, ed. Yossef Rapoport and Shahab Ahmed, New York: Oxford University Press, 2010, pp. 229–246.

Kalābādhī, Abū Bakr Muḥammad al-, *al-Taʿarruf li-madhhab ahl al-taṣawwuf*, ed. Maḥmūd Amīn al-Nawāwī, Cairo: Maktabat al-Kulliyya al-Azhariyya, 1389/1969.

———, *al-Taʿarruf li-madhhab ahl al-taṣawwuf*; trans. Arthur J. Arberry as *The Doctrine of the Sufis*, repr. New York: Cambridge University Press, 1977.

Karamustafa, Ahmet T., *God's Unruly Friends: Dervish Groups in the Islamic Later Middle Period, 1200–1550*, Salt Lake City: University of Utah Press, 1994.

Katz, Steven T., ed., *Mysticism and Language*, New York: Oxford University Press, 1992.

Khadduri, Majid, tr., *Al-Shāfiʿī's* Risāla*: Treatise on the Foundations of Islamic Jurisprudence*, Cambridge: Islamic Texts Society, 1987.

Khalīfa, Ḥājjī, *Kashf al-ẓunūn ʿan asāmī al-kutub wa'l-funūn*, repr., New York: Johnson Reprint Corporation, 1938.

Khaṭīb al-Tibrīzī, Muḥammad b. ʿAbd Allāh al-, *Mishkāt al-maṣābīḥ*, ed. Muḥammad Nāṣir al-Dīn al-Albanī, 3 vols., Beirut & Damascus: al-Maktab al-Islāmī, 1405/1985.

———, *Mishkāt al-maṣābīḥ*, ed. and tr. James Robson as *Mishkat al-Masabih: English Translation with Explanatory Notes*, Lahore: Muhammad Ashraf, 1975.

Kramers, J. H., et al., *Encyclopaedia of Islam*, 11 vols., new edn. (*EI²*), Leiden: E. J. Brill, 1954–2002.

Landolt, Hermann, 'Der Briefwechsel zwischen Kāshānī und Simnānī über Waḥdat al-Wuǧūd,' *Der Islam,* vol. L, no. 1, 1973, pp. 29–81.

Lane, Edward, *Arabic-English Lexicon*, 8 vols., repr., Beirut: Librairie du Liban, 1980.

Lamotte, Virginie, 'Ibn Taymiyya's Theory of Knowledge,' M.A. thesis, McGill University, 1994.

Laoust, H., *Contribution à une étude de la méthodologie canonique de Taḳī-d-Dīn Aḥmad b. Taimīya*, Cairo: Imprimerie de l'Institut français d'archéologie orientale, 1939.

———, *Essai sur les doctrines sociales et politiques de Takī-d-Dīn Ahmad b.*

Taimīya, Cairo: Imprimerie de l'Institut français d'archéologie orientale, 1939.

———, 'La biographie d'Ibn Taimīya d'après Ibn Kaṯīr,' *Bulletin d'études orientales* (*BEO*), vol. IX, 1942, pp. 115–162.

———, 'Le hanbalisme sous le califat de Bagdad (241/855–656/1258),' *Revue des études islamiques* (*REI*), vol. XXVII, 1959, pp. 67–128.

———, 'Le hanbalisme sous les Mamlouks bahrides (658/1260–784/1382),' *REI*, vol. XXVIII, 1960, pp. 1–71.

Madelung, Wilferd, *Religious Trends in Early Islamic Iran*, Albany, NY: Persian Heritage Foundation, 1988.

Madjid, Nurcholish, 'Ibn Taymiyya on *Kalām* and *Falsafa*: A Problem of Reason and Revelation in Islam,' Ph.D. dissertation, University of Chicago, 1984.

Makari, Victor, 'The Social Factor in Ibn Taymiyyah's Ethics,' Ph.D. dissertation, Temple University, 1976.

———, *Ibn Taymiyyah's Ethics: the Social Factor*, California: The Scholars Press, 1983.

Makdisi, George, 'Hanbalite Islam,' in *Studies on Islam*, trans. Merlin Swartz, New York: Oxford University Press, 1981, pp. 216–274.

Makkī, Abū Ṭālib al-, *Qūt al-Qulūb*, 4 vols., Cairo: al-Maktaba al-Ḥusayniyya, 1351/1932.

Mālik b. Anas, *al-Muwaṭṭa'*, ed. Muḥammad ʿAbd al-Bāqī, 2 vols., Cairo: Dār Iḥyā' al-Kutub al-ʿArabiyya, 1986.

Margoliouth, D. S., 'Contribution to the Biography of ʿAbd al-Kadir of Jilan,' *Journal of the Royal Asiatic Society*, April, 1907, pp. 267–310.

———, 'The Devil's Delusion of Ibn al-Jawzi,' *Islamic Culture*, vol. x, July, 1936, pp. 339–368, 633–647; vol. XI, April, 1937, pp. 267–273, 393–403, 529–533.

Marmura, Michael, tr., 'Avicenna: On the Proof of Prophecies and the Interpretation of the Prophet's Symbols and Metaphors,' in *Medieval Political Philosophy: A Sourcebook*, ed. Ralph Lerner and Muhsin Mahdi, New York: The Free Press, 1963, pp. 112–121.

Martin, David Ludwig, 'Al-Fanā' (Mystical Annihilation of the Soul) and al-Baqā' (Subsistence of the Soul) in the Work of Abū al-Qasim al-Junayd al-Baghdādī,' Ph.D. dissertation, Los Angeles, University of California, 1984.

Massignon, L., *La Passion de Husayn Ibn Mansūr Hallāj*, trans. Herbert Mason as *The Passion of al-Ḥallāj: Mystic and Martyr of Islam*, 4 vols., Bollinger Series, vol. XCVIII, Princeton: Princeton University Press, 1982.

McAuliffe, Jane Dammen, 'Quranic Hermeneutics: The Views of al-Tabarī and Ibn Kathīr,' in *Approaches to the History of the Interpretation of the Qur'ān*, ed. Andrew Rippin, Oxford: Clarendon Press, 1988, pp. 46–62.

McCarthy, Richard Joseph, *Freedom and Fulfillment: An Annotated Translation of al-Ghazālī's* al-Munqidh min al-Dalāl *and Other Relevant Works of al-Ghazālī*, Boston: Wayne Publishers, 1980.

Melchert, Christopher, 'The Ḥanābila and the Early Sufis,' *Arabica*, vol. XLVIII, no. 3, 2001, pp. 352–367.

Memon, Muhammad Umar, *Ibn Taymiyyah's Struggle Against Popular Religion: With an Annotated Translation of his* Kitāb iqtidā' aṣ-ṣirāṭ al-mustaqīm li-mukhālafat aṣḥāb al-jahīm, The Hague & Paris: Mouton, 1976.

Michel, Thomas F., 'Ibn Taymiyya's Critique of *Falsafa*,' *Hamdard Islamicus*, vol. VI, no. 1, 1983, pp. 3–14.

———, 'Ibn Taymiyya's *Sharḥ* on the *Futūḥ al-ghayb* of ʿAbd al-Qādir al-Jīlānī,' *Hamdard Islamicus*, vol. IV, no. 2, 1981, pp. 3–12.

Mojaddedi, Jawid A., 'Getting Drunk with Abū Yazīd or Staying Sober with Junayd: The Creation of a Popular Typology of Sufism,' *Bulletin of the School of Oriental and African Studies*, vol. LXVI, no. 1, 2003, pp. 1–13.

Murād, Ḥasan Qāsim, 'Miḥan of Ibn Taymiyya: A Narrative Account based on a Comparative Analysis of Sources,' M.A. thesis, McGill University, Montreal, 1968.

Nadīm, Abū al-Faraj Muḥammad ibn Isḥāq al-, *The Fihrist of al-Nadīm*, ed. and tr. Bayard Dodge, 2 vols., New York: Columbia University Press, 1970.

Nadwi, Abul Hasan Ali, *Saviours of Islamic Spirit*, ed. and tr. Muhiuddin Ahmad., Lucknow, India: Academy of Islamic Research and Publications, 1977.

Nasr, Seyyed Hossein, 'The Qur'ān and *Ḥadīth* as source and inspiration of Islamic philosophy,' in *History of Islamic Philosophy*, ed. Seyyed Hossein Nasr and Oliver Leaman, vol. 1, New York: Routledge, 1996, pp. 27–39.

Nicholson, Reynold, *The Mystics of Islam*, repr., New York: Schocken Books, 1975.

Omari, Racha, el, 'Ibn Taymiyya's "Theology of the Sunna" and his Polemics with the Ashᶜarite,' in *Ibn Taymiyya and His Times*, ed. Yossef Rapoport and Shahab Ahmed, New York: Oxford University Press, 2010, pp. 101–119.

Osman, Yahya, *Histoire et classification de l'oeuvre d'Ibn ᶜArabī*, 2 vols., Damascus: Centre National de la Recherche Scientifique, 1964.

Özervarlı, M. Sait, 'The Qur'ānic Rational Theology of Ibn Taymiyya and his Criticism of the *Mutakallimūn*,' in *Ibn Taymiyya and His Times*, ed. Yossef Rapoport and Shahab Ahmed, New York: Oxford University Press, 2010, pp. 78–100.

Penrice, John, *A Dictionary and Glossary of the Korān*, repr., Karachi: Rahim Brothers, 1987.

Qushayrī, Abū al-Qāsim ᶜAbd al-Karīm al-, *al-Risālat al-qushayrīyya fī ᶜilm al-taṣawwuf*, ed. Zakariyyā al-Anṣārī, Cairo: Maktabat wa-Maṭbaᶜat Muḥammad ᶜAlī Sabīᶜ wa-Awliyā'uh, 1382/1962.

Rahman, Fazlur, *Islam*, London: Weidenfeld & Nicolson, 1966.

Rāzī, Fakhr al-Dīn al-, *al-Tafsīr al-kabīr li'l-imām al-Fakhr al-Rāzī*, Beirut: Dār Iḥyā' al-Turāth al-ᶜArabī, [no date].

Reinert, Benedikt, *Die Lehre vom* tawakkul *in der klassischen Sufik*, Berlin: Walter De Gruyter & Co., 1968.

Sābiq, al-Sayyid, *Fiqh us-Sunnah: az-Zakāh and aṣ-Ṣiyām*, tr. Abdul-Majid Khokhar, Muhammad Saᶜeed Dabas and Jamal al-Din M. Zarabozo, Indianapolis: American Trust Publications, 1412/1991.

Ṣafadī, Ṣalāḥ al-Dīn Khalīl b. Aybak al-, *Kitāb al-wāfī bi'l-wafayāt*, 30 vols., Wiesbaden: Franz Steiner Verlag, 1974.

Saleh, Walid A., 'Ibn Tamiyya and the Rise of Radical Hermeneutics: An Analysis of *An Introduction to the Foundations of Qur'ānic Exegesis*,' in *Ibn Taymiyya and His Times*, ed. Yossef Rapoport and Shahab Ahmed, New York: Oxford University Press, 2010, pp. 123–162.

Ṣāliḥ, Muḥammad Adīb, *Lamaḥāt fī uṣūl al-ḥadīth*, Beirut & Damascus: al-Maktab al-Islāmī, 1405/1985.

Sayyid, Fu'ād, ed., *Fihrist al-makhṭūṭāt*, 3 vols., Cairo: Maṭbaᶜat Dār al-Kutub, 1961–1963.

Schacht, Joseph, *The Origins of Muhammadan Jurisprudence*, Oxford: Clarendon Press, 1959.

Schimmel, Annemarie, *Mystical Dimensions of Islam*, Chapel Hill: University of North Carolina Press, 1975.

Shawkānī, Muḥammad, *al-Qur'ān al-karīm wa-bi'l-hāmish zubdat al-tafsīr min fatḥ al-qadīr wa-huwa mukhtaṣar min tafsīr al-Imām al-Shawkānī*, ed. Muḥammad Sulaymān ʿAbd Allāh al-Ashqar, Kuwait: Wizārat al-Awqāf wa'l-Shu'ūn al-Islāmiyya, 1406/1985.

Sībawayh, ʿAmr ibn ʿUthmān, *Kitāb Sībawayh: Le livre de Sībawayh, traité de grammaire arabe par Sīboūya, dit Sībawayh*, ed. Hartwig Derenbourg, 2 vols., repr., Reinheim, Germany: Druckerei Lokay, [no date].

Sīlī, Sayyid ʿAbd al-ʿAzīz al-, *al-ʿAqīda al-salafiyya bayn al-imām Ibn Ḥanbal wa'l-imām Ibn Taymiyya*, Cairo: Dār al-Manār, 1416/1995.

Sivan, Emanuel, *Radical Islam*, New Haven & London: Yale University Press, 1990.

Speight, R. Marston, 'The Function of *ḥadīth* as Commentary on the Qur'ān, as Seen in the Six Authoritative Collections,' in *Approaches to the History of the Interpretation of the Qur'ān*, ed. Andrew Rippin, Oxford: Clarendon Press, 1988, pp. 63–81.

Stace, W. T., *Mysticism and Philosophy*, Philadelphia & New York: J. B. Lippincott Co., 1960.

Suyūṭī, Jalāl al-Dīn ʿAbd al-Raḥmān al-, *al-Itqān fī ʿulūm al-Qur'ān*, Beirut: Dār al-Fikr, [no date].

Suyūṭī, Jalāl al-Dīn ʿAbd al-Raḥmān al-, and Jalāl al-Dīn Muḥammad al-Maḥallī, *al-Qurān al-karīm bi-tafsīr al-Imāmayn al-Jalālayn*, Beirut: Dār al-ʿIlm li'l-Jamīʿ, [no date].

Swartz, Merlin, 'A seventh century (A.H.) Sunnī creed: The ʿAqīda Wāsiṭīya of Ibn Taymīya,' *Humaniora Islamica*, vol. 1, 1973, pp. 91–131.

Syafruddin, Didin, 'The Principles of Ibn Taymiyya's Qur'ānic Interpretation,' M.A. thesis, McGill University, 1994.

Ṭabarī, Abū Jaʿfar Muḥammad b. Jarīr al-, *Jāmiʿ al-bayān ʿan tafsīr āy al-Qur'ān*, Cairo: Maktaba wa-Maṭbaʿat Muṣṭafā al-Bābī al-Ḥalabī, 1373/1954.

Talmon, Rafael, '"*Al-kalām mā kāna muktafiyan bi-nafsihi wa-huwa ğumla*": A Study in the History of Sentence-Concept and the Sībawaihian Legacy in Arabic Grammar,' *Zeitschrift der Deutschen Morgenländischen Gesellschaft*, vol. CXXXVIII, 1988, pp. 74–98.

Tarābulūsī al-Ḥanafī, ʿAlī b. Khalīl al-, *Muʿīn al-ḥukkām*, Egypt: [no publisher], 1393/1973.

Taylor, Christopher Schurmann, 'The Cult of Saints in Late Medieval Egypt,' Ph.D. dissertation, Princeton University, 1989.

Versteegh, C. H. M., *Arabic Grammar and Qur'anic Exegesis in Early Islam*, New York: E. J. Brill, 1993.

Wansbrough, John E., *Quranic Studies: Sources and Methods of Scriptural Interpretation*, Oxford: Oxford University Press, 1977.

Watt, Montgomery W., *Islamic Philosophy and Theology*, Edinburgh: Edinburgh University Press, 1985.

Weiss, Bernard, *The Search for God's Law: Islamic Jurisprudence in the Writings of Sayf al-Dīn al-Āmidī,* Salt Lake City: University of Utah Press, 1992.

Wensinck, Arent Jan, *Concordance et indices de la tradition musulmane*, 8 vols., repr., Istanbul: Çağrı Yayınları & Tunis: Maison Souhnoun, 1988.

Wolfson, Harry A., *The Philosophy of the Kalam*, Cambridge, MA: Harvard University Press, 1976.

INDEX

al-ʿAbbās, 57, 106
ʿ*abd*, see slave; worshipper
ʿAbd Allāh b. Masʿūd, xxix, cxii, 54
ʿAbd Allah b. al-Mubārak, 100
ʿAbd al-Qādir al-Jilānī, 11, 95–6
ʿAbd al-Wahhāb, cii
Abraham, 14, 33, 37, 105; God's intimate friend, 26, 54, 55–6, 57; model for combatting polytheism, 52–5; perfection of love and worship, lxxxiv–lxxxv, cxviii, 26; the way of Abraham and the way of Pharaoh, 69–71
abrogation, xxviii, xxxiv, cxiii
Abū al-ʿAliyya, xxx
Abū ʿAmr b. al-ʿAlā', xlix
Abū Bakr al-Ṣiddīq, cxiii, cv, cxv, 36, 56, 57, 59, 67, 73
Abū Ḥanīfa, xxv, xli, xlii, xliii, xlix, cviii, cxviii
Abū Hurayra, xcvii, cxii, cxviii
Abū Juhayr al-Darīr, 74, 111
Abū Saʿīd al-Khuḍrī, cxii
Abū Ṣāliḥ Mufliḥ, cii
Abū ʿUbayda Maʿmar b. al-Muthannā, xlix, cxxi
Abū Yaʿlā, xliii
Abū Yūsuf, xlii, cxviii
Abū Zahra, xxxiv
Adam, xlvi, 12–13
ʿ*adl*, see justice
al-Afram, Aqūsh, governor of Damascus, xvi, xviii, ciii
Ahl al-Sunna (People of the *Sunna*), xli, xliv, cxvi, cxvii; a coherent group with common beliefs, xliv; definition, xlv, liv
Ahl al-Sunna wa'l-Jamāʿa (People of the *Sunna* and the Congregation), xxxii, xxxvii, xl, lv, cxvi; creed, lv, 113; definition, xxxix; the saved sect, xxxix–xl
ʿĀ'isha, cxiv
ʿAlī b. Abī Ṭālib, xl, xlii–xliii, lxi, cxv, 105
almsgiving, 1, 4; *zakā*, xlii, cxviii
al-Āmidī, Sayf al-Dīn, lxxv, lxxvii, cxxvi–cxxvii
analogy (*qiyās*), lxxi–lxxii, cx; rational analogy, lxxi, lxxii; syllogism/analogy distinction, lxxvi, cxxvii
Anas b. Mālik, cxviii
angels, 4, 71; worship 2, 3, 31, 91
annihilation, see *fanā'*
al-anṣār, see the Helpers
anthropomorphism (*tashbīh*), xiv, lv, lvi, lviii, lxiv, 96–97, 113
apostasy, 10, 15
ʿ*aql*, see intellect; reason
Arabic grammar, xlvi, xlviii, li, liii, lxviii; *basmala*, 83–4, 116; classification of plurals, cxxxiii; complete sentence, 83–4, 86, 116; grammar of the *dhikr*, 78–81, 85, 86 (innovation, 80, 86); grammarians, xlv, 81, 83, 86, 115, 116; grammatical analysis of the commands to worship, 27–30 (syntactic coordina-

tion, 28); *kalām/qawl* distinction, 81, 115; legitimate supplications, 114; meaningful sentence, 79, 81, 82, 85, 115, 116; meaningful statements, 81–7, 116; technical terminology, xlviii, 85–6, 116, 117; see also Arabic language; Sībawayh, ʿAmr b. ʿUthmān
Arabic language, xlv–liv, lxix; Arabic of the *Salaf*, xlvii–xlviii, l, liii–liv; Arabic script, xlvii, cxx; Arabic/worship relation, xlvi (language control is 'worship' control, xlvi); *dhawq*, l–li, cxxi; exegesis, xlvi; foundation of Ibn Taymiyya's thought, x, xxiv, xxxi; Ḥanbalī School, xlviii–xlix; language of the Qur'ān and the *Ḥadīth*, xlvi, xlvii, xlix, l; linguistic terms, xlvi, xlviii, 86, 102; pre-Islamic period, xlvii; *Risālat al-ʿubūdiyya*, xlv, xlvi; Salafī principles, xlviii, li; *ṣamad*, xlvii–xlviii, cxx; study of Arabic language as a collective duty, xlvii; see also Arabic grammar; language
arrogance (*kibr*), 8, 31, 93; arrogance and polytheism inhibit the will to worship, 48–52; the opposite of faith, 49
asceticism, xi, xii, cxxv, 64, 65; corrupt asceticism, cxvii
al-Asfahānī, Muʿammar b. Ziyād, lxxviii
al-Ashʿarī, Ḥammād b. Abū Sulaymān, lxii, lxxvii, cvi
Ashʿarism, xix, xxv, xxxiv, civ, cxx, cxxvii; acquisition of one's actions, lix, lxii; *kalām*, lxxvii
ʿAtā' b. Abī Rabāḥ, xxix
Austin, R. W. J., 105–106
ʿAwf b. Mālik, 36
awliyā', see saints
Awzāʿī, lxxii

al-Baghawī, Ḥasan b. Masʿūd, xxxv, civ
al-Baghdādī, Abū Manṣūr ʿAbd al-Qāhir, cxviii
Balyānī, cxxix, cxxxii
baqā' (subsistence), xc, cxxxi
Basra, xl, cxxv, 74
Baybars al-Jāshangīr, Mamluk sultan, xix, xxi–xxii, xxii, cvi
beatific vision, lxvii–lxviii, cxxiii–cxxiv, cxxv, cxxix
Bell, Joseph N., cxxix, 101
bidʿa, see innovation
Bilqīs/Queen of Sheba, 53
al-Bisṭāmī, Abū Yazīd, lxxviii, lxxix, cxxviii, 71, 74
Braune, Walther, ci, 96
Brockelmann, Carl, xii, xciv
al-Bukhārī, Muḥammad, cxii, cxx, cxxiii, cxxiv

Calder, Norman, cxi, cxiii
Carter, Michael G., cix, cxx, 117
certainty (*yaqīn*), 2, 19, 91
charity, 1, 28
Chittick, William, cxxxii, 94, 98, 111
Christians, 16, 51, 60, 65, 70, 89; conversion to Islam, xiv; the Gospel, 64; love for God, 64
cognition (*ʿirfān*), 11, 78, 79, 95
the Companions (*ṣaḥāba*), x, xiii, xxxix–xlv, 54, 63, 73; exegesis, xxviii, xxix, xxxvii, xxxviii, cxii; foundation of Ibn Taymiyya's thought, xxiv, xxvi, xxxi, xxxvii, xxxix, cxxiv; overturning the statements and habits of, xlv; Qur'ān, xxvii; *Sunna*, xxvi, xli

contentment, cxxix, 1–2, 12, 13, 35, 63
creation: creation of all things out of nothingness, ix; Creator, 7–8, 16, 53, 77; creed, lv; God/creation distinction, lxvi, lxxx, lxxviii, lxxxiii, lxxxv, xc, xciii, 16, 76, 96, 106, 113; God's immanence in the world, lxv; Ibn ʿArabī, Muḥyī al-Dīn, xciii, cxxix, cxxxii, 94, 96–7; the Muʿtazila, xxxvi; worship (perfection of created being lies in his worshipping of God, 30–1, 48–9; the purpose of the creation, 2, 16)
creed, xviii–xx, xxv, liv; *Ahl al-Sunna*, lxv; *al-ʿAqīda al-hamawiyya al-kubrā*, xiv–xv, xx; *al-ʿAqīda al-wāsiṭiyya*, xviii, lv, lvii, lviii, lxv, lxvii, lxix, cxxiii; *bi-lā kayf*, lxi–lxii, lxiii, xciii; Divine attributes, lv–lvii; Divine Names, lv; intermediate position, liv, lvi, lxiv, cxxxiii, cxxiv; *al-Istiqāma* and Ibn Taymiyya's view of worship, lxx–xciii; oneness, lv–lvi; Salafī creed, xviii, xix, cvi; worship, liv, lv; see also Divine attributes; Divine Names; human volition; Ibn Taymiyya, Aḥmad: religious thought
Curtis, Roy xxxii, xxxiii, cix, cx–cxi, cxii–cxiii

al-Ḍaḥḥāk b. Muzāḥim, xxx, xlviii
al-dalīl wa'l-madlūl, see evidence and indicated meanings
al-Darānī, Abū Sulaymān, lxxvii, cxxix, 74
David, 33
denial, 8, 93
desire: desires are responsible for innovation, 22, 24; *hawā*, xi; hidden polytheism and desires, 67–9; *irāda*, 49; mastery over, 41; tasting faith as opposed to loving one's own desires, 22–4
determinism, see predestination
deviation: deviant exegetes, xxxiii, xxxv–xxxvi, xxxviii, cxv; self-contradictory beliefs, lv, 17–18; *tafsīq*, lxxv, cxxvi; see also innovation
dhawq, see taste
dhikr, see remembrance of God
Dhū al-Nūn al-Miṣrī, 59, 107
disbeliever, ix, 10, 16; hated by God, 64; striving against, 1, 13, 16; *takfīr*, lxxv, cxxvi
disobedience, 11, 70; determinism as excuse for disobedience, 16–19; fatalism, 18; Satan, 3
Divine attributes, xiv, 96; creed, lv–lvii; God's attributes existed in His essence, lvii; God's face and hands, lxiii–liv; God's hearing and seeing, lxiv–lxv; God's immanence in the world, lxv; God's justice, lxi–lxii; God's knowledge, lvii, lviii; God's omnipotence, lxi–lxii; God's speech, xlvi, lxviii–lxx, cxix, cxx (Qur'ān, xix, lxix–lxx, cxxiv); God's transcendence, lxv–lxviii ('rising above the throne', lxvi, lxvii, cxxv); God's will, lvii–lix (creative will, lxxxvi, 7; God's will/human volition relationship, lix, lxi–lxii, 18; volition/creative will distinction, lvii–lix, cxxii); Qur'ān, lvi–lvii; see also creed; Divine attributes, denial of; God; oneness
Divine attributes, denial of (*taʿṭīl*), xxxvi, lvi, lxiii, lxiv, xciii, cxvii,

113; Absolute Being devoid of attributes, xcii; the Muᶜtazila, xcii, cxv, cxxiii
Divine Names, lvi, 53, 96; creed, lv; Ibn ᶜArabī, Muḥyī al-Dīn, cxxxii; nearness to certain names of God, 99; the 'Perfect Man', xcii, cxxxii; Qur'ān, lvi–lvii; see also creed; God
divorce, xxiii, cviii

ecstatic experience (*wajd*), lxxiv, lxxviii, cxxvii–cxxviii; mystical experience, 25, 98, 114; see also intoxication; loss of consciousness; Sufism; union with the divine
ecstatic expression (*shaṭḥ*), lxxviii–lxxxi, lxxxvi, cxxviii, 74; examples of, lxxix; heresy, lxxx; see also Sufism
the Emigrants (*al-muhājirūn*), 73, 111
enmity for God's enemies, 10, 13–14, 43, 44, 51, 75, 77, 78
Epistle on Worship (*Risālat al-ᶜubūdiyya*), viii–ix, xxxii; criteria followed in preparing and presenting the translation, xcv–xcvii; historical circumstances of, xciii–xciv; manuscripts of, xciv; printed editions, xciv–xcv; purpose of, ix–x; Q.II.21, ix, 1, 32; *Sunna*, x; see also Ibn Taymiyya, Aḥmad: writings
evidence and indicated meanings (*al-dalīl wa'l-madlūl*), xxxv–xxxvi, xxxvii–xxxviii, cxv
exegesis (*tafsīr*), xxvi; Arabic language, xlvi; the Companions, statements of, xxviii, xxix, xxxvii, xxxviii, cxii; exegesis/hermeneutics distinction, cx; exegesis of the Qur'ān by the Qur'ān, xxviii, liii; the Followers, statements of, xxviii, xxix–xxxii, xxxiv, xxxvii, xxxviii (inconsistent terminology used by, xxx); four steps of hermeneutics, xxvii–xxxii; *ḥadīth*, xxviii–xxix, xxxi–xxxii, xxxviii, cxii–cxiii; limitations, xxviii; personal opinion, xxxi, xxxvii, xxxviii; the Prophet, xxvii, xxxiv, cxi, cxiv; Salafī principles, xxxiii, xxxviii, xxxix; skills needed for, xxvii–xxix, xxxii, cxii–cxiii; *Sunna*, xxviii; *tafsīr bi'l-ma'thūr*, xxvii; *tafsīr bi'l-ra'y*, xxvii; *uṣūl al-tafsīr*, cx; see also exegetes, classification of
exegetes, classification of, xxxii–xxxviii, xlvi; *Ahl al-Sunna wa'l-Jamāᶜa*, xxxii; deviant exegetes, xxxiii, xxxv–xxxvi, xxxviii, cxv; geographical aspect, cxiii; Kufa, xxxiii; Mecca, xxxiii; Medina, xxxiii, xli; use of correct hermeneutics, xxxiii; xxxviii

faith (*īmān*), 49; *ḥadīth* of Gabriel, li–lii, 4–5; perfecting faith and love, 44–5; tasting faith as opposed to loving one's own desires, 22–4; tasting the sweetness of, 57–9; testimony of faith, cxxviii–cxxix, 4, 10, 77–8, 80, 87, 115; witnessing, lxxxvii, 77–8
Fakhry, Majid, cxxxii
fanā' (annihilation), viii, lxxix, lxxxi, lxxxvi–lxxxvii, 62; contemplation of God's pure essence, lxxxvii; dangers of the annihilation of witnessing, lxxxix; *farq/jamᶜ* relationship, 76–8; Ḥanbalī pietism, lxxxix, xci; Ibn Taymiyya's description of, lxxxviii–lxxxix, cxxx–cxxxi; *istihlāk*, lxxxvii,

lxxxviii, lxxxix, cxxx; loss of consciousness, lxxxix, xci, 73–4; perfection of worship, xc; Ṣūfī descriptions of, lxxxvii–lxxxviii; union with the divine, lxxxviii, lxxxix, 72–3, 110; see also ecstatic experience; Sufism; union with the divine
fanā', types of, lxxxvii, lxxxviii–lxxxix, 71, 109; *fanā'* of existence/condemnable *fanā'*, lxxxvii–lxxxviii, lxxxix, 71, 75–6, 112; *fanā'* of prophets and saints/*fanā'* of the will, lxxxviii, 71; *fanā'* of witnessing/defective *fanā'*, lxxxviii, 71, 72–3, 77, 110 (unity of objectives and will, 110–11)
al-Faqī, Muḥammad Ḥāmid, 109
Fārābī, lxxiii
al-Fāriqī, Zayn al-Dīn, xiv
farq (separation), xc, cxxxi, 76–8, 113
fasting, 1, 4
fatalism, xl, xlix, lx–lxii, cxvii, cxxiii, 19; disobedience, 18
fear, 6, 7, 29, 54, 87, 88; fear of His punishment, 2, 68; love in balance with hope and fear, 59–60
festival, xliv–xlv, 49
figurative speech (*majāz*), xlviii–li, cxxi; *dūna al-majāz*, lxiii; *ḥaqīqa/majāz* dichotomy, xlix, cxx–cxxi
fiqh, see jurisprudence
fiṭra (natural disposition), ix
the Followers (*tābiᶜūn*), xxxix–xlv, 74; exegesis, xxviii, xxix–xxxii, xxxiv, xxxvii, xxxviii; foundation of Ibn Taymiyya's thought, xxiv, xxvi; overturning the statements and habits of, xlv; *Sunna*, xli
the Followers of the Followers (*tābiᶜ al-tābiᶜīn*), xxxix
free will, see human volition
al-Fuḍayl b. ᶜIyād, lxxvii, 27, 74, 99

Gabriel, 4, 28, 33, 92, 108; *ḥadīth* of Gabriel, li–lii, 4–5
ghalaba, see rapture
al-Ghazālī, Abū Ḥāmid, lxxiii, cxx, 97; ecstatic expressions, lxxviii–lxxix
God, 7–8; Creator, ix, lix–lx; God's nearness, lxvii, cxxiii; love for God, lxxxiii–lxxxiv, 1, 5, 6, 44; love of God, 27, 64–5 (God's beloved ones, 57, 61, 107); see also creation; Divine attributes; Divine Names; oneness
good and evil: enjoining good and forbidding evil, 1, 13, 16, 96; good/evil distinction, lxxxii, lxxxiii, lxxxvi, 96
good deed: God's love for 61, 107; righteous deed, 26–7, 66, 87; supplication, 27
greed, 35, 67–8
Gully, Adrian, cxix–cxx, cxxi, 111, 117

ḥadīth, x, 91, 100; authentic *ḥadīth*, xxviii–xxix, lxvii; classification of the scholars of *Ḥadīth*, cxii; exegesis, xxviii–xxix, xxxi–xxxii, xxxviii, cxii–cxiii; formulating opinions in opposition to authentic *ḥadīths*, cxviii; foundation of Ibn Taymiyya's thought, x, xxv, liii; *ḥadīth* of Gabriel, li–lii, 4–5; *ḥaqīqa/majāz* dichotomy, xlix, cxx–cxxi; jurisprudence, lxxv–lxxvi; *khabar al-wāḥid ḥadīth*, lxxv–lxxvi, cxxvi–cxxvii; no figurative meaning, xlviii–xlix, cxx; weak *ḥadīth*, xxix, cxiv
al-Ḥallāj, lxxviii–lxxx, cxxvii–cxxviii
Hallaq, Wael B., cxxi, cxxv, cxxvii, 93, 111

al-Hamadhānī, ʿAyn al-Quḍāt, lxxix, lxxx
Ḥammād b. Zayd, lxxii
Ḥanbalī School, x, xii; criticism by Ibn Taymiyya, cix; development of, cii; Ibn Taymiyya's religious thought, xiii, xviii, xxv, xxxiv, 112; principles of jurisprudence, xliii; principles of theology, law and exegesis, xxxii; Ṭabarī, Muḥammad b. Jarīr, xxxiv, cxiv; see also Ibn Ḥanbal
ḥaqīqa, see literal meaning; reality
al-Harawī, ʿAbd Allāh al-Anṣārī, lxxxvii, cxxx, 107
al-Ḥasan b. ʿAlī, 57, 106
al-Ḥasan al-Baṣrī, xxix, xlii, xlviii
ḥasb, see sufficiency
Heinrichs, Wolfhart, cxx, cxxi
Hell, 15; determinism, 24–5
the Helpers (*al-anṣār*), 73, 111
heresy (*ilḥād*), cv, 75, 76, 80, 87; ecstatic expression, lxxx; Sufism, lxxix, lxxx, cxxvii; *zindīq*, 59, 107
Hermann, Landolt, 96
hope, 2; love in balance with hope and fear, 59–60
ḥubb (love), 57, 59; *ʿishq/ḥubb* distinction, 101–102; *khulla/ḥubb* distinction, 57, 106; worship, 5, 56; see also love
Hūd, 2, 13
Ḥudhayfa al-Marʿishī, lxxvii
al-Hujwīrī, ʿAlī b. ʿUthmān, lxxx, cxxx
ḥulūl, see incarnation
human volition, lix–lxii, 18, 50; causes and potentialities in human acts, lxii; free will, cxv–cxvi (absolute free will, xxxvi, lx, lxi, cxxiii); God's will/human volition relationship, lix, lxi–lxii, 18; *istiṭāʿa*, lx, cxxii–cxxiii; love, 45; obedience, 18; predestination and free will, lxxi, lxxxi, 11–12 (delicate balance of, 19–20); responsibility, lxi–lxii, 18–19; see also creed
humility, 5, 59
hypocrisy, ix, 1, 13, 16, 64, 71, 112

ʿibāda, see worshipping/acts of worship
Iblīs, see Satan
Ibn ʿAbbās, ʿAbd Allāh, xxix, xxxiii, xli, xlviii, lxvi, lxix, cxii, cxiii, 37, 88
Ibn ʿAbd al-Hādī, ix, xciii–xciv
Ibn Abī al-Dunyā, 78, 114
Ibn ʿAqīl, xliii
Ibn ʿArabī, Muḥyī al-Dīn, 98, 105, 106, 115; antinomianism and unity of being, 15, 96; *barzakh*, 96–7; God, xcii, 99 (Divine Names, cxxxii; God and the creation, xciii, cxxix, cxxxii, 94, 96–7); monism, xviii, xix, xxii, cv, cxxix, cxxxii (Ibn Sīnā/Ibn ʿArabī correspondence, xcii); pantheism, xxi; the 'Perfect Man', cxxxii; *waqt*, 99
Ibn ʿAṭiyya, Abū Muḥammad, ix, xxxvii, cxiii, cxiv
Ibn Daqīq al-ʿĪd, xvii, civ
Ibn Fūrak, lxxvii, cxxvii
Ibn Ḥajar al-ʿAsqalānī, Aḥmad b. ʿAlī, 94–5, 111, 113
Ibn Ḥanbal, xxv, xli, cvii, 100; creed, lv–lxx; *ḥaqīqa/majāz* dichotomy, li, cxxi; the Lafẓiyya, cxix; methodology, lxxii, cxi; principles of jurisprudence, xliii; see also Ḥanbalī School
Ibn Jamāʿa, xvii, xx, xxi, civ, cvii
Ibn al-Jawzī, xi–xii, ci, cxviii, 106
Ibn Jinnī, 115
Ibn Kathīr, xvii, xxxiii, cii, ciii, civ,

cvii, cix, cxii–ciii; Ibn Taymiyya's *Muqaddima fī uṣūl al-tafsīr*, cx–cxi
Ibn Kullāb, lxix, lxxvii, cxix, cxxiv
Ibn Makhlūf, xviii, xx, xxi, cvi–cvii
Ibn Manẓūr, Abū Faḍl Jamāl, xcvii, cxxxii–cxxxiii, 92
Ibn Masᶜūd, xxxiii, xlviii, lxix, 29
Ibn al-Mubārak, lxxii
Ibn al-Muraḥḥil, Ṣadr al-Dīn, xix, cv
Ibn al-Qayyim, Muḥammad lxxxvii, lxxxviii, xc, xciv, cxxx, 93, 110, 111, 112; love, 92
Ibn Qudāma, Muwaffaq al-Dīn, x, cxi
Ibn Sabᶜīn, xxii, cv, cxxix, cxxxii, 15
Ibn Ṣaṣarī, Najm al-Dīn, xvii, civ, cvi
Ibn Sīnā, Abū ᶜAlī al-Ḥusayn, lxxiii; the Necessary Existent, xcii
Ibn Sīrīn, xlii
Ibn Taymiyya, Aḥmad: *Banū Taymiyya*, x–xiii; conflicts and trials, xiii–xxiv; death, vii, xxii, xxiv; exile to Egypt, xxi–xxii, lxx, cvii; imprisonment, xx, xxi, xxii–xxiv; lecture, xiv, xxi, cii–ciii; opponents, xvi, xvii, xviii, xix, xxiii, civ–cv, cxx; origin of the name Taymiyya, xcix; social activist and reformer, xiii; see also the entries below for Ibn Taymiyya, Aḥmad
Ibn Taymiyya, Aḥmad: methodology, xxiv–xxvi, xxxvii, liii, liv, cxi; method of debate, viii; revelation and methodology are linked together, xxv; Ṭabarī's methodology, xxxiii–xxxiv, cxiv; see also Ibn Taymiyya, Aḥmad: religious thought
Ibn Taymiyya, Aḥmad: religious thought, liv–xciii; conservatism, vii; a controversial Islamic thinker, vii, lxx; epistemology, xxxii; foundation of, xxiv–xxvi, liii, cxxiv (Arabic language, x, xxiv, xxxi; the Companions, xxiv, xxvi, xxxi, xxxvii, xxxix, cxxiv; the Followers, xxiv, xxvi, xxxvii; *ḥadīth*, x, xxv, liii; Qur'ān, vii, x, xxiv, xxv, xxxi, xxxix, liii, cxxiv, 112; *Sunna*, vii, xxiv, xxv–xxvi, xxxi, xxxix, cxxiv, 112); four steps of hermeneutics, xxii; Ḥanbalī School, xiii, xviii, xxv, xxxiv, 112; misinterpretation of his thinking, vii; orthodox tradition, xxv, xxxix, ciii; Righteous Predecessors, xxxix, liii, cxvi; Salafī principles, liv; see also creed; Ibn Taymiyya, Aḥmad: methodology
Ibn Taymiyya, Aḥmad: writings, vii, xxii; *al-ᶜAqīda al-hamawiyya al-kubrā*, xiv–xv, xviii–xx, cvi; *Dar' taᶜāruḍ al-ᶜaql wa'l-naql*, cxxiv, cxxvi; *al-Istiqāma*, lxx–xciii, cxxiii, cxxiv; *al-Kaylāniyya*, cxix; *Kitāb al-īmān*, xlxix, cxix, cxx; *Kitāb iqtidā' al-ṣirāṭ al-mustaqīm li-mukhālafat aṣḥāb al-jahīm*, xliv; *Muqaddima fī uṣūl al-tafsīr*, xxvi–xxvii, xxx, cx–cxi; *Risāla ilā Naṣr al-Manbijī*, cv; *Ṣiḥḥat uṣūl madhhab ahl al-Madīna*, xl, xli, xlii–xliii, cxviii; *al-Ṣūfiyya wa'l-fuqarā'*, cxvii; see also *Epistle on Worship*
Ibn Taymiyya, Fakhr al-Dīn, x, xcix; Ḥanbalī school, x–xi; Sufism, xi, xii
Ibn Taymiyya, Majd al-Dīn, xii, xiii
Ibn Taymiyya, Sharaf al-Dīn, xii, cii, cvi
Ibn Taymiyya, Shihāb al-Dīn, x, xii–xiii, cii
Ibn Taymiyya, Zayn al-Dīn, xii, ci, cvi
Ibn ᶜUmar, xli, cxii, 32

Ibn al-Zamlakānī, xvi, xviii, cvi
idolatry, lxviii, 15; false deities, 2, 15, 23, 31, 95, 111
Idrīs, xlvi
ignorance, 8, 30, 93; ignorance regarding the love for God, 61–2
iḥsān, see perfect devotion
ijtihād, see independent judgement
al-Ikhnā'ī, Muḥammad b. Abī Bakr, xxiii, cix
ᶜIkrima, xxix, xlviii
ilḥād, see heresy
ᶜilm (knowledge), cxv, 18, 94–5; religion/knowledge relationship, lxxiii–lxxiv; religious knowledge, 60, 97–8; see also knowledge
īmān, see faith
incarnation (*ḥulūl*), xci–xcii, xciii, 16, 75
independent judgement (*ijtihād*), viii, xxxii, xxxix, xlvi, cxvii, cxxv; *ḥaqīqat al-ijtihād*, 45
innovation (*bidᶜa*), lxxi, cix, cxxi, 21–2; beginnings of, xl–xli; desires are responsible for innovation, 22, 24; grammar of the *dhikr*, 80, 86; Ibn Taymiyya's campaign against, xliv; innovated opinion, lxxi; *Kitāb iqtidā' al-ṣirāṭ al-mustaqīm li-mukhālafat aṣḥāb al-jahīm*, xliv; the Muᶜtazila, xxxvii, xliv, xlix (innovated acts of worship, xl); polytheism, 20–1; test for, xliv–xlv; worship, xl, cxvii, 21, 87; see also deviation
intellect (*ᶜaql*), 98; *dalīl ᶜaqlī*, lxxi, cxxv; dual view of, cxxiv; weakness of, 46–7, 60
intention, 47; deeds are based on, 49–50, 66, 80, 103
intercession, xxxvii, 107; intercession of the dead, cviii; the Prophet's intercession, cvii
interpretation (*ta'wīl*), xxix, cvi, 81
intimacy (*khulla*), lxxxiv, lxxxv, 56, 59, 105–106; as the perfection of love, 56; intimate love and intimate friendship, 55–7; see also love
intoxication (*sukr*), lxxx, lxxxiv, cxxxi, 62, 73, 74; sobriety must prevail over, lxxxix, xc, xci, cxxxi; see also *fanā'*
irāda, see volition
ᶜirfān, see cognition
Isaac, 33, 55, 70
al-Isfarāyīnī, Abū Isḥāq, lxxvii, cxxvii
Ishmael, 55
ᶜishq, see passion
islām, see submission
Islamic sects, xxxix–xl, xliv; classification of, xxxii
the Ismāᶜīlīs, 112
ittiḥād, see union with the divine
Izutsu, Toshihiko, lii, xcix

Jābir b. ᶜAbd Allāh, cxii
the Jabriyya, lix–lx, cxvii, cxxiii; see also fatalism
Jacob, 33, 37–8, 52, 55, 70
Jāghān, governor of Damascus, xiv, xv, ciii
the Jahmiyya, xxxv, xl, xliv, cxvii–cxviii, cxxv, 22, 56; love and oneness, 105; oneness, xxxvi
Jalāl al-Dīn al-Qazwīnī, xiv–xv
jamᶜ (joining), xc, cxxxi, 76–8, 113
Jesus, 3–4, 16, 28, 30, 31, 51, 53, 55, 64, 65, 89
Jews, 51–2, 60; Torah, 52–3, 64
jihād, see striving
jinn, 2, 32, 91, 92
Job, 33
joining, see *jamᶜ*
Joseph, 13, 32, 41, 52
al-Junayd b. Muḥammad, lxxvii,

lxxxix, xc, cxxxi, 74, 111, 113
jurisprudence (*fiqh*), xii, lxxv, cxxvi; development of, liv, cx; *ḥadīth*, lxxv–lxxvi; innovated opinion, lxxi; *kalām* and the transformation of jurisprudence into a matter of opinion, lxxv–lxxvi, cxxvi; principles of, xlii, xliii, lxxi
justice (*ʿadl*), xxxvi, cxv–cxvi, 27; God's justice, lxi–lxii; reward and punishment, lix, lx–lxi
Juwaynī, xix, lxxvii, cxxv

Kaʿb b. Mālik, 67
al-Kalābādhī, Abū Bakr Muḥammad, lxxviii, cxxvii, cxxx–cxxxi, 95, 112
kalām (speculative theology), xxv, cix–cx; development of, cx; Ibn Taymiyya's critique of, lxxi–lxxvii (arguing without authority, lxxiv, cxxvi; danger when applied to belief and worship, lxxvi; disagreement over principles, lxxiv, cxxvi; misconceptions about prophethood, lxxii; religion/knowledge relationship, lxxiii–lxxiv; Salafī principles, lxxvi; transformation of jurisprudence into a matter of opinion, lxxv–lxxvi, cxxvi); *khabar al-wāḥid ḥadīth*, lxxv–lxxvi, cxxvi–cxxvii; Sufism/*kalām* link, lxxvii; see also speculative theologian
kalām (speech): animals' speech, xlvi, cxix; divine origin of language, xlvi, cxix–cxx; God's speech, xlvi, lxviii–lxx, cxix, cxx (Qur'ān, xix, lxix–lxx, cxxiv); human speech, xlvi, cxix; *kalām lafẓī*, xix; *kalām manẓūm*, xlvi; *kalām nafsī*, xix
the Karmathians, cxv, 76, 112
Kāshānī, ʿIzz al-Dīn Maḥmūd, 96
Katz, Steven T., cxxviii
Khaḍir, 10, 18, 94–5
al-Khalīl b. Aḥmad, xlv, xlix, l, li
al-Kharā'itī, Jaʿfar, xii, c–ci
Khaṭīb al-Tibrīzī, Muḥammad, cxiv, cxvi
the Khawārij, xvii, xxxvii, xliv, lxxi, cxvi, 107
Khorasan, xl
khulla, see intimacy
al-Khurqānī, Abū al-Ḥasan, 107
al-Khuway, Shihāb al-Dīn, xiv
kibr, see arrogance
Kisā'ī, ix
knowledge: God's knowledge, lvii, lviii; knowledge beyond intellectual understanding, 18, 97; mystical knowledge, 94, 98; reason/revelation relationship, 22, 97–8; see also *ʿilm*; *maʿrifa*
Kufa, xl, xliii; scholars of, xxxiii, lxxii, cxxv
the Kullābiyya, lxxvii, lxxviii

the Lafẓiyya, cxix
Lamotte, Virginie, xxxii
Lane, Edward, cxxii, 92, 96, 97, 108
language: associative indication, xlix–li, cxxi; conventionalist view of language, cxxi; general/specific meanings, li–lii; mystical language, cxxviii; qualified/unqualified statements, lii–liii; symbolic language, lxxii; written language, xlvi; see also Arabic language; figurative speech; literal meaning
Laoust, H., lxii, c, cii, cviii, cix, cx, civ, cvi
legal reasoning (*uṣūl al-fiqh*), xxv, lxxi, cviii

legal school (*madhhab*), viii; agreement among the four imams on methodological principles, xli–xliv; classification of Muslims according to their adherence to, xxxiv–xxxv; institutionalization of, cii; see also Abū Ḥanīfa; Ḥanbalī School; Mālik b. Anas; al-Shāfiʿī, Muḥammad b. Idrīs
lexicographer, xlvii, xcvii
literal meaning (*ḥaqīqa*), xlviii, xlix–l, cxxi; *ḥaqīqa/majāz* dichotomy, xlix, cxx–cxxi
loss of consciousness, lxxxi, lxxxvi, lxxxix, cxxix; classification of people who fell into unconscious state, xci; consciousness in worship, lxxxix–xc, 73–4, 111; see also ecstatic experience; *fanāʾ*
love, 92; the Companions, 63; criteria of, 62–4; erroneous notions of, lxxxvi; fire of, 63, 107–108; hope, fear and, 59–60; how to approach God through, 64–6; human volition, 45; interaction of love, worship and reliance, 47–8; levels of, 5; love and hate for the sake of God, 44, 45–7, 51, 58, 59; love for God, 1, 5, 6, 44 (and His oneness, lxxxiii, lxxxiv); love of God, 27, 64–5 (God's beloved ones, 57, 61, 107); love for the Prophet, 1, 6, 44, 45, 59; love of the Prophet, 56–7; obedience and love, 60–2; passionate love, 5, 39, 40–1, 92, 101–102; perfecting faith and love, 44–5; polytheistic form of love, lxxxiv; see also *ḥubb*; *maḥabba*; worship and love; worship, perfection of

madhhab, see legal school
al-Maghribī, Abū Yaʿqūb, lxxxi
maḥabba (love), 6; perfect love and worship, lxxxiv–lxxxv, 10; perfection of love, 56, 59; unqualified love, lxxxiv, 23, 59; see also intimacy; love
majāz, see figurative speech
the Malāmatiyya, lxxxii, cxxx
Mālik b. Anas, xxv, xli, xlii, xlv, xlix, lxxii, cxviii, cxxv, 114; Mālikī School, xxii, xliii, cviii, cxxv; principles of jurisprudence, xliii; *Sunna*, 26
the Mamluks, xiii, xvi, civ; Islamic law, xviii
al-Manbijī, Naṣr, xviii, xix, xxi, xxii, xxiii, cv
maʿrifa (knowledge/cognizance), 8, 93, 86, 110; *fanāʾ* of witnessing, 72, 110; a gnostic science, 94; realisation and cognizance, 10, 18, 94; see also knowledge
Maʿruf al-Karkhī, lxxvii, 74, 111
Masrūq b. al-Ajdaʿ, xxx
McAuliffe, Jane Dammen, xxxiii, cx, cxi
Mecca, xl; scholars of, xxxiii
Medina, xl, xli, xlii–xliv, cxvii, 46; leading role in propagating the *Sunna*, xlii; scholars of, xxxiii
Melchert, Christopher, cxiv
Memon, Muhammad Umar, xliv, lxxxiii,
messengers, 2, 31, 32, 51–2, 88; see also the Prophet
Michel, Thomas, 95
the Mongols, xiii, xv–xvi, xvii, civ; Ilkhan Ghazan, xv–xvi, xvii, civ
monism, xcii, cxxxii, 87; Ibn ʿArabī, Muḥyī al-Dīn, xviii, xix, xxii, cv, cxxix, cxxxii (Ibn Sīnā/Ibn ʿArabī correspondence, xcii); Sufism, lxxx, lxxxvi, xcii

Moses, lxix, xci, cxviii, 28, 29, 38, 50–1, 52, 55, 70, 79, 81, 94; *ḥadīth* of Adam and Moses, 12–13; mother of, lxxxviii, 72; supplication of, 38
Muʿādh b. Jabal, cxii
Muḥanna b. ʿĪsā, Ḥusām al-Dīn, xx, cvii
Mujāhid b. Jabr, xxix, xlviii
al-muhājirūn, see the Emigrants
the Muji'a, xliv
mukāshafa, see unveiling
the Murji'a, xxxv, xl, cxvi
the Muʿtazila, xxxiv, lxxv; deviant exegesis, xxxv, xxxvi–xxxvii; Divine attributes, denial of, xcii, cxv, cxxiii; five principles, xxxvi–xxxvii, cxv, cxvi; innovation, xxxvii, xliv, xlix (innovated acts of worship, xl); personal opinion, xxxvii, cxv; predestination and determinism, 19; religious knowledge, 97–8
mysticism, xi–xii; attacks against mystics, xviii; mystical experience, 25, 98, 114; mystical knowledge, 94, 98; pantheistic mysticism, xi; philosophical mysticism, xciii, cxxxii, 114; see also Sufism

nafs, see self
al-Nāṣir Muḥammad, Mamluk Sultan, xv, xxii, ciii, civ, cvii–cviii
Nasr, Seyyed Hossein, 93–4
natural disposition, see *fiṭra*
Nicholson, Reynold, cxxviii, cxxxi, 98–9, 107
Niffarī, 98–9
Noah, 2, 13, 27, 28, 32, 33, 52, 88
al-Nūrī, Abū al-Ḥasan, 74

obedience, 5, 6, 70, 87, 88, 89; free will, 18; love and obedience, 60–2; obedience to the law, 96; worshipping, xcvii
oneness (*tawḥīd*), ix, cxv, 113; abstraction of oneness, 74, 75, 111; application of oneness, 48, 76, 95; creed, lv–lvi; declaration of oneness, 10, 95; interrelationship between God's essence, names and attributes, xciii; love for God and His oneness, lxxxiii, lxxxiv; love in balance with hope and fear, 60; the Muʿtazila, xxxvi; philosophers' mathematical oneness, xciii
opinion (*ra'y*), xlvi, cxiii; innovated opinion, lxxi; *kalām* and the transformation of jurisprudence into a matter of opinion, lxxv–lxxvi, cxxvi; 'mere opinion', xxxi, xxxvii; People of Opinion, xxvii, xxxvi, xxxviii, lxxii; personal opinion, xxxi, xxxii, xxxiii, xxxiv, xxxvii, xxxviii, cxiii, cxv

Paradise, 15; determinism, 24–5
passion (*ʿishq*), xi, xii; *ʿishq/ḥubb* distinction, 101–102; passionate love, 5, 39, 40–1, 92, 101–102
patience, 1, 12, 13, 36, 37–8, 65, 96; honourable patience, 37–8
People of the *Sunna*, see *Ahl al-Sunna*
People of the *Sunna* and the Congregation, see *Ahl al-Sunna wa'l-Jamāʿa*
perfect devotion (*iḥsān*), 27; *ḥadīth* of Gabriel, li–lii, 4–5; *iḥsān*, 92; righteous deed, 26
the 'Perfect Man', xcii, cxxxii
Pharaoh, 50–1, 69–71, 76
philosopher, lxxiii, lxxvi–lxxvii, 98; intellect, cxxiv; misunderstanding of prophecy, lxxii–lxxiii; monistic Sufism, xcii; philoso-

phers' mathematical oneness, xciii; philosophical mysticism, xciii, cxxxii, 114
pietism, xi, lxxxix, xci
piety, xii, 3, 13; pious acts, 88
pilgrimage, 1, 4, 84, 85
polytheism (*shirk*), 8, 11–12, 17, 34, 42; Abraham as the model for combatting polytheism, 52–5; arrogance and polytheism inhibit the will to worship, 48–52; hidden polytheism and desires, 67–9; innovation, 20–1; polytheistic form of love, lxxxiv; the sin that God will never forgive, 52
prayer, 1, 4; benefits of, 17, 41–2; call to prayer, 49, 84–5 (*takbīr*, 49); congregational supererogatory prayer, xliv, cxviii–cxix; constant prayer, 27, 29; dispense from, 20, 97; invocation, 17; prayer for the Prophet, 97; prostration, 56, 82; supplication, lxxxv, cxxx, 1, 17, 27–8, 67, 78, 97, 114 (statements concerning remembrance and supplication, 82–3; supplication of Moses, 38; supplication of the Prophet, 38); see also remembrance of God
predestination: classification of humanity and, 7–9; determinism, lviii–lix, cxxii, 5, 20, 21, 22, 24; determinism as excuse for disobedience, 16–19; free will and, lxxi, lxxxi, 11–12 (delicate balance of free will and predestination, 19–20); groups that err concerning *qadar*, 24–6; *ḥadīth* of Adam and Moses, 12–15; *qaḍā'*, cxxii; *qadar*, xl, lviii–lix, cxvii; religious obligations, 9–11
the Prophet, xci; exegetical role, xxvii, xxxiv, cxi, cxiv; following the Prophet, lxxxiii–lxxxiv, 44, 87; God's intimate friend, 55–6; love for the Prophet, 1, 6, 44, 45, 59; Night Journey, xci, 4, 33, 74; obedience to, 88; the 'Perfect Man', cxxxii; perfection of love and worship, lxxxiv–lxxxv, 4; prayer for the Prophet, 97; Prophet's birthday, xlv; Prophet's intercession, cvii; Prophet's love, 56–7; Qur'ān, revealed to, lxix, 4, 33, 92; supplication of the Prophet, 38; visiting the Prophet's grave, xlv
prophets, liii, 2, 52–3, 55, 61, 94; *fanā'*, lxxxviii, 71; prophethood, 55 (misunderstanding of, lxxii–lxxiii); worship xci, 2
punishment, xxxvi, lix, 20, 45; executing the punishment, xxxvi–xxxvii; fear of God's punishment, 2

qaḍā'/qadar see predestination
the Qadariyya, xxxv, lix, cxvii, cxviii, cxxiii, 19
the Qalandariyya, lxxxii
Qatāda b. Diʿāma, xxx, xlviii, cxiii
qiyās, see analogy
al-Qūnawī, al-Ṣadr al-Rūmī, cxxix, cxxxii
Qur'ān, vii, xix, xxvi, lxx; Arabic language, xlvi, xlvii, xlix, l; the Companions, xxvii; Divine attributes, lvi–lvii; Divine Names, lvi–lvii; following the Book, 29; foundation of Ibn Taymiyya's thought, vii, x, xxiv, xxv, xxxi, xxxix, liii, cxxiv, 112; God's speech, xix, lxix–lxx, cxxiv; *ḥaqīqa/majāz* dichotomy, xlix, cxx–cxxi; literal meaning, xlviii–xlix, lxxiii; memorisation of,

xxviii; Qur'ān/*Sunna* relationship, xxv, xxviii; reason/revelation relationship, 22, 97–8; recitation of, xlvi, lxix, cxix, cxxv, cxxix, 1, 29, 38, 74, 82–3 (proper pronunciation, 86); revealed to the Prophet, lxix, 4, 33, 92; *Sunna*, xxv; transcription of, lxix–lxx; uncreated, lxix; ʿUthmān's edition, xxvi; see also exegesis
Qurtubī, cxiii
Qushayrī, Abū al-Qāsim, lxxxvii, cxxviii–cxxix, cxxxi, 107, 113; *kalām*, lxxvii

al-Rabīʿ b. Anas, xxx
rapture (*ghalaba*), 62, 74
the Rawāfiḍ, lxxi
ra'y, see opinion
al-Rāzī, Fakhr al-Dīn, lxxvii, cxx, cxxv, 93
reality (*ḥaqīqa*), 9, 70, 93, 94; existential reality, 9, 10–11, 15, 16, 17, 18, 19; religious reality, 9, 10, 11, 15
reason (*ʿaql*): *ʿaqliyyāt*, 22, 97–8; religious knowledge, 97–8
reliance (*tawakkul*), 2, 6, 24, 25, 29–30, 87–8, 89, 98, 100; begging, 36–7, 100; dispersing of goods, 87–8; interaction of love, worship and reliance, 47–8; working for provisions, 36, 37, 100
religion, 5, 24, 67, 89; principles, 87; religious reality, 9, 10, 11, 15; sincerity of religion, 1, 26–7, 41, 51, 54, 67, 68, 69; the whole of the religion is included in worshipping, 5
religious law: adhering to, 25, 63; commands and prohibitions, 19–20, 22, 62, 87; distraction, disobedience, 25, 98–9; see also obedience
religious scholars, see *ʿulamā'*
remembrance of God (*dhikr*), 1, 41, 42, 72; grammar of the *dhikr*, 78–81, 85, 86 (innovation, 80, 86); repeating a simple word or phrase, 79–81, 114, 116; statements concerning remembrance and supplication, 82–3; see also prayer
repentance, 1, 13, 25, 61
resurrection, 5, 21, 70, 107
the Rifāʿiyya, xviii, lxxxiii
Righteous Predecessors (*al-salaf al-ṣāliḥ,* the *Salaf*), vii, xii, xviii, 12, 59; Arabic of the *Salaf*, xlvii–xlviii, l, liii–liv; concept of, xxxix, cxvi–cxvii; Ibn Taymiyya's religious thought, xxxix, liii, cxvi; methodology of, xxiv
Rightly Guided Caliphs, xxix, xlii
al-Rūmī, Jalāl al-Dīn, cxxviii

Ṣafī al-Dīn al-Ḥindī, cv, cvi
ṣaḥāba, see the Companions
Saʿīd b. Jubayr, xxix, xlviii
Saʿīd b. al-Musayyab, xxix, xlviii
saints (*awliyā'*), 22; *fanā'*, lxxxviii, 71; hierarchy of Ṣūfī saints, c; sobriety in worship, xci
al-salaf al-ṣāliḥ/the *Salaf*, see Righteous Predecessors
the Salafī: orthodoxy, x–xi; Salafī creed, xviii, xix, cvi; Salafī principles, xlviii, li, liii, lv, lxv, lxviii, lxxvi (exegesis, xxxiii, xxxviii, xxxix; Ibn Taymiyya's religious thought, liv)
Ṣāliḥ, 2
Sālim, cxii
Sallār, governor of Egypt, xx, cvi
al-Sarrāj, Abū Muḥammad, xi, c
Satan (Iblīs), 8, 9, 10, 11, 13, 84; disobedience, 3, 32; powerlessness regarding worshippers, 3, 32–3

Schimmel, Annemarie, xi, c, cxxviii, 107–108
self (*nafs*), lxiii, lxvi, cxv; God's 'self', lxvi
separation, see *farq*
al-Shāfiʿī, Muḥammad b. Idrīs, xix, xxv, xli, xlix; *kalām*, lxxii, cxxv; principles of jurisprudence, xliii; Qur'ān/*Sunna* relationship, xlviii; Shāfiʿī School, xviii, xx, xliii, cviii
Shaqīq al-Balkhī, 100
shaṭḥ, see ecstatic expression
al-Shiblī, Abū Bakr, lxxviii, cxxviii, 74
Shīʿī Islam, xvi, xviii, xl, xliv; exegesis, cxv; polemics against the Shīʿa, xlii; the Rāfiḍa, 56, 105; Twelver Shīʿa, cxv–cxvi, 105
al-Shīrāzī, Abū al-Faraj, cii
shirk, see polytheism
Shuʿayb, 2, 25
Shuʿba b. al-Ḥajjāj, xxx–xxxi, cxiii
Shuhda bint Aḥmad, xi
Sībawayh, ʿAmr b. ʿUthmān, xlv, xlix, 81, 85, 115, 116, 117
al-Sijistānī, Abū Bakr, civ
al-Sijistānī, Abū Dāwūd, 67
sin, 20, 21, 97; blatant sin, 20, 21, 26, 27, 40–1, 42, 43, 68, 69; God's hate for major sins 61, 107; polytheism, the sin that God will never forgive, 52
sinner, 7, 12, 107; grave sinner, xxxvii, cxv, cxvi; worshipper, 13
slave (*ʿabd*), 7, 8, 42; desires of the self, 35; slave of wealth, fame, images, leadership, 34, 35, 39, 43, 46, 47; slavery of the heart, 39, 40–1; slavery/worship relationship, 8, 38–40
Solomon, 33, 53
speculative theologian, xxxvii; classification of, lxxvi–lxxvii; innovation, 22; see also *kalām* (speculative theology)
speculative theology, see *kalām* (speculative theology)
speech, see *kalām* (speech)
Speight, R. Marston, xxxiii, cxi, cxiii
Stace, W. T., 114
striving (*jihād*), 44–5, 46, 63, 67; striving against disbelievers, 1, 13, 16
submission (*islām*), 5, 49, 52–3, 87, 89; *fanā'*, xc; *ḥadīth* of Gabriel, li–lii, 4; universal subjugation, 53; worship, 6
subsistence, see *baqā'*
sufficiency (*ḥasb*), 7, 92–3
Sufism, viii, cxxiv; antinomian Ṣūfī groups, lxxxii; Basra, cxvii; classification of Ṣūfīs, lxxvii–lxxviii; forty *abdāl*, xi, c; heresy, lxxix, lxxx, cxxvii; hierarchy of Ṣūfī saints, c; Ibn Taymiyya, Fakhr al-Dīn, xi, xii; Ibn Taymiyya's attacks against, xvii, xviii, lxxxii–lxxxiii, cv–cvi, cxxix; Ibn Taymiyya's critique of, lxxvii–xciii; monism, lxxx, lxxxvi, xcii; mystical Sufism, xvii, cxxiv; state/station, 99; Sufism/*kalām* link, lxxvii; traditional 'sources' of knowledge, lxxiv; traversing and concentration, 25, 99; 'voluntaristic' Sufism, xi; see also ecstatic experience; ecstatic expression; *fanā'*; mysticism
Sufyān b. ʿUyayna, 23, 98
sukr, see intoxication
al-Sulamī, Abū ʿAbd al-Raḥmān, xxxviii, lxxviii, cxi
Sunna, vii, lxx; adhering to, 25–6; Arabic language, xlvi, xlvii, xlix, l; the Companions, xxvi,

xli; exegesis, xxviii; foundation of Ibn Taymiyya's thought, vii, xxiv, xxv–xxvi, xxxi, xxxix, cxxiv, 112; Mālik b. Anas, 26; Medina, xlii; Qur'ān/*Sunna* relationship, xxv, xxviii
Sunnī Islam, x, xlii
Syria, xl

Ṭabarī, Muḥammad b. Jarīr, xxvii, cx, cxi, cxiv, 93; methodology, xxxiii–xxxiv, cxiv
tābiᶜ al-tābiᶜīn, see the Followers of the Followers
tābiᶜūn, see the Followers
tafsīr, see exegesis
Talḥa b. ᶜUbayd Allāh, 79, 114
tashbīh, see anthropomorphism
taste (*dhawq*), l–li, cxxi, 22
taᶜṭīl, see Divine attributes, denial of
tawakkul, see reliance
tawḥīd, see oneness
ta'wīl, see interpretation
Ṭāwūs, Abū ᶜAbd al-Raḥmān, 37, 100
al-Thaᶜlabī, Aḥmad b. Ibrāhīm, xxxv, cxiv
al-Tilimsānī, lxxxi, cv, cxxviii, cxxix, cxxxii
al-Tirmidhī, Abū ᶜĪsā Muḥammad b. ᶜĪsā, 67, 68, 78
al-Tustarī, Sahl b. ᶜAbd-Allāh, lxxvii–lxxviii

Ubayy b. Kaᶜb, cxii
ᶜubūdiyya, see worship
ᶜulamā' (religious scholars): complex relations with the ruling elite, xiv–xv; professionalization of, cii
ᶜUmar b. al-Khaṭṭāb, cxv, 26–7, 35, 38, 45, 67, 73
union with the divine (*ittiḥād*), lxxix, lxxxi, lxxxiv, lxxxix, xci–xcii, xciii, 75, 114; *Ahl al-Ittiḥād*, lxxxviii, xcii, 87; *fanā'* of witnessing, 73; monism, xcii; pantheism, xxi; see also ecstatic experience; *fanā'*; Sufism
unity of being (*waḥdat al-wujūd*), xci–xcii, xciii; antinomianism and, 15, 96, 106; refutation of, xciii
unveiling (*mukāshafa*), 25, 94, 98
Usāma b. Zayd, 57, 106
uṣūl al-fiqh, see legal reasoning
ᶜUthmān b. ᶜAffān, cxv

Van Ess, Josef, cxix, cxxiv
visitation of graves (*ziyāra*), xxiii, xlv, cviii–cix; visiting the Prophet's grave, xlv
volition (*irāda*), 50, 73; Divine volition/Divine creative will distinction, lvii–lix, cxxii; see also human volition

waḥdat al-wujūd, see unity of being
al-Wāḥidī, Abū al-Ḥasan ᶜAlī b. Aḥmad, xxxv, cxiv
wajd, see ecstatic experience
Watt, Montgomery W., cxv, cxvi, cxxii, cxxvii
Wensinck, Arent Jan, 91
wine, 20, 41, 73, 97
worship (*ᶜubūdiyya*), xcvii; Arabic language/worship relation, xlvi; components of, 4–5; consciousness in worship, lxxxix–xc, 73–4, 111; correct worship, 87–9; creed and worship, liv, lv; definition, 1; division of humanity into a hierarchy based on, ix; grammatical analysis of the commands to worship, 27–30; *ijtihād*, forbidden in worship, cxxv; innovation, xl, cxvii, 21, 87; the means of,

24, 25, 48; mystical Sufism, liv–lv; nature of God and worship, liv–lv; obligation to worship God alone, ix, 6, 10, 26, 32, 49, 87, 88–9; the purpose of the creation, 2, 16; Qur'ān, lxx (Q.II.21: ix, 1, 32); slavery/worship relationship, 8, 38–40; sobriety, xci; speculative theology, liv–lv; subjection and self-abasement, xcvii; *Sunna*, lxx; the whole of the religion is included in, 5; see also worship and love; worship, perfection of
worship and love, 5–6; all that God loves is included in worship, 27; *ḥubb*, 5, 56; human's need of God, 48; love for God and His oneness, lxxxiii–lxxxv; interaction of love, worship and reliance, 47–8; intimacy, 56; see also worship, perfection of
worship, perfection of, lxxxiv–lxxxv, 30–3, 48, 51; examples of, 33, 56; perfect love and worship, lxxxiv–lxxxv, 10, 65 (Abraham, lxxxiv–lxxxv, cxviii, 26; the Prophet, lxxxiv–lxxxv, 4); perfection of created being lies in his worshipping of God, 30–1, 48–9; perfection of the *fanā'/baqā'* experience, xc; principles of perfect worship, 26–7, 87; see also worship and love
worshipper (*ʿabd*), xcvii, 3, 5, 10; angels, 2, 3, 31, 91; description of, 2–4, 16–17 (those who walk on earth with reverence, 3, 33); sins of, 13
worshipping/acts of worship (*ʿibāda*), xcvii, cxxxiii, 5; examples of, 1–2, 16–17, 29–30; humility, 5; *ʿibāda*, used in an unqualified way, liii; obedience, xcvii; obligatory acts, 26, 65; recommended acts, 26, 65; voluntary acts, 65

Yaḥyā b. Saʿīd, cxxix
yaqīn, see certainty
Yūsuf b. Asbāt, lxxvii

al-Zamakhsharī, Abū al-Qāsim, xxxvi, xxxvii
Zayd b. Aslam, xxxiii
al-Zubayrī, Jaʿfar b. Muḥammad, cxiv
Zurāra b. Abī Awfā, 74, 111